PHYSICS NOW!

Physics Now!

BRENDAN CASSERLY AND BERNARD HORGAN

Gill & Macmillan

Gill & Macmillan Ltd
Hume Avenue, Park West
Dublin 12
with associated companies throughout the world
www.gillmacmillan.ie
© Brendan Casserly and Bernard Horgan 2000
© Artwork Gill & Macmillan

Design: Identikit Design Consultants, Dublin
Artwork: Blaise Smith, Alanna Corballis
Photo Research: Anne-Marie Ehrlich

ISBN-13: 978 07171 2261 5
ISBN-10: 0 7171 2261 1
Print origination in Ireland by Identikit Design Consultants, Dublin
and Carole Lynch, Dublin

The paper used in this book is made from the wood pulp of managed forests. For every tree felled, at least one tree is planted, thereby renewing natural resources.

All rights reserved.
No part of this publication may be reproduced, copied or transmitted in any form or by any means without written permission of the publishers or else under the terms of any licence permitting limited copying issued by the Irish Copyright Licensing Agency.

Acknowledgments

For permission to reproduce transparencies and photographs
grateful acknowledgment is made to the following:
Mary Evans Picture Library; The Mansell Collection; Planet Earth Pictures;
The Bettman Archive; Image Select; AKG London;
Maynooth College/Fotocraft; Frank Spooner/Gamma Press;
Stephen O'Reilly; Ford Motor Company Ltd; Science Photo Library;
Science and Society Picture Library

Contents

INTRODUCTION   VII

1. Reflection of Light   1
2. Refraction of Light   13
3. Lenses   23
4. Helping the Eye   30
5. Waves   35
6. The Spectrum   46
7. Sound   54
8. Vectors and Scalars   70
9. Linear Motion   75
10. Forces   84
11. Moments   96
12. Energy Sources   102
13. Work, Energy and Power   106
14. Density and Pressure   117
15. Circular Motion   125
16. Heat, Temperature and Thermometers   136
17. Transmission of Heat   147
18. Heat Capacity and Latent Heat   153
19. Static Electricity   168
20. Electric Fields   181
21. Simple Circuits   189
22. Magnetism and Magnetic Fields   204
23. Measuring Resistances   212
24. The Heating and Chemical Effects of an Electric Current   224
25. The Force on a Current-carrying Conductor in a Magnetic Field   232
26. Applied Electricity: Current and Magnetic Fields (Option 2)   238
27. Electromagnetic Induction   248
28. Electromagnetic Induction (Option 2)   260
29. Capacitors and Capacitance   269
30. Semiconductors   278
31. Applied Electricity: Semiconductors (Option 2)   285
32. The Electron   301
33. Photoelectric Emission and X-rays   311
34. Radioactivity   323
35. The Structure of the Atom   336
36. Radioactive Decay   342
37. Uses of Radioisotopes and Radiation Hazards   348
38. Nuclear Energy   358
39. Inside the Atom (Option 1)   369
40. Fundamental Particles (Option 1)   376

ANSWERS TO LONG NUMERICAL QUESTIONS   389
INDEX   392

Introduction

Science is as old as mankind. Science exists because of two things: necessity and curiosity.

Back in the Stone Age people made weapons because they needed to kill animals for food. They needed to keep warm, particularly at night, so they discovered fire. They needed to move things from one place to another, so somebody invented the wheel. The same thing happens today. If there is a problem, scientists try to invent, or discover, something to solve it.

In the nineteenth century, people needed a simple and safe way to light up their homes at night. Thomas Edison studied the problem and invented the electric light bulb. Edison was one kind of scientist, an inventor. Isaac Newton was a different kind of scientist. He studied science not out of necessity but out of curiosity. In the seventeenth century scientists were known as natural philosophers. Newton wanted to understand the world he lived in. He studied the planets and became the first man to understand gravity. He discovered that white light can be split up into different colours by passing it through a thick piece of glass or a drop of water. This is how rainbows are formed.

Because of the work of Edison, Newton and thousands of other scientists, the amount of scientific knowledge available to mankind became so great that it was split up into different branches. Three of those branches – physics, chemistry and biology – are probably being studied in your school. This book is concerned with one of them – physics.

Physics

Physics is about matter and energy. Matter is anything that has mass. Matter can exist in three states: solid, liquid and gas. Energy is the ability to do work. It can exist in many forms, e.g. mechanical energy, light, sound, heat, electrical energy, magnetic energy, chemical energy and nuclear energy. The study of energy is central to all branches of science and in particular to physics. In fact, you will begin by studying light, which is a form of energy. You will do a number of experiments and at the end of each experiment you will write a report.

Reports on experiments

Scientists write reports for two reasons: so that they can share their knowledge with others, and because without a report they may not be able to recall **exactly** what they did and what happened.

When you write a report on an experiment you should use the following headings:

Date:
Aim: What is the purpose of the experiment?
Method: Step-by-step instructions for doing the experiment.
Result: What happened?
Conclusion: What does this show?

ERRORS

Mention the main sources of error in your report. One factor is the accuracy of the instruments you use. If, for example, you use a thermometer graduated in degrees then you can be accurate only to the nearest degree. If the thermometer is graduated in half degrees then you can be accurate to the nearest half degree.

Of course you should try to avoid errors as much as possible, or at least make sure that the percentage error is small. If you are measuring something that is 10 cm long and you make an error of 1 cm then the percentage error is 10%. If you are measuring something that is 1 m long and you make an error of 1 cm then the percentage error is only 1%.

The percentage error can often be reduced by repeating the experiment a number of times and taking an average of the readings. It can also be reduced by designing the experiment so that the quantities to be measured are as large as possible.

The results of an experiment should, where possible, be presented in the form of a chart, table or graph.

Graphs

When drawing graphs you should follow certain rules.

Scale: Use a convenient scale that will give a fairly large graph. Show clearly what is being measured and the units being used on each axis.

Plotting: As a general rule put the independent variable on the *x*-axis and the dependent variable on the *y*-axis.

Example: If a man is running along a road at 5 m per second then the distance travelled depends on the time, so that distance is the dependent variable and should be plotted on the *y*-axis. In fact the distance–time graph should turn out as shown in Diagram 1. The graph is a straight line through the origin, which shows that the two quantities being graphed are directly proportional to each other. (Whatever happens to one happens to the other.)

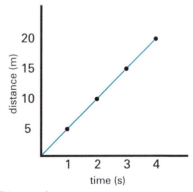

Diagram 1

Shape: If you have studied Boyle's law in Junior Certificate Science or if you have ever pumped up a bicycle, you know that pressure is inversely proportional to volume. (Whatever happens to one, the opposite happens

INTRODUCTION

to the other.) So if you plot a graph of pressure against volume you will get a curved graph as shown in Diagram 2. If you plot P against $1/V$ you will get a straight line through the origin (Diagram 3): this is a much more suitable graph and the deductions from it are much more useful.

The advantage of using a graph as opposed to calculating the mean (average) value is that by drawing the line of best fit you arrive at the average of the most consistent readings.

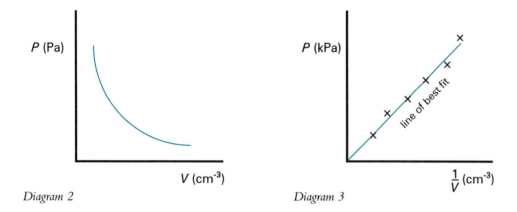

Diagram 2   Diagram 3

Slope: If the experiment involves a formula that contains a fraction, then put the denominator (bottom part of the fraction) on the x-axis and the numerator (top) on the y-axis.

Example: In an experiment on Ohm's law $R = V/I$, so put I on the x-axis and V on the y-axis. Now pick two convenient points on the graph that are as far apart as possible (so as to reduce the percentage error), and get the slope as shown in Diagram 4.

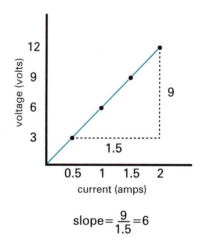

Diagram 4

The following features of the new physics syllabus should be noted.

- Ordinary level students are required to study most of the core. Higher level students must study ALL the core material and either option 1 OR option 2. The higher level material additional to the ordinary level core is clearly marked in the text with a light blue line.

The following diagram may help students with the structure of the syllabus.

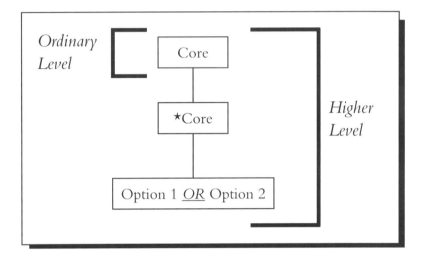

- Ordinary level students are not required to derive the given formulae; they are required to use them to solve problems. Higher level students are required to derive certain formulae and to apply all formulae to solve problems of a more difficult nature

- An asterisk indicates a question for higher level students.

- There is a greater emphasis on science, technology and society – the application of physics, and the technology which physics makes possible, to our work and everyday lives. Students are also required to reflect on the influence of science and technology on society and our environment.

- In order to place the development of physics in an historical context we have included the pen pictures of famous scientists.

- **So as to arrange the syllabus in logical order, and place material in its proper context, Option 2 has been dealt with in three separate chapters, 26, 28 and 31.**

Reflection of Light

CHAPTER 1

Energy would not be much use to us if it could not travel from one place to another. What would be the point of lighting a fire if the heat energy could not travel out of the fire into the room? What good would sunlight be to us if it could not travel from the sun to the earth?

But how does light travel? The answer is in 'straight lines', as you will see if you look at the pinhole camera in the diagram. Now look at the shadow in the second diagram. If light did not travel in straight lines, would there be a shadow?

Reflection

The sun gives out its own light so it is **luminous**. Light bulbs, candles and fires are all luminous. Most things are not luminous. This book is not luminous: you can see it because light is reflected off the book and into your eyes.

Most objects have rough irregular surfaces so that different parts of the surface reflect light rays in different directions. This is called diffuse reflection.

Mirrors have smooth regular surfaces, which give regular reflection. Light is reflected according to the laws of reflection.

1. **The angle of reflection (r) is equal to the angle of incidence (i).**
2. **The incident ray, the normal and the reflected ray are all in the same plane (all three can be drawn on a flat sheet of paper).**

Note that the angle of incidence (i) is between the incident ray and the normal, not between the incident ray and the mirror.

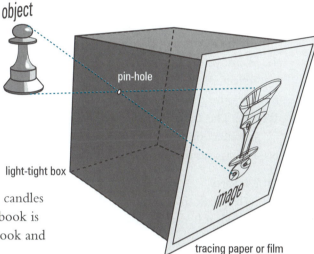

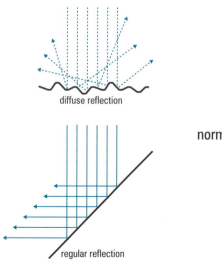

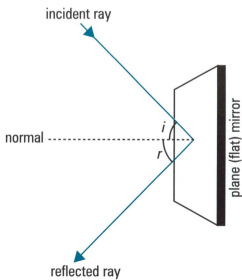

Experiment

AIM: To verify that the angle of incidence equals the angle of reflection.

METHOD
1. Stand a plane mirror vertically on a sheet of paper.
2. Mark the position of the back of the mirror.
3. Shine a ray of light onto the mirror and mark the position of the incident and reflected rays.
4. Remove the mirror and draw in the incident ray, the reflected ray and the normal.
5. Measure the angles of incidence and reflection.

Result: The angle of incidence is equal to the angle of reflection.

6. Repeat for different values of the angle of incidence.

QUESTIONS
1. Why mark the position of the **back** of the mirror?
2. Why is it best to choose large angles of incidence?

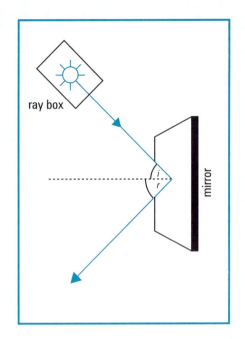

Images

The image we see in a plane mirror is caused by reflection from the back of the mirror, as you can see from the diagram. The rays of light entering the eye seem to come from behind the mirror, so that is where the image is seen.

If you try to find the exact position of the image behind the mirror, you will come up against a rather obvious problem. You cannot go behind the mirror to locate the image since the image can only be seen from the front. To overcome this difficulty, we make use of parallax.

Parallax is the apparent relative movement of two objects due to the movement of the observer.

To demonstrate parallax

Hold two pencils, one in each hand, in front of you, as shown in the diagram. Move your head to one side. Note the apparent relative movement between the two pencils. Now move your head in the opposite direction. Note that in each case the pencil that is further away from your eye appears to move with you. Hold one pencil directly above the other. Move your head to one side. Note that on this occasion there is no relative movement between the two pencils or, to put it another way, the two pencils move together without parallax. This will enable us to locate an image in a plane mirror.

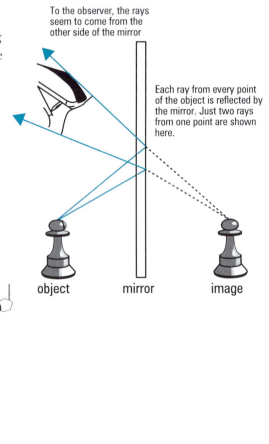

Reflection of Light

Experiment

AIM: To locate an image in a plane mirror.

METHOD

1. Stand the plane mirror M on a sheet of paper.
2. Mark the position of the back of the mirror.
3. Place the object pin O in front of the mirror.
4. Move the tall search pin around behind the mirror until it coincides with the image of O, as seen in the mirror, without parallax.
5. Measure the distance from O to the back of the mirror. Measure the distance from I to the back of the mirror.

Result: Both distances should be the same.

Conclusion: The image is as far behind the mirror as the object is in front of it.

This can also be demonstrated using a sheet of clear glass as shown in the diagram.

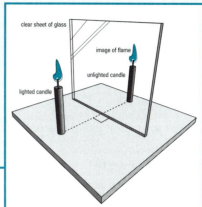

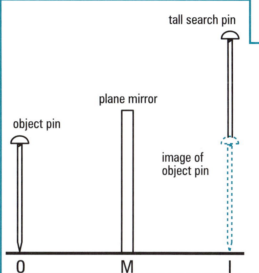

Lateral inversion

If you stand in front of a plane mirror and raise your right hand you will notice that your image raises its left hand. This is known as lateral inversion. One everyday application of this is shown in the photograph.

The periscope

During a golf tournament, someone at the back of the crowd might use a simple periscope to get a better view. A simple periscope can be made as shown in the diagram.

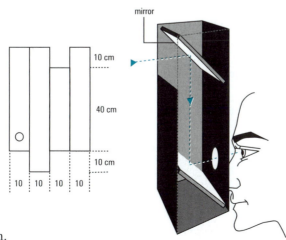

How would this lettering look in the rear view mirror?

3

Real and virtual images

There are two kinds of image, real and virtual. A real image is formed by the **actual** intersection of light rays. It is always **inverted** and can be formed on a screen. A virtual image is formed by the **apparent** intersection of light rays. It is always **erect** and cannot be formed on a screen.

Images formed in plane mirrors are
- virtual
- laterally inverted
- the same size as the object
- as far behind the mirror as the object is in front of it.

When a mirror has a curved surface, this no longer applies. The image may even be in mid-air in front of the mirror, as we shall see.

Uses of plane mirrors

Plane mirrors are used to make rooms look larger and to increase light levels. They are used in clothes shops when shoppers are trying on clothes. They are also used in simple periscopes.

Spherical mirrors

There are two types of curved mirror, concave and convex. If you look into the front of a highly polished spoon you will see an image of yourself upside down. You are looking into a **concave** mirror. If you look into the back of the spoon you will see an image of yourself the right way up. You are now looking into a **convex** mirror.

P is called the pole of the mirror.
C is the centre of curvature.
F is the focus.
FP is the focal length.
CP is the radius of curvature.

CP = 2FP

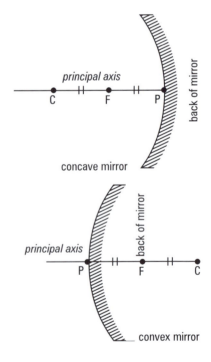

Concave mirrors

Rays of light are reflected from a concave mirror according to the following rules.

1. Rays of light parallel to the principal axis are reflected back through the focus.
2. Rays of light passing through the focus are reflected parallel to the principal axis.
3. Rays of light coming from the direction of the centre of curvature are reflected back along their own path.

REFLECTION OF LIGHT

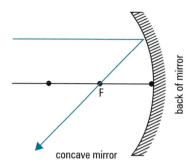
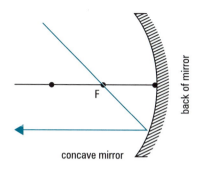
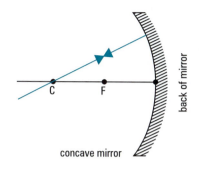

The position, nature (real or virtual) and size of an image depends on the distance of the object from the mirror, as the following ray diagrams show.

Note: In order to find the position of the image, all we need do is to draw, according to the above rules, exact geometrical diagrams of two rays of light coming from the object and find where they meet. This tells us where the image is formed.

OBJECT BEYOND C
The image is:
1. between C and F
2. real
3. inverted
4. smaller than the object.

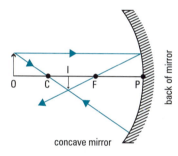

OBJECT AT C
The image is:
1. at C
2. real
3. inverted
4. same size as the object.

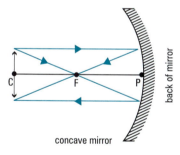

OBJECT BETWEEN F AND C
The image is:
1. beyond C
2. real
3. inverted
4. larger than the object.

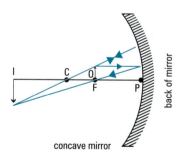

Physics Now!

OBJECT AT F
The image is at infinity.

OBJECT BETWEEN F AND P
The image is:
1. behind the mirror
2. virtual
3. erect
4. larger than the object.

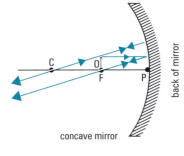
concave mirror

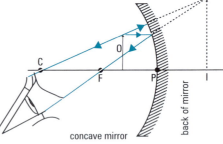
concave mirror

We can also arrive at the position and nature of the image by calculation, using the formulae:

$\frac{1}{f} = \frac{1}{u} + \frac{1}{v}$ and $m = \frac{v}{u}$

f = focal length
u = distance from mirror to object
v = distance from mirror to image
m = the magnification = size of image/size of object

Sign convention

For a real image we take v as positive. For a virtual image v is negative. Focal length is positive for a concave mirror and negative for a convex mirror.

Please read 'Reports on Experiments' and 'Graphs' in the introduction to this book.

Mandatory experiment

AIM: To find the focal length of a concave mirror.

METHOD 1
1. Hold a concave mirror so that the image of a distant object, e.g. a tree, is focused onto a sheet of paper.
2. Measure the distance from the mirror to the paper.
This distance is the focal length of the mirror.

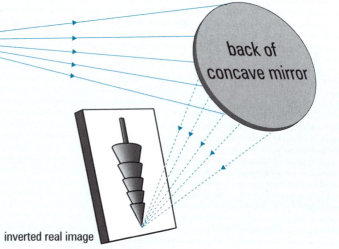

METHOD 2
1. Lay the mirror on a bench, face upwards.
2. Place the pin in a retort stand directly above the mirror.
3. Adjust the pin until the pin and its image move together without parallax.
4. The pin is now at the centre of curvature of the mirror (*see diagram*).

5. Measure the distance from the pin to the pole of the mirror. This distance is the radius of curvature. Half this distance is the focal length.

METHOD 3
1. Set up the apparatus as shown in the diagram.
2. Adjust the position of the screen until a sharp image of the lamp box is formed on it.
3. Measure u and v.
4. Calculate the focal length from the formula $\frac{1}{f} = \frac{1}{u} + \frac{1}{v}$.
5. Repeat for different positions of the lamp box and find the average value of f.

QUESTION
When would you not get an image on the screen?

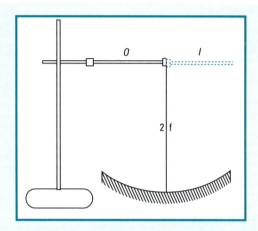

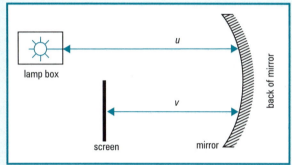

Convex mirrors

Rays of light are reflected from a convex mirror according to the following rules.
1. Rays parallel to the principal axis are reflected so as to appear to be coming from the focus.
2. Rays of light heading towards the centre of curvature are reflected back along their own path.

When an object is placed in front of a convex mirror, the image is always virtual, erect and diminished.

PROBLEM 1
An object is placed 15 cm in front of a concave mirror of focal length 10 cm. Find the position, magnification and nature of the image.

$\frac{1}{f} = \frac{1}{u} + \frac{1}{v}$ $\Rightarrow$ $\frac{1}{10} = \frac{1}{15} + \frac{1}{v}$ $\Rightarrow$ $\frac{1}{10} - \frac{1}{15} = \frac{1}{v}$ $\Rightarrow$ $\frac{1}{30} = \frac{1}{v}$

$\Rightarrow$ $v = 30$ cm

(v is positive as the image is real.)

$m = \frac{v}{u} = \frac{30}{15} = 2$

Answer: A real, inverted image, twice the size of the object, 30 cm from the mirror. The situation can be represented by a ray diagram as shown.

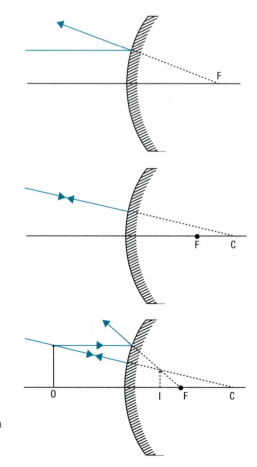

7

Problem 2

A convex mirror of focal length 12 cm forms an image 4 cm from the mirror. Find the position of the object.

$f = -12$ cm, $v = -4$ cm (why negative?), $u = ?$

$\dfrac{1}{f} = \dfrac{1}{u} + \dfrac{1}{v}$ $\qquad$ $\dfrac{1}{-12} = \dfrac{1}{u} + \dfrac{1}{-4}$ $\qquad$ $\dfrac{1}{4} - \dfrac{1}{12} = \dfrac{1}{u}$ $\qquad$ $\dfrac{3}{12} - \dfrac{1}{12} = \dfrac{1}{u}$

$\dfrac{1}{6} = \dfrac{1}{u}$

$u = 6$ cm

The object is 6 cm in front of the mirror.

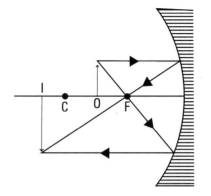

Problem 3

An object placed 20 cm in front of a concave mirror has a real image 3 times the height of the object. Where must the object be placed to form a virtual image 3 times the height of the object?

Stage 1

$u = 20$ cm; $\qquad m = 3 \Rightarrow \dfrac{v}{u} = 3 \Rightarrow \dfrac{v}{20} = 3 \Rightarrow v = 60$ cm.

$\dfrac{1}{f} = \dfrac{1}{u} + \dfrac{1}{v}$

$\dfrac{1}{f} = \dfrac{1}{20} + \dfrac{1}{60}$

$\dfrac{1}{f} = \dfrac{4}{60} = \dfrac{1}{15}$

$f = 15$ cm

Stage 2

$f = 15$ cm; $u = ?$; $v = ?$; $m = 3$; $\dfrac{v}{u} = 3$; $v = 3u$

However, since the image is virtual v is negative.

$\dfrac{1}{15} = \dfrac{1}{u} - \dfrac{1}{3u}$ $\quad \Rightarrow \quad$ $\dfrac{1}{15} = \dfrac{2}{3u}$ $\quad \Rightarrow \quad 3u = 30 \Rightarrow u = 10$ cm

The object must be placed 10 cm in front of the mirror.

Reflection of Light

Uses of concave mirrors
Concave mirrors are used as reflectors in car headlamps, flashlamps, electric bar heaters, etc.

As concave mirrors can give a magnified erect image they can also be used as shaving and make-up mirrors, but be sure your face is inside the focus. (Why?)

A dentist uses specially designed concave mirrors, as shown in the diagram, to examine your teeth.

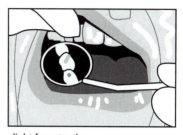

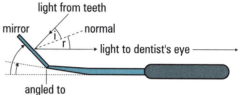

Uses of convex mirrors
Convex mirrors have two advantages:
1. The images formed by convex mirrors are always erect, not inverted.
2. Convex mirrors provide a large field of view, as you can see in the diagram. Convex mirrors of very long focal length (which could be mistaken for plane mirrors) are used as wing mirrors in cars as they give a wide field of view without giving a false sense of distance.

Convex mirrors are also used on buses, in shops and at dangerous junctions as they can, in effect, enable us to see round corners.

A convex mirror being used to 'see around a corner'

Summary
- Light is a form of energy.
- The laws of reflection are:
  1. The angle of reflection (r) is equal to the angle of incidence (i)
  2. The incident ray, the normal and the reflected ray are all in the same plane.
- A real image is formed by the actual intersection of light rays. It can be formed on a screen and is always inverted.
- A virtual image is formed by the apparent intersection of light rays. It cannot be formed on a screen and is always erect.
- A concave mirror forms a virtual image when the object is inside the focus.
- $\frac{1}{f} = \frac{1}{u} + \frac{1}{v}$
- $m = \frac{v}{u}$
- Concave mirrors are used as reflectors in headlamps and also as make-up mirrors and by dentists.
- Convex mirrors give a wide field of view and are used as rear-view mirrors in cars and buses. They are also used in shops and at dangerous junctions.

Short Questions

1. The diagram shows a ray of light being reflected by a plane mirror. Is the angle of reflection (A) 20°, (B) 35°, (C) 55°, (D) 70° or (E) 110°?

2. Is the image in a plane mirror always (A) real erect and diminished, (B) virtual, erect and diminished, (C) real, erect and the same size, (D) virtual, erect and the same size or (E) virtual, erect and laterally inverted?

3. An optician's test card is fixed 80 cm behind the eyes of a patient who looks into a plane mirror 300 cm in front of him as shown in the diagram. Is the distance from his eyes to the image of the card (A) 300 cm, (B) 380 cm, (C) 600 cm, (D) 680 cm or (E) 760 cm?

4. Will a concave mirror form a virtual image if the object is (A) inside the focus, (B) at the focus, (C) between the focus and the centre of curvature, (D) at the centre of curvature or (E) outside the centre of curvature?

5. The diagram shows an object O placed between the centre of curvature C and the focus F of a concave mirror. Is the image formed (A) inside the focus, (B) between the focus and the centre of curvature, (C) at the focus, (D) at the same position as the object or (E) outside the centre of curvature?

6. If an object is placed at a distance 2f from a concave mirror of focal length f, will the image be (A) inside the focus, (B) at the focus, (C) between the focus and the centre of curvature, (D) at the centre of curvature or (E) outside the centre of curvature?

7. An object is placed at a distance of 30 cm from a concave mirror of focal length 15 cm. Is the magnification (A) 0, (B) 0·5, (C) 1, (D) 1·5 or (E) 2?

8. Will a convex mirror form a virtual image (A) only when the object is inside the focus, (B) only when the object is at the focus, (C) only when the object is between the focus and the centre of curvature, (D) only when the object is at the centre of curvature or (E) always?

9. Is a convex mirror often used as an outside rear-view mirror on a car because (A) it has a wide field of view, (B) it has a narrow field of view, (C) the image is always magnified, (D) the image is always real or (E) the image appears the same size as the object?

10. Is the image formed by a shaving or make-up mirror (A) real and erect, (B) real and inverted, (C) virtual and erect, (D) virtual and inverted or (E) virtual and the same size as the object?

11. Light is a form of _____.

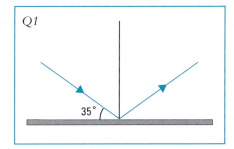

Q1

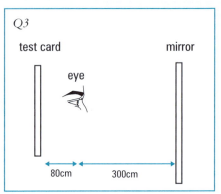

Q3

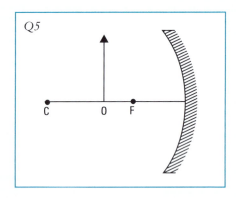

Q5

12. State the laws of refection.
13. A real image is formed by
    _____.
14. A virtual image is formed by
    _____.
15. If an object is at the focus of a concave mirror, the image is formed at _____.
16. Explain the basic physical principle involved in each of the following:
    (a) an electric fire has a polished and curved surface behind the heating element
    (b) a concave mirror is sometimes used by a dentist as a magnifying mirror
    (c) when you are looking from a bright room out into the darkness the window glass acts as a mirror.

LONG QUESTIONS
1. Why are you unable to see an image of yourself in this page?
2. Trace figure 1. Draw two rays to locate the image of the object as seen by the observer.
3. A boy walks towards a plane mirror with a speed of 0.5 m/s. Does the boy's image appear to move towards or away from him? At what speed does the image move?
4. An optician is testing your eyesight in a room which is only 3 metres long. You are sitting at one end of the room. The optical chart is hanging directly above your head. You are looking at its image in a plane mirror hanging on the wall directly opposite you. Why is the optician using this arrangement? Why are the letters on the chart printed backwards?
5. A concave mirror has a focal length of 15 cm. (a) Calculate its radius of curvature. (b) Calculate the position of the image of an object standing (i) 30 cm from the mirror, (ii) 20 cm from the mirror, (iii) 10 cm from the mirror. In each case state the nature of the image formed.
6. A convex mirror of focal length 12 cm forms an image 4 cm from the mirror. Find the position of the object and the magnification.
7. An object is placed 20 cm in front of (a) a convex mirror, (b) a concave mirror, of focal length 10 cm. Compare the images.
8. What magnification is obtained when an object is placed 10 cm in front of a concave mirror and the image is formed 30 cm from the mirror?
9. A man must position his face 10 cm away from a shaving mirror in order to achieve a magnification of 3. What is the focal length of the mirror?

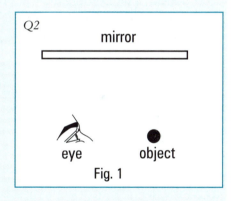

Fig. 1

10. A dentist has a choice of three small mirrors, convex, concave and plane, to examine the back of your teeth. State which she should use to give the best view. Give reasons for this choice rather than the other two.

11. An illuminated object and a concave mirror are used to produce a sharp image of the object on a screen. The corresponding magnifications (linear) and the image distances are given in the table.

Magnification m	0·25	1·5	2·5	3·5
Image distance v (cm)	20	40	56	72

Draw a graph plotting m along the vertical axis and v along the horizontal axis. Use the graph to find the image distance when $m = 1·0$. What is the object distance when $m = 1·0$? What is the focal length of the mirror?

12. In an experiment to measure the focal length of a concave mirror, a student found the position of the real image for various positions of an object. The object distance, u, and the corresponding image distance, v, were measured and the following table was drawn up.

u (cm)	v (cm)	$\frac{1}{u}$ (cm^{-1})	$\frac{1}{v}$ (cm^{-1})
29	64	0·034	0·016
37	43	0·027	0·023
40	41	0·025	0·024
50	35	0·020	0·029

(i) Draw a simple sketch to show how the apparatus might have been arranged in this experiment.
(ii) How might the position of the image have been determined?
(iii) Calculate a value for the focal length f of the mirror using the above data and the equation $\frac{1}{f} = \frac{1}{u} + \frac{1}{v}$.

Refraction of Light

CHAPTER 2

Look at the two cars in the diagram. In the first car the two front wheels hit the mud at the same time, so the car slows down but it does not change direction. In the second car the front wheel on one side hits the mud first and slows down first. This causes the car to change direction.

The same thing happens to light when it passes into a more dense medium (e.g. from air to water) and, for the same reason, the light slows down. (You should remember from Junior Certificate science that light belongs to a group of waves called the electromagnetic spectrum. As for all waves, velocity = frequency × wavelength. In this case the light slows down because the wavelength decreases; the frequency remains the same).

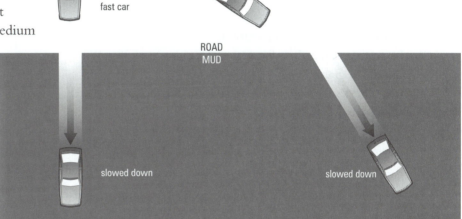

If the light were coming out of the glass into the air it would travel along the exact same path, but in reverse.

Light passing into an optically **more dense** medium is bent towards the normal. Light passing into an optically **less dense** medium is bent away from the normal.

The bending of light rays when they pass from one medium into another is called **refraction**. There are two laws of refraction.

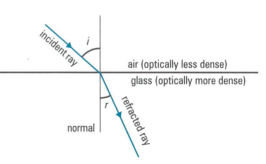

Laws of refraction

1. $\frac{\sin i}{\sin r}$ is constant for two given media (this is called Snell's law).

2. **The incident ray, the refracted ray and the normal are all in the same plane.**

   $\frac{\sin i}{\sin r}$ is known as the refractive index n.

The refractive index from air to glass is simply called the refractive index of glass. The same applies when light passes from air into water or any other medium.

PHYSICS NOW!

Mandatory experiment

AIM: To verify Snell's law.

METHOD

1. Draw the outline of a glass block on a sheet of paper. Remove the block.
2. Draw a normal NO to the side of the block and a line making an angle of incidence of 20° with NO. Replace the block.
3. Stick two pins P and Q on the line.
4. Stick two pins R and S in line with the images of P and Q as seen through the block. Remove block and pins.
5. Join RS and continue it until it meets the outline of the block at B. Join OB.
6. Measure the angle of refraction r.
7. Repeat this procedure for angles of incidence of 30°, 40°, etc. and plot a graph of **sin i** against **sin r**.

Result: The result should be a straight line through the origin, which verifies Snell's law.

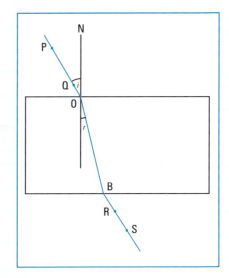

QUESTIONS

1. How would you get the refractive index of the glass block from the graph?
2. What do you notice about the incident and emergent rays?

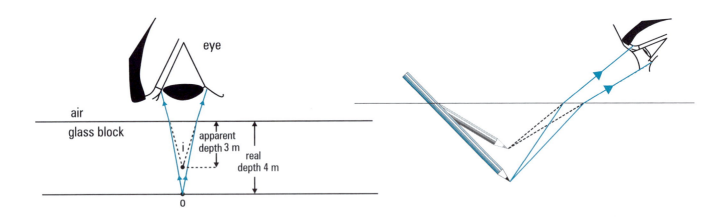

Refraction can produce some curious effects, as you can see from the diagrams.

In the labelled diagram $\frac{\text{real depth}}{\text{apparent depth}} = \frac{4}{3}$, which is in fact the refractive index of water. This gives us an alternative method of finding the refractive index.

refractive index = $\frac{\text{real depth}}{\text{apparent depth}}$

Refraction of Light

Mandatory experiment

AIM: To find the refractive index of a rectangular glass block.

Method

1. Draw a straight line on a sheet of paper.
2. Stand a glass block on end over the line.
3. Move the search pin up and down until it coincides, without parallax, with the image of the line as seen through the block.
4. Fix the search pin to the side of the block and measure the apparent depth.
5. Now measure the real depth of the block.
6. The refractive index = $\dfrac{\text{real depth}}{\text{apparent depth}}$

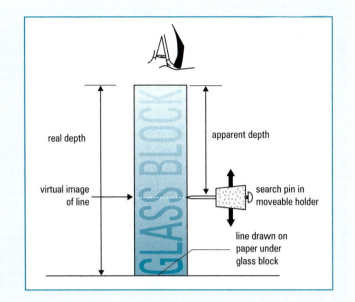

Mandatory experiment

AIM: To find the refractive index of a liquid.

Method

1. Set up the apparatus as shown in the diagram.
2. Move the search pin up and down until it coincides, without parallax, with the image of the line as seen in the liquid.
3. Fix the search pin to the side of the beaker and measure the apparent depth.
4. Measure the real depth of the beaker.
5. Refractive index = $\dfrac{\text{real depth}}{\text{apparent depth}}$

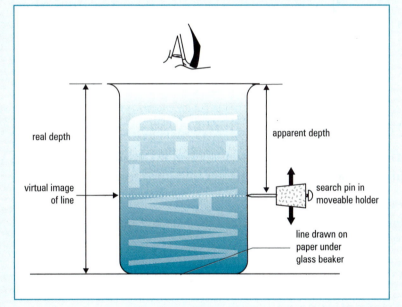

When finding the refractive index for two media, neither of which is air, use the following formula

refractive index from medium 1 to medium 3 = (index from 1 to 2) × (index from 2 to 3).

Problem

The refractive index for glass is $\frac{3}{2}$ and the refractive index for water is $\frac{4}{3}$. What is the refractive index from water to glass?

$_an_w = \frac{4}{3}$, so $_wn_a = \frac{3}{4}$

$_wn_g = {_wn_a} \times {_an_g} = \frac{3}{4} \times \frac{3}{2} = \frac{9}{8}$

Total internal reflection

Total internal reflection can occur only when light is going into a less dense medium and can be demonstrated as shown in the diagram.

When light passes from glass to air it is refracted away from the normal as in (a). As the angle of incidence is increased, the angle of refraction eventually reaches 90°, as in (b). If the angle of incidence increases beyond this value total internal reflection occurs, as in (c).

The critical angle (C) is the angle of incidence in the denser medium corresponding to an angle of 90° in the less dense medium.

From diagram (b), the refractive index from air to glass

$n = \frac{\sin 90°}{\sin C} \Rightarrow n = \frac{1}{\sin C}$

As the refractive index of glass is $\frac{3}{2}$,

$\frac{3}{2} = \frac{1}{\sin C}$

$\sin C = \frac{2}{3} = 0.667 \Rightarrow C = 41°49'$

The critical angle for glass is 41°49'.

Total internal reflection occurs when the angle of incidence in the denser medium is greater than the critical angle.

Problem
Find the critical angle for water if the refractive index of water is $\frac{4}{3}$.

$n = \frac{1}{\sin C} \Rightarrow \sin C = \frac{1}{n} \Rightarrow \sin C = \frac{3}{4} \Rightarrow C = 48°35'$

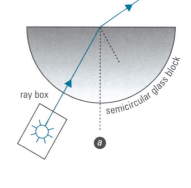
a

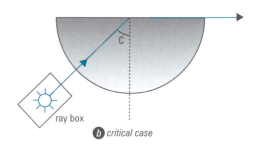
b critical case

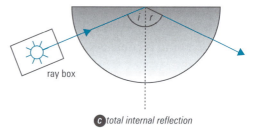
c total internal reflection

Applications

Total internal reflection has some very useful applications. To begin with, glass prisms can be used to turn a ray of light through 90°, 180° and other angles. This fact can be used in the periscope and in binoculars.

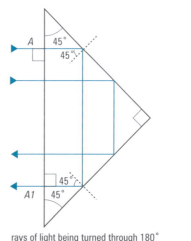
rays of light being turned through 180°

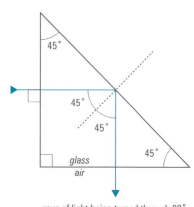
rays of light being turned through 90°

REFRACTION OF LIGHT

1. PERISCOPE
High-quality periscopes use prisms instead of mirrors because prisms give total internal reflection and do not deteriorate with age in the way that mirrors can.

2. PRISM BINOCULARS
The size of the final image in a pair of binoculars depends on the distance travelled by the light within the binoculars. By using two prisms this distance can be increased without increasing the length of the binoculars.

3. REFLECTORS ON BICYCLES
Bicycle reflectors are designed so that the angle of incidence for light trying to pass from the plastic into the air is greater than the critical angle, so total internal reflection occurs and the light is reflected back to the driver of the car as in the diagram. The same idea can be used in reflective road signs.

4. JEWELLERY
Precious stones such as diamonds have to be cut very carefully so that they will produce total internal reflection of light, and sparkle.

5. FIBRE OPTICS
An optical fibre consists of a hair-like thread of glass surrounded by an outer layer of less dense glass. Light is trapped within the core by total internal reflection, as shown in the diagram.

Using optical fibres, light can be piped from one place to another in much the same way as we pipe water from one place to another.

In the communications industry fibre optic cables are being used to replace conventional telephone cables. Electrical signals are converted into pulses of laser light which travel along the fibres. At the other end the light is converted back into electrical pulses. This system has the advantage of being much faster, since the signals travel at the speed of light, the cables are much lighter and easier to handle and they do not need as many signal boosters along the way.

A fibre optic cable: The cable is made of inner and outer layers of glass, in which light travels at different speeds. Total internal reflection occurs at the boundary between these layers. Scratches on the plastic covering will not cause a loss of light, because the light does not reach this part of the fibre.

Fibre optics can be used to destroy tumours. If a tumour grows in a solid organ like the liver, it is almost impossible to remove it by surgery. If a fibre optic cable is passed into the organ, laser light can be directed along it. The laser is directed at the tumour cells, and kills them.

Another application is the **endoscope**. One bundle of optical fibres, called a light guide, carries light into the patient's body. Another bundle of optical fibres, called the image guide, carries light back from inside the body to the observer. The endoscope has been used very effectively to examine and photograph the digestive system, the reproductive system and the tubes leading to the heart. It has made a great deal of exploratory surgery unnecessary.

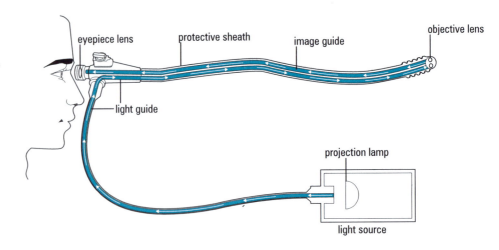

MIRAGES

Mirages usually occur in warm weather when motorists see what appears to be a pool of water on the road. As you can see from the diagram, this is caused by total internal reflection as light from the blue sky tries to pass from the cool upper air through the warm, less dense, air nearer the ground.

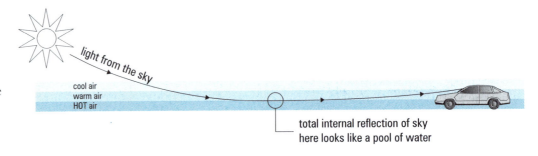

The reason why light bends when going from one medium to another is a change in velocity. This gives us another way of looking at refractive index.

> **refractive index from medium 1 to medium 2 = $\dfrac{\text{velocity in medium 1}}{\text{velocity in medium 2}}$** $\left(n = \dfrac{c_1}{c_2}\right)$

PROBLEM

The speed of light in air is 3×10^8 m s^{-1}. If the refractive index of water is $\frac{4}{3}$, find the speed of light in water.

$$n = \frac{c_1}{c_2} \Rightarrow c_2 = \frac{c_1}{n} \Rightarrow c_2 = (3 \times 10^8) \times \tfrac{3}{4} = 2{\cdot}25 \times 10^8 \text{ m s}^{-1}$$

Refraction of Light

Summary

- Refraction: light bends when it passes from one medium to another medium of different density.
- Laws of refraction:
    1. $\frac{\sin i}{\sin r}$ is constant for two given media.
    2. the incident ray, refracted ray and normal are all in the same plane.
- $n = \frac{\sin i}{\sin r} = \frac{\text{real depth}}{\text{apparent depth}} = \frac{\text{velocity in medium 1}}{\text{velocity in medium 2}}$
- The critical angle is the angle of incidence in the denser medium corresponding to an angle of refraction of 90° in the less dense medium.
- $n = \frac{1}{\sin c}$
- Total internal reflection occurs when the angle of incidence in the denser medium is greater than the critical angle.
- Total internal reflection is used in periscopes, prism binoculars, reflectors and fibre optics (communication and endoscopes).

Short Questions

The refractive index of water is $\frac{4}{3}$. The refractive index of glass is $\frac{3}{2}$.

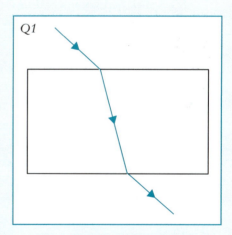
Q1

1. The diagram shows a ray of light passing through a parallel-sided glass block. Are the changes in direction caused by (A) refraction, (B) total internal reflection, (C) dispersion, (D) lateral inversion or (E) reflection?
2. The real depth of a pool is 4 m. Is the apparent depth (A) 1·33 m, (B) 2 m, (C) 2·5 m, (D) 3 m or (E) 4 m?
3. Does a stick held in a pond appear to be bent at the surface because (A) the critical angle for water is 45°, (B) total internal reflection has occurred, (C) light travels faster in water than in air, (D) rays of light from the eye bend into the water, or (E) rays of light from the stick are bent away from the normal at the surface?
4. Given that the refractive index of water is $\frac{4}{3}$, is the critical angle for water approximately (A) 25°, (B) 42°, (C) 45°, (D) 49° or (E) 60°?
5. Given that the refractive index of glass is $\frac{3}{2}$, is the critical angle for glass approximately (A) 25°, (B) 42°, (C) 45°, (D) 49° or (E) 60°?

6. State the laws of refraction.
7. Define 'critical angle'.
8. In the diagram, (a) angle A is called _____; angle B is called _____.
   (b) If medium 2 is air and the values of A and B are 30° and 45° respectively, what is the refractive index of medium 1?
   (c) When would the value of B be less than that of A?
   (d) What name is given to the value of A for which B is 90°?
   (e) When will total internal reflection occur?
   (f) Give one application of total internal reflection.
9. In the diagram, a ray of light enters a semicircular slab of glass at A and leaves it at B. What condition must be fulfilled for the light to follow the path shown?
10. Give one advantage of using a prism instead of a mirror in an optical instrument.
11. Explain the basic physical principles involved in each of the following.
    (a) A glass prism can sometimes be used instead of a plane mirror.
    (b) The real depth of a swimming pool filled with water is greater than the apparent depth.
    (c) A stick partly immersed in water appears to be bent at the water surface.

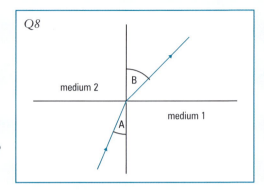
Q8

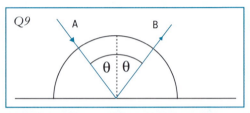
Q9

Long Questions

1. Calculate the angle of incidence in the diagram.
2. A fish appears to be 6 m below the surface of a pond. What depth is the fish really at? ($n = \frac{4}{3}$ for water)
3. A rectangular glass block has a real width of 6·0 cm and an apparent width of 4·0 cm. What is the refractive index of the block? If the block is 3 cm deep, by how much will print over which it is placed appear to be raised?
4. In order to verify Snell's law the student plotted a graph similar to the one shown.
   (a) Name the two quantities which the student plotted on the graph.
   (b) What does this graph tell you about the relationship between the two quantities?
*5. How is the refractive index of a material related to the velocity of light in the material? If the velocity of light in air is 3×10^8 m s^{-1} and the refractive index of glass is 1·5, calculate the velocity of light in the glass.
6. Complete the paths of the two narrow beams of monochromatic light XY shown in the diagrams. The

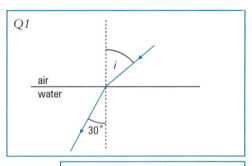
Q1

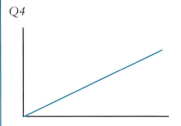
Q4

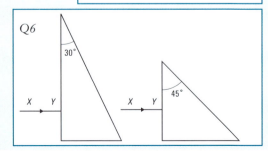
Q6

critical angle of the glass of both prisms is 42°. Explain the meaning of the term 'critical angle'.

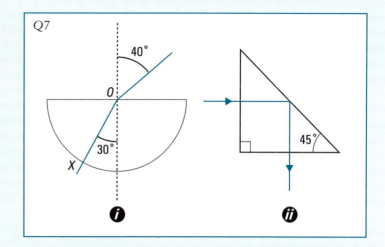

7. In diagram (i): (a) Explain what happens to the ray at X, between X and O, and at O. Why has the emerging ray been refracted?
(b) Calculate the refractive index of the material.
(c) Describe how the apparatus could be used to find the critical angle experimentally. Calculate its value for this material.
(d) Glass prisms are sometimes used to turn light through 90°, as shown in diagram (ii). Would prisms of the material in diagram (i) be able to do the same? Explain.

8. In an experiment to determine the refractive index of water a black line is painted on the bottom of a tall glass container which is then partially filled with water. When someone looks vertically down into the water the black line appears to be closer than it really is. Explain, with the help of a ray diagram, why this is so. The following results were obtained in such an experiment.

Real depth (cm)	8·1	12·0	16·0	20·00
Apparent depth (cm)	5·9	9·1	12·0	15·1

Plot a graph of real depth (y-axis) against apparent depth (x-axis) and hence determine a value for the refractive index of water.

9. The following is part of a report by a student of an experiment to verify Snell's law. 'The glass block was placed on a sheet of paper. The incident ray and the refracted ray were marked on the paper. Two angles were measured. The experiment was repeated for a number of other incident and refracted rays. The measurements were then tabulated.'
(i) Describe how the incident and refracted rays could have been obtained in this experiment. (ii) Show by means of a diagram the angles that were measured. (iii) Indicate the additional steps that should be taken in order to verify Snell's law.

★10. A ray of light was passed through a rectangular glass block and the angles of incidence, i, and refraction, r, were measured. The following table shows the measurements obtained in the experiment.

i (degrees)	12	21	29	40	49	62	70	79
r (degrees)	8	14	19	26	0	36	39	41

Draw a suitable graph and explain how this verifies Snell's law. From the graph determine the refractive index of the glass. Outline an experimental procedure for determining the position of the refracted ray and hence finding the angle of refraction. Explain why placing the block on its edge would have given a less accurate result.

11. A microscope is focused on a mark on a sheet of paper. When a slab of glass 7 cm thick is placed on top of the paper, it is necessary to raise the microscope 1·75 cm in order to bring the mark back into focus. What is the refractive index of the glass?

*12. (a) Explain the terms: refractive index; total internal reflection.
(b) Describe an experiment to measure the refractive index of a liquid.
(c) Use a ray diagram to show that light can be reflected through 180° by a triangular prism.
(d) Calculate the minimum value for the refractive index of the material of the prism for this to occur.
(e) What are optical fibres? Explain how light is transmitted along such fibres and give two uses of them.

*13. A travelling microscope reads 5, 6·84, 9·88 cm when focused on an object in air, the same object covered by a glass slab and the top of the glass slab respectively. Find the refractive index of the glass.

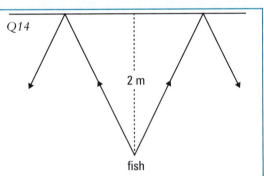

*14. Calculate the radius of the circle on the surface of the water through which the fish in the diagram can be seen if the fish is 2 m below the surface (take the critical angle as 49°).

*15. A small fish is 0·4 m below the surface of a river and 0·3 m out from the vertical bank. The surface of the river is level with the bank. If a fisherman's eyes are 1·5 m above the ground, how far from the bank of the river is he standing when he can just see the fish?

*16. The refracting angle of a glass prism is 45°. What is the least possible angle of incidence of a ray that passes through without undergoing total internal reflection? (Take the refractive index of the glass as 1·5.)

*17. An optical fibre has a core made of glass with a refractive index of 1.460 and a cladding made of plastic of refractive index 1.440. What is the critical angle for the boundary between the glass and plastic?

Lenses

CHAPTER 3

In this chapter we shall study thin lenses. The diagram shows two common types of lens, **converging** (convex) and **diverging** (concave).

When light passes through a lens it is refracted twice, once when it passes from air to glass and once when it passes from glass to air. The effect of this is that a converging lens causes light rays to come together, whereas a diverging lens causes light rays to spread apart.

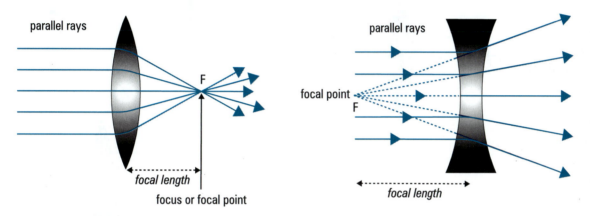

When drawing ray diagrams for converging lenses, remember that

1. **Rays of light parallel to the principal axis are refracted through F, the focus (and vice versa).**
2. **Rays passing through the centre of the lens are undeviated.**

The position, nature and size of the image formed by a converging lens depends on the distance of the object from the lens, as you can see from the ray diagrams.

OBJECT BEYOND 2F

The image is
1. between F and 2F
2. real
3. inverted
4. smaller than the object.

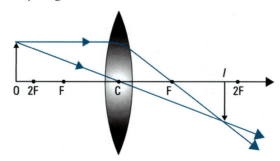

Physics Now!

OBJECT AT 2F

The image is
1. at 2F
2. real
3. inverted
4. the same size as the object.

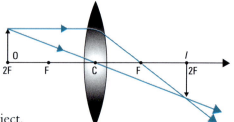

OBJECT BETWEEN 2F AND F

The image is
1. beyond 2F
2. real
3. inverted
4. larger than the object.

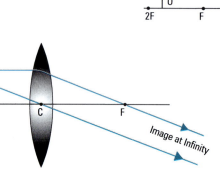

OBJECT AT F

The image is at infinity.

OBJECT INSIDE F

The image is
1. behind the object
2. virtual
3. erect
4. larger than the object.

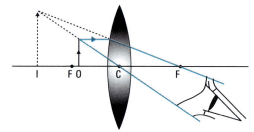

If you had a bright object, lens and screen, as shown in the diagram, could you demonstrate all of the above? Try it and see.
How many failed? Why?

In the case of a diverging lens the image is always virtual, erect and diminished as shown in the diagram below.

Problems involving lenses can be solved by accurate ray diagrams or by using these formulae:

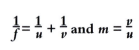

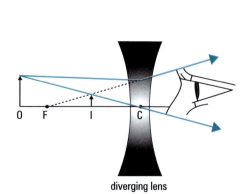

diverging lens

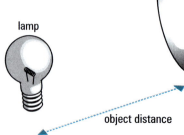

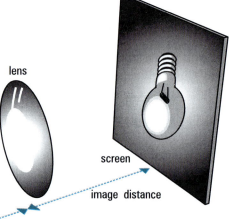

When the object is a long way off, then the image distance is the focal length of the lens.

Sign convention: For a converging lens, f is positive. For a diverging lens, f is negative. For a real image, v is positive. For a virtual image, v is negative.

Problem 1

An object is placed 12 cm from a converging lens of focal length 10 cm. Find the position, nature and size of the image.

$$\frac{1}{f} = \frac{1}{u} + \frac{1}{v} \implies \frac{1}{10} = \frac{1}{12} + \frac{1}{v} \implies \frac{1}{10} - \frac{1}{12} = \frac{1}{v}$$

$$\implies \frac{6}{60} - \frac{5}{60} = \frac{1}{v}$$

$$\implies \frac{1}{60} = \frac{1}{v}$$

$$\implies v = 60$$

$$m = \frac{v}{u} = \frac{60}{12} = 5$$

A real image 5 times the size of the object is formed 60 cm from the lens.

As an exercise, draw an accurate ray diagram to illustrate the above.

Problem 2

A diverging lens of focal length 15 cm forms an image 5 cm from the lens. Find the position of the object.

Diverging lens, so f is negative. Virtual image, so v is negative.

$$\frac{1}{f} = \frac{1}{u} + \frac{1}{v} \implies \frac{1}{-15} = \frac{1}{u} + \frac{1}{-5} \implies \frac{1}{5} - \frac{1}{15} = \frac{1}{u}$$

$$\implies \frac{3}{15} - \frac{1}{15} = \frac{1}{u}$$

$$\implies \frac{2}{15} = \frac{1}{u}$$

$$\implies 7{\cdot}5 = u$$

Answer: 7·5 cm from the lens.

Mandatory experiment

AIM: To find the focal length of a converging lens.

METHOD 1
1. Use the lens to focus the image of a distant object onto a screen.
2. Measure the distance from the lens to the screen. This distance is the focal length of the lens.

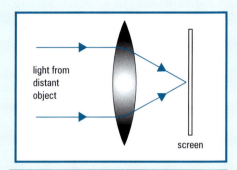

METHOD 2
1. Lay a converging lens on top of a plane mirror.
2. Fix a pin so that it projects horizontally from a retort stand above the lens.
3. Adjust the pin until pin and image move together without parallax. The pin is now on the focal plane of the lens.

Result: the distance from the pin to the centre of the lens gives the focal length.

4. Repeat a number of times and find the average value of f.

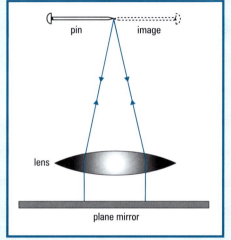

METHOD 3
1. Set up the apparatus as shown in the diagram.
2. Adjust the position of the lens until a sharp image of the slit in the lamp box is formed on the screen.
3. Measure u and v.
4. Calculate f from the formula $\frac{1}{f} = \frac{1}{u} + \frac{1}{v}$.
5. Repeat for different positions of the lamp box and calculate the average value of f.

QUESTIONS
1. If the lamp box and screen are fixed in position there are two positions of the lens for which a sharp image is formed on the screen. Why is this?
2. When will you not get an image on the screen?

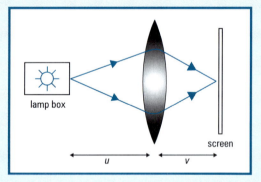

The power of a lens

Opticians often speak about the power of a lens.

$$\text{power} = \frac{1}{\text{focal length in metres}} \quad (P = \frac{1}{f})$$

The power of a lens is measured in **dioptres**, so a converging lens of focal length 20 cm would have a power of $\frac{1}{0.2\text{m}} = 5$ dioptres. You will easily recognise a powerful converging lens: it is much thicker than the lenses you use for experiments.

Lenses

Sometimes a compound lens is formed by placing two lenses of powers P_1 and P_2 in contact. In this case $P = P_1 + P_2$ or $\frac{1}{F} = \frac{1}{f_1} + \frac{1}{f_2}$

Summary

- A converging lens forms a virtual image when the object is inside the focus.
- A diverging lens always forms a virtual, erect, diminished image.
- For a converging lens f is positive.
- For a diverging lens f is negative.
- The power of a lens $P = \frac{1}{f}$.
- For two lenses in contact $P = P_1 + P_2$.

SHORT QUESTIONS

1. Does a converging lens form a virtual image when the object is (A) inside the focus, (B) at the focus, (C) between the focus and the centre of curvature, (D) at the centre of curvature or (E) outside the centre of curvature?
2. An object is placed 12 cm in front of a converging lens of focal length 10 cm. Will the image formed be (A) virtual, upright and magnified, (B) real, upright and diminished, (C) real, upright and magnified, (D) real, inverted and magnified or (E) real, inverted and diminished?
3. An object is placed at a distance of $2f$ from a converging lens of focal length f. Is the magnification of the image (A) 0, (B) 0·5, (C) 1, (D) 1·5 or (E) 2?
4. The diagram shows rays from the top of an object, O, passing through a diverging lens. The lens forms an image of O at I. Which of the following distances is the focal length of the lens? (A) PQ, (B) PR, (C) PS, (D) RS, (E) QS.
5. When a postage stamp is viewed through a converging lens, which of the following could **not** be a description of the image formed? (A) same size and upside down, (B) smaller and upside down, (C) magnified and upside down, (D) magnified and erect, (E) smaller and erect.
6. A virtual magnified image of an object can only be produced by a _____ lens.
7. When an object is at the focus of a converging lens, the image is at _____.
8. In terms of u and v, the focal length f is equal to _____.

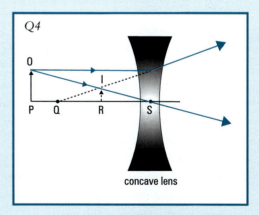

27

LONG QUESTIONS

1. An object is placed 50 cm from a converging lens of focal length 20 cm. Find the position, nature and magnification of the image.
2. How can a converging lens be used as a magnifying glass? An object is placed 30 cm from a diverging lens of focal length 10 cm. Find the position and nature of the image.
3. An object 5 cm high is placed 20 cm from a converging lens of focal length 15 cm. Find the size and position of the image.
4. An object 6 cm high is placed 30 cm in front of a converging lens. A real image is formed 10 cm away from the lens. What are the size of the image and the focal length of the lens?
5. An object 5 cm high is placed 10 cm away from a converging lens of focal length 20 cm. Find the size and position of the image.
6. An object is placed 4 cm from a converging lens, giving a real image 16 cm from the lens. Find the focal length of the lens and the magnification of the image.
7. The diagram shows the relative positions of pieces of apparatus set up to show that a converging lens forms an image on a screen. The image distance V is found for each of 8 different object distances U, the image being clearly focused in each case. The results are listed in the table (in cm).

U	19	21	25	28	32	35	40	50
V	71	52	37	32	28	26	24	21

(a) Plot a graph of V (y-axis) against U (x-axis).
(b) Mark on the graph a point where $U = V$. From the graph find the value of U when $U = V$. Use this value to find the focal length of the lens.

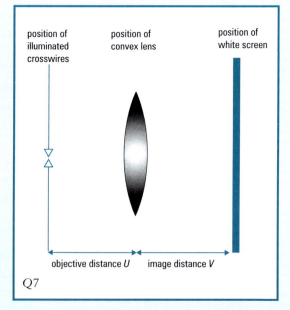

Q7

8. (a) A student wishing to project a magnified image of a 5 cm × 5 cm slide on to a screen uses the arrangement in the diagram. He finds that a clear image appears when the distance between the slide and the lens is 20 cm and the distance between the lens and the screen is 100 cm. Determine (i) the size of the image, (ii) the focal length of the lens. In an attempt to produce a larger image, the student then (1) moves the lens to the right, keeping the slide and the screen in the same position, (2) moves the

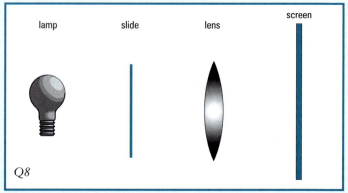

Q8

slide closer to the lens and the screen further from the lens. Will action (1) on its own have the desired effect? Describe what the student would see on the screen as he moved the lens until it was 20 cm from the screen. Would action (2) on its own have the desired effect? Is there any limit to the movement of the slide? If so, what is the limit and what would be the result of passing this limit?
(b) Draw a diagram to show the action of a lens in a simple camera when an image of a distant object is being formed on the film.

9. An object is placed 16 cm from a lens which gives a real, inverted image the same size as the object. What is the focal length of the lens?

10. An object placed 6 cm from a converging lens gives an inverted image magnified three times. Where must the object be placed to give an erect image magnified four times?

11. An object and a screen are 60 cm apart. A converging lens placed between them gives an image on the screen three times the size of the object. Find the focal length of the lens. Find also a second position of the lens to give an image on the screen and calculate its size.

12. An object is placed 15 cm from a screen. When a lens is held 6 cm from the screen, a clear image is formed. At what other distance from the screen can the lens be held so as to form a clear image on the screen?

13. An object is placed 30 cm from a converging lens of focal length 20 cm. If the object is moved 5 cm towards the lens, how far does the image move?

14. A converging lens of focal length 12 cm forms an image which is erect and three times the size of the object. Find the object and image distances.

*15. The diagram shows a lamp box L placed at a fixed distance from a screen S. A converging lens is placed between L and S. Explain why there will, in general, be two positions of the lens for which a sharp image of the opening in the lamp box will be formed on the screen. One of these positions is shown in the diagram. Using the values given on the diagram find:
(i) The distance between the two positions of the lens for which a sharp image is formed on the screen.
(ii) The focal length of the lens.

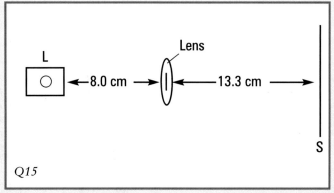
Q15

Helping the Eye

CHAPTER 4

One of the main uses of lenses is to help compensate for defects in the human eye. When a perfect eye is relaxed, the distance from the lens to the retina is equal to the focal length of the lens. This means that rays of light from a distant object, which are practically parallel, are brought to a focus on the retina where a sharp image is formed. As the object moves closer to the eye the ciliary muscles cause the lens to bulge, shortening its focal length so that the image is still formed on the retina. This process is called **accommodation**. When the object comes to a point about 25 cm from the eye, the eye cannot accommodate any further. This is called the **near point**, and the distance from this point to the eye is called the least distance of distinct vision. Any object closer to the eye than this distance cannot be seen properly. (Try this by holding a pencil at arm's length and bringing it slowly towards your eye).

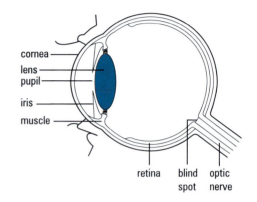

Defects of the eye

1. Myopia or short sight
The eyeball is too long for the lens, so that light from a distant object is not brought to a focus on the retina. This means that distant objects cannot be seen clearly. The remedy is to place a suitable diverging lens in front of the eye as shown in the diagram below.

2. Long sight
In this case the eyeball is too short for the lens. The remedy is to place a suitable converging lens in front of the eye.

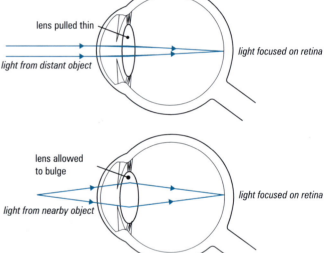

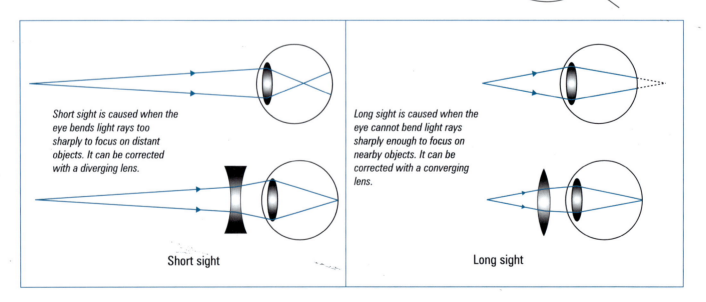

Short sight is caused when the eye bends light rays too sharply to focus on distant objects. It can be corrected with a diverging lens.

Long sight is caused when the eye cannot bend light rays sharply enough to focus on nearby objects. It can be corrected with a converging lens.

Short sight

Long sight

3. Astigmatism

If the cornea of your eye is not perfectly spherical, you suffer from astigmatism. This means that when the eye sees clearly in one plane it cannot see as clearly in other planes. You can test your eyes for astigmatism as shown in the diagram.

As people get older the lenses in their eyes become less flexible, so they cannot change shape (focal length) as much as before. This can lead to problems with reading and with distant vision. One solution is to have two pairs of glasses, one for general use and one for reading. Another solution is **bifocal lenses**, with the top part for distant vision and the bottom part for reading.

an astigmatism chart

If one line in the chart appears distinct and fine, but the other lines appear blurred, then you have this eye defect.

Contact lenses

Many people prefer contact lenses to glasses. Contact lenses appear to be placed directly onto the cornea, but in fact a film of tear fluid forms between the lens and the eye, and the lens is held in place by surface tension. They give better all-round vision than glasses, but they must be cleaned properly to prevent eye infection.

The magnifying glass

Even if your eyes are perfect, they may need help. For example, have you ever tried to read the fine detail on an ordnance survey map? If you have, you know why so many students bring a magnifying glass into a geography exam.

The magnifying glass is a converging lens of short focal length. The lens is held close to the object so that the object is inside the focus of the lens. The result is a virtual, erect and magnified image. The eye is placed close to the lens so that the image is at the near point, thus giving the greatest magnification.

The microscope

The magnifying glass is fine for studying ordnance survey maps, but would not do for blood cells. What we need in this case is a microscope. As shown in the diagram, the first lens (the objective lens) forms an image inside the microscope. The microscope is adjusted so that this image is just inside the focus of the eyepiece lens. The eyepiece lens now acts as a magnifying glass and the final image is formed at the near point.

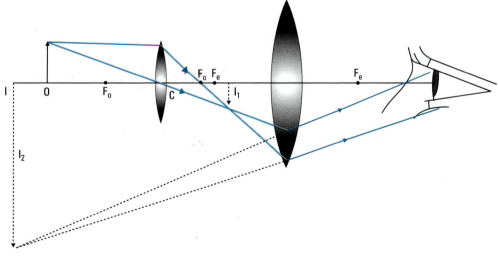

Physics Now!

The Astronomical Telescope

If you look at the diagrams on page 24 you will see that a single lens cannot produce a magnified image of a distant object, but two lenses can. This is what happens in a telescope. The details are given in the diagram. When the final image is formed at infinity it can be viewed with a relaxed eye, thus avoiding eye strain. The telescope is now in **normal adjustment**.

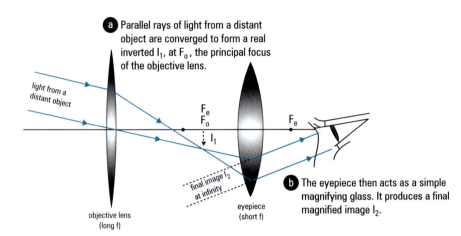

a Parallel rays of light from a distant object are converged to form a real inverted I_1, at F_o, the principal focus of the objective lens.

b The eyepiece then acts as a simple magnifying glass. It produces a final magnified image I_2.

The Slide Projector

A slide projector involves the use of a concave mirror and lenses.

As you can see from the diagram, a concave mirror is used to reflect light back towards the slide and two lenses are used to concentrate light on the slide.

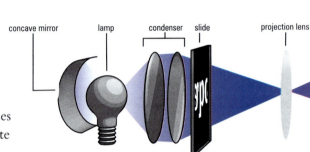

The Spectrometer

A spectrometer is used to study light. It consists of the following parts.

1. A **collimator C**, which is a tube with a slit **S** at one end and a converging lens at the other. In practice the slit should be at the focus of the lens so that light entering the slit will emerge from the lens as a parallel beam.
2. A **telescope T** with crosswires in its eyepiece.
3. A **circular scale** which is marked in degrees and has a vernier scale attached.
4. A **table** which rotates and can be levelled with three screws.

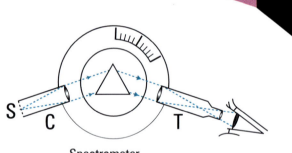

Spectrometer

Before use, the spectrometer must be adjusted as follows:
1. adjust the eyepiece until the crosswires are clearly seen
2. focus the telescope on a distant object
3. place a lamp in front of the slit and place the telescope in line with the collimator
4. adjust the width of the slit to give a fairly narrow beam of light, and adjust the telescope until the image of the slit coincides with the crosswires without parallax
5. level the table.

Helping the Eye

The camera

Despite the fact that it can have the faults mentioned above, and some others besides, the eye is a wonderful organ. In designing the camera, people have tried, to an extent, to copy the eye. There are, however, certain marked differences.

To begin with, a camera lens is rigid so the focal length cannot be changed. Instead the light is focused on the film by moving the lens in or out.

The amount of light entering the camera is controlled in two ways. First, the diaphragm can be adjusted to vary the size of the **aperture** through which the light passes.
This is similar to the way in which the iris controls the amount of light entering the eye, although the iris is more flexible than the diaphragm. The amount of light entering the camera can also be controlled by varying the amount of time for which the shutter remains open (the shutter speed). Finally, the image formed on the film is permanent, whereas the image formed on the retina is not.

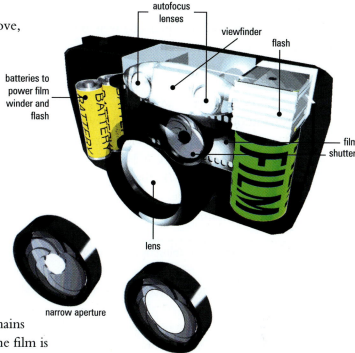

Summary

- ◆ Accommodation means that the eye focuses objects at different distances from it onto the retina by changing the shape, and hence the focal length, of the lens.
- ◆ A converging lens acts as a magnifying glass if the object is placed inside the focus.
- ◆ A simple microscope has two converging lenses of short focal length.
- ◆ An astronomical telescope has two converging lenses, an objective of long focal length and an eyepiece of short focal length.

Short Questions

1. In the eye, is the image formed on (A) the iris, (B) the retina, (C) the cornea, (D) the lens or (E) none of these?
2. A part of the eye that does not change its shape when focusing objects at different distances but is responsible for a large proportion of the refraction of light rays from an object is (A) the retina (B) the pupil, (C) the lens, (D) the cornea or (E) the iris?
3. Is the image formed in the eye (A) real, inverted and diminished, (B) virtual, inverted and diminished, (C) real, inverted and magnified, (D) virtual, inverted and magnified or (E) real, erect and diminished?

4. Your friend can read perfectly well, but cannot see the board unless she sits on the front row in class.
   (A) Is she short sighted or long sighted?
   (B) What type of lenses — converging or diverging — would an optician prescribe for her?
5. A point of similarity between the eye and the camera is that they both (A) focus their image in the same way, (B) have concave lenses, (C) have shutters of variable speed, (D) contain fluids or (E) form an inverted image on their light-sensitive surface?
6. Normal adjustment means that _____.

7. In an astronomical telescope the intermediate image is always _____.

8. In an astronomical telescope the final image is always _____.

9. The main difference between the objective and the eyepiece in a compound microscope is that _____.

10. When a compound microscope is used the object must be _____ the focus of the object lens.

11. With reference to the simple diagram of the spectrometer, answer five of the following.
    (a) Name the parts labelled A and B.
    (b) What is the function of part A?
    (c) What part of the spectrometer is represented by the letter D?
    (d) Part A contains a lens C. What type of lens is it?
    (e) When the spectrometer has been properly adjusted the distance from the slit to the lens C should be equal to _____.

    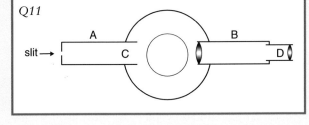

    (f) When a diffraction grating is placed on the spectrometer table a series of images may be observed. What adjustment should be made to the spectrometer if the images are found to be too faint? _____.

Waves

CHAPTER 5

Our main source of energy is the sun, but the sun's energy would be of little use to us if it could not travel to the earth. One very important way in which energy travels is by means of waves.

Types of waves

Imagine a number of small boats anchored in a pool. The water at the centre of the pool is disturbed. The particles of water at the centre of the pool begin to vibrate. These in turn cause neighbouring particles to vibrate and the disturbance travels, in the form of waves, towards the edge of the pool. The important thing to notice is that, as the waves move towards the edge of the pool, the boats don't go anywhere. They simply rise and fall as the water particles beneath them vibrate up and down. In other words, the disturbance moves horizontally but the particles vibrate vertically. This type of wave is called a **transverse wave**. It can be demonstrated using a slinky as shown in the diagram.

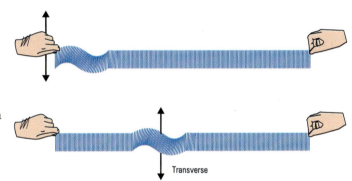

Transverse waves are waves that travel perpendicular to the direction of vibration of the particles.

All the waves in the electromagnetic spectrum, including **light waves**, are transverse waves.

The slinky can also be used to demonstrate another type of wave. In this case the wave travels parallel to the direction of vibration of the particles.

Longitudinal waves are waves that travel parallel to the direction of vibration of the particles.

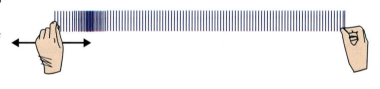
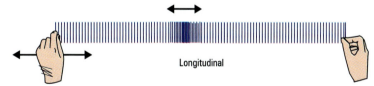

Sound waves are longitudinal.

SEISMIC WAVES

Another type of wave is that produced by an earthquake. Enormous amounts of energy are released by earthquakes. The energy travels by seismic waves. The primary waves are longitudinal waves that move through rocks (and water) at speeds up to 5 kilometres per second. The secondary waves produced by these waves are transverse waves moving at about 3 kilometres per second through rocks. When

35

both types of wave reach the surface they produce a destructive transverse wave on the surface at speeds of 3 kilometres per second.

We can learn a great deal about waves by mathematical calculations and by experiments. For mathematical purposes, waves can be represented as shown in the diagram.

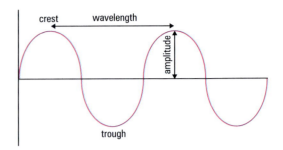

The **amplitude** (*a*) of a wave is the greatest displacement from rest.

The **frequency** (*f*) is the number of waves passing a fixed point per second. One wave per second = 1 **hertz** (Hz).

The **wavelength** (λ) is the distance from one crest to the next.

If an object has a frequency of 5 hertz it will send out 5 waves per second. If each wave is 66 m long the front of the first wave will have travelled 330 m in one second. From the diagram we can see that

velocity = frequency × wavelength

$c = f \times \lambda$

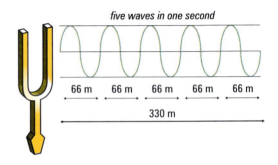

This formula applies to **all** waves.

Problem 1
Radio Atlantic 252 broadcasts on 252 metres. If the velocity of radio waves in air is 3×10^8 m s^{-1}, what is the frequency of the waves?

$$f = \frac{c}{\lambda} = \frac{3 \times 10^8}{252} = 0{\cdot}0119 \times 10^8 \text{ Hz} = 1190 \text{ kHz}$$

Interference

If two trains arrived at the same point at the same time they would crash. On the other hand, if you sit listening to a band playing music the sound waves from the different instruments do not crash. Instead they merge or combine. What happens when they combine is called interference.

Interference means that when two or more waves meet the resultant displacement is equal to the algebraic sum of the individual displacements.

This can be demonstrated using a ripple tank and two dippers as shown in the diagram. Let the dippers vibrate slowly and watch what happens when the two sets of circular waves overlap. Note in particular what happens when the crest of one wave overlaps (1) the crest of another wave, (2) the trough of another wave.

If the two waves are in phase (in step) when they meet, the result is constructive interference.

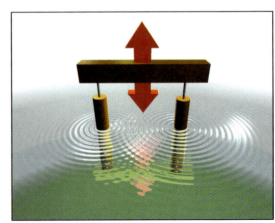

Constructive interference occurs when two waves combine to give a wave of larger amplitude.

If the two waves are out of phase when they meet, the result is destructive interference.

Destructive interference occurs when two waves combine to give a wave of smaller amplitude.

The most interesting effect of all can occur when waves from coherent sources meet.

Coherent sources are sources that have the same frequency and are in phase with each other.

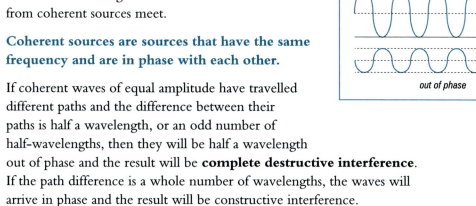

If coherent waves of equal amplitude have travelled different paths and the difference between their paths is half a wavelength, or an odd number of half-wavelengths, then they will be half a wavelength out of phase and the result will be **complete destructive interference**. If the path difference is a whole number of wavelengths, the waves will arrive in phase and the result will be constructive interference.

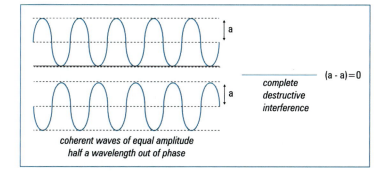

The wave theory of light

About 1680 a Dutchman called Christiaan Huygens said that light travelled from one place to another by means of a wave motion.

REFLECTION ON THE WAVE THEORY

A plane wave front AB strikes a plane mirror as shown in the diagram. While B is travelling to C, the wavelet from A will reach D. The same applies to other points between A and C. So AB is the incident wavefront and DC is the reflected wavefront.

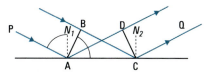

REFRACTION ON THE WAVE THEORY

A wavefront AB strikes an air-to-water surface as shown in the diagram. The wavelet from A has arrived at D by the time B arrives at C. The new wavefront DC now continues to travel in the direction AD in the water.

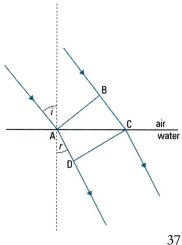

The wave theory was in conflict with the **corpuscular theory** put forward by Isaac Newton in 1660. The corpuscular theory says that light is composed of high-speed particles emitted by luminous bodies. According to this theory, light would travel faster in a more dense medium. According to the wave theory, it would travel more slowly in a more dense medium.

Also, if the wave theory were correct, it should be possible to get two light waves to meet and produce darkness (complete destructive interference). Two things happened that tilted the balance in favour of the wave theory.

1. A scientist called Foucault showed that light slowed down when it entered a more dense medium.
2. In 1802 Thomas Young succeeded in producing interference patterns with light.

Young's experiment

It is extremely difficult to get two coherent light sources. Young overcame this problem by placing a screen with two slits in it in front of a single lamp. The arrangement and the effect are shown in the diagram.

Interference patterns can be demonstrated using a laser beam as shown in the diagram. This has the advantage that there is no need to darken the room, but be careful when using a laser. Follow the safety instructions exactly.

You can also demonstrate interference of **sound waves** by using a signal generator and two speakers. (Remember, interference applies to all waves, not just light waves). However, problems can arise if you try this in a room, particularly a small room, due to the reflection of sound off the walls and ceiling.

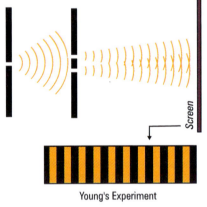
Young's Experiment

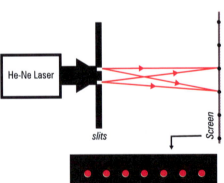

Interference patterns

Have you ever seen oil or petrol floating on the surface of water? If you look at it from different angles you see different colours. What you are looking at is an interference pattern. Interference patterns can also be seen in soap bubbles.

Christiaan Huygens (the Netherlands) 1629–1693
Although he studied astronomy and built the first pendulum-driven clock, Huygens is best remembered for proposing the wave theory of light.

Thomas Young (England) 1773–1829 *studied the eye and became aware of the causes of astigmatism and of the fact that the lens changes shape in order to focus. He also suggested that light is composed of only three primary colours. He is best remembered for proving experimentally that light has a wave nature by demonstrating interference and diffraction of light. He also suggested that light* **waves** *are transverse.*

Diffraction

If you are standing in the school corridor and two of your friends are talking loudly round the corner, you can hear what they are saying but you cannot see them. In other words, sound waves travel round corners but light waves do not, at least not normally. In fact, light waves can also spread round corners in certain circumstances. The fact that waves can spread round corners can be demonstrated using a ripple tank as shown in the diagram. In the first case some slight bending of the waves occurs but in the second case, when the width of the gap is about the same as the wavelength of the waves, the waves spread out round the corners of the obstacle.

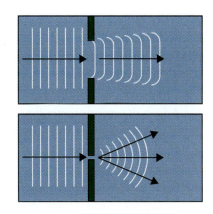

The spreading of waves into the geometric shadow of an obstacle is called diffraction.

It is not necessary to have a gap for diffraction to occur. If waves strike the edge of an object secondary waves can spread out from that edge, so diffraction can occur at the edge of an object.

The longer the wavelength, the greater is the diffraction.

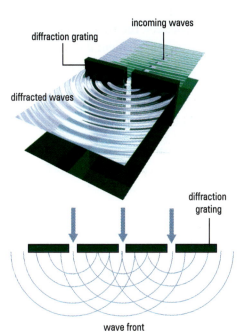

THE DIFFRACTION GRATING

A diffraction grating consists of a large number of parallel lines ruled on a piece of transparent material. (Think of Young's experiment with a large number of slits). Light cannot pass through the lines, but it can pass through the spaces between them. This means that the spaces act as a series of parallel slits. The diagram shows what happens when a beam of monochromatic light (light of one wavelength) falls normally on the grating. Diffraction occurs at each slit.

Consider rays that emerge in a direction making an angle θ with the grating. If the path differences between these rays when they are brought together by a converging lens are whole numbers of wavelengths, then they will meet in phase (constructive interference). The result will be the first bright image on the left. This is also referred to as the first bright fringe or the first-order image. Another group of parallel rays making an angle greater than θ with the normal will form a second-order image, and so on. The distance between adjacent slits is known as the grating element (d).

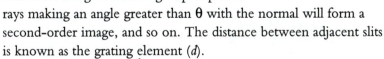

From the diagram, $\dfrac{\lambda}{d} = \sin \theta \Rightarrow \lambda = d \sin \theta$, which is the condition for the formation of the first-order image. In the case of the second-order image, $2\lambda = d \sin \theta$.

In general, $n\lambda = d \sin \theta$. This formula can also be used for Young's slits.

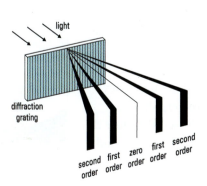

Physics Now!

Mandatory experiment

AIM: To measure the wavelength of monochromatic light using a diffraction grating.

METHOD

1. Adjust the spectrometer for parallel light.
2. Place the telescope in line with the collimator.
3. Clamp the grating on the table at right angles to the collimator.
4. Rotate the telescope to the left until the crosswires are on the first-order image. Note the angle.
5. Repeat for the first-order image on the right. The difference between the two readings gives 2θ.

The grating element d is indicated on the grating.

Result: λ can now be calculated from the formula $n\lambda = d \sin \theta$.

6. Repeat the experiment for the second-order image on each side. Take the average value for λ.

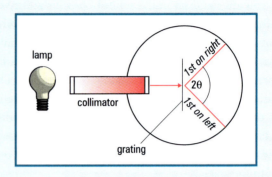

QUESTION

What determines the number of images seen in the telescope?

PROBLEM

Monochromatic light falls normally on a diffraction grating having 500 lines per mm. If the second-order image occurs at an angle of 30° to the normal, find the wavelength of the light.

5×10^2 lines per mm $= 5 \times 10^5$ lines per m

$d = \dfrac{1}{5 \times 10^5}$

$2\lambda = d \sin \theta$

$\lambda = \dfrac{d \sin \theta}{2} = \dfrac{1 \times 0.5}{5 \times 10^5 \times 2} = 0.5 \times 10^{-6}$ m $= 500 \times 10^{-9}$ m

$= 500$ nanometres (nm)

RADIO AND TV WAVES

Radio and TV waves can be diffracted. However, if you are listening to FM radio the VHF (very high frequency) waves have very short wavelengths and therefore do not diffract very well round

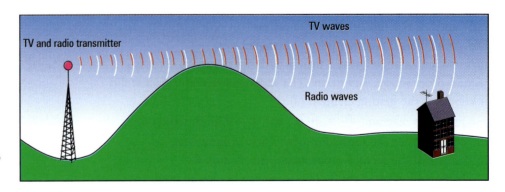

hills. UHF (ultra-high frequency) waves, which are used for TV, have even shorter wavelengths and diffract even less. This can cause poor reception in valleys. Radio waves with long wavelengths diffract well.

Polarisation

Light waves are transverse, which means that they vibrate at right angles to the direction in which they are travelling. From the diagram we can see the vibrations radiate out like a disc from the centre of the wave path. When the light meets the polariser, only vibrations in the direction *ab* will pass through. The light has now been **polarised**, which means that its vibrations are confined to one plane.

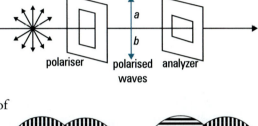

This effect is used in sunglasses, because it reduces the amount of light getting through and it also cuts out the glare when light is reflected from the surface of water in a swimming pool or lake.

Polarisation can be demonstrated using two pieces of polaroid material (e.g. two lenses from an old pair of polaroid sunglasses). Simply let the two pieces of polaroid material overlap. If the intersection lets light through, turn one of the pieces through 90°. This should stop light getting through.

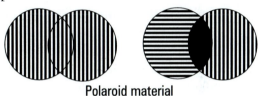

Polaroid material

STRESS POLARISATION

If you look through polaroid sunglasses at a transparent material that is under stress you will see a number of lines crossing the material. This is called stress polarisation. Look at the windscreen of a car, for example. One application of stress polarisation is that architects make plastic models of buildings and study them to find any points of stress.

Radio and TV waves are polarised before being transmitted. This makes them less liable to interference, but it is essential that your aerial be turned into the correct plane to receive them.

Only transverse waves can be polarised.

Summary

- Transverse waves are waves that travel perpendicular to the direction of vibration of the particles.
- Longitudinal waves are waves that travel parallel to the direction of vibration of the particles.
- velocity = frequency × wavelength
- Interference means that when two or more waves meet, the resultant displacement is equal to the algebraic sum of the individual displacements.
- Constructive interference occurs when two waves combine to give a wave of larger amplitude.
- Destructive interference occurs when two waves meet to give a wave of smaller amplitude.

PHYSICS NOW!

- Coherent sources are sources that have the same frequency and are in phase.
- The spreading of waves into the geometric shadow of an obstacle is called diffraction.
- The longer the wavelength, the greater is the diffraction.

SHORT QUESTIONS

1. Is the basic difference between transverse and longitudinal waves a difference in (A) amplitude, (B) direction of vibration, (C) frequency, (D) the medium through which they travel or (E) wavelength?
2. When longitudinal waves pass through a medium, do the particles of the medium oscillate (A) up and down, (B) parallel to the direction of the wave, (C) to and fro, (D) perpendicular to the direction of the wave or (E) at 45° to the direction of the wave?
3. Was the wave theory of light proposed by (A) Young, (B) Huygens, (C) Newton, (D) Michelson or (E) Snell?
4. A transverse wave is drawn to scale in the diagram. What is the wavelength of this wave? (A) 1 cm, (B) 2 cm, (C) 4 cm, (D) 8 cm or (E) 12 cm.

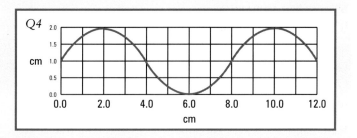

5. Transverse waves are waves that _____.
6. Longitudinal waves are waves that _____.
7. Velocity = _____ × _____
8. Two sources are coherent if they _____.
9. Constructive interference occurs when _____.
10. Complete destructive interference can occur only between _____.
11. Diffraction is _____.
12. When the vibrations of a wave are confined to one plane, the wave has been _____.
13. Light is an example of a _____ wave; sound is an example of a _____ wave.
14. _____ waves cannot be polarised.
15. Explain the basic physical principle involved in the following.
    (a) You can hear round corners but you cannot see round corners.
    (b) Polaroid material is used in the lenses of sunglasses.

*16. When light from a certain light source S is passed through a diffraction grating and onto a screen, Fig. 1, pairs of red and green lines, X and Y, are seen on the screen. Which of the following statements is correct?
(A) X is red because the wavelength of red light is less than the wavelength of green light.
(B) X is green because the wavelength of green light is less than the wavelength of red light.
(C) Y is green because the wavelength of green light is less than the wavelength of red light.
(D) Y is red because the frequency of red light is less than the frequency of green light.
(E) X is green because the frequency of green light is less than the frequency of red light.

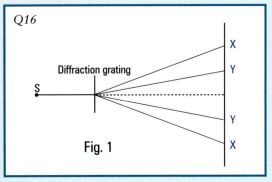

Long Questions

1. The following is part of a student's account of an experiment to measure the wavelength of monochromatic light. 'The apparatus was set up as shown in the diagram. After the apparatus had been adjusted a number of measurements were taken. From these measurements the wavelength of the light was calculated.' (a) Show, by means of a labelled diagram, a suitable arrangement of apparatus in this experiment.
(b) State the measurements that the student would have taken in the experiment. (c) How can these measurements be used to calculate the wavelength of monochromatic light?

*2. In order to demonstrate a 'Young's fringes' interference pattern with sound waves, two loudspeakers X and Y are set close to each other as shown in the diagram, each producing 'in step' sound waves of the same loudness and frequency. The equipment is set up on a playing field. An observer walking in front of the speakers hears maximum loudness only at points A, B, C, D and E, and minimum loudness between these points.
(a) Why is it not satisfactory to perform this experiment inside a room?
(b) (i) Sound waves always arrive at C in step. Why?
(ii) Sound waves always arrive at B in step. Why?
(iii) Sound waves always arrive at A in step. Why?
(c) (i) If AX = 11 m and AY = 10 m, what is the wavelength of the sound used? (ii) If the frequency of the note emitted is 660 Hz, what is the velocity of sound in air? (Show your working.)

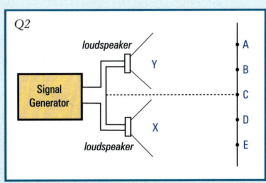

(d) How would the spacing of the maxima, at the same distance from the speakers, be affected if the frequency of the sound were increased? Explain your answer.

3. If you were carrying out an experiment to measure the wavelength of monochromatic light using a spectrometer, what step(s) would you take in each of the following cases?
   (a) If the images seen in the telescope were very faint.
   (b) If the cross-wires were unclear.
   (c) If the images on one side were above the centre of the eyepiece.

   In using a spectrometer to measure the wavelength of sodium light with a diffraction grating which had 500 lines per mm, the following readings were noted for the positions of the images: 243°30', 217°15', 200°, 182°45' and 163°30'.
   (i) One of the angles was read wrongly. Which one was it? Give a reason for your answer. (ii) Calculate the wavelength of the light used.

4. A diffraction grating has 6,000 lines per cm. The first order image is at an angle of 20°. Find the wavelength of the light.

5. A diffraction grating has 500 lines per mm. Monochromatic light of wavelength 650 nm is incident normally on the grating. At what angle is the first-order image, and how many orders of images are there?

6. A diffraction grating of 6,000 lines per cm is illuminated with sodium light. With the telescope fixed on the first-order image on the left, the reading is 130°. The reading for the first-order image on the right is 171°24'. What is the wavelength of the light?

7. Using the same diffraction grating as in question 6, the second-order spectrum of light of wavelength 645 nm coincides with the third-order spectrum of light of a different wavelength. What is the wavelength of the second light?

8. Light of wavelength 600 nm falls on a diffraction grating. The first-order image is formed at an angle of 20° to the normal. What is the grating element?

★9. What is the reading indicated by the spectrometer scales shown in diagram (a) and enlarged in diagram (b)?

   In an experiment, one of the first-order images was found at the position shown in the diagram and the other was found at a reading of 68°50'. Given that the diffraction grating has 600 lines per mm, calculate the wavelength of the light used. Why should the position of the second- and third-order images also be obtained?

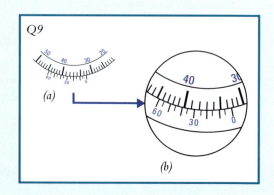

Q9
(a)
(b)

*10. The following is part of a student's account of an experiment to measure the wavelength of monochromatic light.
'The apparatus was arranged to that a number of bright images could be observed. The angular positions, θ, of five of these images were determined. The results obtained are shown in the table. The diffraction grating had 400 lines per mm.'

n	2	1	0	1	2
θ/degree	28.5	14.0	0.0	14.4	28.8

Describe the apparatus which might have been used in this experiment. Explain how the apparatus would have been arranged and how the angular positions of the image would have been determined. Use all the data given in the table to calculate a value for the wavelength of the light. The values for the angular positions of the images on the right of the central image are larger than the corresponding ones on the left. Suggest a possible reason for this and give two other factors which might have affected the accuracy of the experiment.

The Spectrum

CHAPTER 6

In 1660 Isaac Newton allowed a narrow beam of white light to strike a glass prism and found that the white light was split into seven colours: red, orange, yellow, green, blue, indigo and violet. The resultant band of colour is called a **spectrum**, and the splitting of white light is called **dispersion.**

Dispersion is the splitting up of white light into its constituent colours.

The reason for dispersion is as follows: different-coloured lights have different wavelengths. As the light travels from one medium to another the long wavelengths are refracted less and the short wavelengths are refracted more, and so the colours are separated slightly from each other.

Isaac Newton (England) 1642–1727 One of the greatest scientists of all time. He is best remembered for three laws of motion, the law of universal gravitation, the separation of white light into its constituent colours, the corpuscular theory of light and the reflecting telescope.

Primary colours

Although white light can be split up into seven colours, white can be produced by mixing red, green and blue light in the proper proportions.

Red, green and blue are called primary colours.

All other colours are a combination of these and are called secondary colours.

Complementary colours are a primary colour and a secondary colour that together give white (e.g. blue and yellow).

The addition of colours can be demonstrated using three coloured spotlights, or flashlamps with coloured filters, as shown in the diagram. The addition of colours is used in stage lighting and television sets.

A red book will reflect red light if red light or light containing red falls on it. If light that does not contain red falls on it, it reflects no light and appears black.

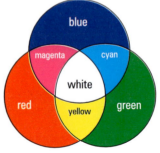

A pure spectrum

The spectrum obtained by Newton was an impure spectrum in that the different colours overlapped to a considerable degree. A pure spectrum can be obtained as shown in the diagram.

A rainbow is caused by the dispersion of light by raindrops. Light is also dispersed by precious gems. In both cases the dispersion is due to a combination of

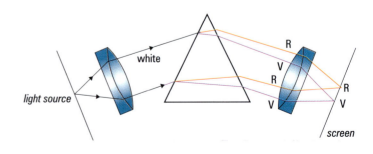

The Spectrum

refraction and total internal reflection.

Light falling on a compact disc is reflected in a diffraction pattern according to the formula $d \sin \theta = n\lambda$. Each wavelength is reflected at a different angle, so we can see colours when white light is reflected from the surface of a compact disc.

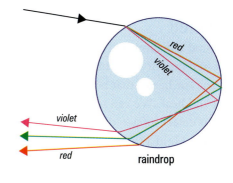

Dispersion by a grating

When white light falls on a diffraction grating, the different colours contained in white light are diffracted by different amounts. This means that the light is not only diffracted but also dispersed. The result is a series of spectra as shown in the diagram. Note that red light, which has the longest wavelength, is deviated most and violet (shortest wavelength) is deviated least. This is the exact opposite to the dispersion produced by a prism. Also, there is a lot of overlapping in the spectrum produced by the prism but not in the spectrum produced by the diffraction grating. Note that no spectrum is formed directly behind the grating, because the path difference between all the waves here is zero.

Dispersion by diffraction: long wavelengths diffracted most.
Dispersion by refraction: long wavelengths refracted least.

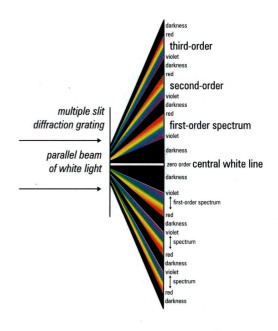

The electromagnetic spectrum

In 1865 the Scottish physicist James Clerk Maxwell suggested a new theory of light. He said that light waves were really vibrating electric and magnetic fields. He also suggested that this **electromagnetic radiation** might exist at wavelengths greater than visible light and shorter than visible light. This was confirmed when the German scientist Heinrich Hertz demonstrated that electromagnetic radiation with longer wavelengths than light did exist: radio waves. The full range of the electromagnetic spectrum is given in the diagram. The light to which our eyes are sensitive is only a tiny part of the spectrum. All electromagnetic waves are fundamentally the same, but some have high frequency and short wavelength (e.g. X-rays) while others have low frequency and long wavelength.

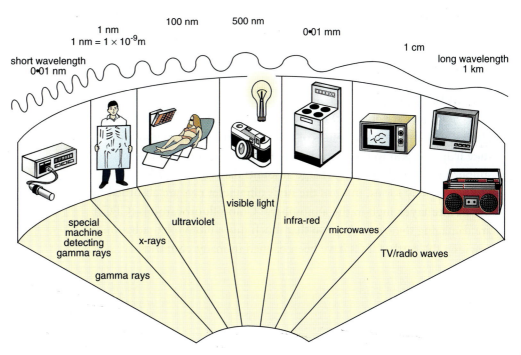

47

Infra-red

Infra-red radiation is given off by warm objects. Your body gives off infra-red rays. It is the infra-red radiation from the sun, a coal fire or an electric bar heater that heats you up. An electric light bulb gives out light and heat. We can see the light but not the infra-red rays (heat).

To detect infra-red radiation, set up the apparatus shown in the diagram. Hold a thermopile in the region just beyond the red. (A thermometer with a blackened bulb may work.) Note how the temperature rises.

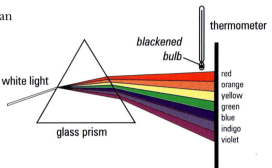

APPLICATIONS OF INFRA-RED RADIATION
1. It has a heating effect and is used to help heal damaged muscles.
2. Using infra-red sensitive film, doctors take photographs called **thermographs**. These can help detect circulation problems (if the thermograph is bluer, the skin is cooler). They can also be used to detect tumours.
3. Your remote control uses an infra-red beam to control your TV or video.
4. If there is a burglar alarm in your school, it is probably designed to detect infra-red given out by an intruder.
5. Fire-fighters use infra-red viewers to search for unconscious people in smoke-filled buildings or under rubble.
6. Special infra-red glasses can be used for night vision, and infra-red cameras can be used to photograph animals at night without disturbing them.
7. The atmosphere lets in short-wavelength infra-red rays which heat up the earth. The earth then gives out longer wavelength infra-red rays but carbon dioxide in the air keeps these rays in and thus keeps the earth warm. This is called the **greenhouse effect**. Scientists are concerned that too much carbon dioxide is being released into the atmosphere and that the average temperature of the earth is rising.

Can you identify the animal in this infra-red photograph?

Ultraviolet

Ultraviolet rays are given off by the sun and also by electric arcs used in electric welding. Small amounts of ultraviolet radiation are good for us, as they help our skin to produce vitamin D, but large amounts can cause sunburn or even skin cancer. Large amounts damage our eyes.

Fortunately for us, most of the sun's ultraviolet rays are absorbed by the **ozone layer** high in the atmosphere. Chlorofluorocarbons (CFCs) are damaging the ozone layer so that much more ultraviolet radiation is reaching the earth. CFCs have been banned in many countries.

TO DETECT ULTRAVIOLET RADIATION

Hold a white cloth that has been washed in a detergent just beyond the violet region of the spectrum. (A quartz prism must be used, as glass absorbs UV radiation.) Alternatively you can hold the cloth in front of a UV lamp.

APPLICATIONS OF ULTRAVIOLET RADIATION

1. Some substances **fluoresce**: they absorb ultraviolet rays and convert the energy to visible light rays. This is what happens in a fluorescent light tube.
2. Some washing powders contain chemicals (called brighteners) which fluoresce. This is why white clothes that have been washed in these powders appear so bright under the UV lamps in a disco.
3. Security pens contain special ink which you can use to write your name on your personal stereo etc. This is invisible in ordinary light but shows up clearly under UV light.

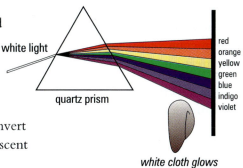

Microwaves

What we call microwaves are in fact radio waves of short wavelength. They have two main uses, communication and cooking.

1. COMMUNICATION

The first radio waves used by humans were long waves. They were refracted and eventually totally internally reflected by layers of different density in the atmosphere, so they could be received thousands of miles away. Unfortunately, the reception was not always good as the different layers in the atmosphere change rapidly when the temperature changes.

Microwaves are not refracted much by the atmosphere; in fact they practically travel in straight lines. This means that microwaves can carry information on the earth's surface from transmitter to receiver, but to do this transmitter and receiver must be in 'line of sight' of each other. Because of the curvature of the earth's surface they must be, on average, within 40 miles of each other. However, by using a series of transmitters and receivers signals can be sent right across the country.

For communication over longer distances microwaves can be sent from the surface of the earth to satellites and back again.

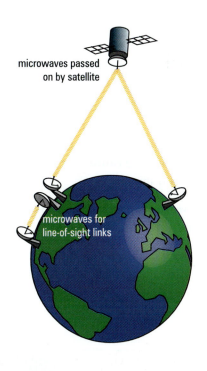

2. COOKING

In a microwave oven the microwaves are produced by a magnetron and guided to a metal stirrer which reflects the waves into the oven. Microwaves are reflected by metal but absorbed by water, sugar and fat molecules in food. This causes the food to heat up and cook very rapidly. The door has a wire mesh to reflect microwaves back into the oven and a safety switch that turns off the microwave if the door is opened.

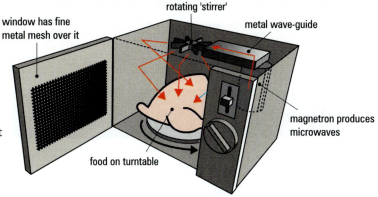

Emission spectra

If you heat some sodium chloride in a Bunsen flame its atoms become excited and it emits yellow light which is the same as the light given out by sodium street lamps. This is called an emission spectrum.

An emission spectrum is a spectrum given out by a substance when its atoms are excited.

If you examine this light with a spectrometer you will see that it consists of a number of lines. A **line** spectrum is emitted by a monatomic gas.

A molecular gas, such as oxygen, emits a **band** spectrum, i.e. a series of lines arranged in bands.

If you examine the spectrum emitted by a filament lamp you will see that it is **continuous**. A continuous spectrum is emitted by a hot solid or liquid.

Since no two elements emit the same spectrum, substances can be analysed by heating them and studying the spectrum produced to see what elements are present.

Absorption spectra

There are a number of dark lines in the spectrum of the sun. This means that many wavelengths are missing because they were absorbed by gases in the sun's atmosphere. A German scientist, Joseph von Fraunhofer, measured the wavelengths of these lines, which later became known as **Fraunhofer lines**. This type of spectrum is called an absorption spectrum.

An absorption spectrum is a spectrum that is continuous except for certain missing wavelengths.

Since a gas will absorb exactly the same wavelengths as it would emit when heated, the missing wavelengths tell us what gases are in the sun's atmosphere. It was in this way that helium was discovered in the sun's atmosphere before it was found on earth.

Joseph von Fraunhofer (Germany) 1787–1826
Contrary to popular belief, the dark lines in the spectrum of the sun were not discovered by Fraunhofer, but he was the one who measured their wavelengths. For this reason the lines became known as Fraunhofer lines.

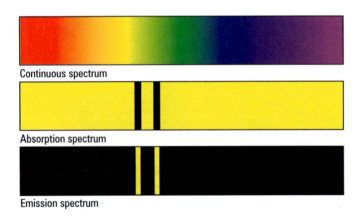

Lasers

A laser tube produces a beam of light in which all the waves are of the same frequency and in phase. As a result of constructive interference, a beam of high-energy light is produced. This narrow beam can be controlled with great precision.

USES OF THE LASER

Laser beams are used in eye surgery to treat a detached retina. The beam, which passes through the cornea and lens without damaging them, is focused on the retina and welds it into place.

The laser has replaced the scalpel in many cases. As it cuts through flesh the heat seals the cut blood vessels almost instantly so there is very little bleeding.

Computer-controlled lasers can cut through up to 50 layers of cloth at a time with great speed and accuracy. Your jeans were probably cut out in this way. Lasers can also cut through steel.

A laser beam scans the underside of a compact disc, converting the information stored there into electrical impulses which are later converted to sound.

Laser beams are also used at supermarket checkouts to scan barcodes.

Theodore Harold Maiman (USA) 1927– developed the first successful LASER at Hughes Research Laboratories, Miami, Florida.

Summary

- Dispersion is the splitting up of white light into its constituent colours.
- The primary colours are red, green and blue.
- Complementary colours are a primary colour and a secondary colour that together give white.
- An emission spectrum is a spectrum given out by a substance when its atoms are in an excited state.
- An absorption spectrum is a spectrum that is continuous except for certain missing wavelengths.
- Fraunhofer lines are dark lines in the spectrum of the sun due to absorption.

SHORT QUESTIONS

1. The diagram shows a ray of light incident on a triangular glass block. As the ray or rays pass through the prism, which of the following statements is correct? (A) The blue ray is deviated more than the red ray. (B) The red ray is deviated more than the blue ray. (C) No dispersion of the ray occurs. (D) Dispersion occurs only as the ray comes out of the prism. (E) The ray passes through undeviated and undispersed.

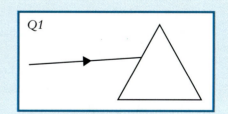

2. Which of the following are not complementary colours? (A) yellow and blue, (B) yellow and cyan, (C) green and magenta, (D) red and cyan, (E) red and turquoise.

3. If a white screen is illuminated by red light from a slide projector and simultaneously with blue light from a second projector, will the screen appear (A) magenta, (B) white, (C) cyan, (D) black or (E) yellow?
4. Dispersion is _____.
5. The primary colours of light are _____.
6. Define complementary colours.
7. If a body reflects no light it appears to be _____.
8. Compared with the speed of radio waves in air, is the speed of light waves in air (A) more than twice as great, (B) much greater but not twice as great, (C) almost the same, (D) much smaller but not half as great or (E) less than half as great?
9. Which of the following have the shortest wavelength? (A) radio waves, (B) gamma rays, (C) infra-red rays, (D) visible light or (E) microwaves.
10. Do visible light waves differ from ultraviolet waves in that they (A) travel more slowly, (B) travel more quickly, (C) do not require a carrying medium, (D) vibrate transversely or (E) have longer wavelengths?
11. Which of the following types of wave has the highest frequencies? (A) X-rays, (B) infra-red, (C) light, (D) ultraviolet or (E) radio.
12. Which of the following cannot be polarised? (A) infra-red rays, (B) radio waves, (C) X-rays, (D) sound waves or (E) ultraviolet rays.
13. Which one of the following lists of electromagnetic radiation is in order of increasing wavelength and decreasing frequency?
(A) Gamma radiation, ultraviolet radiation, infra-red radiation, radio waves.
(B) Ultraviolet radiation, gamma radiation, infra-red radiation, radio waves.
(C) Gamma radiation, infra-red radiation, ultraviolet radiation, radio waves.
(D) Radio waves, infra-red radiation, ultraviolet radiation, gamma radiation.
(E) Radio waves, ultraviolet radiation, infra-red radiation, gamma radiation.
14. Give two properties of infra-red radiation.
15. Give two properties of ultraviolet radiation.
16. Define an emission spectrum.
17. Define an absorption spectrum.
18. What are Fraunhofer lines?
19. Give an example of a continuous spectrum.

★20. A line spectrum is obtained from a certain light source. Which of the following statements is *not* correct?
(A) The position of the lines depends on the frequency of the light.
(B) The number of lines depends on the energy levels of the atoms of the source.
(C) The colours of the lines depend on the speed of the light.
(D) The colours of the lines depend on the wavelength of the light.
(E) The positions of the lines depend on the energy levels of the atoms of the source.

LONG QUESTIONS

★1. Explain the basic physical principles involved in the following.
(a) Fluorescent lamps produce more light than filament lamps of the same power.
(b) In a disco, bluish-violet light often causes clothes to glow.
(c) Sunlight passed through ordinary glass cannot produce a sun tan.

★2. A witness to a car accident, which occurred in a street lit by sodium lamps, gave this account. 'A green car pulled out from the kerb into the path of a red car causing it to swerve into a black car.' Evidence gathered the following day by the police suggested that the car which pulled out was blue-green, the car which swerved was blue and the car it crashed into was magenta. Was the witness right? Explain.

Sound

CHAPTER 7

Hold one end of a ruler firmly on a bench. Make the other end vibrate. Listen to the sound.

Stretch an elastic band between your fingers and pluck it.

Place your fingertips against the front of your throat and speak. Can you feel the vibrations?

In order to produce sound, something must vibrate.

The wave nature of sound

Connect a microphone to an oscilloscope as shown in the diagram. Strike a tuning fork to make it vibrate, and hold it in front of the microphone. A **transverse** wave will appear on the screen with the same frequency as the **longitudinal** sound wave produced by the tuning fork.

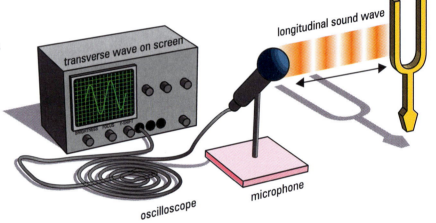

Characteristics of sound

From early childhood we learn to distinguish different sounds from each other. Sounds differ in three ways:
(a) **pitch**, (b) **loudness**, (c) **quality** or **timbre**.

Strike a low-frequency tuning fork and listen to the sound. Now hold it in front of the microphone and look at the wave on the screen. Repeat this using a high-frequency tuning fork. Clearly, **the pitch depends on the frequency**.

Strike a tuning fork, listen to the sound and hold it in front of the microphone. Now strike the fork much harder and repeat. Clearly, **the loudness depends on the amplitude**.

If someone plays a note on the piano and then plays the same note on a violin, you can tell them apart quite easily because there is a difference in quality or timbre. **The quality depends on the wave form.** The different wave forms produced on the screen are shown in the diagram.

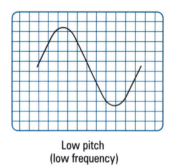

Low pitch (low frequency)

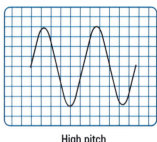

High pitch (high frequency)

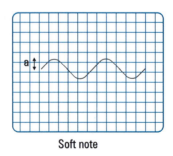

Soft note

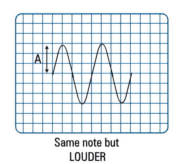

Same note but LOUDER

Sound

A tuning fork produces a pure note, i.e. a note of one frequency only. Notes produced by musical instruments such as the piano and violin consist of a basic frequency and a number of other frequencies which are multiples of the basic frequency. The lowest frequency is called the **fundamental frequency**. The other frequencies are called **harmonics**.

Harmonics are frequencies that are multiples of the fundamental frequency.

Sometimes the fundamental frequency is called the **first harmonic** and all the other harmonics are called **overtones**.

The wave form you see on the screen and the sound you hear are produced by **interference** between the fundamental and the overtones. Different instruments produce different overtones and therefore different sounds.

If a sound contains a number of frequencies that are not related to each other, we do not hear a musical note; we hear noise.

An electronic synthesiser enables you to mix whatever frequencies you want. In this way you can imitate various instruments or create an entirely new sound.

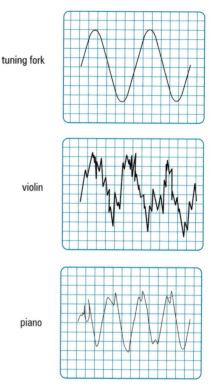

Ultrasonics

Humans can hear sounds with frequencies between 20 Hz and 20 kHz. These are known as the **audio frequencies**. As we get older we become less sensitive to high frequencies. Sound waves with frequencies above 20 kHz are called **ultrasonics**. A dog whistle is a simple example of an ultrasound: it can be heard by dogs but not by humans.

Ultrasounds have many uses

1. *Sonar.* This system can be used to find the depth of the sea. A ship sends out high-frequency waves and times how long it takes them to return. Sonar is also used by fishermen to detect shoals of fish. Ultrasound sonar systems are used to communicate with submarines travelling under water.

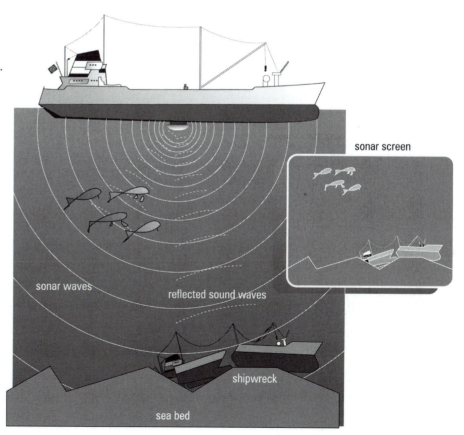

PHYSICS NOW!

2. *Ultrasound scanning.* Ultrasound is beamed into the body. Echoes are produced as the sound meets different tissues such as bone and muscle. These echoes can be used to build up an image on a screen of the stomach, a baby in the womb, etc. This system is much safer than X-rays.

3. Just as the vibrations from a pneumatic drill can be used to break up concrete, focused ultrasound shock waves can be used to break up painful kidney stones. The tiny pieces can then be passed out of the kidneys in the urine.

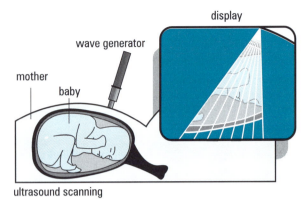

4. Ultrasound is used to clean metals. The intense vibrations of ultrasound shake the dirt off the metal surface.

5. Dentists use ultrasound to clean hardened plaque from patients' teeth.

6. Ultrasound can be used to weld plastics.

How sound travels

Sound waves are longitudinal waves, they are not electromagnetic waves. Sound waves travel through a medium by disturbing its particles. Without a medium they cannot travel, as the following simple experiment shows.

Set the bell ringing. Slowly evacuate the air from the jar. As you continue doing this the hammer can still be seen striking the gong, but the sound gets fainter and fainter. This shows that sound needs a medium through which to travel.

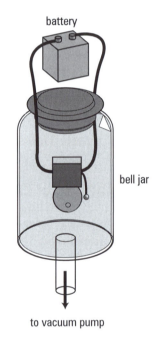

Resonance

The molecules of a substance are never motionless. Even in a solid the molecules can vibrate. The molecules have a natural frequency of vibration which varies from one substance to another. Molecules of glass, for example, have a certain natural frequency of vibration. If a singer can produce a note of the same natural frequency as the glass molecules, then the glass will shatter. This effect is called **resonance**.

Resonance is the response of a body to vibrations of its own natural frequency.

A simplified explanation of what happens is that since the frequency of the note is the same as the natural frequency of vibration of the glass molecules, constructive interference occurs leading to vibrations of much larger amplitude, which cause the glass to shatter.

Resonance is a transfer of energy between two bodies with the same natural frequency.

A pendulum has a natural frequency of vibration which depends on its length, so it can be used to demonstrate resonance as shown in the

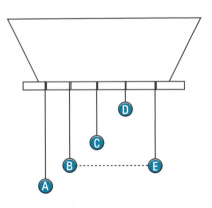

56

diagram. The heavy pendulum E is set in motion. This causes the others to vibrate, but the one that vibrates most is B. This is because B and E have the same length and therefore the same natural frequency of vibration.

RESONANCE CAN CAUSE PROBLEMS
Much of the damage done by earthquakes is due to resonance between buildings, or the ground under them, and the seismic waves from the earthquake. Resonance also occurs between the microwaves in a microwave oven and the food molecules, but care must be taken to ensure that there is no resonance between the microwaves and the molecules of the materials from which the oven is made.

USEFUL EFFECTS OF RESONANCE
Security tags in shops contain electronic circuits tuned to oscillate at a certain frequency. Radio transmitters at the doors send out waves of the same frequency. If anyone attempts to bring the tag out the door, resonance takes place and an alarm is set off.

A stethoscope is used to listen to sounds from inside the body, in particular sounds from the heart and lungs. Sounds from the lungs are of a higher frequency than those from the heart. The head of the modern stethoscope consists of two cones, one closed and one open. The diaphragm of the closed cone has a high natural frequency of vibration and resonates with the high frequency sounds from the lungs. When listening to the heart the doctor presses the open cone against the skin and uses the skin as a diaphragm. By varying the pressure of the cone on the skin, the skin can be tuned to resonate with the heartbeat, giving a louder sound.

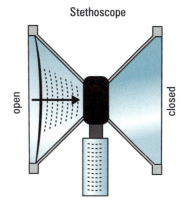

(a)

Beats

Sound waves can be reflected, as shown in diagram (a), and refracted, as shown in diagram (b). They can also be diffracted, which is why sound waves travel round corners.

Interference of sound can be demonstrated as follows. Take two tuning forks of the same frequency. Place a little plasticine on one prong of one of them to lower its frequency. Sounded individually, each emits a clear continuous note but when they are sounded together the sound rises and falls regularly. The maxima are called beats. The number of beats per second is the difference between the two frequencies, $f_1 - f_2$. If the number of beats per second were zero, the two notes would have the same frequency. This technique of eliminating beats is used by piano tuners to check that two notes are of the same frequency.

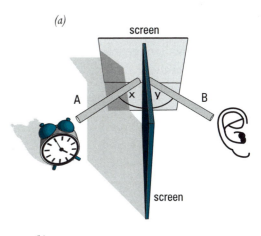

(b)

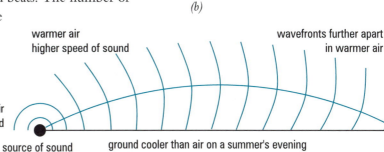

Interference by reflection

The vibrating tuning fork in the diagram sends out progressive waves along the string. On reaching the pulley they are reflected back along the string, having suffered a phase change of half a wavelength. We now have two wave trains of equal amplitude and frequency travelling in opposite directions. As a result of interference a pattern of **stationary waves** or **standing waves** is formed. Certain points in the string are at rest and do not vibrate at all. These are called **nodes** (N). Other points vibrate with maximum amplitude. These are called **antinodes** (A). The distance between successive nodes is half a wavelength. The distance between a node and an antinode is a quarter of a wavelength.

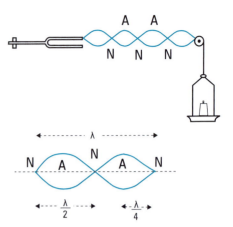

Vibrations in pipes

The music produced by tin whistles, trumpets and other wind instruments is an example of vibrations in pipes.

If a tuning fork is sounded over the mouth of a closed pipe, stationary waves are set up as shown in the diagram. There is always a node at the closed end of the pipe and an antinode at the open end. Note also that only odd multiples of the fundamental frequency are produced.

In the case of an open pipe, as shown in the diagram, odd and even multiples are produced.

Resonance, nodes and antinodes can all be demonstrated using a device called Kundt's tube, as shown in the diagram. The rod is clamped in the centre and set vibrating by stroking it with a cloth that has been sprinkled with resin. By adjusting the position of the piston P the air column can be made to resonate with the rod.

The lycopodium powder is disturbed at the antinodes and settles at the nodes.

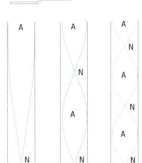

Stationary waves in a closed pipe

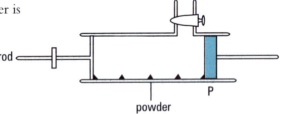

Stationary waves in an open pipe

Mandatory experiment

AIM: To measure the velocity of sound using a resonance tube.

METHOD
1. Strike a tuning fork of known frequency and hold it over the air column in the tube.
2. Slowly raise the tube until the sound reaches a maximum. This is called the first position of resonance. (The antinode is not exactly at the top of the tube but a small distance, known as the end correction, above it.)
3. Measure the distance l.
4. Take the end correction as being 0·3 times the diameter of the tube.

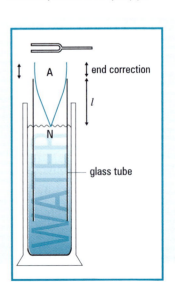

SOUND

5. $\frac{\lambda}{4} = (l + 0.3d) \Rightarrow \lambda = 4(l + 0.3d)$
6. The velocity c can now be calculated from the formula
   $c = f\lambda$, where f is the frequency of the fork.

The velocity of sound in air is approximately 330 m s^{-1}.

QUESTIONS
1. Would you use a tuning fork of very low frequency to do this experiment? Why?
2. If you got an answer of 82·5 m s^{-1}, what mistake would you have made?

Velocity of sound in other media

The velocity of sound in a medium depends on the density and elasticity of the medium. The velocity of sound in air is approximately 330 m s^{-1}. It is independent of the pressure but proportional to the square root of the absolute temperature. The velocity of sound in water is about 1,480 m s^{-1}. In iron it is about four times as great.

Vibrations in strings

The music produced by guitars, violins and other string instruments is an example of vibrations in strings.

The sonometer is used to study the vibrations of stretched strings. The length of string free to vibrate is varied by varying the distance between the bridges. The tension in the string is varied by varying the mass, and therefore the weight, at M.

Mandatory experiment

AIM: To investigate the variation of the fundamental frequency of a string with length.

METHOD
1. Set the tension of the string at a convenient value and leave it fixed.
2. Strike a tuning fork of known frequency on a block of wood and place it in contact with bridge A.
3. Adjust B until the paper rider is thrown off the string. The string is now in resonance with the fork and emits a note of the same frequency. Measure l.
4. Repeat this procedure with forks of different frequencies and enter your results in the table.

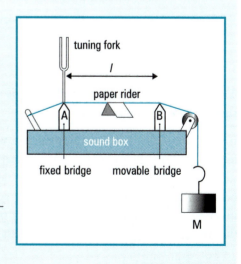

f (Hz) l (m) $\frac{1}{l}$ (m^{-1})

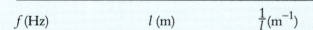

Result: fl should have the same value in all cases. So fl is constant, or $f \propto \frac{1}{l}$.

5. If you have been able to get 5 or more readings, draw a graph of f against $\frac{1}{l}$. You should get a straight line through the origin.

Conclusion: $f \propto \frac{1}{l}$.

The frequency of a stretched string is inversely proportional to its length.

Mandatory experiment

AIM: To investigate the variation of the fundamental frequency of a string with tension.

METHOD
1. Set the length of the string at a convenient value and leave it fixed.
2. Strike a tuning fork of known frequency on a block of wood and hold it in contact with the bridge A.
3. Adjust the tension until the paper is thrown off the string. Note the tension.
4. Repeat this procedure with a number of forks of different frequency. Enter your results in the table.

f (Hz)	T (N)	$\sqrt{T}$ (N$^{\frac{1}{2}}$)

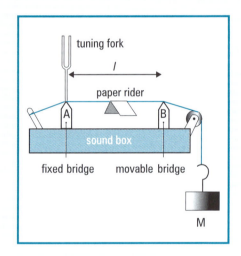

5. Plot a graph of f against $\sqrt{T}$.

Result: A straight line through the origin.

Conclusion: $f \propto \sqrt{T}$.

The frequency of a stretched string is directly proportional to the square root of the tension.

If you look at the strings on a guitar you will see that the lowest frequency string is made of heavy material while the highest frequency string is made of light material. This would imply an inverse relationship between the mass of the string and the frequency. In fact the frequency is inversely proportional to the square root of the mass of a unit length of the string. ($f \propto \frac{1}{\sqrt{\mu}}$ where μ is the mass of a unit length of the string.)

Putting all three factors together, we find that in the case of the fundamental frequency

$$f = \frac{1}{2l}\sqrt{\left(\frac{T}{\mu}\right)}$$

Vocal chords

We speak by forcing air through a gap in our vocal chords. The frequency of the sound depends on
(1) the length of the chords: a man's voice has a lower frequency than a woman's because his vocal chords are longer
(2) the degree of tension of the chords: the greater the tension, the greater is the frequency
(3) the mass of the chords: the greater the mass, the lower is the frequency.

These are the same factors as affect the frequency of any vibrating string. The sound produced by the vocal chords is increased by using the throat, mouth and nose as resonators. Altering the shape of the lips, mouth and tongue also modifies the sounds.

The Doppler effect

Have you ever noticed that as an ambulance approaches you the sound increases in pitch, and as it goes away from you the sound decreases in pitch? This effect was predicted by Christian Doppler in 1845. He said that when a source of sound waves (or light waves) is moving, a change in frequency should be observed.

The Doppler effect is the change in the frequency of a wave due to relative motion between the wave and the observer.

This can best be explained with the help of two diagrams. In the first diagram the source S is stationary. An observer at A and an observer at B receive waves of the same wavelength and the same frequency.

In the second diagram the source is moving towards A and away from B. The observer at A receives waves of reduced wavelength and **increased frequency**. The observer at B receives waves of increased wavelength and **reduced frequency**.

If c is the velocity of the waves, u is the velocity of the source, f is the frequency of the waves emitted by the source and f' is the frequency of the waves received by the observer, the formula for the Doppler effect is

$$f' = \frac{fc}{(c \pm u)}$$

Christian Johann Doppler (Austria) 1803–1853

proposed that when a source of sound, or light, was moving a change of frequency would be observed. This became known as the Doppler effect.

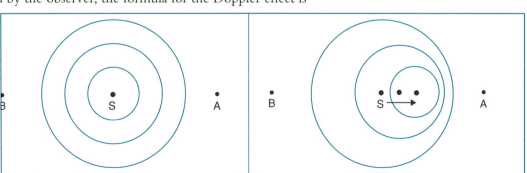

PHYSICS NOW!

The formula is best explained by an example.

PROBLEM

A train whistle emits a sound of frequency 500 Hz as the train approaches a station at a velocity of 40 m s^{-1}. Calculate the change in pitch of the sound as the train passes through the station.

(Velocity of sound in air = 340 m s^{-1})

(a) As the train approaches, $f' = \dfrac{fc}{(c-u)} \Rightarrow f' = \dfrac{(500 \times 340)}{(340 - 40)} \Rightarrow f' = 566$ Hz

(b) As the train leaves, $f' = \dfrac{fc}{(c+u)} \Rightarrow f' = \dfrac{(500 \times 340)}{(340 + 40)} \Rightarrow f' = 450$ Hz

Change in frequency = 566 − 450 = 116 Hz

The Doppler effect is used by police in speed traps. It is used in air navigation and in tracking satellites. Scientists study the movement of stars by studying the light that comes from them. Photographs of the spectra of distant galaxies show that certain characteristic lines have shifted towards the red end of the spectrum. This **red shift** is caused by the Doppler effect and tells us that these galaxies are moving away from us rapidly.

Sound intensity

The term 'sound intensity' is used to describe the amount of sound energy passing through a particular point.

Sound intensity is the energy per second passing through 1 square metre held at right angles to the direction in which the sound is travelling.

From this definition it follows that the unit of sound intensity is the **watt per metre squared (W m^{-2})**.

Imagine somebody holding up an empty picture frame, 1 metre squared, and measuring the amount of sound energy passing through it per second. Now you have the idea. The term 'loudness' is sometimes used, but it is not an exact term. For example, a pop record may sound very loud to you but to a person who is partially deaf it doesn't sound loud at all.

A sound intensity of 10^{-12} W m^{-2} is known as the threshold of hearing because, at a frequency of 1 kHz, a sound of this intensity should just be audible to the average human ear. The intensity of any other sound **relative** to this threshold intensity can be expressed in units called **bels**.

The bel is a very large unit, so the **decibel (dB)** is used in practice. The range of sound intensities experienced by the human ear is so great that it takes a logarithmic scale to accommodate them (the alternative would be to use numbers with 12 or more digits).

The relative increase in intensity is 1 B if $I_2 = 10I_1$.

The relative increase in intensity is 2 B if $I_2 = 10^2 I_1$.

The relative increase in intensity is n B if $I_2 = 10^n I_1$.

This implies that $\dfrac{I_2}{I_1} = 10^n$, and $\log_{10} \dfrac{I_2}{I_1} = n$.

Number of bels $= \log_{10} \dfrac{I_2}{I_1}$

PROBLEM

When a student switches on her radio the sound intensity in her room increases from 10^{-8} W m^{-2} to 10^{-5} W m^{-2}. What is the relative increase in intensity?

Number of bels $= \log_{10} \dfrac{I_2}{I_1} = \log_{10} \dfrac{10^{-5}}{10^{-8}} = \log_{10} 10^3 = 3$ bels $= 30$ dB

Sound intensity level

If we take 10^{-12} W m^{-2} as our basic unit and apply it to the above formula, we get

intensity level $= \log_{10} \dfrac{I}{10^{-12}}$ B

or in decibels

$10 \left(\log_{10} \dfrac{I}{10^{-12}} \right)$ dB

PROBLEM

The sound intensity in a factory is 4×10^{-5} W m^{-2}. If the sound intensity doubles what is the effect on the sound intensity level?

Old intensity level $= \log_{10} \dfrac{(4 \times 10^{-5})}{10^{-12}}$
  $= \log_{10}(4 \times 10^7)$
  $= \log_{10}(4) + 7$
  $= 7 \cdot 6$ B
  $= 76$ dB

New intensity level $= \log_{10} \dfrac{(8 \times 10^{-5})}{10^{-12}}$
  $= \log_{10}(8 \times 10^7)$
  $= \log_{10}(8) + 7$
  $= 7 \cdot 9$ B
  $= 79$ dB

Clearly doubling the sound intensity increases the sound intensity level by 3dB.

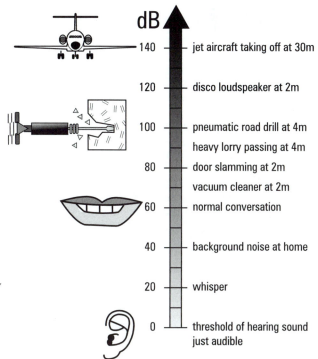

Physics Now!

Noise pollution

Noise can reduce the quality of life. For example, noise from heavy traffic can make life unpleasant for people living nearby. So can noise from discos. Discos often have noise levels of over 100 dB. This can damage your hearing. Using headphones to listen to loud music can have the same effect. Once the sensitive nerves in the cochlea (part of the ear) are damaged they cannot be repaired.

Some countries have introduced laws limiting the noise dose. Even then, people working near noisy machines should wear earplugs.

A microphone does much the same job as the human ear, i.e. it converts sound energy into electrical impulses. The difference is that microphones, particularly the moving coil type, have a very even response over most of their frequency range whereas the ear has not. The frequency response of the human ear is at its best for sounds in the frequency range from 2 to 4 kHz. Since health inspectors visiting factories, discos, etc. are concerned about possible damage to the ear, they need to use sound level meters which respond in a similar way to the ear. The scale used on these meters is frequency weighted. In other words it is adapted to the ear's frequency response. The unit on this scale is the **dB(A)** so it is known as the dB(A) scale or the A scale.

Interference is being used increasingly to reduce noise levels. A microphone picks up some of the sound. Its phase is changed by half a wavelength. It is then amplified and fed back through a speaker to interfere destructively with the sound in the factory, hall, etc.

In a large hall, reflected sound can take a long time to die away. This is a particular problem in concert halls. The **acoustics** (sound characteristics) of a hall can be improved by using curtains, carpets and soft materials to absorb sound.

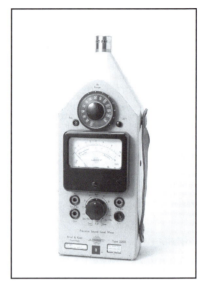

This sound level meter can be used to read sound levels in factories, discos, etc.

Sound waves and light waves

We can now compare and contrast light waves and sound waves.

Light waves	Sound waves
electromagnetic, which means they are due to varying electric and magnetic fields	due to vibrating particles
can be polarised	cannot be polarised
do not need a medium	need a medium
transverse	longitudinal
can be reflected and refracted and are subject to interference	can be reflected and refracted and are subject to interference
can be diffracted	diffract more due to their longer wavelength
travel in air at 3×10^8 m s^{-1}	travel in air at 330 m s^{-1}

Alexander Graham Bell (Scotland/USA) 1847–1922 invented the telephone. He was trained in public speaking and in teaching the deaf to speak. He also studied anatomy and physiology, which gave him some ideas for the telephone. He invented a number of other devices, including one that transmitted sound using light waves.

Summary

- The pitch of a note depends on the frequency.
- The loudness depends on the amplitude.
- Harmonics are frequencies that are multiples of the fundamental frequency.

- The quality of a note depends on the wave form (fundamental plus overtones).
- Resonance is the transfer of energy between two bodies of the same natural frequency.
- The Doppler effect is the change in the frequency of a wave due to relative motion between the source and the observer.
- Sound intensity is the energy per second flowing through one square metre held at right angles to the direction in which the sound is travelling.
- The unit of sound intensity is the watt per metre squared.

SHORT QUESTIONS
1. Is the speed of sound greatest in (A) a vacuum, (B) air, (C) water, (D) steel or (E) sand?
2. Is all sound caused by (A) electromagnetism, (B) electricity, (C) transverse waves, (D) sine waves or (E) vibrations?
3. Which of the following statements is not true?
   (A) The speed of sound is constant.
   (B) Interference occurs in sound.
   (C) The pitch of a note depends on its frequency.
   (D) Sound requires a medium.
   (E) The human ear is sensitive to a particular range of frequencies.
4. Is the physical factor that affects the pitch of a note (A) the speed of sound in air, (B) the amplitude of the vibration (C) the frequency of the vibration, (D) the density of the surroundings or (E) the number of overtones?
5. Is the loudness of a sound always reduced when there is a reduction in (A) wavelength, (B) amplitude, (C) frequency, (D) period or (E) velocity?
6. A transistor radio was placed in a glass container. When all the air was removed from the container the radio was not heard. Was this because (A) radio waves cannot pass through a vacuum, (B) sound waves require a medium, (C) transistor circuits will not function in a vacuum, (D) the lack of pressure prevents the loudspeaker of the radio from moving, or (E) the glass absorbed all the sound emitted?
7. Which of the following does not apply to sound waves?
   (A) They transmit energy. (B) They result from vibration.
   (C) They are propagated by a series of compressions and rarefactions. (D) They travel fastest in a vacuum.
   (E) They can be diffracted.
8. In a medium where the velocity of sound is 45 m s^{-1}, will a source of frequency 150 Hz produce waves with a wavelength of (A) 0·3 m, (B) 0·5 m, (C) 3·0 m, (D) 5 m or (E) 10 m?

9. The diagram shows two paths taken by sound waves from a firework, which emits a flash and a bang, to an observer. The velocity of sound in air is taken as 340 m s^{-1}. Does the observer hear (A) two sounds at the same time, (B) one sound instantaneously and another 2 seconds later, (C) one sound after 1 second and another after 2 seconds,
(D) one sound after 2 seconds and another after 4 seconds, or
(E) one sound after 1 second and another after 4 seconds?

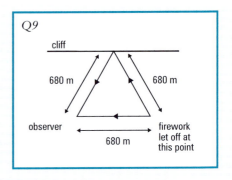

10. The pitch of a note depends on _____.
11. The loudness of a note depends on _____.
*12. The unit of sound intensity is the _____.
13. What are harmonics?
14. What is resonance?
15. The frequency of a stretched string is _____ to its length.
*16. The frequency of a stretched string is _____ of the tension.
17. As a source of sound moves towards an observer, the frequency _____. This is known as _____.
*18. The fundamental frequency of a uniform stretched string is 200 Hz. If the tension of the string is increased by a factor of 4, its new fundamental frequency will be _____.
*19. Explain the basic physical principle involved in each of the following.
(a) The note from a tin whistle changes depending on where the musician puts her fingers.
(b) A dog whistle cannot normally be heard by humans.
(c) When a tuning fork is set vibrating and then rotated slowly close to the ear, the sound varies from loud to soft.
(d) The timekeeper of a race watches for the flash of the starter's gun.

LONG QUESTIONS
Take the velocity of sound in air as 330 m s^{-1} unless told otherwise.
1. What is the frequency of sound waves of wavelength 0·3 m?
2. Which of the following does not travel at the same speed as radio waves? (i) Light, (ii) Sound, (iii) X-rays.
3. A loudspeaker produces sound waves of frequency 1320 Hz. What will be their wavelength in air?
4. The timekeeper of a 100 m race stands near the finishing tape and starts his stopwatch on hearing the bang from the starting pistol. Calculate the error in his timing.
5. Two tuning forks of 480 Hz and 512 Hz are sounded together. What is the frequency of the beats?

*6. An organ pipe 2 m long is open at both ends. What is the fundamental frequency? What is the first overtone? What is the second overtone?

7. 'All waves may show <u>diffraction</u> and <u>interference</u> effects but not all waves may be <u>polarised</u>.'
Explain the underlined terms.
What type of wave is a sound wave?
Describe a laboratory experiment to measure the speed of sound in air.
The diagram represents a wave motion. What is (i) The amplitude, (ii) The wavelength, of the wave?
If it takes the wave in the diagram a time of 0.5 s to travel a distance of one wavelength calculate:
(i) The velocity of the wave; (ii) The frequency of the wave.

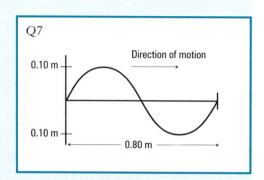
Q7

*8. A resonance tube open at both ends is 10 m long. Find the frequency of the second harmonic if the speed of sound in air is 340 m s^{-1}.

9. The frequency of the note emitted by a sonometer wire vibrating transversely is 300 Hz. What will be the frequency of the note when the length of the wire is reduced by one-third without changing the tension?

*10. A sonometer wire was tuned to a fundamental frequency of 250 Hz. The vibrating wire was then under a tension of 10 N and was 87 cm long. Calculate how to tune the wire to a fundamental frequency of 375 Hz by adjusting its (i) length only, (ii) tension only.

11. While the tension of a vibrating string was kept constant, its length was varied in order to tune the string to a series of tuning forks. The results obtained were as follows.

Frequency of fork (Hz)	256	288	320	384	512
Length of string (cm)	78·1	69·5	62·5	52·1	39·1

By the appropriate use of the above readings, obtain a straight-line graph and hence determine (a) the relationship between the frequency of vibration and the length of the stretched string, (b) the frequency of an unmarked fork that was in tune with 41·7 cm of the string.

*12. The diagram shows a sonometer. A, B and C are three triangular wedges, and W is a weight. What is the effect on the pitch of the note produced by the wire, when plucked, of (a) increasing AB and keeping W the same, (b) keeping AB the same and increasing W, (c) keeping both AB and W the same and using wire of the same material but greater cross-section?

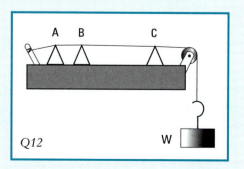
Q12

*13. The apparatus in the diagram was used in an experiment to investigate the relationship between the frequency of a string and the tension in the string. (a) State the function of the parts labelled A and B in the diagram. (b) How could the frequency of vibration of the string have been measured? (c) Why should A not be moved during the experiment? (d) Write an expression to show the relationship between the frequency of vibration of the string and the tension in the string. (e) Sketch the graph you would expect to obtain from this experiment.

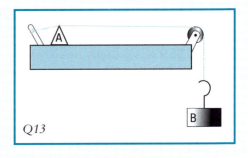
Q13

*14. The speed of sound in air may be measured in a laboratory experiment by setting up stationary waves. Explain how stationary sound waves can be produced and give a method for the detection of the nodes (or antinodes). Hence, show how the speed of sound in air is measured. If the frequency of the waves is increased, how is the distance between the nodes (or antinodes) changed? Explain how this change may affect the accuracy of the experiment. Given that the speed of sound in air is 340 m s^{-1} and that the distance between successive nodes (or antinodes) is 33 cm, calculate the frequency of the waves.

*15. A car travelling at 20 m s^{-1} passes a stationary observer. If the car emits a sound of frequency 500 Hz, what frequency does the observer hear (a) as the car approaches, (b) as the car moves away from him?

16. (Part (c) of this question should be left until after chapter 15 is studied.) (a) Describe an experiment to show that sound is a wave motion. Explain the physical principles underlying each of the following:
(i) sounds can be heard more clearly on a cold night than on a warm day, (ii) a glass can be shattered by a singer singing a high note.
(b) When the source of a note moves past a stationary observer, the pitch of the note seems to change. What name is given to this phenomenon?
*(c) A whistle which is emitting a note of 1 kHz is whirled in a horizontal circle on the end of a string 12 m long at a constant angular speed of 50 rad s^{-1}. What are the highest and lowest frequencies heard by a person standing some distance away? (Speed of sound in air = 340 m s^{-1}.)

17. Explain the terms (i) natural frequency, (ii) resonance. Explain the physical principles underlying each of the following. (a) A tuning fork placed on a sonometer may cause the sonometer wire to vibrate.
(b) The pitch of a note from a train whistle is higher to a

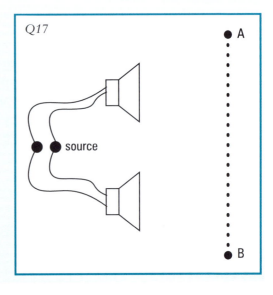
Q17

person standing near the track when the train is approaching than when it is going away.

(c) A note of a particular frequency played on a piano sounds different from a note of the same frequency played on the guitar.

The diagram shows two loudspeakers, both of which are connected to the same source, e.g. a signal generator. State what a person walking slowly from A to B would hear, and explain how this phenomenon occurs.

★18. Explain the principles involved in each of the following.
(i) Two tuning forks are fixed side by side. One is set vibrating and then stopped. The other is then found to be vibrating.
(ii) The diagram shows two sheets, A and B, of a certain type of transparent material placed parallel to each other in front of a light source, S. A is fixed and B can be rotated on its stand while kept parallel to A. It is observed that when B is rotated through 90° no light passes through the two sheets of material. Could this be done with sound?

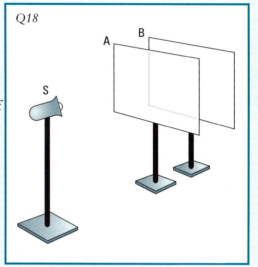

Q18

★19 How may it be shown experimentally that sound is a wave motion? A train's whistle emits a continuous note of frequency 640 Hz as it approaches a person standing near the track. To the person the frequency of the note appears to be 720 Hz.
(i) Explain, with the aid of a diagram, why the frequency of the note appears higher to the person standing near the track.
(ii) Calculate the speed of the train. (Speed of sound in air = 340 m s^{-1}.)

★20. Explain the term resonance. Give an example of resonance. Outline a laboratory experiment to measure the speed of sound in air.
Explain, with the aid of a diagram, why a sound wave may change direction when it enters a medium of different density. Give an example.
State the factors on which the natural frequency of a stretched string depends. Give the units in which these factors are measured.
State the relationship between the natural frequency of the stretched string and any two of the factors which you have given.
Explain how one of these factors could be changed, while keeping the others constant, so as to double the frequency of vibration of the string.

Vectors and Scalars

CHAPTER 8

A car is being driven round a track. At A its velocity is 60 km/h due west, at B it is 60 km/h due south, and at C it is 60 km/h due north. Notice that when we are given the velocity of the car we get two details: the magnitude, e.g. 60 km/h, and the direction, e.g. due south.

Any quantity that has both magnitude and direction is a vector.

Velocity, force, etc., are vectors. Not all quantities have direction.

Any quantity that has magnitude only is a scalar.

Time, volume, mass, etc. are scalars.
The addition or subtraction of scalars is a simple matter, e.g. 3 seconds + 4 seconds = 7 seconds. However, in adding vectors to find their resultant, we must take direction into account, e.g. a woman starting from A walks 3 km due east. She then walks 4 km due north. The resultant displacement from A is not 7 km but 5 km, as can be seen from the diagram.

N.B. Displacement is a vector having both distance and direction.
It is clear from the above examples that the addition of vectors is not as simple as the addition of scalars.

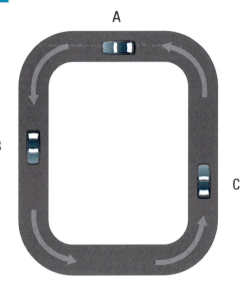

Composition of vectors

If the vectors are along the same line, they can be added or subtracted by simple arithmetic, as indicated in diagrams 1 and 2. If, however, they are not along the same line, their resultant will not be equal to the simple sum of the two vectors; it will be less than their sum. Also, it will lie in a different direction, as indicated in diagram 3.

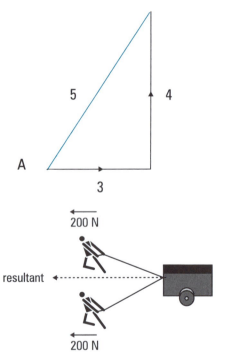

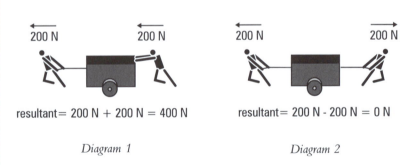

Diagram 1   *Diagram 2*   *Diagram 3*

We can find the resultant of two perpendicular vectors by drawing a rectangle to scale.

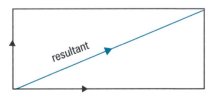

Problems can be solved by accurate drawing or by calculation.

Problem

Find the resultant of a force of 3 units due north and a force of 4 units due east.

(a) By drawing:
Answer: A force of 5 units 37° north of east.

(b) By calculation:

$R^2 = 3^2 + 4^2 = 25 \Rightarrow R = 5$

$\tan \theta = \frac{3}{4} = 0\cdot 75 \Rightarrow \theta = 36°52'$

Answer: A force of 5 units 36°52' north of east.

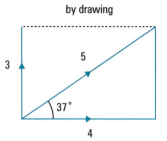
by drawing

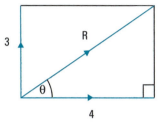
by calculation

Experiment

AIM: To find the resultant of perpendicular vectors.

Method

1. Set up the apparatus as shown in the diagram.
2. Fix the two upper Newton balances in position.
3. Pull on the lower balance until the strings from the upper balances are perpendicular to each other.
4. Fix the lower balance in position.
5. Mark off lengths OC and OB to scale to correspond to the readings on the upper balances.
6. Complete the rectangle OCDB.
7. The diagonal OD represents the resultant of the two forces applied by the upper balances and should correspond to the reading on the lower balance.

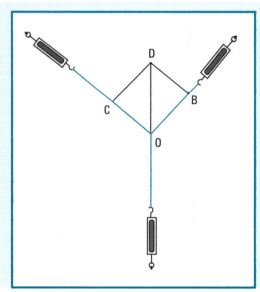

Problem

A boat that can travel 5 kilometres per hour in still water is to cross a river from south to north at right angles to the current, which flows due east at 2 kilometres per hour.

(i) In what direction must the boat be headed?
(ii) How long will the crossing take if the river is 2 km wide?

In this case we know one component: 2 kilometres per hour due east. We also know that the resultant of the river current and the force exerted by the boat's engine must point straight across the river. We even know the magnitude of the other component vector, the velocity of the boat (5 kilometres per hour). What we do not know is the direction of this vector.

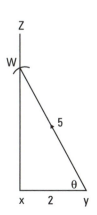

71

(i) By drawing
Draw *xy* two units long due east to represent the velocity of the current. Draw *xz* perpendicular to *xy*. With *y* as centre and 5 as radius, cut *xz* at *w*. Join *yw*.
By measurement, θ = 66°. By calculation, $\cos\theta = \frac{2}{5} = 0.4$
⇒ θ = 66°25'.
The boat must be headed at an angle of 66°25' to the bank against the current.

(ii) The time taken is the distance travelled in any direction divided by the velocity in that direction. From the diagram, the velocity straight across is |*xw*|.

$|xw| = \sqrt{5^2 - 2^2} = \sqrt{21}$

Time = (distance straight across)/(velocity straight across) = $\frac{2}{\sqrt{21}}$

= 0·436 hours

Resolution of vectors

If two vectors can be replaced by a single vector, called their resultant, it stands to reason that the reverse is also true. So a vector can be **resolved** (split) into two components. The most convenient components of vectors are those at right angles to each other.

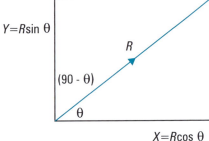

$\frac{x}{R} = \cos\theta \Rightarrow x = R\cos\theta$

$\frac{y}{R} = \cos(90° - \theta) = \sin\theta \Rightarrow y = R\sin\theta$

So vector *R* can be resolved into two components perpendicular to each other: *R*cos θ and *R*sin θ. For example, a force of 5 units acts in a direction 60° north of east. Its component due east is

5cos 60 = 5(0·5) = 2·5.

A vector has no component in a direction at right angles to itself. For example, if we consider a force of 10 units acting due east, its component due north is 10cos 90° = 10(0) = 0.

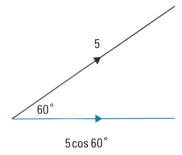

PROBLEM

Resolve the vectors in the diagram into two perpendicular directions.
Total Due North is 5 + 3 sin 60° - 2 sin 20° = 5 + 2.598 - 0.68 = 6.918.
Total Due East is 6 + 3 cos 60° + 2 cos 20° = 6 + 1.5 + 1.879 = 9.379.

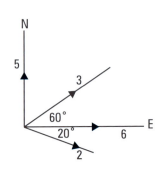

Summary

- Any quantity that has both magnitude and direction is a vector.
- Any quantity that has magnitude only is a scalar.
- If two vectors are represented by two adjacent sides *ab* and *ad* of a rectangle *abcd*, the diagonal *ac* represents their resultant.
- A vector has no component at right angles to itself.

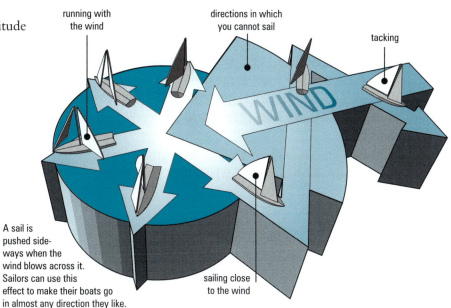

A sail is pushed sideways when the wind blows across it. Sailors can use this effect to make their boats go in almost any direction they like.

Using vectors

Short Questions

1. Which of the following is not a vector: (A) displacement, (B) mass, (C) velocity, (D) momentum, (E) acceleration?
2. Which of the following is a scalar: (A) acceleration, (B) energy, (C) force, (D) momentum, (E) velocity?
3. Which of the objects in the diagram has the greatest resultant force acting on it?
★4. A man applies a force of 50 N at an angle of 60° to the horizontal. The component of this force in the horizontal direction is _____.

Long Questions

★1. Find the magnitude and direction of the resultant in each of the following cases. (a) 12 newtons due north and 16 newtons due east, (b) 90 newtons due west and 120 newtons due south, (c) 17 newtons due west and 11 newtons due north.
★2. A body is acted on by a force of 20 N due south and a force of 50 N due east. Find the magnitude and direction of a third force required to keep the body in equilibrium.
★3. A woman is pulling a roller across a lawn. When the handle is horizontal, the force required is 500 N. What force is required if the handle is at an angle of 60° to the horizontal?
★4. (a) State, with a brief explanation, whether it is possible, given forces of 3 N and 8 N, to produce a resultant force of (i) 5 N, (ii) 15 N, (iii) 8 N. (b) An elephant is dragging a tree trunk along a horizontal surface by means of an attached rope

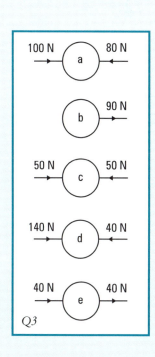

Q3

which makes an angle of 30° with the horizontal. The tension in the rope is 4000 N.

(i) By scale drawing, or otherwise, determine the horizontal force exerted by the rope on the tree trunk.

(ii) Determine the vertical component of the force exerted by the rope on the tree trunk. Explain why it serves a useful purpose.

(iii) Name the other forces that act on the tree trunk and show clearly the directions in which they act.

Linear Motion

CHAPTER 9

Displacement is the distance of a body from a fixed point in a particular direction.

A person starting at a point A and running due east at 6 m s^{-1} for 10 s will undergo a displacement of 60 m due east. The person might be thought to have had a velocity of 6 m s^{-1}, but this statement is not true. The person had a speed of 6 m s^{-1} but a velocity of 6 m s^{-1} **due east**. In other words, speed is a scalar; velocity is a vector.

Velocity is speed in a given direction.
Velocity is the rate of change of displacement.

It is unlikely that a man would be able to continue to run with a steady velocity of 6 m s^{-1} due east. If he had to run uphill he would probably run more slowly, and he would probably run faster downhill. Therefore he would be constantly changing velocity and so would be accelerating.

Acceleration is the rate of change of velocity.

PROBLEM
A car takes 5 s to increase its velocity from 10 metres per second to 25 metres per second. What is the acceleration of the car?

Acceleration = change in velocity/time taken = $\dfrac{15 \text{ m s}^{-1}}{5 \text{ s}}$ = 3 m s^{-2}

Acceleration is measured in metres per second squared.

As we said in chapter 8, velocity is a vector. Since acceleration is the rate of change of velocity, it follows that acceleration is also a vector. A vector changes if either its magnitude or its direction changes. For example, in chapter 8 we mentioned a car going round a circular track at a steady rate of 60 km/h. It was constantly changing direction, so it was accelerating.

In order to solve problems involving uniform acceleration, we need to derive three equations of motion. In these equations, we shall use the following notation.

u = initial velocity, v = final velocity, a = acceleration,
s = displacement, t = time.

Change in velocity per second = acceleration

$\dfrac{(v-u)}{t} = a \quad \Rightarrow \quad v - u = at$

$\quad\quad\quad\quad \Rightarrow \quad v = u + at \quad (1)$

75

Displacement = average velocity × time $= \frac{(u+v)}{2} \times t$

$$= \frac{(u + u + at) \times t}{2}$$

$$= (u + \tfrac{1}{2} at) \times t$$

$$s = ut + \tfrac{1}{2} at^2 \quad (2)$$

From (1), $t = \frac{(v-u)}{a}$

Displacement = average velocity × time

$s = \frac{(v+u)}{2} \times \frac{(v-u)}{a} \Rightarrow s = \frac{(v^2 - u^2)}{2a} \Rightarrow v^2 - u^2 = 2as$

$$\Rightarrow v^2 = u^2 + 2as \quad (3)$$

Care must be taken to use standard units with the above equations of motion.

Problem

A body accelerates uniformly from rest and travels 1200 m in the first 30 seconds. Find the acceleration and the final velocity of the body.

$u = 0$, $s = 1200$ m, $t = 30$ seconds, $v = ?$, $a = ?$

(1) $s = ut + \tfrac{1}{2} at^2 \Rightarrow 1200 = 0 + \tfrac{1}{2} a(900) \Rightarrow 1200 = 450a \Rightarrow \tfrac{8}{3} = a$

(2) $v = u + at \Rightarrow v = 0 + (\tfrac{8}{3})(30) \Rightarrow v = 80$

Answer: 8/3 m s^{-2} and 80 m s^{-1}

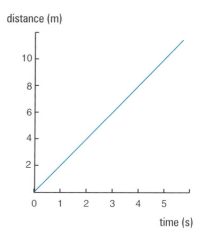

Distance–time graphs

Look at the two distance–time graphs in the diagram. The first represents a body moving with constant velocity. We can get the velocity by getting the slope of the graph. The slope is 2, which means the velocity is 2 m s^{-1}.

The second represents accelerated motion. In this case the velocity is changing all the time, so there is no single value for the velocity. We can get the velocity at a particular point by getting the slope of the tangent at that point.

Problem

A body starts from rest and accelerates at 5 m s^{-2} for 4 seconds. Its velocity remains constant for the next 10 seconds and it finally comes to rest with uniform retardation after a further 5 seconds. Find the total distance travelled.

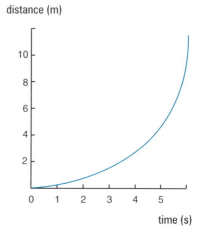

LINEAR MOTION

Stage 1
$u = 0, v = ?, a = 5 \text{ m s}^{-2}, t = 4 \text{ s}, s = ?$
$s = ut + \frac{1}{2}at^2 \Rightarrow s = 0(4) + \frac{1}{2}(5)(16) \Rightarrow s = 0 + 40$
$s = \mathbf{40 \text{ m}}$
$v = u + at \Rightarrow v = 0 + (5)(4) \Rightarrow v = 20 \text{ m s}^{-1}$

Stage 2
$v = 20 \text{ m s}^{-1}, t = 10 \text{ s}$

distance = velocity × time = **200 m**

Stage 3
$u = 20 \text{ m s}^{-1}, v = 0, a = ?, s = ?, t = 5 \text{ s}$
$v = u + at \Rightarrow 0 = 20 + a(5) \Rightarrow -20 = 5a \Rightarrow -4 = a$
$v^2 = u^2 + 2as \Rightarrow 0 = (20)^2 + 2(-4)s \Rightarrow 0 = 400 - 8s \Rightarrow s = \mathbf{50 \text{ m}}$

Total distance is 40 + 200 + 50 = **290 m**.

Velocity–time graphs

The velocity–time graph for the above example is shown in the diagram. Note that **velocity** is given by the height of the graph, **acceleration** is given by the slope of the graph, **distance** travelled is given by the area under the graph.

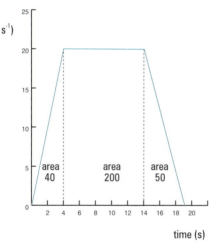

PROBLEM
The driver of a train travelling at 108 km/h sees another train 3 km ahead of him travelling at 90 km/h in the same direction on the same track. Find the least acceleration necessary to avoid a collision.

In this question we are dealing with relative motion, so we can consider one train as being at rest and the other as approaching it at 18 km/h (i.e. 108 − 90). So in effect the train needs to reduce its velocity from 18 km/h to zero in a distance of 3 km or less.
(18 km/h = 5 m s^{-1})

$v^2 = u^2 + 2as \Rightarrow 0 = 5^2 + 2a(3 \times 10^3) \Rightarrow 0 = 25 + 6a \times 10^3 \Rightarrow$
$-25 = 6a \times 10^3 \Rightarrow -\dfrac{25}{(6 \times 10^3)} = a \Rightarrow a = -4.166 \times 10^{-3} \text{ m s}^{-2}$

Reaction Times and Stopping Distances

When a driver sees something which requires him or her to brake, it takes time to react. The time lag between seeing and braking is called the **reaction time**. Reaction times range from 0.2 s to 0.8 s. **Reaction distance** is the distance travelled during the reaction time.

Reaction distance = reaction time x average speed during this time

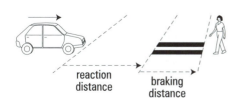

Braking distance is the distance travelled by a vehicle when the brakes are applied.

Stopping distance = reaction distance + braking distance

On average it takes about 0.75 seconds for a driver to react to an emergency. In this time a car travelling at 60 km/h will cover 12.6 metres. At 100 km/h, which is the national speed limit in Ireland, this increases to 19.5 metres! Remember 19.5 metres is the reaction distance, the distance covered *before* the driver brakes.

Reaction times increase if the driver has been drinking. Reflexes and co-ordination are slower. After drinking some drivers feel overconfident and are inclined to take risks, especially by driving too fast.

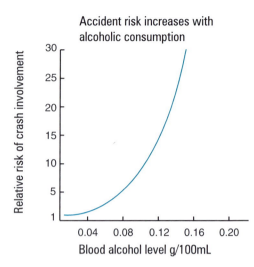
Accident risk increases with alcoholic consumption

Acceleration due to gravity

The air is first removed from the tube by means of a vacuum pump. The tube is then inverted and the coin and feather fall at the same speed.

If the air were not removed from the tube, the feather would fall more slowly than the coin, but this would be caused by air resistance, not by the difference in weight between the feather and the coin.

Ignoring air resistance, the acceleration due to gravity is the same for all bodies at the same place.

A body falling freely experiences an acceleration (*g*) towards the centre of the earth. As this acceleration is uniform at a given place, the equations of motion apply to it. The value of *g* is usually taken as 9·8 m s^{-2}.

g always acts downwards.

If *g* is acting in the same direction as the velocity of a body, then *g* is taken as positive. If it acts in the opposite direction to the velocity of the body, *g* is taken as negative.

If a body is thrown vertically upwards with an initial velocity *u*, its velocity decreases by *g* units per second until it becomes zero. At this stage the body is at its highest point. However, the acceleration due to gravity continues to operate and the body moves downwards. When the body passes through the initial point of projection, its velocity is *u* once again, but in the opposite direction.

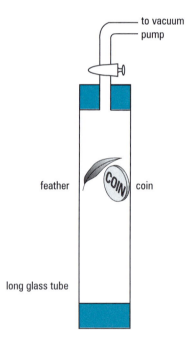

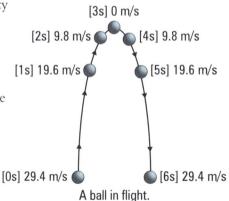

A ball in flight.
The velocity changes by 9.8 m/s every second

LINEAR MOTION

PROBLEM
With what velocity must a body be projected vertically upwards in order to reach a maximum, height of 50 m?

$u = ?$
$v = 0$
$s = 50$ m
$a = -9.8$ m s^{-2}
$t = ?$

$v^2 = u^2 + 2as$
$0 = u^2 + 2(-9.8)(50)$
$0 = u^2 - 980$
$u^2 = 980$
$u = \sqrt{980}$
$u = 31.304$ m s^{-1}.

PROBLEM
A stone is dropped from the top of a building 490 m high. Find
(1) the time it takes to reach the ground.
(2) the velocity with which it strikes the ground.

$u = 0$
$v = ?$
$s = 490$ m
$a = 9.8$ m s^{-2}
$t = ?$

(1) $v^2 = u^2 + 2as$
$v^2 = 0 + 2\,(9.8)(490)$
$v^2 = (9.8)(490)$
$v = 98$ m s^{-1}.

(2) $v = u + at$
$98 = 0 + 9.8t$
$t = 10$ s

Galileo Galilei
(Pisa, Italy) 1564–1642
discovered that all bodies would fall at the same speed except for air resistance. He made an astronomical telescope that is the basis for many modern telescopes. He supported Copernicus' view that the sun is the centre of the universe, but was forced by the pope to renounce this. Although he did not progress as far as Newton, he could be regarded as having done the groundwork for modern mechanics.

Mandatory experiment

AIM: To investigate the relationship between period and length for a simple pendulum (and hence to calculate g).

METHOD
1. Attach the pendulum bob to one end of a light thread and clamp the other end of the thread between two pieces of cork.
2. Set the pendulum swinging through a small angle and take the time for 50 oscillations.
3. Find the periodic time T for one oscillation.

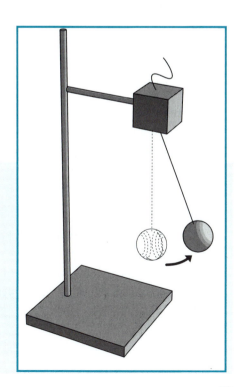

4. Carefully measure l, the distance from the cork to the centre of the pendulum bob.
5. Repeat for different values of l.
6. Plot a graph of T^2 against l. A straight line through the origin implies that $l \propto T^2$. The slope of this graph gives the value of $\frac{l}{T^2}$. g can now be calculated from the formula $g = \frac{4\pi^2 l}{T^2}$.

QUESTIONS
1. Why should you use a light thread and a dense pendulum bob?
2. Why should the pendulum only be allowed to swing through a small angle?

Mandatory experiment

AIM: To measure g by free fall.

METHOD

1. With the switch K in position 1, the ball bearing is attached to the electromagnet with a small piece of paper between them.
2. When the switch is thrown to position 2 the ball bearing is released and the centisecond timer T starts.
3. When the ball bearing hits the trapdoor the timer stops. The time for the free fall is now known.
4. Repeat a number of times and take the minimum time, t.
5. Measure s carefully.
   $(s = ut + \frac{1}{2} at^2)$

In this case $u = 0$ so that $s = \frac{1}{2} gt^2 \Rightarrow g = \frac{2s}{t^2}$.
g can now be calculated.
Note: s should be at least 1 m.

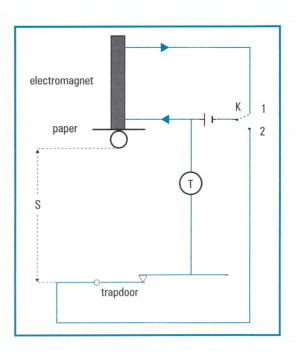

Summary

- Displacement is the distance of a body from a fixed point in a given direction.
- Velocity is speed in a given direction.
- Acceleration is rate of change of velocity.
- $v = u + at$, $\quad s = ut + \frac{1}{2} at^2$, $\quad v^2 = u^2 + 2as$

Short Questions

1. A car travels 9 km in 15 minutes. Is its average velocity in m s^{-1}: (A) 0·6, (B) 2·25, (C) 9·25, (D) 10, (E) 15?
2. A car takes 6 s to increase its velocity from 10 m s^{-1} to 22 m s^{-1}. Is its acceleration in ms^{-2}: (A) 2, (B) 6, (C) 10, (D) 12 or (E) 22?
3. A car starts from rest with uniform acceleration of 4 m s^{-2}. Is its velocity in m s^{-1} after 3 s: (A) 0·75, (B) 1·33, (C) 3, (D) 4 or (E) 12?
4. A ball is dropped from rest. What is its speed after 3 seconds? (A) 15 m s^{-1}, (B) 25 m s^{-1}, (C) 30 m s^{-1}, (D) 45 m s^{-1}, (E) 90 m s^{-1}.
5. A stone is dropped from rest from the top of a tall building. Is the fraction (distance fallen after 4 seconds)/(distance fallen after 2 seconds) approximately (A) $\frac{1}{4}$, (B) $\frac{1}{2}$, (C) $\frac{2}{1}$, (D) $\frac{4}{1}$ or (E) $\frac{16}{1}$?
6. Define velocity.
7. Define acceleration.
8. What is the initial velocity given to an object to raise it vertically to a height of 20 m if g is taken as 10 m s^{-2}?
9. Give an example of a body that is accelerating while still moving at a constant speed.
*10. Give an example of a body that has acceleration but no velocity.

Long Questions

1. A body starting from rest accelerates at 4 m s^{-2}. How far does it travel in 5 seconds? How long does it take to travel 100 m?
2. A car with an initial velocity of 20 m s^{-1} reaches a velocity of 50 m s^{-1} in a distance of 300 m. Find its acceleration and the time taken.
3. A body moving with a velocity of 30 m s^{-1} is acted on by a retardation of 6 m s^{-2}. How far does it travel before coming to rest, and how long does this take?
4. A body starts from rest and travels with uniform acceleration in a straight line for 2 seconds. If its velocity at the end of this time is 10 m s^{-1}, find the acceleration of the body and the distance travelled.
5. What is meant by saying that velocity is a vector quantity? Could a body travelling in a circle have uniform velocity? A car starting from rest moves with uniform acceleration. If it covers the first 100 m in 6 seconds, how long will it take to cover the second 100 m?
6. A body starts from rest and moves with an acceleration of 2 m s^{-2} in a straight line. How long does it take to travel the first 50 m? How far does it travel in the first 10 seconds?

7. A man driving a car at 108 km/h sees a woman wheeling a pram across the road 90 metres ahead of him. His reaction time is 0.7 seconds. After he brakes the car stops in 5 seconds. Does he avoid hitting her? If he had observed the national speed limit of 100 km/h would it have made any difference?

8. The diagram represents the motion of somebody walking along a straight road.

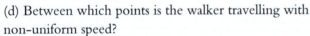

(a) Between which two points on the graph is the walker travelling with uniform speed away from his starting point? Calculate the uniform speed at this stage.
(b) Between which two points is the walker travelling with uniform speed towards his starting point? Calculate the speed at this stage.
(c) Between which points is the walker stationary? For how long a time over the whole motion shown is the walker stationary?
(d) Between which points is the walker travelling with non-uniform speed?
(e) How far does the walker go in the first 50 seconds?
(f) How far does he go in the second 50 seconds?
(g) If he had continued at this rate, how long would he have taken to get 1,000 metres from his starting point?

9. In a laboratory experiment the velocity of an object was measured at various times and the following table was drawn up.

Velocity (m s^{-1})	0·42	0·79	1·16	1·53	1·90	2·27	2·64
Time (s)	0	1·5	3·0	4·5	6·0	7·5	9·0

(a) List the apparatus that might have been used in the experiment.
(b) Draw a graph, using the above data, showing how the velocity of the object varied with the time.
(c) Use the graph to calculate the acceleration of the object.

*10. The following results were obtained by a student in an experiment to measure g, the acceleration due to gravity, using a simple pendulum.

Length (m)	0·2	0·4	0·6	0·8	1	1·2	1·4	1·6
Time for 30 oscillations (s)	27	37·8	46·5	53·7	60·6	66·0	70·8	76·4

Draw a suitable graph and hence determine the value of g.
(a) Why should the amplitude of the oscillations be kept small?
(b) As the length of the pendulum was increased, the number of oscillations timed could have been reduced. Explain.

★11. A car accelerates uniformly from rest and reaches a velocity of 15 m s^{-1} after 3 seconds. It then moves with constant velocity for 5 seconds, and finally decelerates uniformly to rest in 5 seconds. Find the total distance travelled (a) by calculation, (b) by graph.

12. An object starting from rest falls freely and strikes the ground in 7 seconds. Find the velocity with which the object strikes the ground, and the distance travelled in the last second of its fall.

★13. A ball is thrown vertically upwards with an initial velocity of 20 m s^{-1}. Find (a) the maximum height reached,
(b) the velocity at a point halfway up,
(c) the time taken for the ball to hit the ground (neglect the height of the thrower).

★14. A ball is allowed to fall from a height of 405 m and at the same time another ball is thrown vertically upwards with an initial velocity of 90 m s^{-1}. At what height will the two balls meet? (Take $g = 10$ m s^{-1}.)

★15. A stone which is projected vertically upwards from the ground passes a window sill after 5 seconds and again after 7 seconds. Find the initial velocity of the stone and the height of the window sill. (Take $g = 10$ m s^{-1}.)

Forces

CHAPTER 10

If you cycle you are exerting a force. This force causes the bicycle to move. If you exert a greater force the bicycle moves faster. If you turn the handlebars you are exerting a force which causes the bicycle to change direction. By applying the brakes you apply a force which causes the bicycle to stop. So a force can change the speed or direction of a body.

Force is that which alters, or tends to alter, the motion of a body in magnitude or direction.

Force is measured in newtons.
Note: Force can also change the shape of a body or the volume of a gas.

Look at the two objects in the diagram. The first object will not move because the forces acting on it are balanced. The second object will move because the forces are unbalanced. **An unbalanced force causes motion.**

 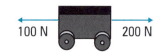

WEIGHT
Every body on earth is acted on by a force which pulls it towards the centre of the earth.

The force with which the earth attracts a body is called the weight of the body.

Since weight is a force, it is measured in newtons.

MASS
Many people use the words 'weight' and 'mass' as if they meant the same thing. They don't.

The mass of a body is the amount of matter in it

or the mass of a body is its resistance to change of its existing motion. Mass is measured in kilograms.

Momentum
It is much easier to stop a car travelling at 50 km h^{-1} than it is to stop a bus travelling at the same velocity. The reason is that, although they are moving at the same velocity, the bus has a much larger mass. The quantity of motion in a body is the product of its mass and its velocity, and is called its momentum.

Momentum is the product of the mass and the velocity of a body.

FORCES

For example, a body of mass 5 kg moving at 12 m s^{-1} has a momentum of 60 kg m s^{-1}.

Much of what we know about the relationships between force, mass, weight and momentum is due to the work of Isaac Newton who, in 1687, published his laws of motion.

Newton's laws of motion

1. A body remains at rest or moving with uniform velocity in a straight line unless an unbalanced force acts on it.
2. The rate of change of momentum is proportional to the force causing it and takes place in the direction of that force.
3. To every action there is an equal and opposite reaction. Action and reaction never act on the same body.

From Newton's second law, force ∝ rate of change of momentum.
$F \propto$ mass × rate of change of velocity
$F \propto ma$
$F = kma$

Now if $F = 1$, $m = 1$ and $a = 1$, then $k = 1$, giving

$F = ma$
Force = mass × acceleration

This leads to the definition of the unit of force: the newton.

A newton is that force which gives an acceleration of 1 m s^{-2} to a mass of 1 kg.

Mandatory experiment

AIM: to show that $a \propto F$.

METHOD

1. The metal strip is drawn back and released so that it vibrates back and over.
2. The trolley is caused to accelerate from rest by placing suitable masses in the scalepan. As the trolley moves, the pen B draws a succession of complete waves on a paper sheet placed on top of the trolley.
3. The first four waves are ruled off on the paper. (The number of waves need not be four, but four is convenient.)
4. The distance s moved by the trolley while these four waves were being traced out is measured. The time (t) taken for the trolley to move this

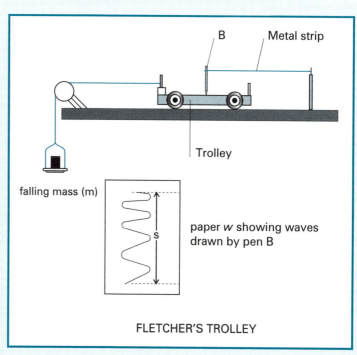

FLETCHER'S TROLLEY

85

distance is 4 times the period of the vibrating strip.
(If the period is not known it can be readily calculated.)
5. The acceleration of the trolley can now be found from the formula $s = \frac{1}{2}at^2 \Rightarrow a = \frac{2s}{t^2}$.

The experiment is repeated a number of times, varying the accelerating force F in each case by varying the mass in the scalepan.

A graph of F against a gives a straight line through the origin, showing that $a \propto F$.

Newton's second law underlines the difference between mass and weight. Since force = mass × acceleration, **weight = mass × g.**

On earth, weight (in newtons) = mass (in kilograms) × 9·8

Gravitation

Gravitation is the attraction that all masses in the universe have for each other. In 1680 Newton published his law of gravitation.

Law of gravitation: The force of attraction between any two bodies is proportional to the product of their masses and inversely proportional to the square of the distance between them.

$$F \propto \frac{(m_1 m_2)}{d^2} \Rightarrow F = \frac{(Gm_1 m_2)}{d^2}$$

G is called the **universal constant of gravitation**
($G = 6.67 \times 10^{-11}$ N m^2 kg^{-2}).

The solar system

The solar system consists of the sun and the 9 planets orbiting it. The enormous gravitational pull of the sun keeps the other planets orbiting the sun. The gravitational pull of the earth keeps its moon orbiting it. The gravitational pull of the moon is so weak that it cannot even hold an atmosphere in place, and so has no atmosphere. However, because the moon is much closer to the earth than the sun is, and orbits the earth, it has a great effect on the seas and causes the regular flow of tides. Tides are caused by a combination of the steady gravitational pull of the sun, the gravitational pull of the moon as it orbits the earth, and the rotation of the earth on its axis.

Weightlessness

Astronauts who travelled a great distance from the earth escaped the earth's gravitational pull and were weightless: there was no gravitational pull on their bodies. Astronauts orbiting the earth feel weightless and float around the space shuttle. This is because their orbit can be resolved into an acceleration at a tangent to the earth and acceleration due to gravity towards the earth. The astronauts and the shuttle are in a state of continuous free fall, and so feel weightless.

Different planets

G has the same value everywhere in the universe. g is the acceleration due to gravity on any particular planet. Different planets have different masses and different radii. It follows that the acceleration due to gravity g varies from one planet to another.

PROBLEM

If you have a mass of 60 kg, what weight is your weight on (i) Earth (ii) The moon.
(i) Weight = mass x g = 60 x 9.8 = 588 N.
(ii) Weight = mass x g - 60 x 1.96 = 117.6 N.

It follows from this example that if you weigh 600 N on earth you would weigh only 120 N on the moon.

Impulse

Another way of looking at Newton's second law is as follows.

$F = ma \Rightarrow F = \frac{m(v - u)}{t} \Rightarrow \mathbf{Ft = mv - mu}$

Ft is known as the **impulse**, so this formula can be stated in words as

impulse = force × time = change in momentum

This formula is useful for problems involving force and time.

PROBLEM

A body of mass 5 kg moving at 2 m s^{-1} has its velocity increased to 6 m s^{-1} in 3 seconds under a constant force. Find the force.

$Ft = mv - mu \Rightarrow F \times 3 = 5 \times 6 - 5 \times 2 \Rightarrow 3F = 20 \text{ N} \Rightarrow F = \frac{20}{3} \text{ N}$

Applications

What would happen if you kicked a cement block as hard as you could? Right, you would probably break your toe. But why?

Let us assume that your foot has a mass of one kilogram and is travelling at 10 m s^{-1}. Suppose your foot is in contact with the block for one hundredth of a second.

$Ft = mv - mu \Rightarrow F \times \frac{1}{100} = 1 \times 0 - 1 \times 10 \Rightarrow F \times \frac{1}{100} = 10 \Rightarrow F = \mathbf{1000 \text{ N}}$

The **shorter** the contact time, the **greater** is the force, and vice versa.

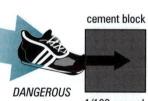

cement block

DANGEROUS

1/100 second

football

SAFE

1/10 second

Road safety

Designers have applied this idea to motor safety. Over half of all serious road accidents occur when a car runs into an obstacle (a wall, a truck, etc.) and decelerates rapidly. This short contact time results in a very large force. By designing a car so that the front crumples gradually on impact, the collision time is increased and the force reduced. Serious injuries can also occur when a car is struck from the rear. For this reason modern cars are designed so that the front and rear both crumple gradually on impact, but the cage (the part containing the passengers) is rigid.

Sport

This idea is also applied in sport, but in a completely different way. When a tennis player is serving she wants to increase the momentum of the ball as much as she can. This means that she wants the **impulse** to be as large as possible. Assuming she is hitting the ball as hard as she can, she is using her maximum force; but if she cannot increase this force she can increase the contact time between the ball and the racket by following through. This increases the impulse and so increases the momentum. The same argument applies in golf, hurling and all ball games.

Seat belts

According to Newton's first law, a body remains at rest or moving with uniform velocity in a straight line unless an unbalanced force acts on it. If you are a passenger in a fast moving car which comes to a sudden stop, you will continue moving with uniform velocity in a straight line out through the windscreen! A seat belt provides the unbalanced force that prevents this from happening. Seat belts are designed to stretch slightly to increase the contact time and so reduce the force of the belt on you. If you are sitting in a stationary car and another car runs into the back of it your head remains stationary but the rest of your body is suddenly pushed forward by the car seat. If you are in a moving car and another car runs into the back of it your head remains moving at the same speed as before but the rest of your body is accelerated. In either case you may experience what is known as 'whiplash'. A headrest may prevent this.

Increasing the collision time reduces the force

Conservation of momentum

In the diagram, two snooker balls moving in opposite directions collide. When they collide they exert a force F on each other for a short time t. From Newton's third law, the forces are equal and opposite. The contact time t is the same for both so the impulses are equal but opposite. This means that the changes in momentum are equal but opposite. In other words, the momentum gained by one ball is equal to the momentum lost by the other. This is the principle of conservation of momentum.

Principle of conservation of momentum:

If no external force acts on a system of colliding bodies, the total momentum of the bodies remains constant.

Mathematically, $m_1u_1 + m_2u_2 = m_1v_1 + m_2v_2$.

PROBLEM
A gun of mass 8 kg fires a bullet of mass 4 g with a velocity of 400 m s^{-1}. What is the velocity of recoil of the gun?

Total momentum before = total momentum afterwards.
$0 = 0{\cdot}004 \times 400 + 8v \Rightarrow -8v = 1{\cdot}6 \Rightarrow v = -0{\cdot}2$ m s^{-1},
i.e. 0·2 m s^{-1} backwards.

Mandatory experiment

AIM: To verify the principle of conservation of momentum.

Apparatus: In this experiment we use an air track. This is a hollow box with a large number of holes through which air can be blown. This enables riders to move along on a cushion of air with the minimum of friction. If light falls on the photo transistor, the timer is inoperative. However, if the beam of light is interrupted, the timer operates.

METHOD
1. Level the air track.
2. Find the mass of each complete rider.
3. Set up the apparatus as shown in the diagram.
4. Give the first rider a slight push to set it in motion. As it passes the first photo transistor, the beam of light is interrupted and the transit time measured.
5. On impact the pin penetrates the plasticine and the two riders move along together. The new transit time is recorded as the card interrupts the beam of light striking the second photo transistor.

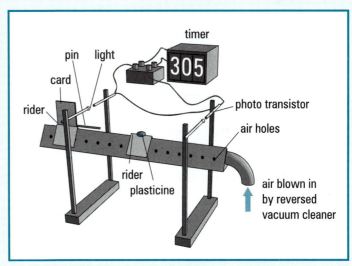

You should find that mass of first rider × velocity before impact = combined mass of riders × velocity after impact.
A typical set of readings would be as follows:
mass of 1st rider = 0·2 kg,
mass of 2nd rider = 0·18 kg,
length of card = 0·1 m,
transit time for 1st rider = 0·15 s,
transit time for both riders = 0·285 s.

$$\text{momentum before impact} = \frac{(0{\cdot}2 \times 0{\cdot}1)}{0{\cdot}15} = 0{\cdot}1333 \text{ kg m s}^{-1}$$

$$\text{momentum after impact} = \frac{(0{\cdot}38 \times 0{\cdot}1)}{0{\cdot}285} = 0{\cdot}133 \text{ kg m s}^{-1}$$

The above equipment with a single rider can also be used to measure velocity.

Mandatory experiment

AIM: To measure the velocity of a body.

METHOD
1. Give the rider a slight push in order to set it moving.
2. The transit time for the card gives the time it takes the rider to travel 0·1 m.
3. $\frac{\text{Distance}}{\text{time}}$ gives the velocity.

The air track with a single rider can also be used to measure the acceleration.

Mandatory experiment

AIM: To measure the acceleration of a body.

METHOD
1. Place the photo transistors one metre apart for convenience.
2. Give the first rider a push in order to set it moving.
3. Note the transit time as it passes the first photo transistor. This is the time it takes to travel 0·1 m. $\frac{\text{Distance}}{\text{time}}$ gives the initial velocity u.
4. Repeat for the second photo transistor to get the final velocity v.
5. The distance s is 1 metre.
6. Calculate the acceleration from the formula $v^2 = u^2 + 2as$.

Why do you think the change in velocity between the two photo transistors is so small?

Jet planes and rockets

Blow up the balloon. Release the neck of the balloon: the balloon flies forward. This can be explained on the basis of Newton's third law. The force exerted by the air rushing out of the neck of the balloon gives rise to an equal and opposite force which causes the balloon to move forwards. It can also be explained on the basis of the law of conservation of momentum. When you hold the balloon in your hand, its momentum is zero. When the neck of the balloon is released, the air rushing out has a certain momentum. The balloon itself develops the same momentum but in the opposite direction, so that the overall momentum is still zero. It is not surprising that the action of the balloon can be explained on the basis of Newton's third law and also on the basis of the law of conservation of momentum, since these two laws are closely related. They also offer an explanation for the working of jet engines and rockets.

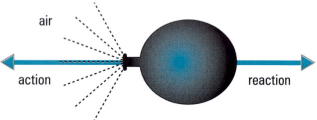

The hot gas rushes from the exhaust of the jet engine with great velocity. This causes the engine and the aeroplane to move forward. The rocket works in much the same way. The exhaust gas has a very high velocity, and consequently a very large momentum. This gives the rocket an equal momentum in the opposite direction. Jet planes cannot be used in outer space, since they depend on air taken in from the outside for their oxygen supply. Rockets, on the other hand, carry their own oxygen in liquid form.

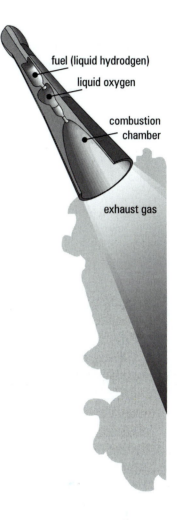

Sport

If you were teeing off in a game of golf, you would try to drive the ball as far as possible. To do this you would use a club called a driver. The head of a driver has a large mass which means that the momentum before impact is big. This means that the momentum after impact will also be big and the ball, being of small mass, will travel a considerable distance.

Summary

- A force is that which alters, or tends to alter, the motion of a body in magnitude or direction.
- The force with which the earth attracts a body is called the weight of the body.
- The mass of a body is the amount of matter in it.
- Momentum is the product of the mass and the velocity of a body.
- Force = mass × acceleration.
- Weight = mass × g.
- Principle of conservation of momentum: If no external force acts on a system of colliding bodies, the total momentum of the bodies remains constant.

SHORT QUESTIONS

1. Is the force, in newtons, necessary to give an acceleration of 2 m s^{-2} to a mass of 6 kg (A) 0·33, (B) 2, (C) 3, (D) 6 or (E) 12?
2. Is the force, in newtons, necessary to give an acceleration of 5 m s^{-2} to a mass of 500 g (A) 2·5, (B) 5, (C) 100, (D) 500 or (E) 2,500?
3. Which one of the following statements is **not** correct?
  (a) Force could be measured in newtons using a spring balance. (b) Weight could be measured in newtons using a spring balance. (c) Length could be measured in metres using a ruler. (d) Mass could be measured in newtons using a beam balance. (e) Time could be measured in seconds using a stopclock.

4. The acceleration due to gravity on the surface of the moon is 1.7 m s^{-2}. The weight of a 4 kg mass on the surface of the moon is
   (A) 0.4 N
   (B) 2.4 N
   (C) 4.0 N
   (D) 6.8 N
   (E) 39.2 N
5. Which of the following statements correctly describes what happens when two bodies collide? (a) Momentum may or may not be conserved, depending on the type of collision. (b) Kinetic energy may or may not be conserved, depending on the type of collision. (c) There is always some loss in the total momentum. (d) There is always some loss in the kinetic energy. (e) Kinetic energy is always conserved.
*6. At a certain instant during a rocket's journey to Mars the booster rocket is fired, doubling the speed and halving the mass. If the original momentum of the rocket is P units, is the new momentum (A) $\frac{P}{4}$ units, (B) $\frac{P}{2}$ units, (C) P units, (D) $2P$ units or (E) $4P$ units?
*7. Which of the following is a unit for momentum? (A) kg m s^{-1}, (B) kg m s^{-2}, (C) kg m^{-1} s, (D) kg m s^{2}, (E) kg m s^{-2}.
8. State the principle of conservation of momentum.
9. What is the relationship between force and momentum?
10. Explain the basic physical principles involved in the following.
    (a) A rocket changes its velocity by expelling a gas.
    (b) When one car is being towed by another, there is a greater chance of the tow rope breaking if the towing car moves off suddenly rather than gradually.
    (c). If the brakes are applied suddenly to a car travelling at speed, the use of a safety belt reduces the risk of injury to a passenger.
11. When a tennis ball is struck by a racquet its momentum changes by 1·6 kg m s^{-1} in a particular direction. If the ball is in contact with the racquet for 0·1 s, what is the average force exerted by the racquet on the ball?
12. (a) Why is it useful to extend collision time?
    (b) Explain two ways in which modern car designs extends collision time for head-on accidents.
    (c) Apart from the features you have mentioned in your answer to part (b), what other safety features are found on modern cars?

Long Questions
1. What acceleration is produced in a body of mass 2,000 g by a force of 5 N?

2. A body of mass 5 kg has its velocity reduced from 50 m s^{-1} to 12 m s^{-1} in 10 seconds. What average force has acted on the body? How far has it travelled during this time?
3. State Newton's second law of motion. What force is necessary to give to a body of mass 5 kg an acceleration of 3 m s^{-2}?
4. A car of mass 1,000 kg travelling at 10 m s^{-1} is brought to rest in a distance of 20 m by a constant retarding force. Calculate the retarding force and the time taken for the car to come to rest.
5. A body of mass 60 kg is acted on by a constant force of 80 newtons. How long will it take the body to attain a velocity of 50 m s^{-1} from rest?
6. (a) What is meant by the expression 'the force of gravity'?
   (b) A man has a mass of 60 kg. Calculate what he will weigh (i) on earth, where $g = 10$ m s^{-2}; (ii) on Jupiter, where $g = 25$ m s^{-2}.
   (c) What will be his mass on Jupiter?
   (d) From which planet (earth or Jupiter) would it be easier to launch a small satellite? Give a reason for your answer.
7. In a laboratory experiment the velocity of a body was measured at various times. The following table shows the data obtained in the experiment.

Velocity/m s^{-1}	0.38	0.70	1.04	1.40	1.78	2.12	2.46	2.80
Times/s	0	1.5	3.0	4.5	6.0	7.5	9.0	10.5

(i) Draw a labelled diagram showing how the apparatus might have been arranged in this experiment.
(ii) Using the above data draw a graph on graph paper of velocity against time.
(iii) From the graph find the acceleration of the body.

8. Sketch the apparatus which you would use in a laboratory experiment to demonstrate that acceleration is proportional to force when mass is constant.
State the measurements which should be made in the experiment.
Describe how you would make these measurements.
Sketch the sort of graph which you would expect to obtain from the experiment.
A body of mass 10 kg accelerates uniformly from rest to a speed of 20 m s^{-1} in a time of 5 seconds.
Calculate
(i) The acceleration of the body during this time.
(ii) The force required to produce the acceleration.
(iii) The distance travelled by the body in this time.

9. A man of mass 100 kg skating at 12 m s^{-1} collides with a man of mass 80 kg at rest. Both move off together after the collision. Find their common velocity.

10. A girl of mass 45 kg running at 7 m s^{-1} jumps on a sled which is at rest. If girl and sled move off at 5 m s^{-1}, find the mass of the sled.

*11. In an experiment to measure acceleration, a constant force was applied to a body so that it moved over a sheet of paper, marked with vertical lines 1 mm apart. As the body moved it left marks on the paper at intervals of $\frac{1}{50}$ s, as shown in the diagram. Calculate the average velocity of the body between A and B. Hence, or otherwise, determine a value for the acceleration of the body.

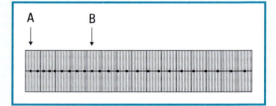

Describe any one type of apparatus that can be used in an experiment to measure acceleration. Mention one precaution that should be taken, when using the apparatus, to ensure a more accurate result.

*12. In an experiment to verify Newton's second law, a constant force was applied to a body of mass 200 g and the resulting acceleration was determined. Additional masses, *m*, were placed on the body and the acceleration was found in each case, the applied force being kept constant throughout. The following results were obtained.

a (cm s^{-2})	148	102	68	58	52	40	34
m (g)	0	100	200	300	400	500	600

Draw a suitable graph on graph paper and hence explain how these results verify Newton's second law. From the graph calculate the magnitude of the force applied to the body. Sketch a labelled diagram of an apparatus that might have been used in this experiment.

13. Define force. State Newton's second law of motion. Describe a laboratory experiment to illustrate Newton's second law of motion.

A body of mass 2 kg accelerates uniformly from rest to a velocity of 8 m s^{-1} in a time of 4 seconds. Calculate (a) the acceleration of the body during this time, (b) the force required to produce the acceleration.

*14. State Newton's second law and show how it leads to a quantitative definition of force. Describe how you would show experimentally that the acceleration of a body is proportional to the force acting on it.

A body leaves a point A and moves in a straight line with constant velocity of 36 m s^{-1}. Seven seconds later another body, of mass 2 kg, at rest at A is acted on by a constant force of 4 N and moves in the same direction as the first body. How long will it take the second body to catch up on the first body?

15. The relationship between the acceleration of a body and its mass was investigated by applying a constant force to a body of mass 150 g and then measuring the acceleration. The mass of the body was increased by placing additional masses on top of the body and the acceleration was found in each case. The values obtained for the additional masses, *m*, and the corresponding accelerations, *a*, are shown in the following table.

m/g	0	50	100	150	200	250	300	350
a/cm s^{-2}	125	90	74	61	50	47	40	35

Explain how the constant force in this experiment might have been applied.

Draw a suitable graph to show the relationship between the acceleration of the body and its mass.

From the graph calculate the value of the constant force which was applied to the body.

Explain how the effect of friction might have been taken into account in this experiment and give one other precaution which might have been taken to ensure a more accurate result.

Moments

CHAPTER 11

A metre stick can be balanced on one finger if the finger is placed at the correct point. In a box of chocolates, each chocolate has its own weight and the chocolates are all in different positions, but the box of chocolates can be balanced on one finger.

The point at which the whole weight of a body appears to act is called its centre of gravity.

To find the centre of gravity of a piece of cardboard, slowly move the cardboard out over the edge of the bench. Draw a line where the cardboard just balances. Turn the cardboard sideways and repeat. Draw a second line. Turn the cardboard again and repeat. Draw a third line. The point of intersection of the three lines is the centre of gravity.

States of equilibrium

(a) STABLE
Tilt the flask slightly. This **raises its centre of gravity**. Now let it go: it will not fall over.

(b) UNSTABLE
Tilt the flask slightly. This **lowers its centre of gravity**. Now let it go: it will fall over.

(c) NEUTRAL
Move the flask slightly. There is **no change in the height of its centre of gravity**. Now let it go: it will stay in its new position.

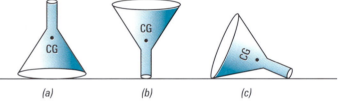

Stable design

There is a difference between stable equilibrium and stable design. Did you notice that when you tilted the flask in diagram (b) the vertical line through its centre of gravity moved outside its base? This means that it is unstable. It is unstable because its base is too narrow and its centre of gravity is too high. It is clear from the diagrams that the principle of stable design is to have a **low centre of gravity and a wide base**.

Levers

Hold a rod horizontally and hang a mass on it as shown in the diagram. Move the mass further and further away from your hand, and try to keep the rod horizontal. Repeat this with a heavier mass. The turning effect you feel depends on the force (weight) and the distance from your hand.

96

MOMENTS

If the centre of gravity of the leaning tower of Pisa were not directly above the base, the tower's weight would create a turning effect which would cause the tower to topple over. However, not all turning effects are bad. Without turning effects we could not use the many levers that make our lives so much easier. For example, the door in the diagram is a lever. When it is pushed it turns on its hinges and opens. The door is called the **load**, the force we use to push the door open is called the **effort** and the hinge is called the **fulcrum**.

A lever is a rigid body that is free to rotate about a fixed point, called a fulcrum.

The turning effect of a force is called the **moment** of the force.

The moment of a force about a point is force × perpendicular distance from the point to the line of action of the force.

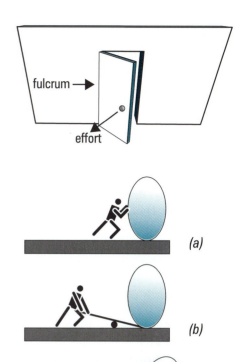

In diagram (a) the man is unable to move the stone. In (b) he uses a lever and fulcrum but still cannot move the stone, because the lever is too short. In (c) he moves the stone with a longer lever.

In (c) the turning effect is $500 \times 2 = 1{,}000$ N m.

Torque

In engineering, a moment or turning effect is called a **torque**. Mechanics use a tool called a torque spanner. This enables them to measure the torque being applied when tightening engine nuts. Tightening them too much can cause damage.

The following are some approximate torque values.

Torque required to turn a door handle: 0·3 N m
Torque required to loosen a wheel nut: 5 N m
Torque produced by a car engine: 150 N m

Conditions for equilibrium

Look at the seesaw in the diagram. The boy's moment about the support is $350 \times 2 = 700$ N m. The girl's moment about the support is $400 \times 1 = 400$ N m. Clearly, the seesaw is not in equilibrium. The boy's side is about to go down.

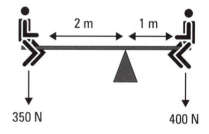

Now look at the metre stick in the diagram.

Anti-clockwise moments		Clockwise moments
$(20 \times 20) + (10 \times 10)$	=	(50×10)
$400 + 100$	=	500
500 N m	=	500 N m

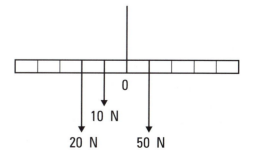

The metre stick is in equilibrium. The sum of the clockwise moments about O equals the sum of the anti-clockwise moments about O. This is an example of the principle of moments.

97

Physics Now!

Principle of moments: When a body is in equilibrium, the sum of the clockwise moments about any point is equal to the sum of the anti-clockwise moments about that point.

Another way of putting this is that the **vector** sum of the moments about any point is zero.

Now look at the plank in the diagram. This is a uniform plank 4 m long, weighing 200 N. It is supported symmetrically by two supports A and B. The force with which the plank presses down on A is 100 N, therefore, by Newton's third law, the reaction of A is 100 N. The same applies at B. Two things should be noted here.

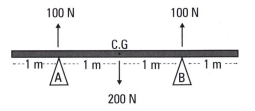

(a) Taking moments about A: 100 N × 2 m = 200 N × 1 m
    Taking moments about B: 100 N × 2 m = 200 N × 1 m
(b) The total force upwards (100 + 100) = the total force downwards (200)

From this it is clear that there are two conditions for equilibrium.
Condition 1: The principle of moments must apply. **(Vector sum of moments about any point is zero.)**
Condition 2: The sum of the forces in any direction must equal the sum of the forces in the opposite direction. **(Another way of saying this is that the *vector* sum of the forces in any direction is zero.)**

Mandatory experiment

AIM: To investigate the laws of equilibrium for a set of coplanar forces.

Method
1. Find the mass of a metre stick and hang it from a stand.
2. Adjust the thread until the metre stick is balanced. The thread is now at the centre of gravity of the metre stick.
3. Hang a number of masses on the metre stick and adjust their positions until the metre stick balances.
4. Calculate the moments about O.

Result: The sum of the clockwise moments equals the sum of the anti-clockwise moments.

5. Leaving the masses as they are, hang the metre stick from a suitable spring balance.

Result: The reading on the spring balance equals the sum of all the weights, including the weight of the metre stick (remember, weight = mass × g).
Conclusion: The two laws of equilibrium have been obeyed.

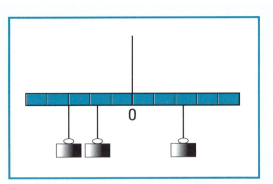

Question
Does the length of each thread matter?

MOMENTS

Couples

When you steer a bicycle round a bend with both hands on the handlebars, you usually apply two equal but opposite forces as in the diagram. Such a pair of equal parallel forces is called a couple. When you unscrew the top off a bottle you are applying a couple.

The moment of a couple is the product of one of the forces and the perpendicular distance between the two. Couple $T = F \times d$.

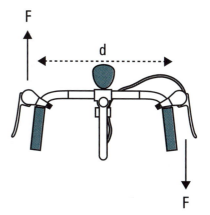

Video recorders, cassette decks and record players each contain an electric motor. When current flows through a coil of wire inside the motor, a couple is produced which causes the coil to spin.

If you did any experiments on electricity in Junior Certificate science you probably used an ammeter. This was a moving coil meter, so called because when current flows through the coil inside the meter a couple acts on the coil, causing it to rotate and move the needle over the scale.

A couple cannot be replaced by a single force; it can only be balanced by another couple.

Summary

- The point at which the whole weight of a body appears to act is called its centre of gravity.
- A lever is a rigid body that is free to rotate about a fixed point called the fulcrum.
- The moment of a force about a point is the force × the perpendicular distance from the point to the line of action of the force.
- The principle of moments states that when a body is in equilibrium the sum of the clockwise moments about any point is equal to the sum of the anti-clockwise moments about that point.
- The conditions for equilibrium are (a) the principle of moments must apply, (b) the vector sum of the forces in any direction is zero.
- The moment of a couple is the product of one of the forces and the perpendicular distance between the two.

SHORT QUESTIONS

1. To find the weight of a jar of berries, a girl set up the apparatus in the diagram. What result did she get? _____

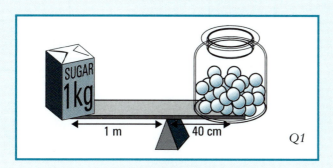

Q1

2. In the diagrams the arrows indicate the position of the load, effort or fulcrum. Label each one correctly.

3. The diagram shows a shape cut from plywood of uniform thickness. Which of the points A, B, C, D and E is the most likely position of the centre of gravity?

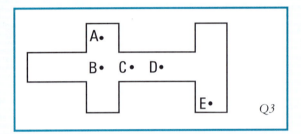

Q3

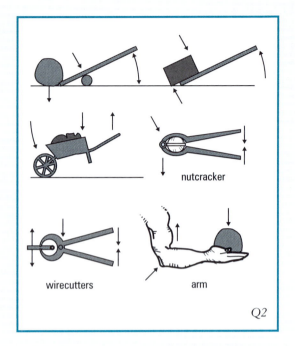

Q2

4. The diagram shows a rigid bar which is in equilibrium and is supported at its centre of gravity. Is the mass X (A) 20 kg, (B) 45 kg, (C) 2 kg, (D) 1·5 kg or (E) 0·5 kg?

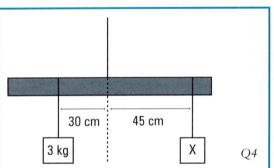

Q4

5. The diagram shows a uniform metre stick which is balanced with a body of mass 2 kg at the 20 cm position. What is the position of the body of mass 4 kg?
   (A) 55 cm
   (B) 65 cm
   (C) 70 cm
   (D) 85 cm
   (E) 90 cm

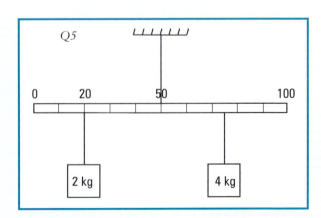

Q5

MOMENTS

LONG QUESTIONS

1. State the principle of moments.
   The diagram shows a uniform metre stick of mass 0·1 kg which is in equilibrium under the action of a number of forces. Calculate the weight of the metre stick. Use the information given in the diagram to to explain how this arrangement can be said to verify the principle of moments.

2. A uniform plank 6 metres long has a mass of 50 kg and is supported symmetrically on two trestles 4 metres apart. Find the maximum weight of a man who can stand on one end of the plank without causing it to overbalance.

3. A uniform plank of mass 20 kg and length 4 m is supported by vertical ropes at each end and used as a scaffold. A man of mass 75 kg stands 1 m from one end and a 15 kg pile of bricks is placed so that its centre of gravity is 3 m from the same end. Find the tension in each rope.

4. A nut must be tightened to a torque of 70 Nm.
   (a) What force must you put on the end of the spanner to reach this torque?
   (b) What would be the advantage of sliding a 96 cm tube over the end of the spanner, and pulling on the end of that?

* 5. In an experiment to verify the principle of moments a number of forces were applied to a metre stick as shown in the diagram. The metre stick was horizontal and in equilibrium when the forces were applied at the positions shown in the diagram. The centre of gravity was found to be at the 50 cm mark. Using the data given on the diagram calculate the weight of the metre stick.
   Explain how the arrangement shown in the diagram verifies the principle of moments.

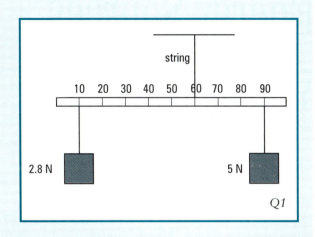
Q1

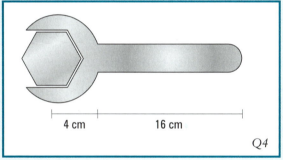
Q4

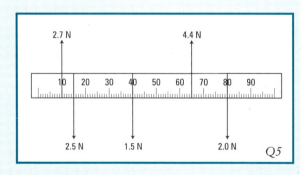
Q5

Energy Sources

CHAPTER 12

You are late for school—again! You eat your breakfast quickly then grab your schoolbag, which you packed the night before, and dash out the door. You cycle along the road and up to the top of church hill. With a sigh of relief you coast down the far side and in through the school gates, and screech to a halt at the bicycle shed.

'All very interesting,' you might say, 'but what has all this got to do with energy?'

As you cycled along the road the **chemical energy** stored in your food was converted into **kinetic energy**. Cycling up the hill some of your **kinetic energy** was converted to **potential energy**. Going down the other side the **potential energy** was converted back into **kinetic energy** and finally, as you applied the brakes and screeched to a halt, the **kinetic energy** was converted to **heat energy** and **sound energy**. So you see, energy plays a big part in your life from day to day. But what exactly is energy, how many different kinds of energy are there, and where did it all come from in the first place?

Energy is the ability to do work.

Energy is measured in units called joules.

Types of stored energy

POTENTIAL ENERGY
The water behind the dam has energy stored in it because of its position. It can run down through the channel and cause the turbine to spin. This can be used to make electricity.

The elastic band has energy stored in it because of its condition (it is stretched).

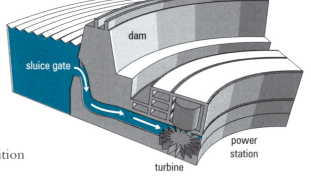

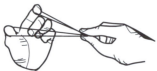

Potential energy is energy that something has because of its position or condition.

CHEMICAL ENERGY
All the things in the diagram have chemical energy stored in them.

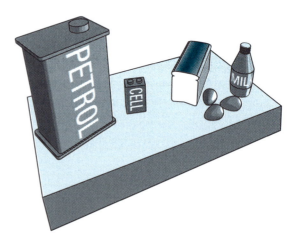

ENERGY SOURCES

NUCLEAR ENERGY
The substances in the diagram are radioactive. They have nuclear energy stored in them. This energy can be released in a nuclear power station and used to make electricity.

Other forms of energy (not stored)

KINETIC ENERGY
The car and the hammer have energy because they are moving.

Kinetic energy is energy that something has because it is moving.

HEAT ENERGY
The water in the kettle has heat energy. If it gets hot enough it will turn to steam. Steam can make things move.

ELECTRICAL ENERGY
The ESB supplies us with electrical energy. When we use a cell or a battery we convert chemical energy to electrical energy. A bulb gives out light energy. A radio gives out sound energy.

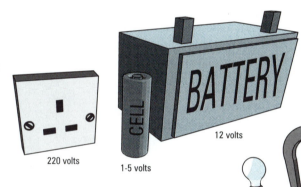

A magnet has magnetic energy. It makes the pins move.

Where energy comes from
All of our energy came, in the first place, from the sun. What happens in the Sun is that matter is converted into energy according to the formula $E=mc^2$ where c is the speed of light. Millions of years ago dense tropical forests grew in many parts of the world. The trees took in energy from the sun and changed it into chemical energy. Other smaller plants also took in energy from the sun. Animals got their energy by eating the plants. As time went by, many changes occurred on the surface of the earth and the remains of plants and animals became buried under the ground and the seas. The pressure changed them into coal, oil and natural gas. The energy stored in coal, oil and natural gas is being used today to keep cars, trucks, trains and factories going.

It is important to realise that, when we eat our food, we are gaining energy but **we are not creating energy**. Neither are we destroying the energy stored in the food: we are simply changing it from one form to another.

Physics Now!

Energy cannot be created or destroyed, it can only change from one form to another.

This is known as the law of conservation of energy.

Many of the things that are most useful to us in our daily lives change energy from one form to another. Electric cookers change electrical energy to heat energy. Light bulbs change electrical energy to heat and light energy.

Energy sources

One of our main sources of energy is fossil fuels, i.e. coal, oil, peat and natural gas. The trouble is that these fuels are non-renewable, which means that they are not being replaced in nature so the supply will eventually run out. For this reason we have to look for alternatives. These alternatives have the advantage of being renewable, but they also have disadvantages.

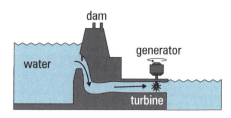
Hydroelectricity

Wind energy

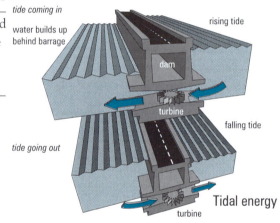
Tidal energy

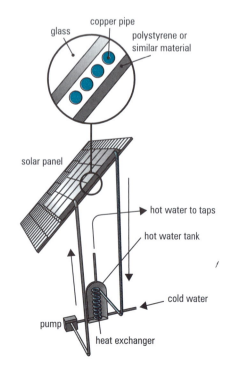

Energy source	How the energy is produced	Disadvantages
Hydroelectricity	A dam built across a river forms a lake. Water flowing through the dam turns a generator to produce electricity	Not all rivers and lakes are suitable
Wind energy	Large windmills are used to turn a generator	Expensive; low output; only a few areas are suitable. Windmills can be unsightly if located in scenic areas
Tidal energy	A dam built across an estuary forms a lake behind it which fills and empties with the tides. The fast-flowing water turns generators	Expensive to build. Few areas are suitable
Solar energy	The sun's energy is trapped by solar panels and used to heat water. Another kind of solar panel contains cells that convert solar energy into electricity	The energy is most needed in winter, when sunshine is weakest
Biomass	Fast-growing plants are used to make alcohol, which can be used instead of petrol	Very large areas of land are needed

The question of whether nuclear energy should be regarded as renewable or non-renewable is far too complicated to be dealt with at this stage, but the whole question of nuclear energy will be dealt with in detail later.

Summary

- Energy is the ability to do work (measured in joules).
- Energy cannot be created or destroyed; it can only change from one form to another.
- Fossil fuels such as coal, oil, peat and natural gas are non-renewable.
- Hydroelectricity, wind energy, tidal energy, solar energy and biomass are renewable.

SHORT QUESTIONS
1. Define energy.
2. Define potential energy.
3. Define kinetic energy.
4. What is meant by renewable and non-renewable?
5. What is biomass?
6. What energy conversions take place in (i) a television set, (ii) a Bunsen burner, (iii) a washing machine, (iv) a car, (v) an electric hair dryer?
7. What energy conversion takes place in a nuclear reactor?
8. The sun's energy is responsible for world stocks of coal, oil and natural gas. Explain.
9. Explain the basic physical principle involved in each of the following.
   (a) When a fast-moving car is brought to rest by braking, the brakes become hot.
   (b) The water at the bottom of a waterfall is slightly warmer than that at the top.
   (c) A bicycle dynamo produces less light as the bicycle slows down.

Work, Energy and Power

CHAPTER 13

Work is done when a force moves a body. The man pushing the trolley in the diagram is clearly doing work. But how can we calculate how much work he has done?

1. The greater the force necessary to move the trolley, the more work the man does.
2. The further the man pushes the trolley, the more work he does.

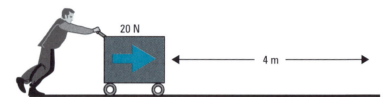

work = force multiplied by distance moved in the direction of the force ($W = Fs$)

Work is measured in units called joules, e.g. if the man in the diagram uses a force of 20 newtons to move the trolley a distance of 4 metres, then he has done

$20 \times 4 = 80$ joules of work

A joule is the work done when a force of 1 newton moves its point of application 1 metre in the direction of the force.

The mass of the brick in the diagram is 3 kilograms. But the weight of the brick is 3×9.8 newtons. This is the force pulling the brick towards the earth, so a person must exert an equal force upwards to lift the brick, i.e. 3×9.8 newtons. If he lifts the brick 2 metres off the ground then the work done is force × distance, i.e. $3 \times 9.8 \times 2$ joules = 58.8 joules.

Energy

Energy has already been defined as the ability to do work. For this reason energy, like work, is measured in joules.

MECHANICAL ENERGY

There are two types of mechanical energy.

Potential energy is energy that a body has due to its position or mechanical condition.

The block in the diagram will move down towards the ground, raising the bucket as it goes. In this way the block is doing work. It is able to do work because it has potential energy due to its position h metres above the ground. How much work can it do?

Work = force × distance. The force pulling it towards the ground is its weight mg. So the work it can do is mgh.

Potential energy (E_P) = mgh

If you wind up an alarm clock, the hands will keep moving for 24 hours.

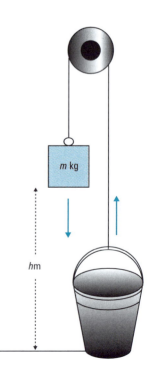

106

Work, Energy and Power

In this case the work of moving the hands is done by a spring. The spring has potential energy because of its condition: it is wound tight.

It is important to realise that the energy the block has is the work done on it in raising it h metres above the ground. Similarly, the energy the clock spring has is the work done in winding it up.

Kinetic energy
Any moving body has energy because it is moving.

Energy due to motion is called kinetic energy.
Kinetic energy $(E_k) = \frac{1}{2} mv^2$

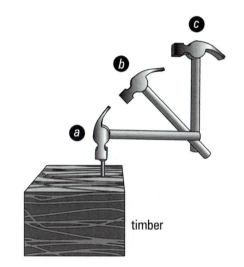

1. Hold a nail upright on a piece of timber and place the face of a hammer on top of it. The hammer does no work because it has no energy.
2. Raise the hammer above your head. The hammer now has potential energy because of its position.
3. Bring the hammer down swiftly on the nail. As the hammer moves down, its potential energy changes into kinetic energy. If you strike the nail a number of times, you will feel the nail getting hot. On impact, the kinetic energy of the hammer changes to heat (and sound etc.). This example illustrates how energy changes from one form to another.

Another example is the simple pendulum.

1. When the pendulum is at its highest point A, the potential energy is maximum, the kinetic energy is zero.
2. As the pendulum swings from A to B the potential energy changes completely to kinetic energy.
3. As it swings from B to C the kinetic energy changes back to potential energy.

The principle of conservation of energy states that energy can neither be created nor destroyed; it merely changes from one form to another.

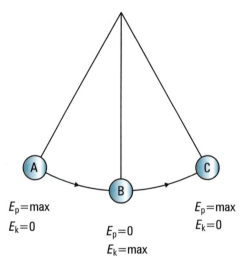

When we do work we are changing energy from one form to another.

Problem 1
A body of mass 8 kg at rest on a smooth horizontal plane is acted on by a constant force for 0·5 min. If the velocity of the body at the end of that time is 25 m s^{-1}, find (a) the force, (b) the distance travelled, (c) the work done on the body, (d) the final kinetic energy of the body.

(a) $u = 0$, $v = 25$ m s^{-1}, $s = ?$

$t = 30$ s, $a = ?$

$v = u + at \Rightarrow 25 = 0 + a \times 30 \Rightarrow a = \frac{5}{6}$ m s^{-2}

$F = ma = 8 \times \frac{5}{6} = \frac{20}{3}$ N

(b) $s = ut + \frac{1}{2}at^2 \Rightarrow 0 + \frac{1}{2} \times \frac{5}{6} \times 900 = 375$ m

(c) $W = Fs = \frac{20}{3} \times 375 = 2{,}500$ J

(d) Since the body starts from rest, its final kinetic energy is the work done on it, which is 2500 joules. Alternatively, $E_k = \frac{1}{2}mv^2 = \frac{1}{2}(8)(25)^2 = 2{,}500$ joules.

Problem 2

A bullet of mass 20 g is fired into a block of wood of mass 380 g lying on a smooth table. The block moves off with a velocity of 10 m s^{-1}. Find the velocity of the bullet and the kinetic energy before and after the impact.

momentum before = momentum after
$0 \cdot 02 \times v = (0 \cdot 02 + 0 \cdot 38) \times 10$
$0 \cdot 02 \times v = 0 \cdot 4 \times 10 \Rightarrow v = 200$ m s^{-1}

Total E_k before impact = $\frac{1}{2} \times 0 \cdot 02 \times 200^2 = 400$ J

Total E_k after impact = $\frac{1}{2} \times 0 \cdot 4 \times 10^2 = 20$ J

Note: Momentum is conserved but **kinetic** energy is not: 380 joules of energy is converted to heat and sound.

Problem 3

A block of wood of mass 2 kg is suspended by a fine vertical string 1 m long. A bullet of mass 10 g travelling at 100 m s^{-1} is fired horizontally into the block and becomes embedded in it. Calculate the maximum inclination of the string to the vertical.

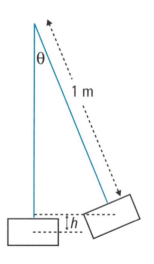

By the law of conservation of momentum:

$2 \cdot 01v = 0 \cdot 01 \times 100 \Rightarrow 2 \cdot 01v = 1 \Rightarrow v = \frac{1}{2 \cdot 01}$ m s^{-1}

$h = 1 - 1\cos\theta = 1 - \cos\theta$

E_k at bottom = E_p at top

$0 \cdot 5m \times \frac{1}{(2 \cdot 01)^2} = m \times 9 \cdot 8 \times (1 - \cos\theta)$

$\frac{1}{(2 \times 4 \cdot 04 \times 9 \cdot 8)} = 1 - \cos\theta$

$0 \cdot 012 = 1 - \cos\theta$

$\cos\theta = 1 - 0 \cdot 012 = 0 \cdot 988$

$\theta = 8°54'$

Power

If you had a high-powered car you could drive from Cork to Dublin. If you had only a low-powered car you could still drive from Cork to Dublin. So what are the advantages of the high-powered car over the low-powered car? One of the main advantages is that it could get you to Dublin in a shorter time. This gives us our first indication of what scientists mean by the word 'power'. Power is concerned not just with the work that is being done, but with the rate at which it is being done. The rate at which work is done is called power.

$$\text{Power} = \frac{\text{work done}}{\text{time taken}}, \text{ or}$$

power is the amount of work done per second

Anything that does work is converting energy from one form to another, so we can also say that power is the rate at which energy is converted from one form to another.

Power is measured in watts: 1 watt = 1 joule per second

e.g. a 100 watt lamp converts electrical energy to light and heat at the rate of 100 J s^{-1}.

PROBLEM 4

A boy of mass 50 kg walks steadily up a flight of stairs to the top of a building 40 m high. If the time taken is 2 minutes, what is the power of the boy?

Force = mass × acceleration = 50 × 9·8 = 490 N
Work = force × distance = 490 × 40 = 19,600 J

$$\text{Power} = \text{work done per second} = \frac{19,600}{120} = 163{\cdot}33 \text{ watts}$$

Here is an easy way to estimate your own power.
1. Find your weight in newtons.
2. Measure the vertical height of a flight of stairs (measure the height of one step and multiply by the number of steps).
3. Run up the stairs as fast as you can and time yourself in seconds.
4. Your power = $\dfrac{(\text{weight} \times \text{height of stairs})}{\text{time in seconds}}$

Were you tired after running up the stairs? Now you understand why there are lifts in tall buildings and escalators in multi-storey shopping centres.

Here is another way to estimate your power.
Take a convenient mass and hold it at shoulder level. Extend your arm straight up in the air and measure the height through which you have raised the mass. Now measure how long it takes you to do this 15 times going as fast as you can.

PHYSICS NOW!

Your power = $\dfrac{15mgh}{t}$

Machines

We use machines to help us do work. There are a number of reasons for this. Some machines produce a much greater force than we could produce on our own (e.g. a lever). Other machines do work for hours without getting tired. In fact, machines convert energy from one form to another and deliver the output energy in the form of work. However, some of this work is not useful. In other words, there is no such thing as a 100% efficient machine.

EFFICIENCY

The efficiency of a machine is a measure of how good it is at converting energy without waste. In science the efficiency of a machine is defined as follows.

efficiency = $\dfrac{\text{power output}}{\text{power input}} \times 100\%$

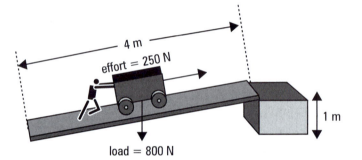

To understand how this operates, consider one of the simplest machines of all, the **ramp** or **inclined plane**.

Suppose the man in the diagram pushes the load up the ramp in 20 seconds.

Useful work done = 800 N × 1 m = 800 J

Power output = $\dfrac{800 \text{ J}}{20 \text{ s}}$ = 40 W

Actual work done = 250 N × 4 m = 1000 J

Power input = $\dfrac{1000 \text{ J}}{20 \text{ s}}$ = 50 W

Efficiency = $\dfrac{(40 \times 100\%)}{50}$ = 80%

The other 200 J is lost as heat due to friction.

Friction

If a car fails to start, the usual procedure is to push it. Sometimes it can be quite difficult to get the car to start moving, but it is much easier to keep it moving once it begins to move. The reason it is difficult to get the car to start moving in the first place is friction between the tyres and the road.

Friction is a force that opposes relative motion between two bodies in contact.

Friction always opposes motion.

Friction arises because there is no such thing as a perfectly smooth surface. Even two surfaces that appear smooth to the naked eye and feel smooth to the touch will look like this under the microscope.

It is obvious that if one of these bodies is moved over the other it will experience a resistance due to friction.

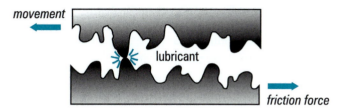

INVESTIGATING FRICTION
Rub your hands together very quickly. Can you feel them heating up? This heat is caused by friction.

Put some soap solution on your hands. Now rub them together very quickly. Do they heat up? Not very much? That is because there is very little friction. You used soap as a lubricant to reduce friction between your hands. **Lubricants are substances that reduce friction.**

Experiment
AIM: To investigate friction.

METHOD
1. Attach a spring balance to a block of wood and pull until the block just begins to move. Note the reading on the balance.
2. Attach some sandpaper to the bottom of the block and repeat.

Result: a greater force is needed.

3. Remove the sandpaper and put some grease on the bottom of the block.

Result: a smaller force is needed.

Conclusion: Lubricants reduce friction.

4. Now: (a) turn the block on edge so that the surface in contact with the bench is smaller; (b) put some slotted masses on top of the block. What difference do these changes make?

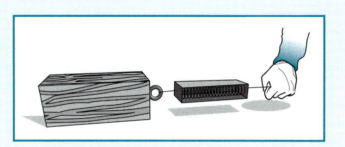

STATIC AND DYNAMIC EQUILIBRIUM
In an earlier chapter we saw that a metre stick could be in equilibrium under the action of a number of coplanar forces. Since the metre stick is not moving, it is in **static equilibrium**.

When a car is travelling at constant speed, the forces acting on it are balanced. In other words, the force provided by the engine is balanced by friction between the road and the tyres and air resistance. Since the car is moving, this is a case of **dynamic equilibrium**.

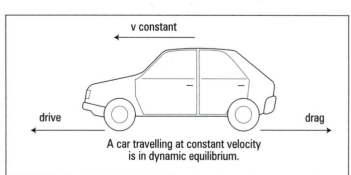

A car travelling at constant velocity is in dynamic equilibrium.

Viscosity

Viscosity is resistance to flow in fluids.

Friction is not confined to solids. It also occurs in fluids (liquids and gases). We can show this very simply.

Take two beakers. Put some water in one and some engine oil in the other. Pour out some of the water. Pour out some of the oil. Notice that the oil flows much more slowly than the water. Scientists say that oil has a higher viscosity than water.

This is caused by friction or viscous drag between the layers of molecules in the fluid. The difference in viscosity between water and engine oil can be demonstrated much more effectively as follows.

Fill a tall graduated cylinder with water. Drop a small ball bearing into the water and use a stopwatch to time its descent. Now drop a similar ball bearing into an identical cylinder filled with engine oil and time its descent. Note that the second ball bearing sinks much more slowly. The demonstration might be even more effective if the two ball bearings were dropped simultaneously.

Much study on the effects of viscous drag on small spheres falling through fluids was carried out by Sir George Stokes in the last century. He found that they experienced a retarding force F which depended on their velocity, their radius and the viscosity of the fluid. A sphere falling through a fluid has three forces acting on it.
1. its weight W acting downwards
2. an up-thrust U due to displaced fluid (Archimedes' principle)
3. a frictional force F acting upwards.

W and U are constant, but F increases with velocity.

So, as the sphere begins to fall, it accelerates. But as its velocity increases, F increases, until a stage is reached where $U + F = W$. At this stage the net force on the sphere is zero. According to Newton's first law, the sphere will now continue to fall with a uniform velocity known as its terminal velocity. This is another case of dynamic equilibrium. People who jump from airplanes and free-fall reach a terminal velocity. After they open their parachutes they reach a lower terminal velocity.

A body moving through a gas, such as air, also experiences a frictional force. This is why a feather falling freely is slower than a coin unless, of course, they are both falling in a vacuum. However, gases are much less viscous than liquids. This is why the hovercraft works so well. The hovercraft engine blows air downwards so that the craft moves along on a cushion of air, not on water. This reduces friction quite considerably and enables the hovercraft to achieve a much greater velocity than conventional water-craft. The air track used in the experiment to demonstrate the law of conservation of momentum makes use of the same idea.

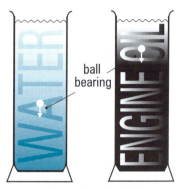

tall graduated cylinder

George Stokes (Ireland) 1819–1903, born in Skreen, Co. Sligo, was a mathematician whose law of viscosity in 1851 described the motion of a sphere through a viscous fluid. He also explained fluoresence.

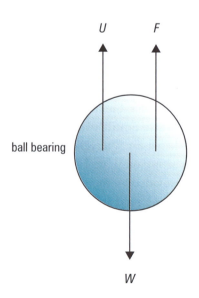

WORK, ENERGY AND POWER

Advantages and disadvantages of friction

Friction is both useful and troublesome. On the one hand, if it were not for friction between your shoes and the ground you would find it impossible to walk: you would slip and fall, as happens in icy weather. But for friction between tyres and the road, cars would be impossible to control. Friction between brake pads and wheel causes your bicycle to stop. On the other hand, friction between the moving parts of an engine could cause the metal to wear out quickly, or the metal might become so hot due to friction that it melted, causing the engine to seize up. A lubricant such as engine oil prevents this from happening.

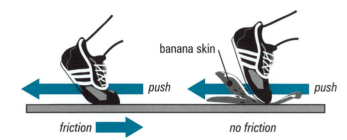

A liquid film between two surfaces usually reduces friction. Oil reduces wear in engines. Graphite is also used as a lubricant, because its layers of atoms slide easily over one another. A layer of air can be used to separate surfaces and reduce friction, as in the case of the hovercraft.

Summary

- Work = force × distance moved in the direction of the force.
- A joule is the work done when a force of one newton moves its point of application one metre.
- Potential energy is energy that a body has due to its position or mechanical condition.
- Kinetic energy is energy due to motion.
- Power is the amount of work done per second.
- 1 watt = 1 J s^{-1}.
- Friction is a force that opposes relative motion between two bodies in contact.
- Viscosity is resistance to flow in fluids.

SHORT QUESTIONS

1. When a moving car is brought to rest by applying the brakes, the kinetic energy of the car (A) does not change, (B) is changed to potential energy, (C) is changed mostly to heat energy in the brakes, (D) is all transferred to the passengers, (E) is all absorbed by the road.
2. The unit of energy is (a) the watt (W), (b) the joule (J), (c) the kelvin (K), (d) the pascal (Pa), (e) the farad (F).
3. A block of wood is pulled along a horizontal bench at a constant speed of 15 m s^{-1} by a force of 8 N. How much work is done against friction in 6 seconds? (A) 720 J, (B) 120 J, (C) 48 J, (D) 20 J, (E) 3·2 J.
4. A body of mass 5 kg at a height of 2 m above the ground has a potential energy of (A) 2 J, (B) 2·5 J, (C) 9·8 J, (D) 10 J, (E) 98 J.

5. How much work is done when a mass weighing 400 N is lifted 3 metres? (A) none, (B) 403 N m, (C) 1,200 J, (D) 1,200 W, (E) 133 J.
6. A body 5 m above the ground has a potential energy of 980 J. Its mass is (A) 5 kg, (B) 5 N, (C) 9·8 kg, (D) 20 kg, (E) 98 kg.
7. A body at rest 5 m above the ground has a potential energy of 490 J. When it is released and has fallen a distance of 3 m its kinetic energy is (A) 98 J, (B) 196 J, (C) 245 J, (D) 294 J, (E) 300 J.
8. The work done in kJ, taking g to be 10 m s^{-2}, when an object of mass 100 kg is dropped through a distance of 5 m is (A) 0·05, (B) 5, (C) 20, (D) 105, (E) 5,000.
*9. The unit of work, the joule, is equivalent to (A) kg m s^{-2}, (B) kg m s^{-1}, (C) N m s^{-2}, (D) N m, (E) N s^{-1}.
10. A mouse of mass 0·03 kg runs 2 m up a curtain in 4 s. Its power, in watts, is (A) $0.03 \times 2 \times 4$, (B) $\frac{(0.03 \times 2)}{4}$, (C) $\frac{(0.03 \times 4)}{2}$, (D) $\frac{(0.03 \times 9.8 \times 2)}{4}$, (E) $\frac{(0.03 \times 9.8 \times 4)}{2}$.
11. Calculate the kinetic energy of a car of mass 1,000 kg moving with a velocity of 5 m s^{-1}.
12. Give two examples of the importance of friction in everyday life.
*13. When a car of mass 1,000 kg accelerates from rest to a speed of 20 m s^{-1} in 8 s, the average power developed by the engine is _____.
14. Work can be defined as the product of _____ and _____.

LONG QUESTIONS
1. A body of mass 20 g is moving at 50 m s^{-1}. What is its kinetic energy?
2. What work is done when a mass of 50 kg is raised through a height of 5 m?
3. A pump raises 100 litres of water through 10 metres in 5 minutes. What is the power of the pump? (Take 1 cm^3 = 1 g.)
4. A stone of mass 150 g is thrown vertically upwards with a velocity of 2 m s^{-1}. Find its kinetic energy and potential energy at its highest point, and halfway up.
5. An engine has to lift a pile driver of mass 400 kg through a distance of 2 metres in 3 seconds. What power must it have?
6. A catapult gives 10 joules of energy to a stone of mass 50 g. What is the initial velocity of the stone?
7. How much work is done when a body of mass 50 kg is pulled a distance of 6 m by a force of 3 newtons?
8. A boy of mass 60 kg climbs to the top of a flight of stairs which has 20 steps. If each step is 15 cm high, find the work done. If it takes the boy 10 seconds to get to the top, what is his power?

9. A ball of mass 100 g falls from a height of 2 m and rebounds to a height of 1·5 m. Find (a) the kinetic energy as it strikes the floor, (b) the kinetic energy at the instant it leaves the floor.

10. State Newton's second law of motion. Describe an experiment to verify that acceleration is proportional to force. Explain how the effect of friction might be overcome in this experiment.

*11. State what is meant by (i) energy, (ii) power. Give the unit in which each is measured.
A car of mass 1,000 kg, starting from rest, increases its velocity to 15 m s^{-1} over a time of 5 seconds. Calculate:
(i) The kinetic energy of the car at the end of the 5 seconds.
(ii) The average power generated in giving the car this velocity over this time.

12. State the principle of conservation of energy.
A car of mass 1,200 kg is moving with a velocity of 15 m s^{-1}.
What is the kinetic energy of the car?
The car is brought to a stop by applying the brakes. Calculate the force needed to bring the car to a stop in a distance of 50 m. Name the main form of energy into which the kinetic energy of the car is converted as it is brought to a stop.

*13. Define (i) energy, (ii) momentum. Describe an experiment to verify the principle of conservation of momentum. A radioactive nucleus, initially at rest, emits an alpha particle of mass $6·8 \times 10^{-27}$ kg to produce a new nucleus of mass $3·67 \times 10^{-25}$ kg. Explain how the principles of conservation of momentum and energy apply to this reaction. Calculate the ratio of the speed of the alpha particle to the speed of the new nucleus. Given that their total mass, when at rest, is $9·50 \times 10^{-30}$ kg less than the mass of the original nucleus, calculate their total initial kinetic energy and hence the speed of each. Note: The last part of this question should not be done until chapter 38 has been studied. (Speed of light in vacuum $c = 3·00 \times 10^8$ m s^{-1}.)

*14. A machine lifts a load of 50 kg vertically upwards at 2 m s^{-1}. If the machine is 80% efficient, find its nominal power.

*15. A body of mass 5 kg moving at 10 m s^{-1} strikes a stationary body of mass 3 kg and adheres to it. Find (a) the velocity of the combined mass after the impact, (b) the change in kinetic energy due to the impact.

*16. A body of mass 10 kg moving at 5 m s^{-1} collides with a body of mass 4 kg at rest. The two masses move on together. Find the change in kinetic energy due to the collision.

*17. A pump raises 30 kg of water per minute to a height of 5 m, and produces a muzzle velocity of 20 m s^{-1}. What is the power of the pump?

★18. A bullet of mass 10 g travelling at 450 m s^{-1} passes through a block of wood 5 cm thick. If it emerges from the wood with a velocity of 150 m s^{-1}, find the average retarding force exerted on the bullet by the wood.

★19. A bullet of mass 5 g travelling at 100 m s^{-1} penetrates a block of wood and comes to rest in one hundredth of a second. Find how deeply it penetrates the wood, and the average retarding force exerted on it.

★20. Define (i) energy; (ii) momentum.
A block of wood of mass 5 kg is suspended by a fine vertical wire of length 2 m. A bullet of mass 40 g is fired horizontally into the wood and becomes embedded in it. If the impact causes the wire to swing through an angle of 3° to the vertical, calculate the velocity of the bullet before impact.
($g = 9.8$ m s^{-1}, cos 3° = 0.9986)

Density and Pressure

CHAPTER 14

In diagram (a) we are comparing the mass of aluminium and lead. Is this a fair comparison? We should compare the same volume of each substance as in diagram (b).

Scientists say that the density of lead is 11·2 g cm^{-3} and the density of aluminium is 2·7 g cm^{-3}.

The mass of a unit volume of a substance is called its density.

If a piece of iron of mass 39 g has a volume of 5 cm^3, what is its density?

The mass of 5 cm^3 = 39 g

$\Rightarrow$ the mass of 1 cm^3 = $\dfrac{39 \text{ g}}{5 \text{ cm}^3}$ = 7.8 cm^{-3}

$\Rightarrow$ the density of iron is 7·8 g cm^{-3}

Density = mass/volume

Mathematically we can now say that $\rho = \dfrac{m}{V}$, where ρ is the density and V is the volume.

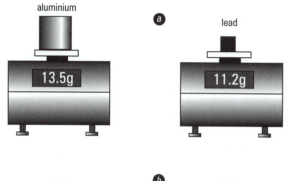

Experiment

AIM: To find the density of an irregular solid.

METHOD
1. Use a balance to find the mass of the solid.
2. Fill the overflow can with water and allow the excess to drip away.
3. Place a graduated cylinder under the spout.
4. Lower the solid gently into the overflow can. The volume of water that overflows into the cylinder equals the volume of the solid.
5. Now divide the mass by the volume to get the density.

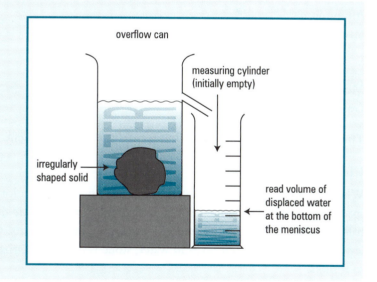

Engineers need to measure the density of substances such as steel and concrete to make sure that the load is not too great for the supports. Geologists need to measure the density of rocks to identify them.

Experiment

AIM: To find the density of a liquid.

METHOD
1. Find the mass of an empty beaker.
2. Using a pipette, place 100 cm³ of liquid in the beaker.
3. Find the mass of the beaker plus the liquid.
4. Subtract the mass of the beaker from this to get the mass of the liquid.

Result: density = $\frac{\text{mass}}{100 \text{cm}^3}$.

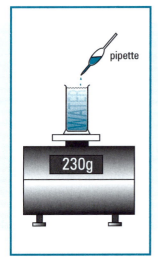

Milk inspectors measure the density of milk to make sure it has not been watered down or is not of poor quality. Excise inspectors measure the density of beer to find the percentage of alcohol. Alcohol is less dense than water, so the lower the density the greater is the percentage of alcohol in the beer.

Some common densities in g cm⁻³

Aeroboard	0·02
Oak	0·65
Methylated spirits	0·8
Ice	0·92
Water	1
Ebony	1·1
Aluminium	2·7
Steel	7·9
Copper	8·9
Lead	11·2
Mercury	13·6
Gold	19

The SI unit of density is kg m⁻³, but g cm⁻³ is more convenient.

Floating and density

When the air in a balloon is heated, it expands and takes up a lot more space. As a result it becomes less dense. Since the hot air inside the balloon is less dense than the cold air outside, the balloon floats. Cork is less dense than water so it floats in water; stone is more dense than water so it sinks.

A body will float in a fluid if it is less dense than the fluid.

Pressure

Fill your schoolbag with books and hang it from your shoulder by a strap. Now hang it from your shoulder by a length of string. Feel the

Density and Pressure

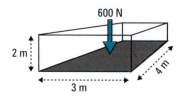

difference? The weight is the same but the force is now pressing on a smaller area, so the pressure is greater because **pressure = $\frac{\text{force}}{\text{area}}$**.

Pressure is force per unit area.

The weight of the block in the diagram is 600 N. The base area is 3 cm × 4 cm = 12 cm². The pressure = $\frac{\text{force}}{\text{area}} = \frac{600 \text{ N}}{12 \text{ cm}^2} = 50 \text{ N cm}^{-2}$.

But when the block is standing on end the pressure = $\frac{600 \text{ N}}{6 \text{ cm}^2} = 100 \text{ N cm}^{-2}$.

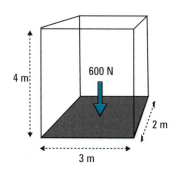

Atmospheric pressure

We live at the bottom of a sea of air called the earth's atmosphere. The air, like everything else, has weight. Since it has weight it exerts pressure. The following simple demonstrations show this.

1. Fill a tumbler to the brim with water.
2. Cover it with a sheet of cardboard.
3. Invert the tumbler holding the cardboard in place.
4. Remove your hand. The water remains in the tumbler.

1. Place a little water in the bottom of a tin can.
2. Boil the water until the steam has driven all the air out of the can.
3. Carefully seal the can and cool it until the steam condenses, leaving a vacuum inside the can.

Result: The atmospheric pressure on the outside causes the can to collapse inwards.

Note: This experiment can be done very effectively using an empty soft drink can and some plasticine, but wear a padded glove to protect your hand.

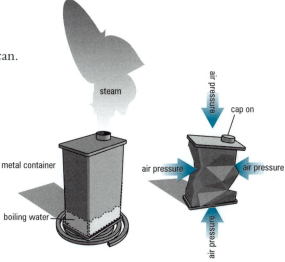

We have seen that the atmosphere exerts pressure. One way in which this pressure can be measured is to find out how much mercury the pressure of the atmosphere will support.

A mercury barometer enables us to compare atmospheric pressures from one day to the next. We can calculate the atmospheric pressure as follows.

Consider a column of mercury of height 76 cm and base area 1 cm². The volume of the mercury is 76 cm³.
The mass is volume × density = 76 × 13·6 = 1033·6 g = 1·0336 kg
The weight = mass × g = 1·0336 × 9·8 = 10·13 N.
Since the pressure is force per unit area, the actual pressure is

$$\frac{10\cdot13 \text{ N}}{1 \text{ cm}^2} = \frac{10\cdot13 \text{ N}}{1 \times 10^{-4} \text{ m}^2} = 10\cdot13 \times 10^4 \text{ N m}^{-2}$$

$$= 1\cdot013 \times 10^5 \text{ N m}^{-2}$$

Pressure can be measured in several other units, e.g. the pascal.

1 pascal (Pa) = 1 N m^{-2}

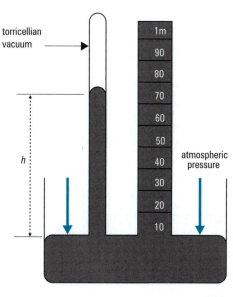

The atmospheric pressure now becomes 1.013×10^5 pascals or, more commonly, **1013 hectopascals**. High atmospheric pressure generally indicates dry weather; low pressure indicates wet weather.

Air moves from areas of high pressure to areas of low pressure. In nature this causes winds.

In a vacuum cleaner a motor-driven fan lowers the pressure inside the machine. This causes air from the higher pressure area outside to rush in, carrying dust with it.

When you inhale, your diaphragm reduces the pressure inside your lungs, causing air to be drawn in.

The aneroid barometer

Variations in pressure cause the top of the corrugated box to move up and down, causing the needle to move over a scale.

Since the atmospheric pressure decreases with height above the earth, a barometer can be adapted to measure height. A barometer used for this purpose is called an **altimeter**.

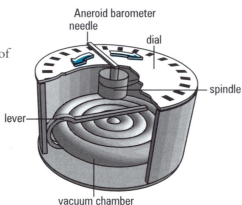

Blaise Pascal (France) 1623–1662 *was a scientist and philosopher. He invented a calculating machine and developed the theory of probability. He also proposed Pascal's law, which applies to pressure in fluids. A pressure of 1 newton per metre squared is called a pressure of one pascal.*

Pressure in fluids

The experiment illustrated in the diagram can be done very simply by filling a tall plastic bottle with water, screwing the top on, making three holes in the side of the bottle and then removing the top. Note that the nearer the hole is to the bottom, the further out the water shoots.

In other words: **the greater the depth, the greater is the pressure**.

Another simple experiment is illustrated in the second diagram. Starting with the balloon skin just below the surface, note the increase in pressure as the depth increases.

By turning the thistle funnel round in different directions we can show that the pressure acts equally in all directions.

The jet of water where the pressure is greatest (at the bottom of the bottle) squirts out farther than water from near the top

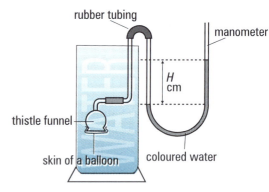

Pressure and density

Open the clip, put the rubber tube in your mouth and suck until the liquids rise up the tube. Then, keeping the tube in your mouth, close the clip. The atmospheric pressure supports 30 cm of methylated spirits but only 24 cm of water. This is because water is more dense than methylated spirits. **The greater the density, the greater is the pressure**.

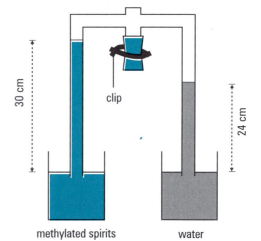

Density and Pressure

As well as the depth and the density, pressure depends on the acceleration due to gravity *g* since, for a fixed mass, *g* determines the weight. So **pressure depends on depth, density and the acceleration due to gravity**.

Mathematically, $P = h\rho g$.

Applications

The fact that pressure is transmitted to all parts of a fluid is used in any machine that has a hydraulic system.

In the diagram, a force of 20 N is applied to the small piston of cross-sectional area 0·01 m².

Pressure = $\dfrac{20 \text{ N}}{0·01 \text{ m}^2}$ = 2000 Pa

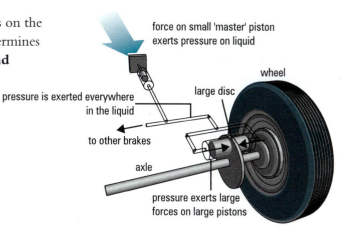

This pressure is transmitted through the fluid to the larger piston of cross-sectional area 0·1 m².

Pressure = 2000 Pa = $\dfrac{200 \text{ N}}{0·1 \text{ m}^2}$

So, a relatively small force of 20 N applied to the brake pedal is magnified into a force of 200 N which pushes the brake pads against the disc, causing a frictional force that stops the axle turning.

Remember, once again, you never get more energy (work) out of a machine than you put in. All that happens is that you apply a small force over a larger distance to produce a large force over a smaller distance. The brake pedal travels about 10 times as far as the brake pads.

Another application of this principle is in the hydraulic car jack. Also, a mechanical digger uses the same idea.

Fluid pressure can be dangerous. A diver who is deep under water experiences a large pressure. If she rises to the surface too quickly the rapid change from high pressure to low pressure can cause bubbles of air in the bloodstream, which lead to a condition known as 'the bends'.

Archimedes' Principle

Did you ever teach anyone how to swim? If you did you know that you can support them quite easily in the water by simply placing one hand under them even if they are as heavy as you are. This is an example of Archimedes' Principle.

Archimedes Principle: A body wholly or partly immersed in a fluid experiences an upthrust equal in magnitude to the weight of the fluid displaced.

Another way of saying this is:

When a body is partly or wholly immersed in a fluid, the apparent loss in weight equals the weight of the fluid displaced.

Archimedes (Greece) 298BC–212BC was the greatest mathematician of ancient times. He lived at Syracuse in Sicily and was killed during its capture by the Romans in the Second Punic War. Archimedes invented an enormous catapult and a concave mirror to focus the heat of the sun on the sails of attacking ships, to help defend Syracuse. He invented the Archimedes' screw, still used to transfer grain. Archimedes made many original contributions to geometry. He is known for his discovery on the weight of a body immersed in a liquid (Archimedes' Principle).

Experiment

AIM: To verify Archimedes' Principle.

METHOD
1. Hang a solid object on a spring balance and note the weight.
2. Set up the apparatus as shown in the diagram and note the weight of the beaker.
3. Lower the object slowly into the water and wait until the overflow has stopped running into the beaker.
4. Note the weight of the displaced water. It should be equal to the apparent loss in weight of the solid object.

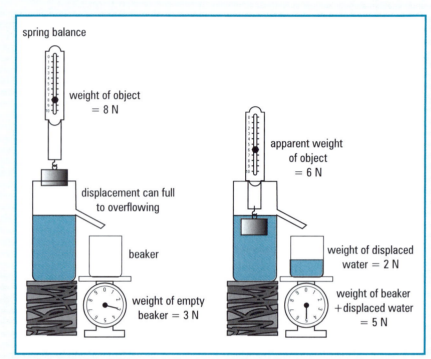

Pressure increases with depth and, as is clear from the diagram, the pressure is greatest at the bottom of the block, so it experiences an upthrust.

The block of wood is less dense than water, so it displaces its own weight of fluid without being wholly immersed. At this stage it experiences an upthrust equal to its own weight, so it floats. This is a special case of Archimedes' Principle known as the **law of flotation**.

A floating body displaces its own weight of fluid.

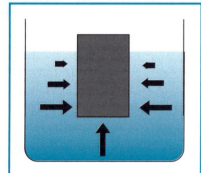

The hydrometer

One practical application of the law of flotation is in the use of a hydrometer.

Allow the hydrometer to float in the liquid. The density can be read off on the scale at the level of the liquid surface. The more dense the liquid, the less the hydrometer sinks.

A special hydrometer is used to check the density of the acid in a car battery. The rubber bulb is used to suck acid from the battery into the glass tube. The density can then be read from the hydrometer floating in the acid. The density in a fully charged battery should be $1\cdot28$ g cm^{-3}. If the density falls below $1\cdot15$ g cm^{-3}, the battery may be permanently damaged.

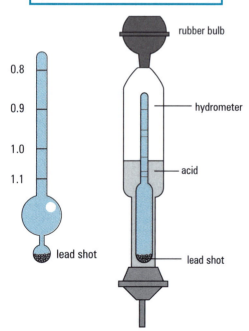

DENSITY AND PRESSURE

Summary

- The mass of a unit volume of a substance is called its density.
- Pressure is force per unit area.
- The unit of pressure is the pascal (1 Pa = 1 N m^{-2}).
- Pressure in a liquid depends on depth and density.
- Archimedes' Principle: A body partly or wholly immersed in a fluid experiences an upthrust equal to the weight of the fluid displaced.
- Law of flotation: A floating body displaces its own weight of fluid.

SHORT QUESTIONS

1. A body of mass 28 kg has a density of 4 kg m^{-3}. Its volume in m^3 is (A) 0·14, (B) 4, (C) 7, (D) 28, (E) 112.
2. Below the surface of a liquid, the pressure acting in the liquid (A) decreases as the depth increases, (B) increases as the depth increases, (C) is independent of the depth, (D) is the same for all liquids at a particular depth, (E) depends only on the temperature of the liquid at a particular depth.
3. The law of flotation states that (A) a floating body displaces its own mass of fluid, (B) a floating body displaces its own volume of fluid, (C) a floating body displaces its own weight of fluid, (D) a floating body has no weight, (E) the density of a floating body is the same as that of the fluid in which it floats.
4. The diagram shows a solid block L floating in water. The block floats because (A) the density of the block is greater than the density of water, (B) the density of the block is the same as the density of water, (C) the upthrust on the block is equal to the force of gravity acting on the block, (D) the upthrust of the block is equal to the air pressure acting on the top, (E) the volume of the block is too large to allow it to sink.

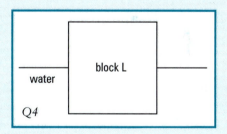

*5. On a certain day the height of the mercury column in a mercury barometer is 74·0 cm. Given that the density of mercury is 1·36 × 10^4 kg m^{-3}, and taking g as 9·81 m s^{-2}, the atmospheric pressure is (A) 9·87 × 10^6 Pa, (B) 9·87 × 10^5 Pa, (C) 9·87 × 10^4 Pa, (D) 1·01 × 10^5 Pa, (E) 1·01 × 10^6 Pa.
6. The cabin of an aircraft flying at high altitude is 'pressurised'. Give a reason for this.
7. Archimedes' Principle states that _____.
8. Pressure in a liquid depends on _____.
9. A pressure of 1 N m^{-2} is known as _____.
10. _____ will not float in mercury.

LONG QUESTIONS

1. A piece of aluminium has a mass of 1·5 kg. Find its volume, given that the density of aluminium is 2·7 g cm^{-3}.

2. A rectangular block of copper has dimensions 10 cm, 8 cm and 6 cm. Find the mass of the block, given that the density of copper is 8·9 g cm^{-3}.

3. 50 g of a liquid of density 1·2 g cm^{-3} is mixed with 40 g of a liquid of density 0·9 g cm^{-3}. What is the density of the mixture?

4. The following table gives the pressure in fresh water at different depths below the surface:

Depth (m)	0	1	3	5	7	9	11
Pressure (N cm^{-2})	10·1	11·1	13·1	15·1	17·1	19·1	21·1

   (a) Draw a graph of pressure against depth. (b) What does the graph tell you about the way pressure varies with depth?
   (c) Why is the pressure 10·1 N cm^{-2} at the surface?
   (d) From your graph, find the depth at which the pressure is double that at the surface. (e) Would the pressure in sea water at this depth have a different value? Explain your answer.
   (f) Draw a section through a reservoir wall and explain the shape of the section. (g) Does the thickness of a reservoir wall at any level depend on the surface area of the reservoir?

5. In the diagram, the area of piston A is 25 cm^2 and that of piston B is 2000 cm^2. A 5 kg mass is placed on A. What is the downward force on A? What is the pressure on the oil under A? What is the pressure on the oil under B? What is the upward force on B?

6. Describe and explain the design features of a common hydrometer. If it is intended to be used over the range of densities 0·70 to 1·00, indicate simply the appearance of its scale.

★7. An open tank is full of water. If 6·8 cm of water evaporates from the tank, what change in the atmospheric pressure will be necessary to restore the pressure on the sides of the tank to its previous value?

8. A girl loads her boat with some steel pipes and rows out into the middle of a small pond. She then throws the pipes, one by one, overboard. What happens to the water level on the side of the boat? Does the water level in the pond rise, fall or stay the same? Explain. Design your own experiment to test your answer in the classroom. Write down your results. They may surprise you!

Circular Motion

CHAPTER 15

N.B. This entire chapter is higher course.

Radians

The Arabs measured angles in degrees. A complete circle was 360°, a half circle was 180° and so on.

The Greeks measured angles in radians. One radian is the angle subtended at the centre of a circle by an arc of length 1 radius.

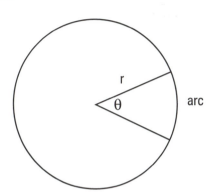

Angle in radians = length of $\frac{\text{arc}}{\text{radius}}$ ($\theta = \frac{s}{r}$)

In the case of a complete circle: angle in radians = $\frac{2\pi r}{r} = 2\pi$

Uniform circular motion

When a body is in uniform circular motion, the periodic time (T) is the time for one complete revolution.

The velocity can be viewed in two ways. We can consider the angle being swept out in one second. This is called the **angular velocity (ω)**.

The angular velocity is the rate of change of angle measured in radians per second ($\omega = \frac{\theta}{t}$)

The periodic time T is the time for one complete revolution. In this case the angle in radians is 2π. So the periodic time is $\frac{2\pi}{\omega}$.

$$T = \frac{2\pi}{\omega}$$

We can also consider the distance moved along the arc in one second. This is called the **linear velocity (v)**.

The angle in radians = length of arc/radius $\Rightarrow \theta = \frac{\text{length of arc}}{r}$

$\Rightarrow$ length of arc = $r\theta$

$v = \frac{\text{(length of arc)}}{t} = \frac{r\theta}{t} = r\omega$

$$v = r\omega$$

Problem

A particle is travelling at a constant speed round a circle of radius 20 cm. If the particle does 5 revolutions per second, find its angular and linear speed.

$\omega = 2\pi \times 5 = 10\pi = 31\cdot 4$ rad s^{-1}

$v = r\omega = 0\cdot 2 \times 31\cdot 4 = 6\cdot 28$ m s^{-1}

125

PHYSICS NOW!

Centripetal force

Fasten a rubber bung or a ball of plasticene® to a piece of string and whirl it round in a circle. Why is it moving in a circle? Newton's first law says that a body will move with uniform velocity **in a straight line** unless an external force acts on it. The external force in this case is the tension in the string. This force acts **towards the centre** of the circle and is called the **centripetal force**.

A body is kept moving in a circle by a resultant force, called the centripetal force, acting towards the centre of the circle.

It is very important to realise that the centripetal force is the **cause** of the circular motion, not the result of it.

To demonstrate this, whirl the ball of plasticine round in a circle. Now release the string. The ball flies off at a tangent, as shown in the diagram. Once the centripetal force is removed the ball no longer moves in a circle, but in a straight line.

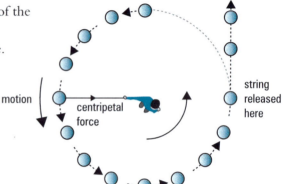

This idea is almost as old as mankind. It was used by David to kill Goliath with a sling shot.

The moon is held in orbit round the earth by the centripetal force provided by the pull of gravity. The planets are held in orbit round the sun in the same way. A knowledge of the scientific principles involved has enabled hammer throwers to improve their performance. The idea is used in a spin dryer. The clothes are held in orbit by the drum, but the water can escape at a tangent through the holes in a drum.

Friction is a very important centripetal force. Sideways friction between the tyres and the road is the centripetal force that keeps a car moving round the bend. If this force is inadequate, because the car is moving too fast or the force is reduced by water, oil or ice on the road, the car does not go round the bend but keeps going straight on!

If you use a larger ball of plasticine you have to apply greater force. If you want the ball to move faster you must apply a greater force. If you use a shorter string you must apply a greater force. So the centripetal force required depends
1. directly on the mass of the body
2. directly on the speed of the body
3. inversely on the radius of the circle.

Circular Motion

Force and acceleration

If a body is in uniform circular motion, its velocity is constant in magnitude **but not in direction**. So it has an acceleration.

$$a = r\omega^2 \text{ or, since } \frac{v}{r} = \omega, \text{ acceleration } = \frac{v^2}{r}$$

$$a = \frac{v^2}{r}$$

The force F necessary to keep a body of mass m moving in a circle is therefore

$$F = \frac{mv^2}{r} \text{ or } mr\omega^2$$

Problem

An electron of mass 9×10^{-31} kg circles the nucleus of an atom with a linear velocity of 3×10^6 m s^{-1}. The radius of its circular path is 6×10^{-10} m. Find the acceleration towards the centre and the centripetal force.

$$a = \frac{v^2}{r} = \frac{(3 \times 10^6)^2}{(6 \times 10^{-10})} = \frac{(9 \times 10^{12})}{(6 \times 10^{-10})} = 1\cdot5 \times 10^{22} \text{ m s}^{-2}$$

$$F = \frac{mv^2}{r} = 9 \times 10^{-31} \times 1\cdot5 \times 10^{22} = 1\cdot35 \times 10^{-8} \text{ N}$$

Planetary motion

In 1609 Kepler published his laws of planetary motion.
1. The planets move in elliptical orbits round the sun as one focus.
2. The line joining the sun and the planets sweeps out equal areas in equal time intervals.
3. The square of the periodic time of a planet is proportional to the cube of its mean distance from the sun.

Gravitation

Gravitation is the attraction that all masses in the universe have for each other. In 1680 Newton published his law of gravitation.

Law of gravitation: The force of attraction between any two bodies is proportional to the product of their masses and inversely proportional to the square of the distance between them.

$$F \propto \frac{(m_1 m_2)}{d^2} \Rightarrow F = \frac{(Gm_1 m_2)}{d^2}$$

G is called the **universal constant of gravitation** ($G = 6\cdot67 \times 10^{-11}$ N m^2 kg^{-2}).

Johannes Kepler (Germany) 1571–1630 used the astronomical observations of Tycho Brahe to propose the three laws of planetary motion. Kepler developed telescopes, invented a magnifying eyepiece and discovered a way of measuring the magnifying power of lenses.

PHYSICS NOW!

The solar system

The solar system consists of the sun and the nine planets orbiting the sun. The enormous gravitational pull of the sun keeps the other planets orbiting it. The gravitational pull of the earth keeps its moon orbiting it. The gravitational pull of the moon is so weak that it cannot even hold an atmosphere in place, and so has no atmosphere. However, because the moon is much closer to the earth than the sun is, and orbits the earth, it has a great effect on the seas and causes the regular flow of tides. Tides are caused by a combination of the steady gravitational pull of the sun, the gravitational pull of the moon as it orbits the earth, and the rotation of the earth on its axis.

Weightlessness

Astronauts who travelled a great distance from the earth escaped the earth's gravitational pull and were weightless: there was no gravitational pull on their bodies. Astronauts orbiting the earth feel weightless and float around the space shuttle. This is because their orbit can be resolved into an acceleration at a tangent to the earth and acceleration due to gravity towards the earth. The astronauts and the shuttle are in a state of continuous free fall, and so feel weightless.

G and g

Consider a body of mass m on the surface of a planet of mass M and radius r. The force pulling the body towards the centre of the planet is mg.

But the force of attraction between the two bodies is $\frac{GMm}{r^2}$

$$\Rightarrow mg = \frac{GMm}{r^2} \Rightarrow \frac{g}{G} = \frac{M}{r^2}$$

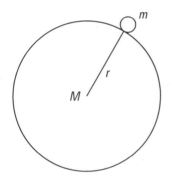

Different planets

G has the same value everywhere in the universe. g is the acceleration due to gravity on any particular planet. Different planets have different masses and different radii. It follows that the acceleration due to gravity g varies from one planet to another.

$$g = \frac{GM}{r^2}$$

$$\frac{(g \text{ on planet 1})}{(g \text{ on planet 2})} = \frac{GM_1}{r_1^2} \times \frac{r_2^2}{GM_2} \Rightarrow \frac{g_1}{g_2} = \frac{M_1 r_2^2}{M_2 r_1^2}$$

PROBLEM

Given that the acceleration due to gravity on earth is 9.8 m s^{-2}, find the acceleration due to gravity on the moon if the mass of the moon is one eightieth that of the earth and the radius of the moon is one quarter that of the earth.

Circular Motion

$$\frac{g_m}{g_e} = \frac{M_m r_e^2}{M_e r_m^2} \Rightarrow \frac{g_m}{9.8} = \frac{1}{80} \times \frac{16}{1} = \frac{1}{5} \Rightarrow g_m = \frac{9.8}{5} = 1.96 \text{m s}^{-2}$$

It follows from this example that if you weigh 600 N on earth you would weigh only 120 N on the moon. On some planets the pull of gravity is so weak that it could not even hold their atmosphere in place. As a result they have no atmosphere.

Astronauts travelling between planets experience weightlessness if they are not within the gravitational field of any planet.

Kepler's third law

Consider a body of mass m in circular orbit of radius r round a central body of mass M.

Let the periodic time be T. Gravitational force = centripetal force.

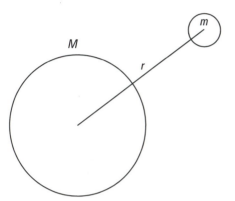

$$\frac{GMm}{r^2} = mr\omega^2 = mr \times \frac{4\pi^2}{T^2} \Rightarrow T^2 = \frac{4\pi^2 r^3}{GM}$$

which, mathematically, is Kepler's third law.

Satellites in orbit

Gravitational pull provides the centripetal force necessary to maintain a satellite on a circular path. The further out the orbit, the lower is the gravitational pull and the speed required to keep the satellite from falling to earth. When a satellite is put into orbit, its speed is carefully chosen so that its weight supplies exactly the right centripetal force to keep it in that particular orbit.

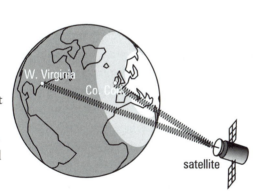

One of the greatest advances in the field of communications has been the use of communication satellites. Basically what happens is that a signal is transmitted from the earth's surface to a satellite and from there to somewhere else on the earth's surface. For this to succeed, the satellite must always be directly above a particular point on the earth's surface. In other words, the period of the satellite must be the same as the period of rotation of the earth, i.e. 24 hours. Such a satellite is said to be in a **geostationary** or **parking orbit**.

Problem

Given that the mass of the earth is 6×10^{24} kg and the radius of the earth is 6.4×10^6 m, calculate the height above the earth's surface of a satellite which is in a geostationary orbit.

$$\frac{4\pi^2 r^3}{GM} = T^2 \Rightarrow r^3 = \frac{GMT^2}{4\pi^2} = \frac{6.67 \times 10^{-11} \times 6 \times 10^{24} \times (24 \times 3{,}600)^2}{4 \times 3.14^2}$$

$$= 7.575 \times 10^{22} \text{ m}^3 \Rightarrow r = 4.231 \times 10^7 \text{ m}$$

The height above the earth's surface is the radius of the satellite's orbit minus the radius of the earth.

$h = 4·231 \times 10^7 - 6·4 \times 10^6 = 3·591 \times 10^7$ m

Stretching materials

Over 300 years ago Robert Hooke conducted a series of experiments to see how the extension of a material and the stretching force were related. He did experiments similar to the following.

Experiment

AIM: To study the extension of a spiral spring.

METHOD
1. Set up the apparatus as shown in the diagram, making sure that the load is just enough to keep the spring taut.
2. Add an extra mass and note **the extension**.
3. Continue adding masses until you have at least seven readings.
4. Draw a graph of extension against load.

Result: The result is a straight line through the origin.
Conclusion: The extension is directly proportional to the load.

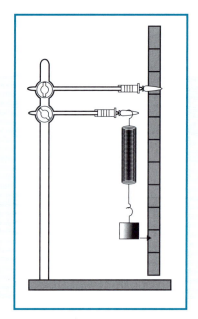

When a stretching force is applied to the spring, a **restoring force** in the opposite direction comes into play. The restoring force is proportional to the displacement (**F = −ks**).

The above conclusion is reasonable within the limits of the experiment. However, if you continue to increase the load a point is reached where the graph changes shape as shown in the diagram. If the load is now removed the spring will not return to its original shape.

The ability of the spring to return to its original shape is called **elasticity**. If the spring is stretched too far it cannot return to its original shape: it has been stretched beyond its **elastic limit**. Hooke summarised what he had learned in a law known as Hooke's law.

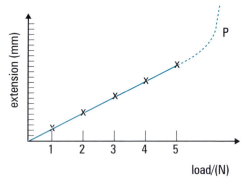

Provided the spring is not extended beyond its elastic limit, the extension is proportional to the load.

Hooke's law applies to car springs, bed springs and steel girders. Graphs of extension against load are studied by construction engineers. The fact that the extension is proportional to the load allows the spiral spring to be used as a spring balance.

Circular Motion

Simple harmonic motion

If you pull the mass in the diagram downwards and release it, it will oscillate up and down about its mean position O. The greater its displacement from O, the greater is its acceleration towards O. If you allow the pendulum in the diagram to swing through a small angle, the greater its displacement from O the greater is its acceleration towards O. This type of motion is called simple harmonic motion.

The motion of a body is simple harmonic motion if its acceleration towards a particular point is directly proportional to its displacement from that point.

In terms of Hooke's law, the restoring force is proportional to the displacement. Mathematically

$$F = -ks \implies ma = -ks \implies a = \left(\frac{-k}{m}\right)s$$

For convenience this is usually written as $a = -\omega^2 s$. **This is a mathematical definition of simple harmonic motion.** The minus indicates that the body begins to retard as it passes through O, the centre of its motion.

If you suspend a bar magnet from a wooden stand and allow it to swing freely, it will execute simple harmonic motion before coming to rest in a north-south direction. A tuning fork and a guitar string also execute simple harmonic motion, as does a simple pendulum.

The path of a simple pendulum forms part of the circumference of a circle, so the periodic time $T = \frac{2\pi}{\omega}$.

This formula applies to all simple harmonic motion. In the case of the simple pendulum **moving through a small angle**, the angular velocity depends on the length of the pendulum and the acceleration due to gravity g. So the formula for the periodic time of a simple pendulum becomes

$$T = 2\pi \sqrt{\left(\frac{l}{g}\right)}$$

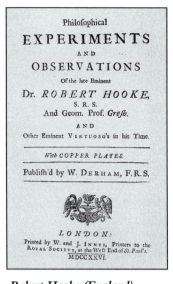

Robert Hooke (England) 1635–1703 was an assistant to Robert Boyle and helped him to discover the gas law (Boyle's law). Hooke discovered the law of elasticity – that the extension of an elastic body is proportional to the force applied – called Hooke's law. He also did some work on light and combustion, and demonstrated that air was necessary for respiration.

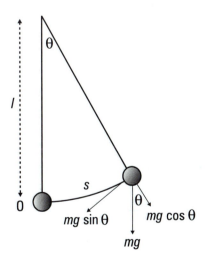

Problem

A body of mass 0.5 kg executes simple harmonic motion. If it has a period of 2 seconds, find
(a) its frequency;
(b) the restoring force when the displacement is 5 cm.

(a) Frequency $= \frac{1}{T} = \frac{1}{2}$ Hz
(b) $F = ma = m\omega^2 S = 0.5 \left(\frac{2\pi}{2}\right)^2 (0.05)$
$= 0.025\pi^2 \approx 0.2465$ N.

Summary

- For a body in circular motion, the periodic time T is the time for one complete revolution.
- The angular velocity is the rate of change of angle measured in radians per second.
- $T = \dfrac{2\pi}{\omega}$
- $\omega = \dfrac{\theta}{t}$
- $v = r\omega$
- Acceleration $= r\omega^2$ or $\dfrac{v^2}{r}$
- $F = \dfrac{mv^2}{r}$ or $mr\omega^2$
- A body is kept in circular motion by a resultant force, called the centripetal force, acting towards the centre of the circle.
- Law of gravitation: The force of attraction between any two bodies is proportional to the product of their masses and inversely proportional to the square of the distance between them ($F = \dfrac{Gm_1 m_2}{d^2}$).
- The motion of a body is simple harmonic motion if its acceleration towards a particular point is proportional to its displacement from that point. Mathematically, $a = -\omega^2 s$.

Short Questions

1. When a body is thrown vertically upwards and reaches its greatest height: (A) its velocity is zero and its acceleration is zero, (B) its velocity is zero and its acceleration is not zero, (C) its velocity is not zero and its acceleration is downwards, (D) its velocity is not zero and its acceleration is upwards, (E) its velocity is zero and its acceleration is upwards.
2. Define angular velocity.
3. A car of mass 900 kg is driving round a circular track with a constant linear speed of 10 m s^{-1}. If the radius of the track is 30 m, the centripetal force is (A) 10 N, (B) 30 N, (C) 900 N, (D) 2,700 N, (E) 3,000 N.
4. Given that the mass of the earth is $6 \cdot 0 \times 10^{24}$ kg and that $G = 6 \cdot 7 \times 10^{-11}$ N m^2 kg^{-2}, the radius of the orbit of a satellite in geostationary orbit round the earth will be approximately: (A) $4 \cdot 24 \times 10^7$ m, (B) $4 \cdot 24 \times 10^7$ km, (C) $6 \cdot 0 \times 10^7$ m, (D) $6 \cdot 7 \times 10^7$ m, (E) $40 \cdot 2 \times 10^7$ m.
5. The weight of a body is W at a point on the earth's surface where the radius of the earth is r. At which of the following heights above the surface of the earth will the weight of the body be $\dfrac{W}{4}$? (A) $\dfrac{r}{2}$, (B) r, (C) $2r$, (D) $3r$, (E) $4r$.

6. Give an example of a body that is accelerating while it moves at constant speed.
7. The mass of a body is 5 kg on the surface of the earth. What is its weight on the surface of the moon? (Take g on the moon as $1 \cdot 6$ m s^{-2}.)
8. When a particle is executing simple harmonic motion, its (A) displacement is proportional to its velocity, (B) velocity is inversely proportional to its displacement, (C) velocity is proportional to its acceleration, (D) displacement is inversely proportional to its acceleration, (E) displacement is proportional to its acceleration.
9. Give an equation that defines simple harmonic motion.
10. The period of a simple pendulum is (A) directly proportional to its length, (B) directly proportional to the square root of its length, (C) directly proportional to its length squared, (D) inversely proportional to its length squared, (E) inversely proportional to the square root of its length.

LONG QUESTIONS

1. Explain each of the following.
   (a) If you swing a bung around your head on a piece of elastic, the length of the elastic changes when you change the speed of the bung.
   (b) A roller-coaster can loop-the-loop if it is going fast enough.
   (c) Cycle racing tracks are steeply banked, sloping towards the inside of the curve.
2. What supplies the centripetal force when:
   (a) A train goes around a corner?
   (b) An aircraft banks? (Think carefully about this one.)
   (c) The earth orbits the sun?
3. A body of mass $0 \cdot 5$ kg is moving in a horizontal circle at constant speed. In what direction is the body being accelerated? If the acceleration is 25 m s^{-2}, what is the horizontal force acting on the body?
4. State Newton's law of gravitation. If the acceleration due to gravity on the surface of the earth is $9 \cdot 8$ m s^{-2}, and the radius of the earth is $6 \cdot 4 \times 10^6$ m, calculate the acceleration due to gravity at a height of 8×10^5 metres above the surface of the earth.
5. Calculate the acceleration due to gravity on the surface of a certain planet given that the acceleration due to gravity on the surface of the earth is $9 \cdot 8$ m s^{-2}, (radius of earth/radius of planet) = $\frac{15}{8}$ and (mean density of earth/mean density of planet) = $\frac{10}{7}$.
6. Give an expression for (i) Newton's law of gravitation, (ii) the relationship between G, the gravitational constant, and g, the acceleration due to gravity. Describe an experiment

to determine the value of *g*. Explain what is meant by centripetal force. Derive an expression for the periodic time of a satellite in a circular orbit round the earth in terms of its height above the earth and the radius and mass of the earth. The radius of the planet Neptune's orbit round the sun is 30 times that of the earth's orbit. Calculate the time taken for Neptune to make one complete orbit of the sun.

7. Two students test the centripetal force equation $F = \frac{mv^2}{R}$ with the arrangement shown in the diagram. The idea is to rotate the mass on the end of the thread in a horizontal circle, keeping the radius *R* constant. This is done by keeping the paper flag attached to the thread stationary just below the tube. The lower weights provide the tension in the thread.
   (a) In what direction does the centripetal force act?
   (b) How is the size of the centripetal force found in this experiment?
   (c) Describe how *R* could be measured.
   (d) Describe how the time *t* for one revolution would be measured.
   (e) Why does the speed of the rotating mass equal $\frac{2\pi R}{t}$?
   (f) If $m = 0.01$ kg, $v = 2$ m s^{-1} and $R = 0.5$ m, what should the centripetal force be?

8. Define simple harmonic motion. The diagram shows a simple pendulum in a position where its displacement from the vertical is θ. Show, on a sketch, the forces acting on the bob of the pendulum in this position. Hence, derive an expression for the acceleration of the bob in a direction perpendicular to AB.

9. Calculate the mean density of the earth, assuming that $G = 6.66 \times 10^{-11}$ units and the radius of the earth is 6.37×10^3 km.

10. Show that the gravitational constant $G = \frac{gr^2}{M}$ where *M* is the mass of the earth, *r* is the radius of the earth and *g* is the acceleration due to gravity. Find the acceleration due to gravity at a height of 1.6×10^6 m above the surface of the earth given that the acceleration due to gravity on the surface of the earth is 9.8 m s^{-2} and the radius of the earth is 6.4×10^6 m.

11. Show that the square of the periodic time of a planet is proportional to the cube of its mean distance from the sun.

12. The diagram shows a simple pendulum with a length of 85 cm. Use the principle of conservation of energy to calculate the maximum speed of the pendulum bob. Explain why the motion of this pendulum should not be considered to be simple harmonic motion.

13. A particle travels from A to B along the arc of a circle of radius 60 cm and centre O, as shown in the diagram. Calculate
    (i) the distance travelled,
    (ii) the displacement undergone by the particle.

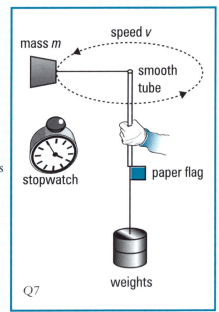
Q7

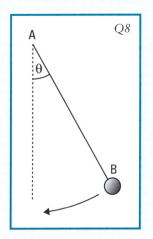
Q8

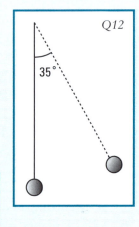
Q12

Q13

14. A satellite is in a circular orbit of radius r around a body of mass M, Fig. 3. Show that the period of the satellite is given by
$$T^2 = \frac{4\pi^2 r^3}{GM}$$

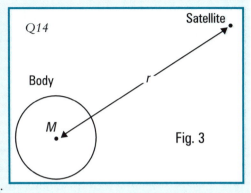

Fig. 3

The planet Jupiter is a satellite of the sun and the radius of its orbit around the sun is 7.8×10^{11} m. Given that the mass of the sun is 2.0×10^{30} kg calculate the time taken for Jupiter to make one complete orbit of the sun.
(Speed of light in vacuum, $c = 3.0 \times 10^8$ m s^{-1}, 1 year = 3.2×10^7 s; $G = 6.7 \times 10^{-11}$ Nm^2 kg^{-2}.)

15. State the principle of conservation of momentum and describe an experiment to verify it.
The direction in which a spacecraft is travelling can be changed by expelling a small mass of gas from it.
A spacecraft travelling with a certain velocity in the direction OA expels a mass of gas in the direction OB. Copy the diagram and show on it a possible direction for the new velocity of the spacecraft and explain why expelling the gas changes the velocity of the spacecraft.

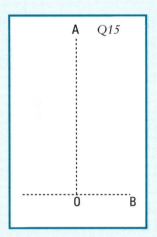

16. Define the term centripetal acceleration.
State the principle of conservation of energy as it applies to a freely falling body.
The diagram shows a body of mass 0.24 kg attached to a fixed point P by a light string of length 0.80 m. when the body is at A, vertically below P, it is given an initial horizontal velocity of 5.0 m s^{-1} as shown in the diagram. It then follows a circular path to position B. When the body is at B calculate:
(i) the velocity of the body;
(ii) the centripetal acceleration of the body;
(iii) the force exerted by the string on the body.
(Take the acceleration due to gravity, $g = 9.8$ m s^{-2}.)

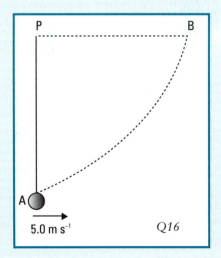

Heat, Temperature and Thermometers

CHAPTER 16

We already know that heat is a form of energy and that energy can change from one form to another. In fact a great deal of energy ends up as heat: some of it useful, some of it not. For example, in a car engine some of the chemical energy stored in petrol is turned into heat energy. This is useful, up to a point, because as the engine heats up it becomes more efficient. On the other hand, if the engine overheats it could be severely damaged, so a cooling system must be included. Before going any further, let us take a look at the effects of heat on solids, liquids and gases.

Experiment

AIM: To show the effect of heat on a solid.

METHOD
1. Check that the ball, when cold, will just pass through the ring.
2. Heat the ball strongly. Note that it can no longer pass through the ring.
3. Allow the ball to cool. Note that it can pass through the ring once again.

Conclusion: This shows that solids expand when heated.

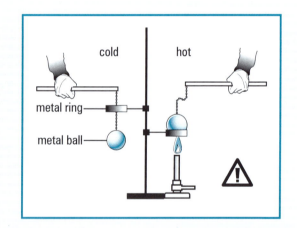

In addition to expanding, solids may change colour when heated. For example, an iron bar may become red-hot or even white-hot.

The bimetallic strip

A bimetallic strip is made of two different metals riveted together. When it is heated, one metal expands more than the other. This causes the strip to bend. The strip straightens out again when it cools. This has a number of applications.

The thermostat

A thermostat is a device used to maintain a steady temperature in a room, an oven, a boiler, etc. In the case of the electric iron, the required temperature is selected by means of the temperature selection knob. The

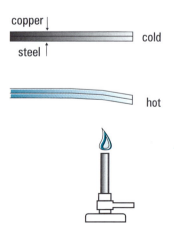

Heat, Temperature and Thermometers

position of the knob determines how much the bimetallic strip must bend in order to open the contacts and thus break the circuit. When the iron is switched on, current flows through the strip to the heater circuit. By the time the iron has reached the selected temperature, the strip will have bent sufficiently to open the contacts and cut off the current to the heater circuit. As the strip cools down it will straighten again, remaking the circuit. This process is repeated as the iron is used.

Thermostats are used to control the temperature of an electric oven or a central heating boiler.

A bimetallic strip can also be used to set off an alarm once a certain temperature is reached, as you can see from the diagram.

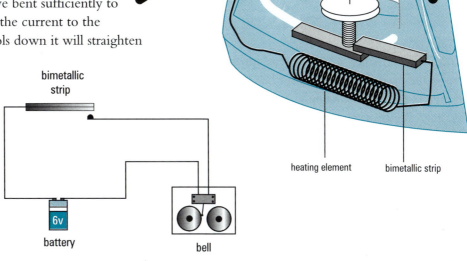

Experiment

Aim: To show that liquids expand when heated.

METHOD
1. Fill the flask to the top with coloured water.
2. Set up the apparatus as shown in the diagram.
3. Heat the liquid and watch it expand up the tube.
4. Cool the liquid: it contracts.

Conclusion: Liquids expand more than solids when they are heated.

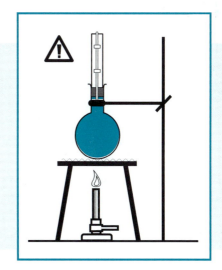

Water

Most liquids expand when they are heated and contract when they are cooled. Water is somewhat different.

When water is cooled it contracts, but when the temperature reaches 4°C it begins to expand again. So water has its greatest density at 4°C. From 4°C to 0°C the water expands and becomes less dense. As a result, ice floats in water.

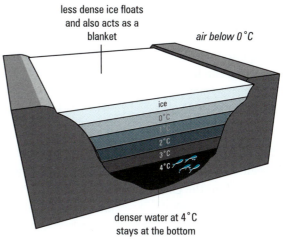

137

PHYSICS NOW!

Sprinklers

Many large buildings such as supermarkets and carpet showrooms have sprinkler valves on their ceilings. The flow of water is prevented by a sealed glass capsule almost full of liquid. When there is a fire the liquid expands and breaks the capsule, releasing the water.

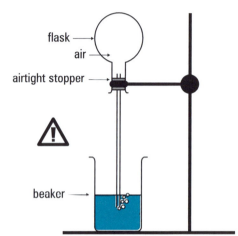

a sprinkler

Gases

Gases also expand when heated, as you can see if you hold the flask shown in the diagram between your hands. Even the heat from your hands makes the gas expand enough to bubble up through the water. As we have already seen, the fact that gases expand when heated, and so become less dense, is used in hot-air balloons.

Thermometers

The simplest type of thermometer contains mercury sealed in a glass tube. This type of thermometer works on the principle that liquids expand when they are heated and contract when they are cooled. The scale used on this thermometer is called the **Celsius** scale.

Experiment

AIM: To calibrate a mercury thermometer.

METHOD
1. Place the thermometer in a funnel of melting ice. Mark the mercury level as 0°C.
2. Place the thermometer above some water in a flask and heat the water until it boils. Mark the mercury level as 100°C.
3. The length between the two marks can now be divided into 100 equal parts, each representing 1°C.
4. In this case the scale can be marked permanently on the thermometer, so we can use the thermometer by simply reading the temperature from the scale.

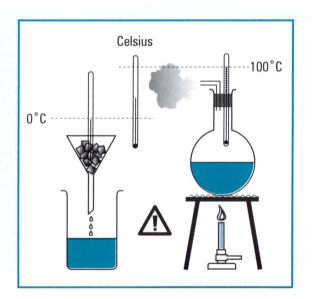

Other liquids

The two liquids commonly used in thermometers, mercury and alcohol, are compared in the following table.

MERCURY	ALCOHOL
1. Measures from −39 to 357°C	1. Measures from −112 to 78°C
2. Takes in little heat	2. Takes in more heat than mercury
3. Easily seen	3. Must be coloured
4. Does not stick to the glass	4. Sticks to the glass
5. Expands less than alcohol	5. Expands more than mercury

The use of water in thermometers was rejected because water does not expand evenly, sticks to the glass, is a poor conductor, boils at 100°C and freezes at 0°C.

Temperature and heat

We have used the word 'temperature' several times, but what exactly is temperature, what does it measure and why is it so important?

The reason it is so important is that it determines whether or not heat will flow and which way it will flow. Heat will flow from one body to another only if there is a difference in temperature between them. For example, if you fill a glass with water from the cold tap, add some ice and then stick your finger into the water, your finger will feel cold. This is because heat is flowing from your finger into the water.

If you now get a glass of warm water, about 50°C, and dip your finger into it your finger will feel warm. This is because heat is flowing from the water into your finger even though there is a lot more heat in your body than there is in the glass of water. Heat will always flow from the higher temperature to the lower temperature, just as water flows from the higher level to the lower level. So you could say that **temperature indicates the level of heat (hotness) in a body, not the amount of heat**.

When we heat a body we are giving it energy. This energy is shared between the molecules of the body. As the temperature rises, the kinetic energy of the molecules rises. There is in fact a direct relationship between the absolute temperature and the average kinetic energy of the molecules.

Measuring temperature

We use a thermometer to measure temperature. There are many different kinds of thermometer, but all thermometers contain a substance that has a thermometric property.

A thermometric property is a property that changes measurably as the temperature changes.

In addition to having a substance with a thermometric property, a good thermometer should:
1. be accurate
2. have a wide range
3. be sensitive
4. be quick to reach thermal equilibrium
5. have a low heat capacity (it should take only a little heat from the body whose temperature it is measuring).

PHYSICS NOW!

Establishing a scale of temperature
The principles underlying the establishment of a scale of temperature are that we need the following.
1. Two fixed points: These must be two temperatures that can be reproduced easily, e.g. the melting point of ice and the boiling point of water.
2. A body that has a thermometric property: e.g. the volume of a liquid, the pressure of a gas at constant volume, the electrical resistance of a piece of platinum wire.
3. Division of the fundamental interval: The fundamental interval is the interval between the fixed points. On the Celsius scale the fundamental interval is divided into 100 equal parts.

The thermocouple
If two wires made of different metals are joined together at both ends and the two junctions are at different temperatures, an emf (voltage) is generated and a current flows. Since the emf changes as the temperature difference changes, it can be used as a thermometric property. This type of thermometer is called a thermocouple. The emf produced is very small and requires a very sensitive meter (millivolts).

Anders Celsius (Sweden) 1701–1744 is best remembered for his study of astronomy and for devising a scale of temperature using the freezing point of water as 0°C and the boiling point of water as 100°C.

Mandatory experiment
AIM: To draw the calibration curve of a thermometer using a mercury thermometer as a standard.

METHOD
1. Set up the apparatus as shown in the diagram.
2. Read the temperature and the voltage.
3. Raise the temperature of the water by 10°C.
4. Read the temperature and the voltage.
5. Repeat this procedure until you have got at least 7 readings.
6. Plot a graph of temperature against voltage.

This experiment can be carried out for a variety of thermometric properties.

Other thermometers
In addition to the liquid in glass thermometers (mercury and alcohol) and the thermocouple, there are several other types of thermometers. One is the constant-volume gas thermometer, which is dealt with later in this chapter. The thermometric property is the pressure of a gas at constant volume. Another is the platinum resistance thermometer, which is dealt with later in the book. The thermometric property in this case is the resistance of a piece of platinum wire. Thermometers based on different

Heat, Temperature and Thermometers

thermometric properties do not agree with each other except at the ice point and the steam point. The reason for this is that the change in length of a column of mercury caused by a change in temperature of 1°C may not correspond to the change in pressure of a gas at constant volume, the change in resistance of a piece of wire or the change in emf of a thermocouple. This does not mean that any of these thermometers is giving the wrong temperature. Each is giving the correct temperature as defined by its own particular thermometric property.

Experiment
AIM: To compare two thermometers based on different thermometric properties.

METHOD
1. Take the readings of a thermometer at the ice point and the steam point.
2. Draw a straight line graph between the two points.
3. Repeat for a thermometer based on a different thermometric property.
4. Compare the values obtained for an unknown temperature from each of these graphs.

Pressure and volume at constant temperature

The relationship between the pressure and the volume of a gas at constant temperature was first investigated by Robert Boyle in 1660.

Boyle used a J-tube, as shown in the diagram. Mercury was poured into the tube so that the mercury levels were the same on both sides. More mercury was added until the difference in levels was 760 mm of mercury. In doing this Boyle had doubled the pressure on the trapped air. As a consequence, he noticed that he had compressed the air into half its volume. Further experiments showed that as the pressure was trebled the volume was divided by three, and so on. He stated the relationship as follows.

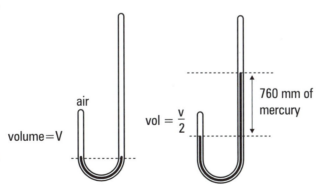

Robert Boyle (Lismore, Co. Waterford) 1627–1691 designed a vacuum pump which he used to show that a feather and a piece of lead will fall at the same speed in a vacuum and that sound cannot travel in a vacuum. He also studied gases and discovered the relationship now known as Boyle's law. He is sometimes referred to as the father of modern chemistry. Perhaps his greatest contribution to science was the development of what is known as the scientific method.

Boyle's law: At constant temperature the pressure of a fixed mass of gas is inversely proportional to its volume (pV is constant).

We can verify Boyle's law using more modern equipment.

Mandatory experiment

AIM: To verify Boyle's law.

METHOD

1. Set up the apparatus as shown in the diagram.
2. Open the tap and pump up the oil as far as possible or until the gauge reaches its maximum reading. Close the tap.
3. Wait a few minutes before reading the pressure and the volume.
4. Open the tap slightly until the pressure falls to a convenient reading. Close the tap, wait a few minutes and read the new pressure and volume.
5. Repeat step 4 about seven times, and plot a graph of p against $\frac{1}{V}$. The result should be a straight line through the origin.

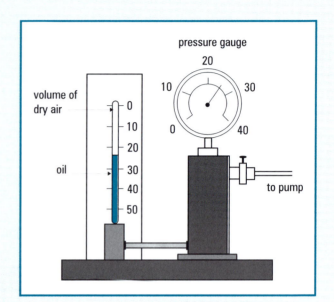

QUESTIONS

1. If no pump is connected and the tap is open, what will the gauge read?
2. Why must you wait before taking readings?
3. Why is the pressure plotted against the inverse of the volume?
4. What difference would it make if the temperature of the room rose during the experiment?

AN IDEAL GAS

An ideal gas is a gas that obeys Boyle's law exactly at all temperatures and pressures. In fact there is no such gas, but the behaviour of real gases at low pressure approaches the behaviour of an ideal gas.

Pressure and temperature at constant volume

Boyle did an experiment to investigate the relationship between the pressure and the volume of a gas at constant temperature, and drew a graph as stated above. Other scientists investigated the relationship between the pressure and temperature of a gas at constant volume, and got graphs similar to the one in the diagram. They produced the graph to the left and discovered that it cut the temperature axis at **−273·15°C**.

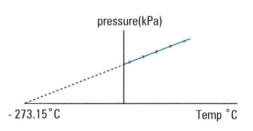

They studied the graph carefully and concluded that, as the temperature dropped, the pressure dropped until, at a temperature of −273·15°C, **the gas exerted no pressure at all**.

Furthermore, if the temperature dropped below −273·15°C the gas would exert **a negative pressure**, which was **impossible**. It was this that first led scientists to consider that there might be an **absolute zero of temperature at −273·15°C**.

Heat, Temperature and Thermometers

The Kelvin scale
Since thermometers based on different thermometric properties give different temperatures, scientists decided to choose one thermometric property as a standard. According to Boyle's law, pV is constant for a fixed mass of gas at constant temperature, but pV changes with temperature. This led Lord Kelvin to suggest that pV for an ideal gas should be taken as the standard thermometric property. The scale of temperature based on pV of an ideal gas as its thermometric property is called the **ideal gas scale** or the **Kelvin scale**. This scale is also referred to as the **absolute** scale, because it begins at absolute zero. On this scale the symbol T is used for temperature and the unit of temperature is the kelvin (K).

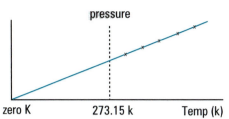

The kelvin scale

Celsius and Kelvin
It follows from the above that

$0°C = 273 \cdot 15$ K
$-273 \cdot 15°C = 0$ K

This last temperature is known as 'absolute zero'. For all but the most accurate work, absolute zero is taken as $-273°C$.

It is clear from a comparison of the two scales that to change from Celsius to Kelvin we add 273, e.g. $17°C = 17 + 273 = 290$ K.

William Thompson, Lord Kelvin (Belfast) 1824–1907 proposed that no temperature lower than $-273 \cdot 15°C$ could exist. He referred to this temperature as 'absolute zero'. He proposed a temperature scale with this temperature as its zero. This scale is called the ideal gas scale or the Kelvin scale. The unit of temperature on this scale is the kelvin (K).

Constant-volume gas thermometer
The instrument in the diagram is called a manometer. It is used to measure pressure. The pressure is the height difference plus the atmospheric pressure. If a manometer is connected to a glass bulb, we have a constant-volume gas thermometer. The mercury must always be brought back to B before taking a reading to ensure that all readings are at constant volume.

Advantages of a constant-volume gas thermometer: accurate, sensitive, very wide range.

Disadvantages: large, cumbersome, large heat capacity, slow to reach thermal equilibrium.

It is used only as a standard for calibrating other thermometers.

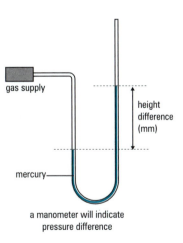

a manometer will indicate pressure difference

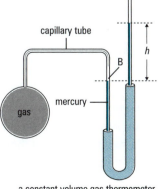

a constant volume gas thermometer

143

PHYSICS NOW!

Summary

- Heat is a form of energy.
- Temperature is a measure of how hot a body is.
- A thermometric property is a property that changes measurably with temperature.
- The principles underlying the establishment of a scale of temperature are: two fixed points, a body with a thermometric property, division of the fundamental interval.
- Boyle's law: At constant temperature the pressure of a fixed mass of gas is inversely proportional to its volume (pV is constant).
- An ideal gas is a gas that obeys Boyle's law exactly. Many gases approach the ideal at successively lower pressures.
- On the ideal gas (or Kelvin) scale, temperature is defined as $T \propto pV$.

SHORT QUESTIONS

1. Which of the following cannot be used as a thermometric property? (A) volume, (B) temperature, (C) pressure, (D) resistance, (E) emf
2. To measure the temperature of boiling water, you could not use: (A) a mercury-in-glass thermometer, (B) an alcohol-in-glass thermometer, (C) a constant-volume gas thermometer, (D) a thermocouple, (E) a resistance thermometer.
3. On the ideal gas (Kelvin) scale the thermometric property is: (A) pressure, (B) volume, (C) temperature, (D) pressure × volume, (E) volume × temperature.
4. Which of the following is not an advantage of mercury over alcohol in thermometers? (A) easily seen, (B) measures up to 357°C, (C) quick to respond, (D) takes in little heat, (E) freezes at −39°C.
5. The temperature 373 K on the Kelvin scale is equivalent to _____ on the Celsius scale.
6. State Boyle's law.
7. What temperature is called absolute zero?
8. The diagram shows a constant-volume gas thermometer. Answer the following. (a) What is meant by a thermometric property? (b) On which thermometric property is the constant-volume gas thermometer based? (c) Why is it used as the standard thermometer? (d) What is the significance of the mark B? (e) Why is T a capillary tube?
9. The graph in the diagram was obtained in an experiment to verify Boyle's law. Clearly label the X and Y axes.
10. (i) What is meant by a thermometric property? _____
_____.

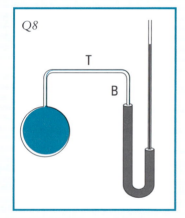

Q8

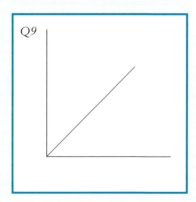

Q9

(ii) The arrangement shown in the diagram can be used as a thermometer.
What is the thermometric property on which this type of thermometer is based?
_____.

(iii) When the arrangement shown in the diagram is being used as a thermometer the galvanometer shows a deflection if junction A is either _____ or _____ than junction B.

(iv) On the Celsius temperature scale the two fixed points are the _____ of water and the _____ of water.

(v) The temperature of a beaker of water on the Celsius is 20°C. What is the temperature of the water on the Kelvin scale? _____

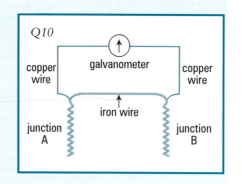

Long Questions

1. Why does a metal spoon at 0°C feel colder than a plastic spoon at the same temperature?
2. In an experiment to verify Boyle's law, the following readings were taken of the pressure and the corresponding volume of a fixed mass of gas at constant temperature.

Pressure (kPa)	100	140	180	220	260	300	340
Volume (cm³)	10·4	7·4	5·8	4·7	4·0	3·5	3·1

   Draw a suitable graph and explain how this verifies Boyle's law. Suggest how the pressure of the gas could have been measured in this experiment.
3. In the case of the electric iron at the beginning of this chapter
   (i) What material might the handle be made of? Why?
   (ii) What might the base be made of? Why?
   (iii) How does the thermostat work?
   (iv) How does the temperature control screw work?
   (iv) Why do you need to be able to set this screw at different temperatures?
4. According to Boyle's law, the pressure of a fixed mass of a gas is inversely proportional to its volume, provided that the temperature of the gas remains constant. Write down an equation for this law.
   Draw a labelled diagram of the apparatus which you would use to verify Boyle's law.
   What measurements would you take in an experiment to verify Boyle's law?
   How would you use these measurements to verify Boyle's law?

5. In a report on a laboratory experiment to verify Boyle's law a student wrote:
'The purpose of this experiment was to investigate the effect of pressure on the volume of a definite mass of gas at constant temperature. When all the readings had been taken a graph was plotted.'
(i) Draw a labelled diagram of the apparatus which may have been used in the experiment.
(ii) Explain how the pressure of the gas could have been measured.
(iii) The following table shows the data which the student obtained in the experiment.

Pressure/kilopascals	100	140	180	220	260	300	340
Volume/cm^3	14.3	10.0	7.7	6.7	5.6	4.8	4.2

Plot a graph on graph paper of pressure against 1/volume.
What conclusion may be drawn from the graph?

Transmission of Heat

CHAPTER 17

Heat would be of little use to us if it could not travel from one place to another. It does this in three ways.

1. Conduction

Conduction is the way in which heat travels through a substance from one particle to the next (but the particles themselves do not travel).

In the diagram we are comparing copper, aluminium, iron and glass to see which conducts heat best.

Note that, generally speaking, metals are good conductors; non-metals are bad conductors. Poor conductors are known as insulators.

Just how good a conductor copper is can be demonstrated using a fine copper gauze and a Bunsen burner.

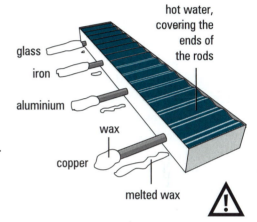

1. Light the gas below the gauze. The gauze conducts the heat away, thus preventing the gas above the gauze from reaching ignition temperature. (Ignition of the gas above the gauze eventually takes place when the gauze becomes red-hot.)
2. In the second case, light the gas above the gauze only.

This was the basis of the Davy lamp, in which a cylinder of copper gauze prevented methane gas on the outside from reaching ignition temperature. These lamps are no longer used by miners, but they are used by safety inspectors since the flame develops a bluish glow in the presence of methane.

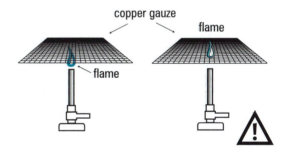

Liquids are not good conductors of heat, as the following experiment shows.

1. Heat the water at the top of the test-tube.
2. Even when the water at the top boils, the ice at the bottom does not melt. This shows that liquids are poor conductors of heat.

If you heat the water in the top part of the hot water cylinder in your hot press, the heat is not conducted down into the water below, so the water on the top remains hot.

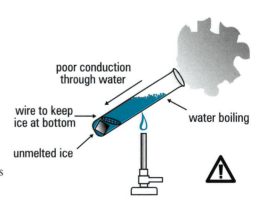

Gases are even poorer conductors than liquids. Air is a very poor conductor. Loose-knit woollen jumpers and string vests keep our bodies warm because the pockets of trapped air act as insulators. The same applies to cavity walls in houses.

147

Physics Now!

2. Convection

It is very important for us to be able to heat water. We use it for cooking, washing, etc. But water is a very poor conductor of heat, so how do we heat it? The answer is that it heats by convection. The particles nearest the heater heat up and move away, carrying the heat with them.

Convection means that heat is carried through liquids and gases by the movement of heated particles.

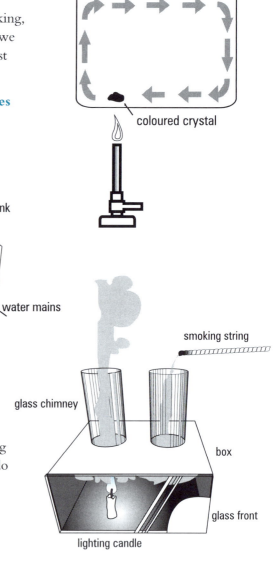

Convection currents in liquids and gases can be demonstrated as shown in the diagrams. We often say that a room is heated by radiators, but it is in fact heated by convection. This can be demonstrated by holding a small piece of tissue paper over a hot radiator and letting it go. The air above the radiator is being heated and rises, carrying the paper with it. As the air cools, it drops down again.

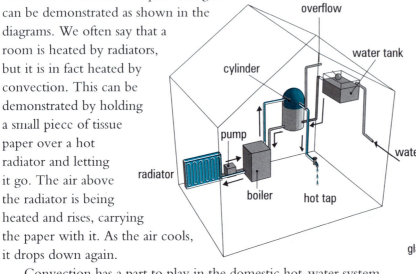

Convection has a part to play in the domestic hot-water system. Many houses have a combined domestic hot-water and central heating system. In practice a pump is included, as convection currents alone do not cause the water to circulate efficiently.

3. Radiation

Most people know that a lens can be used to magnify things. It does this by bending the rays of light so that they all come together. We know this because we can see that the light is concentrated on one spot.

We cannot see heat rays, but we can show that the lens also bends heat rays so that they all come together at one spot.

Try this experiment on a sunny day. First focus on the white part of a newspaper. Then focus on the black part.

Heat radiation is the transfer of energy by means of electromagnetic waves.

The ability of different surfaces to radiate and to absorb radiated heat can be investigated as follows.

148

Transmission of Heat

Experiment

AIM: To show that dark surfaces are better at radiating heat than bright surfaces.

METHOD
1. Set up the apparatus as shown in the diagam.
2. Take the temperature every two minutes.

Result:
The temperature falls faster in the dark can. (There is a fairly big difference to begin with, but as the temperature of the water in the black can drops quickly so does the temperature difference between the can and the room, so the rate of heat loss slows down until finally there is little difference between the two cans.)

Conclusion: Dark surfaces are better at giving out heat than bright surfaces are.

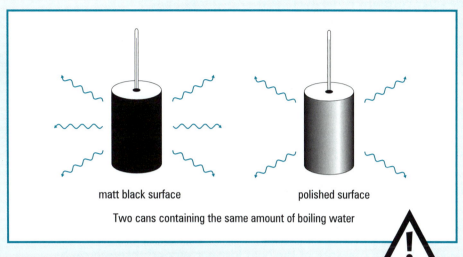

matt black surface   polished surface

Two cans containing the same amount of boiling water

Which coin drops off first in the diagram? Dark surfaces are better at taking in heat than bright surfaces are.

Dark surfaces are better than bright surfaces at radiating and absorbing heat.

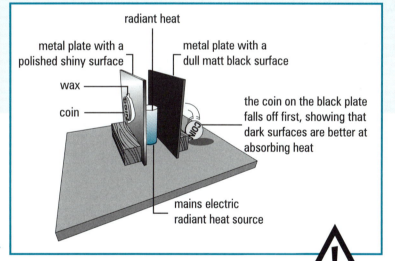

Fire-fighters wear silvery suits so as to reflect heat. In hot countries people wear white clothes and paint their houses white to reduce the absorption of heat from the sun. In the same way petrol tanks, factory roofs and flat asphalt roofs on houses are painted silver.

Cooling fins on motorbikes are painted matt black so as to radiate heat from the engine.

Solar panels are painted matt black to maximise the absorption of heat.

In many countries solar panels are used to heat water. Water is circulated through tubes attached to copper panels. The panels have a black matt finish to maximise their ability to absorb radiated heat. The panels are placed on the roof for maximum exposure to sunshine.

Of course, how effective these solar panels are depends, in part, on the amount of heat energy falling on them.

149

Physics Now!

The solar constant is the average energy per second falling normally on 1 m^2 of the earth's atmosphere. This is also known as solar irradiance.

(The value is $1{\cdot}4 \times 10^3$ W m^{-2}.)

The amount of this energy that actually reaches any point on the earth's surface depends on the weather conditions at that point.

Energy from the sun can also be converted to electricity by solar cells. Indeed, you may own a pocket calculator that is solar powered.

Insulation and U-values

About 25% of the heat lost in a house goes through the roof, 35% goes through walls, 10% through windows and 15% through the floor.

The U-value is a measure of the heat lost per second through each square metre for each 1 K difference in temperature between the inside and the outside.

The unit of U-value is the watt per metre squared per kelvin (W m^{-2} K^{-1}). Clearly, the U-value is affected by the degree to which insulating material (fibreglass, mineral wool, polystyrene, etc.) is used. Insulation reduces the U-value.

	U-value
Tiled roof (uninsulated)	2·5
(with 55 mm fibreglass wool)	0·4
Single block wall	3·6
Cavity wall	1·5
(with 50 mm insulation)	0·5

Thermocouple and thermopile

If the junction between copper wire and iron wire is heated, an electric current flows. This is called the thermoelectric effect. Such a junction can be used to detect heat radiation. However, a more efficient device is a thermopile. This consists of a large number of junctions. The effect is greater if the metals used are antimony and bismuth. For even greater efficiency, the entire device is mounted at the end of a wide collecting cone. The junctions can be blackened to aid absorption of heat.

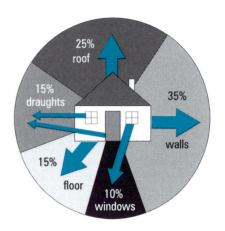

SAVE ENERGY

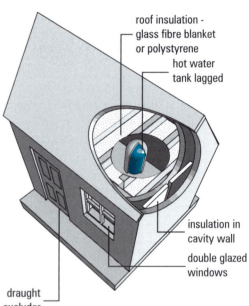

WITH INSULATION!

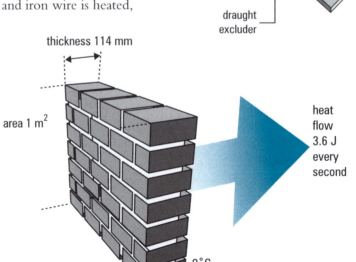

Transmission of Heat

A thermopile mounted at the end of a collecting cone can be used to test the U-value at various places on the outside surface of a building. Another factor here is what is called the 'surface layer'. For example, all else being equal, a house with a rough finish should retain heat better than a house with a smooth finish. This is because of air trapped by the rough surface.

The vacuum flask (Dewar flask) is designed to prevent heat travelling by conduction, convection or radiation. Can you see how it does this?

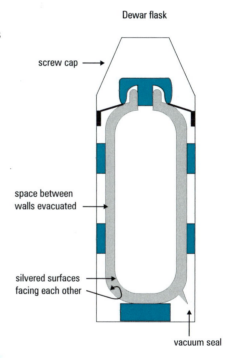

the thermopile

Dewar flask

Summary

- Conduction is the way in which heat travels through a substance from one particle to the next (but the particles themselves do not travel).
- Convection is the way in which heat is carried through a fluid by the movement of heated particles.
- Heat radiation is the transfer of energy by means of electromagnetic waves.
- Dark surfaces are better than bright surfaces at radiating and absorbing heat.
- The solar constant is the average energy per second falling normally on 1 m² of the earth's atmosphere. The value is 1.4×10^3 W m^{-2}.
- The U-value is a measure of the heat lost per second through each square metre for every 1 K difference in temperature between the inside and the outside. The unit of U-value is the W m^{-2} K^{-1}.
- Insulation reduces the U-value.

Short Questions

1. Which of the following illustrates the use of a good conductor of heat? (A) double glazing of windows, (B) straw used to cover plants in frosty weather, (C) fibreglass roof insulation, (D) cooling fins on engines, (E) wooden pan handles.
2. Which of the following is the best conductor of heat? (A) copper, (B) iron, (C) timber, (D) glass, (E) plastic.
3. A string vest can keep you warm in winter because _____.
4. A string vest can keep you cool in summer because _____.
5. The diagram represents the kettle of an automatic tea-maker. After the water boils it rushes out of the tube. The **main** reason for this is that (A) convection currents are set up in the water, (B) steam pressure builds up above the water, (C) the water expands when it is heated, (D) the tube

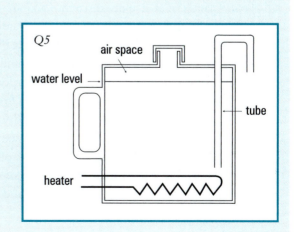

Q5

expands when it is heated, (E) the air above the water expands.
6. Convection takes place (A) only in solids, (B) only in liquids, (C) only in gases, (D) in solids and liquids, (E) in liquids and gases.
7. The solar constant is (A) the speed of light from the sun, (B) the energy per second from the sun falling normally on a square metre of the earth's atmosphere, (C) the time it takes the earth to move round the sun, (D) the distance from the earth to the sun, (E) the power emitted by the sun.
8. Additional insulation will _____ the U-value of a structure.
9. If a structure has a _____ U-value it is a good _____.
10. How does a Dewar flask prevent heat from travelling by conduction, convection and radiation?
11. Explain the basic physical principles involved in each of the following.
    (a) A thermos flask can be used to keep ice from melting.
    (b) On a cold day, the bare metal handlebars of a bicycle feel colder than the plastic handgrips.
    (c) Putting a meshed metal fireguard in front of a fire reduces the amount of heat reaching the room.
    (d) People wear white clothes in both hot and cold climates.

Long Questions
1. Unlike a conventional kettle which is wide, low and made of metal, a jug kettle is narrow, high and made of plastic. What advantages does this give to the jug kettle?
2. What colour is best for giving out heat? Are the radiators in your home, or school, painted this colour? Why or why not?
3. Here is an extract from an advertisement for solar panels. 'Flat solar panels of area approximately 1 m^2 are fixed to the roof. The front glazing is 4 mm glass and each collector contains 7 m of copper tubing which is painted matt black. The tubing is backed with an aluminium foil reflector and fibreglass is used as insulation. A copper waterway is incorporated which circulates water (with the aid of a pump) from the solar panels to the water tank and back again.' (A) Why are copper pipes used? (B) Why are the copper pipes painted black?
(C) Why is insulation needed in the back of the panel?
(D) Explain how the panel acts in a way similar to a greenhouse. Be sure to talk about short and long infrared rays.

Heat Capacity and Latent Heat

CHAPTER 18

It is much more difficult to heat some substances than others, as we shall now show.

Place a certain mass of alcohol in one test-tube and the same mass of water in another. Support both of them in a large beaker of water. Heat the water gently. Note the rate at which the temperature rises in each test-tube.

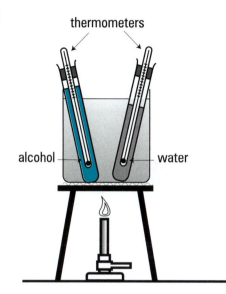

Conclusion: It is easier to raise the temperature of alcohol than to raise the temperature of water. (It is even easier to raise the temperature of a metal such as copper.)

The heat capacity of a body is the amount of heat required to raise the temperature of the body by 1 K.

However, when making comparisons, we must be careful to have the same mass of each substance. The mass we usually deal with is the kilogram.

The amount of heat required to raise the temperature of 1 kg of a substance by 1 K is called its specific heat capacity.

Specific heat capacities ($J\ kg^{-1}\ K^{-1}$)

Water	4200	Concrete	850	Brass	380
Alcohol	2400	Iron	460	Mercury	140
Aluminium	900	Copper	400	Lead	130

EXAMPLE

How many joules of heat are required to raise the temperature of 5 kg of copper by 3 K?

It takes 400 J to raise 1 kg by 1 K
It takes 2,000 J to raise 5 kg by 1 K
It takes 6,000 J to raise 5 kg by 3 K (Answer: 6,000 J)

We could have arrived at this answer much more quickly as:
$5 \times 400 \times 3 = 6,000$ J.

In other words,

the amount of heat gained or lost = mass × specific heat capacity × change of temperature ($Q = m \cdot c \cdot \Delta\theta$)

where Q is the heat energy, m is the mass of the body, c is the specific heat capacity and $\Delta\theta$ is the change in temperature.

PROBLEM

How much heat is required to raise the temperature of 10 kg of water from 20°C to 50°C?

$10 \times 4200 \times 30 = 1{,}260{,}000 \text{ J} = 1{,}260 \text{ kJ}$

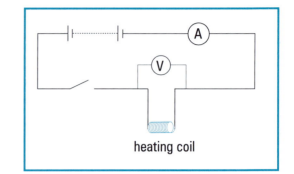

The following experiments are done using a joulemeter, but if a joulemeter is not available the circuit in the diagram can be used.

The energy supplied is then equal to current × voltage × time.

Mandatory experiment

AIM: To find the specific heat capacity of a metal.

METHOD

1. Find the mass of the block of metal.
2. Set up the apparatus as shown in the diagram.
3. Read the initial temperature on the thermometer, and zero the joulemeter.
4. Allow current to flow until a temperature rise of at least 5 K has been achieved.
5. Wait a minute for the heat to spread throughout the metal block before taking the final temperature.

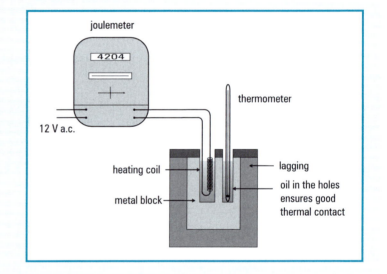

PROBLEM

The following is a typical set of readings.
Mass of aluminium block   500 g
Initial temperature   12°C
Final joulemeter reading   4,204 J
Final temperature   21·5°C
Find the specific heat capacity of the metal.

heat energy supplied = heat gained by aluminium
$4204 = 0{\cdot}5 \times c \times 9{\cdot}5$
$c = 885 \text{ J kg}^{-1} \text{ K}^{-1}$

Heat Capacity and Latent Heat

Mandatory experiment

AIM: To find the specific heat capacity of water.

Method
1. Find the mass of the calorimeter.
2. Find the mass of the calorimeter plus the water.
3. Set up the apparatus as shown in the diagram.
4. Note the initial temperature of the liquid.
5. Zero the joulemeter and allow current to flow until a temperature rise of at least 5 K has been achieved.
6. Note the final temperature and the final joulemeter reading.
7. The specific heat capacity can be calculated from the equation heat supplied = heat gained by calorimeter + heat gained by water

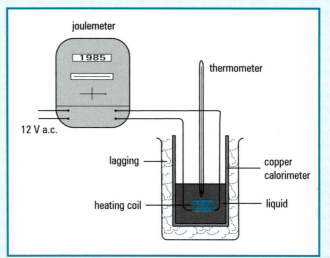

Questions
1. Should you wait for a few minutes after switching off before taking the final temperature?
2. Why is it assumed that the temperatures of the liquid and the calorimeter are the same?
3. Explain why using a larger mass of water while supplying the same amount of energy might have produced a less accurate result.

Problem

The following is a typical set of readings for a liquid other than water

Mass of copper calorimeter	50 g
Mass of calorimeter + liquid	130 g
Initial temperature	12°C
Final joulemeter reading	1,985 J
Final temperature	21°C
Specific heat capacity of copper	400 J kg^{-1} K^{-1}

Find the specific heat capacity of the liquid.

heat supplied by joulemeter = heat gained by calorimeter + heat gained by liquid

Let c be the specific heat capacity of the liquid.

$1985 = (0.05 \times 400 \times 9) + (0.08 \times c \times 9)$
$1985 - 180 = 0.72c$
$1805 = 0.72c$
$c = 2,507 \text{ J kg}^{-1} \text{ K}^{-1}$

The specific heat capacity of the liquid is 2,507 J kg^{-1} K^{-1}.

PROBLEM

The temperature of the water at the bottom of a waterfall is 1 K higher than the temperature at the top. Find the height of the waterfall. (Specific heat capacity of water is 4,200 J kg^{-1} K^{-1}).

Potential energy of the water at the top is *mgh* joules.
Heat gained by the water in falling is $m \times 4200 \times 1$ joules

$\Rightarrow \quad m \times 9\cdot 8 \times h = m \times 4200 \times 1$

$\Rightarrow \quad h = \dfrac{4200}{9\cdot 8} = 428\cdot 5$ metres

PROBLEM

A 300 watt electric drill is used to drill a hole in an iron bar of mass 1 kg. If 80% of the energy used appears in the iron as heat, calculate the rise in temperature of the iron in 20 seconds (specific heat capacity of iron is 460 J kg^{-1} K^{-1}).

300 watts = 300 joules per second $\Rightarrow$ 6,000 joules in 20 seconds.
80% = 4,800 joules
heat gained by the bar = $1 \times 460 \times \theta = 4800$

$\Rightarrow \quad \theta = \dfrac{4200}{460} = 10\cdot 4$ K

Applications

Water has a high specific heat capacity. This makes it useful for storing and carrying heat energy. For example, when water is heated in a central heating boiler a large amount of heat is stored in it and carried round to taps and radiators where it is needed.

Night storage heaters store heat in concrete blocks. Concrete has a lower specific heat capacity than water but it is more dense, so the same mass of concrete takes up less space. The blocks are heated by electric elements which use cheaper night-time electricity. This stored energy is released slowly during the day.

The heat stored in the sea during the day is released at night, which is why island countries such as Ireland do not suffer the extremes of temperature that some other countries do.

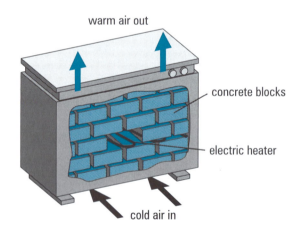

Latent heat

Normally when we heat a substance we expect the temperature to rise. In other words, we expect the thermometer to show the effects of the heat. That is why we can learn so much from the following simple experiment.

1. Place a large amount of ice in a beaker and take the temperature.
2. Heat the ice gently and record the temperature in a table at regular intervals up to boiling point.

Heat Capacity and Latent Heat

3. Keep taking the temperature. What do you notice from the table?
4. Draw a graph of temperature against time.

Conclusion: When the temperature of the ice reaches 0°C it begins to melt. The temperature remains at 0°C until all the ice has melted, even though it is taking in heat.

When all the ice has melted, the temperature of the water rises gradually to 100°C, at which point the water begins to boil. The temperature remains at 100°C until all the water has evaporated.

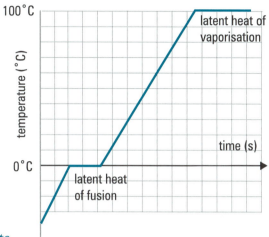

There is no change of temperature during a change in state.

Latent heat is the heat involved when a substance changes state without changing temperature.

The specific latent heat of a substance is the amount of heat needed to change the state of 1 kg of the substance without a change of temperature.

Heat energy needed to change state: $Q = ml$

where Q is the heat energy, m is the mass of the body and l is the specific latent heat.

The specific latent heat of fusion of ice is the amount of heat needed to change 1 kg of ice to water without a change of temperature.

The latent heat of fusion of ice is 336,000 joules per kilogram or 336 kJ kg^{-1}.

The specific latent heat of vaporisation of water is the amount of heat needed to change 1 kg of water to steam without a change of temperature.

The latent heat of vaporisation of water is 2,270,000 joules per kilogram or 2,270 kJ kg^{-1}.

Mandatory experiment

AIM: To find the specific latent heat of fusion of ice.

METHOD
1. Place some small lumps of ice in water and keep taking the temperature until it reaches 0°C.
2. In the meantime find the mass of a calorimeter.
3. Add some slightly warmed water to the calorimeter and find the mass of the calorimeter plus water.
4. Lag the calorimeter as shown in the diagram and take the initial temperature.

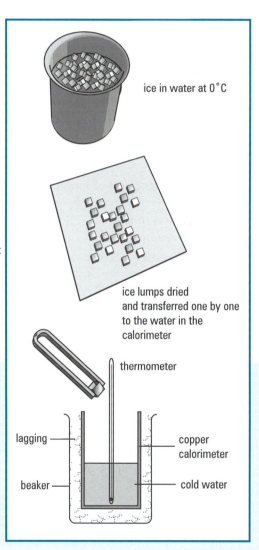

157

5. Dry the lumps of ice on blotting paper and add them, one at a time, to the water.
6. When all the ice has been added, stir until it dissolves and take the final temperature.
7. Find the mass of calorimeter + water + melted ice.
8. The specific latent heat of fusion of ice can be got from the equation:
heat needed to melt ice + heat needed to raise the temperature of resulting water = heat lost by calorimeter + heat lost by water

QUESTIONS
1. What are the main sources of error in this experiment?
2. Why do you dry the ice before adding it to the water?
3. Why should the water be warm before the ice is added?

PROBLEM

The following is a set of readings for the above experiment.

Mass of copper calorimeter	50 g
Mass of calorimeter + water	145 g
Initial temperature	25°C
Final temperature	5°C
Mass of calorimeter + water + melted ice	= 170 g

Find the specific latent heat of fusion of ice.

heat gained by ice in melting	+ heat to raise resulting water by 5°C	= heat lost by calorimeter	+ heat lost by warm water
$(0.025 \times l)$	$+ (0.025 \times 4{,}200 \times 5)$	$= (0.05 \times 400 \times 20)$	$+ (0.095 \times 4{,}200 \times 20)$
$0.025l$	$+\ 525$	$=\ 400$	$+\ 7{,}980$
$0.025l$	$=\ 8{,}380 - 525$		
$0.025l$	$=\ 7{,}855$		
l	$= \dfrac{7{,}855}{0.025}$	$= 314{,}200$ J	$= 314.2$ kJ kg^{-1}

Joseph Black (Scotland) 1728–1799 studied specific heat and latent heat and showed that carbon dioxide differs from air. He taught at the Universities of Glasgow and Edinburgh.

One of the first scientists to appreciate the importance of latent heat was a Scotsman called Joseph Black. As far back as 1770 Black put forward the following argument.

In winter we sometimes have large amounts of snow and ice even though the temperature is only a few degrees below 0°C. Even when the temperature of the atmosphere rises above 0°C it can take some time for

Heat Capacity and Latent Heat

the snow and ice to clear. In fact, the thaw takes place gradually over a period of days or even weeks. This is due to the fact that, apart from the amount of heat it takes to raise the temperature to 0°C, it takes a further 336 kilojoules of heat to melt each kilogram of ice.

Mandatory experiment

AIM: To find the specific latent heat of vaporisation of water.

METHOD
1. Weigh the calorimeter.
2. Weigh the calorimeter and water.
3. Take the temperature of the water.
4. Set up the apparatus as shown in the diagram.
5. Allow steam to pass into the water in the calorimeter until the temperature has risen by about 20°C to 25°C.
6. Finally, reweigh the calorimeter and contents to find the mass of steam condensed.
7. The specific latent heat of vaporisation of water can be found from the equation:

heat lost by steam + heat lost by resulting water = heat gained by calorimeter + heat gained by water

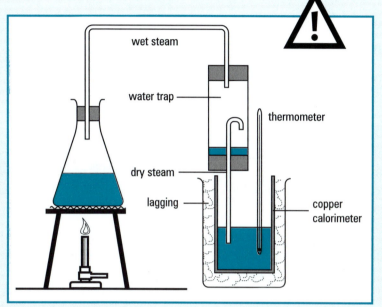

QUESTIONS
1. Would it help to cool the water before passing the steam into it?
2. Should you stir the water before taking the final temperature?

PROBLEM
The following is a set of readings from the above experiment.

Mass of copper calorimeter	50 g
Mass of calorimeter + water	145 g
Initial temperature	22°C
Final temperature	43°C
Mass of calorimeter + water + steam	148·5 g

Find the specific latent heat of vaporisation of water.

heat lost by + heat lost by	= heat gained by + heat gained
steam in resulting water	calorimeter by water
condensing	

$0.0035 \times l + 0.0035 \times 4200 \times 57 = 0.05 \times 400 \times 21 + 0.095 \times 4200 \times 21$

$0.0035l \quad + 837.9 \quad\quad\quad = 420 \quad\quad\quad + 8379$

$0.0035l \quad = 8,799 - 837.9$

$0.0035l \quad = 7,961.1$

$l \quad\quad = \dfrac{7,961.1}{0.0035} \quad = 2,274,600 \text{ J} \quad = 2,275 \text{ kJ}$

Problem

How much heat is needed to change 2 kg of ice at 0°C to 2 kg of steam at 100°C?

(a) To change 2 kg of ice at 0°C to water at 0°C = 2 × 336 = 672 kJ
(b) To raise the temperature of 2 kg of water from 0°C to 100°C = 2 × 4200 × 100 = 840 kJ
(c) To change 2 kg of water at 100°C to steam at 100°C = 2 × 2,270 kJ = 4,540 kJ

Total = 672 + 840 + 4,540 = 6,052 kJ

Applications

If you place a drop of methylated spirits on the back of your hand it quickly evaporates, leaving your hand feeling cold. This is because the methylated spirits took the latent heat of vaporisation needed to change it from liquid to vapour from your hand.

Perspiration cools your body in much the same way. Perspiration consists of salt and water. When the water evaporates it takes its latent heat of vaporisation from your skin and cools you down.

When you put ice in a drink the ice takes its latent heat of fusion from the drink and cools it down.

Heat pumps

When a liquid evaporates it takes its latent heat of vaporisation from its surroundings. When the vapour condenses it gives its latent heat of vaporisation to its surroundings. This is the principle of the heat pump.

A heat pump takes heat from one area and transfers it to another. The most common heat pump is the domestic refrigerator. A fluid that evaporates easily is sealed inside a system of pipes. Outside the fridge a compressor pump compresses the vapour and causes it to condense. As it condenses it gives out its latent heat of vaporisation.

Inside the fridge it takes its latent heat of vaporisation from its surroundings and evaporates.

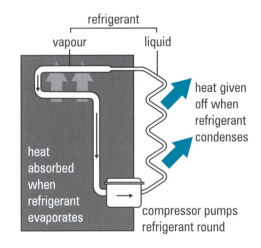

Heat Capacity and Latent Heat

Kinetic theory

We know that if we heat ice it melts, and if we continue to heat the water it eventually boils, but what exactly is happening inside? Scientists have a theory called the kinetic theory to answer this question.

In a solid the molecules are packed very tightly. They have very little freedom of movement but they can vibrate a little. When the solid is heated the molecules gain energy and can move about more freely. If we continue to give energy to the molecules they will be able to move about with complete freedom. On the basis of this theory we can say that the temperature is proportional to the average kinetic energy of the molecules or, putting it the other way round, that the average kinetic energy of the molecules is indicated by the temperature.

Is there any evidence to support this theory? Yes there is, as the following simple test shows.

In this case the molecules of ammonia move faster than those of hydrochloric acid because they are lighter. As a result the molecules meet approximately two-thirds of the way along the tube to form a white cloud of ammonium chloride.

More experimental evidence is provided by **Brownian motion**. A small box is filled with smoke and illuminated from the side. The smoke particles, observed through a microscope, are seen to be in random motion. The higher the temperature, the faster they move. The smoke particles are continually being bombarded by air particles, which are too small to be seen.

Robert Brown (Scotland) 1773–1858 observed an erratic zigzag motion of microscopic pollen particles in water. Later experiments showed that the motion became faster when the temperature was raised. Brownian motion is evidence for the existence of particles (i.e. molecules) in water and other matter.

Controlling the boiling point and melting point

So is that it? When the molecules of a solid gain enough energy it changes into a liquid, and when the molecules of a liquid gain enough energy it changes into a gas? These things happen at certain temperatures and there is nothing we can do about it? Not so!

Mix some salt into a beaker of water and heat it until it boils. Take the temperature.

Impurities raise the boiling point of water.

In the apparatus shown in the diagram, when the water boils close the clip and note the temperature. When the

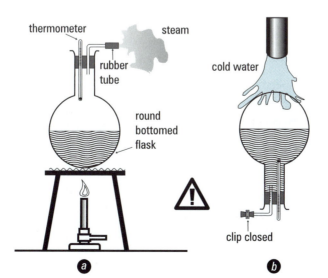

161

water has stopped boiling turn the flask upside down and pour cold water over it. The water begins to boil again at a lower temperature.

Reducing the pressure lowers the boiling point of water.

The opposite also applies: increasing the pressure raises the boiling point. This idea is used in a pressure cooker. Because the pressure is about twice the normal atmospheric pressure the water boils at 120°C and the food cooks much faster.

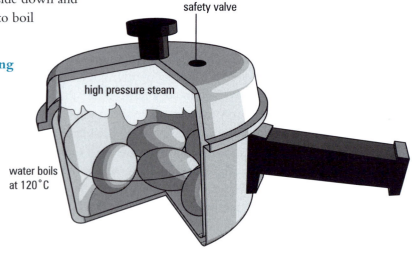

Increasing the pressure raises the boiling point of water.

So much for the boiling point: what about the melting point?
Press two ice cubes together as hard as you can and hold them for a minute or so. Now release them. They are stuck together. Increasing the pressure caused the ice to melt; reducing the pressure caused the water to freeze again.

Increased pressure lowers the melting point of ice.

Summary

- Specific heat capacity: the amount of heat required to raise the temperature of 1 kg of a substance by 1 K.
- The amount of heat gained or lost by a body = mass × specific heat capacity × change of temperature.
- The specific latent heat of fusion of ice is the amount of heat needed to change 1 kg of ice to water without a change of temperature.
- The specific latent heat of vaporisation of water is the amount of heat needed to change 1 kg of water to steam without a change of temperature.
- Reduced pressure lowers the boiling point of water.
- Increased pressure lowers the melting point of ice.

SHORT QUESTIONS
1. 2 kg of a substance which has a specific heat capacity of 4,000 J kg^{-1} K^{-1} is heated from 20°C to 50°C. The energy required is: (A) 15 kJ, (B) 36 kJ, (C) 160 kJ, (D) 240 kJ, (E) 400 kJ.
2. When a heater giving out 10,000 J min^{-1} is placed in 2 kg of a liquid, the temperature–time graph shown in the diagram is obtained. What is the specific heat capacity of the liquid in J kg^{-1} K^{-1}? (A) 33·3, (B) 8·33 × 10^2, (C) 3·00 × 10^4, (D) 5·00 × 10^4, (E) 7·50 × 10^5.

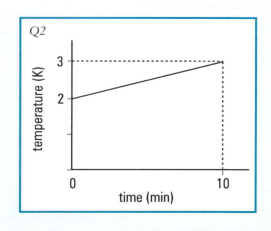

3. It takes 360 J of energy to raise the temperature of 100 g of a substance by 10°C. The specific heat capacity of the substance is (A) 3·6 J, (B) 36 J, (C) 360 J, (D) 3,600 J, (E) 36,000 J.

★4. A piece of iron of mass m and specific heat capacity c and a piece of aluminium of mass $2m$ and specific heat capacity $2c$ each received the same quantity of heat. The temperature of the aluminium rose by 8 K. By how much did the temperature of the iron rise? (A) 2 K, (B) 4 K, (C) 8 K, (D) 16 K, (E) 32 K.

5. The unit of specific latent heat is (A) J kg^{-1} K^{-1}, (B) J kg^{-1} K, (C) J kg K^{-1}, (D) J kg^{-1}, (E) J K^{-1}.

6. An ice cube of mass 30 g melts and remains at 0°C. The specific latent heat of ice is 336 J g^{-1}. The heat gained by the ice from the atmosphere is (A) 112 J, (B) 306 J, (C) 366 J, (D) 5,040 J, (E) 10,080 J.

7. Specific latent heat is defined as _____.

8. Give one practical application of latent heat.

9. The amount of heat energy gained or lost by a body is _____ × _____ × _____.

10. There is no change of _____ during a change of _____.

11. Explain the basic physical principles involved in each of the following.
    (a) Milk can be boiled very quickly by passing a jet of steam through it.
    (b) Potatoes cook faster in water to which salt has been added.
    (c) Water boils at a lower temperature on top of a mountain.
    (d) Perfume dries quickly when applied to the skin.

Long Questions

1. A piece of metal of mass 2 kg and specific heat capacity 440 J kg^{-1} K^{-1} cools from 150°C to 50°C. Find the amount of heat lost.

2. How many joules of heat are produced by a 3 kW heater in 1 hour?

3. An electric heater raises the temperature of 1 kg of water from 20°C to 100°C in 3 minutes. Neglecting heat loss, what is the power rating of the heater?
   (Specific heat capacity of water is 4,200 J kg^{-1} K^{-1}.)

4. How much heat is needed to raise the temperature of 5 kg of lead from 20°C to 50°C? (Specific heat capacity of lead = 126 J kg^{-1} K^{-1}.)

5. The diagram shows the essential parts of a simple refrigerator circuit.

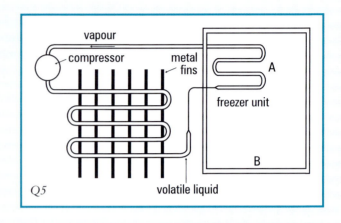

(a) Explain carefully what is happening in the pipes at A, stating clearly why this achieves the desired result.
(b) Why is A situated at the top of the refrigerator?
(c) Why are the fins metal, and what is their purpose?
(d) Name another machine in which metal fins are used to achieve the same purpose.
(e) The walls of the cabinet, B, are sometimes filled with crinkled aluminium foil. Why?
(f) A person who leaves open the refrigerator door to cool the room on a hot day in summer will not succeed. Give the reasons for this.
(g) Explain why a chest-type deep freezer (lid at top) is thought to be more efficient than an upright type (door at side).

6. A waterfall is 80 m high. By how much is the temperature of the water raised in falling from top to bottom? (Specific heat capacity of water is 4,200 J kg^{-1} K^{-1}.)

7. In a simple experiment to determine the specific heat capacity of aluminium, a 50 W immersion heater is inserted in a 2 kg block of aluminium, which also holds a thermometer, as shown.

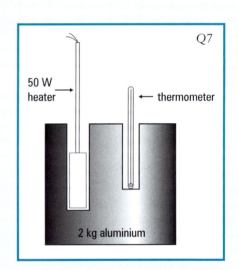

(a) How much heat is supplied by the heater every second?
(b) How much heat is supplied by the heater in 5 minutes?
(c) Why would the temperature of the block be measured more accurately if a little oil were poured into the thermometer hole?
(d) It is found that the temperature of the block rises 8 K in 5 minutes. Neglecting heat losses, calculate from this the value of the specific heat capacity of aluminium.

8. The following is an account of an experiment to measure the specific latent heat of fusion of ice. 'Crushed ice cubes were added to water which was slightly warmer than room temperature, and contained in a well-lagged calorimeter. The temperature of the water was measured before and after the addition of the ice. The mass of the calorimeter and contents was also determined.' The following measurements were obtained.

Mass of calorimeter	60 g
Mass of calorimeter + warm water	175 g
Mass of calorimeter + contents after addition of ice	195 g
Temperature of warm water	26·5°C
Temperature of ice	0°C
Temperature of calorimeter and contents after addition of ice	12·7°C

Given that the specific capacity of water is 4,200 J kg^{-1} K^{-1} and that the specific heat capacity of the material of the calorimeter is 390 J kg^{-1} K^{-1}, use the measurements given above to
(a) find (i) the heat lost by the calorimeter, (ii) the heat lost by the warm water
(b) calculate the specific latent heat of fusion of ice. What was the reason for using crushed ice? State a possible source of error in this experiment.

★9. In an experiment to measure the specific latent heat of vaporisation of water, steam was passed into cold water in an aluminium calorimeter. The following results were obtained.

Mass of calorimeter	30·5 g
Mass of calorimeter + water	81·1 g
Temperature of cold water	16°C
Temperature of steam	100°C
Mass of calorimeter + water + steam	82·2 g
Final temperature of water	28°C

Given that the specific heat capacity of aluminium is 910 J kg^{-1} K^{-1} and that of water is 4,180 J kg^{-1} K^{-1}, calculate the specific latent heat of vaporisation of water. What is the advantage of cooling the water before adding the steam? Give two other precautions that might have been taken to ensure a more accurate result.

10. If a waterfall is 500 m high, calculate the rise in temperature of the water after falling, assuming all the kinetic energy gained is converted into heat. (Specific heat capacity of water is 4,200 J kg^{-1} K^{-1}.)

11. A litre of boiling water is poured into a copper kettle which is at a temperature of 10°C. If the final temperature of the kettle and the water is 75°C, what is the mass of the kettle? (Specific heat capacity of copper = 400 J kg^{-1} K^{-1}.)

12. 500 g of copper is dropped into 50 g of water at 20°C. If the final temperature is 40°C, what was the initial temperature of the copper?

13. 200 g of ice at 0°C is added to 1 kg of water at 50°C. What is the final temperature? (Specific latent heat of ice is 3.4×10^5 J kg^{-1}.)

14. 2·5 g of steam at 100°C is passed into 5 kg of water at 10°C. What is the final temperature? (Specific latent heat of steam is $2 \cdot 3 \times 10^6$ J kg^{-1}.)
15. A car of mass 1,500 kg travelling at 30 m s^{-1} is brought to rest. How much heat is generated in the brakes?
16. A car of mass 1,500 kg travelling at 20 m s^{-1} is brought to rest. If each of the four brakes has a mass of 5 kg, find their average rise in temperature. (Take the specific heat capacity of the brakes as 400 J kg^{-1} K^{-1}.)
17. An electric heater is embedded in a block of metal of mass 1 kg and specific heat capacity 450 J kg^{-1} K^{-1}. If the heater is attached to a 12 volt supply and takes a current of 6 amperes, by how much will the temperature of the metal rise in 5 minutes?
18. A 60 watt electric heater is immersed in 95 cm^3 of water. The temperature of the water rises from 11°C to 20°C in one minute. When the water is replaced by the same mass of oil, the temperature rises by 18°C in 1 minute. Find
    (a) the specific heat capacity of the water
    (b) the specific heat capacity of the oil.
19. A 200 watt electric drill is used to drill a hole in a block of metal of mass 1 kg. Assuming that 80% of the energy is converted to heat in the metal, find the rise in temperature in 10 seconds. (Specific heat capacity of the metal is 500 J kg^{-1} K^{-1}.)
20. In a report of an experiment to compare the specific heat capacities of water and of copper a student wrote the following.
    'The test-tube containing copper rivets at a temperature of 100°C was emptied into the cold water in the copper calorimeter and the highest temperature reached by the water was noted. The following were the measurements obtained in the experiment.'

Mass of copper rivets	9.8 g
Mass of empty calorimeter	60 g
Mass of calorimeter and cold water	98.6 g
Initial temperature of hot copper rivets	100°C
Initial temperature of calorimeter and cold water	16.2°C
Final temperature of calorimeter, rivets and water	23.8°C

(i) How might the rivets have been heated to 100°C?
(ii) Calculate (a) The mass of the cold water; (b) The fall in temperature of the copper rivets; (c) The rise in temperature of the water and the calorimeter.

(iii) State one possible source of error in the experiment.

The specific heat capacity of copper is 3.9×10^2 J kg^{-1}, and the specific heat capacity of water is 4.2×10^3 J kg^{-1} K^{-1}. Calculate the quantity of heat

(i) lost by the copper rivets;

(ii) gained by the cold water.

*21. Define specific latent heat.

Describe an experiment to measure the specific latent heat of fusion of ice.

Conduction, convection and radiation are three methods of transferring heat. Give a brief explanation of each.

Explain the principles involved in each of the following.

(i) The U-valve of a structure is reduced by adding insulation to it.

(ii) On a hot day the sea is usually colder than the land.

(iii) The human body is cooled by perspiring.

(iv) On a hot day the water at the surface of a still lake or pond is usually warmer than the water some distance below the surface.

*22. Define (i) specific heat capacity, (ii) specific latent heat.

Describe an experiment to measure the specific heat capacity of a liquid *or* a solid.

A saucepan containing water is left boiling on a cooker in a kitchen for some time. As the water evaporates from the saucepan and then condenses the temperature of the air in the kitchen is raised.

Explain how this process of evaporation and condensation raises the temperature of the air in the kitchen and give another method by which energy is transferred from the saucepan of water to the air.

Given that the volume of air in the kitchen is 15.6m^3 and that water is evaporating from the saucepan at a rate of 0.65g per second calculate:

(i) The rate at which energy is transferred from the water in the saucepan by evaporation;

(ii) The rise in temperature of the air caused by the evaporation and condensation in 5 minutes, assuming that 10% of the transferred energy is absorbed by the air.

(Specific heat capacity of air = 1.0×10^3 J kg^{-1} K^{-1}; specific latent heat of vaporisation of water = 2.3×10^6 J kg^{-1}; density of air = 1.2 kg m^{-3}.)

Static Electricity

CHAPTER 19

Did you ever get a shock when getting out of a car or when you touched a metal pipe? You were not in contact with any live electricity wires, so where did the electricity come from? A few simple experiments can show you how substances get an electric charge and how electric charges accumulate on them.

Put some very small pieces of paper on your bench. Bring a plastic rod close to the papers: nothing happens. Now rub the plastic rod against your jumper and bring it close to the papers. The plastic attracts the papers because the plastic is charged.

Adjust a tap so that a very thin stream of water flows from it. Bring a plastic rod close to the water: nothing happens. Now rub the plastic rod and hold it close to the water. The stream of water bends and moves towards the rod.

attraction
aluminium foil

Electric charges are produced by rubbing together two different materials.

Rub a balloon against your jumper. Now put it close to the wall or the ceiling of the room: it stays there. This is another example of electric charges. Many other effects, such as a plastic comb lifting your hair (particularly if you have fine hair), show these electric charges.

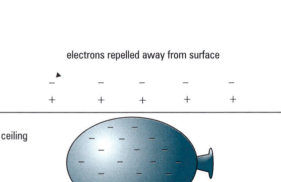
electrons repelled away from surface
ceiling
negative balloon

Experiment 19.1

AIM: To demonstrate the forces between electrical charges.

METHOD:
1. Rub a perspex (clear plastic) rod with a duster and hang it from a wooden stand.
2. Rub another perspex rod with a duster and bring it close to the first.

Result: The rods push away from each other.

3. Rub a polythene rod (white plastic) with a dry duster and suspend it from the stand.
4. Rub another polythene rod with the duster and bring it close to the first.

Result: They push away from each other.

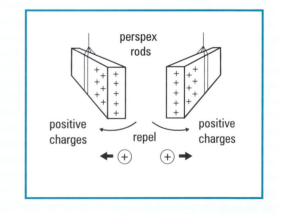
perspex rods
positive charges — repel — positive charges

5. Now bring the polythene rod close to the suspended perspex rod.
Result: The rods move towards each other.
Conclusion: There are two different types of charge: positive and negative.

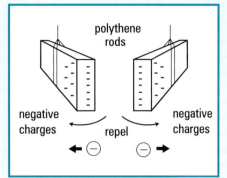
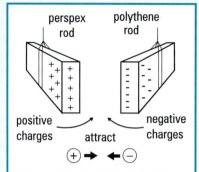

Like charges repel each other, unlike charges attract each other.

Where do charges come from?

To explain how electric charges accumulate on substances, we need to know something about the structure of the atom. All atoms are made up of three different sorts of sub-atomic particles: protons, neutrons and electrons. Protons have a positive electric charge, have a mass of 1 atomic mass unit (a.m.u.) and are part of the dense central core of the atom: the nucleus. Neutrons have no electric charge, have a mass of 1 a.m.u. and are also part of the nucleus. Electrons have a negative electric charge, a mass of $\frac{1}{1,840}$ a.m.u. and are found whizzing around the nucleus in definite orbits.

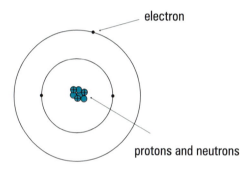

Lithium atom

	Proton	Neutron	Electron
Mass	1 a.m.u.	1 a.m.u.	$\frac{1}{1,840}$ a.m.u.
Charge	+1	0	−1
Location	nucleus	nucleus	orbits around nucleus

In a neutral atom the number of electrons equals the number of protons. Only the protons and electrons have an electric charge. The protons are situated in the core of the atom and so cannot move. Only the electrons on the outside of some atoms can move.

When you rub two dissimilar substances together, one rubs some electrons off the other. When you separate them, one substance has more electrons than it normally would and so is negatively charged; the other has fewer electrons than before and is positively charged.

A body becomes positively charged when it loses electrons.
A body becomes negatively charged when it gains electrons.

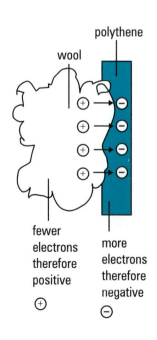

PHYSICS NOW!

The perspex rod in the experiments above was positively charged when rubbed, and the polythene rod was negatively charged. When we charge substances by rubbing and separating them, we get equal but opposite charges.

Conductors and insulators

If you tried to produce electric charges by rubbing a metal biro with a cloth, you would not succeed. This is because the metal is a conductor. Conductors are substances through which electric charges can pass freely. Any charges produced on a conductor flow to earth.

All the substances on which you produced charges are insulators. Insulators are substances through which electric charges cannot pass. The charges produced on them cannot move and so stay where they are produced: **static electricity**.

Thales of Miletus (Greece) c.600 BC *produced static electricity by rubbing together amber and silk. The word electricity comes from the Greek word elektron, which means 'amber'.*

CONDUCTORS

Many solids, liquids and gases can conduct electricity. Solid conductors are usually metals. These contain loosely-bound electrons which are free to move through the metal and so carry electricity. Conductors in a liquid state are usually solutions of salts, called electrolytes. These contain positive and negative ions. The ions carry the electricity by moving through the solution. Molten salts (salts that have been melted) also conduct electricity by the movement of ions.

Gases are normally not conductors. However, they can conduct electricity when the voltage is high and the gas pressure is low. They conduct electricity by the movement of electrons and ions.

Conductor	Current carriers	Examples
Solid	Electrons	Copper, aluminium
Liquid	Positive and negative ions	Salt water, copper sulphate solution
Gas	Electrons and ions	Fluorescent and neon gas tubes

INSULATORS

If you look at the plastic handle of a phase-tester screwdriver you may see 500 V stamped on it. This means that the plastic part of the screwdriver is a satisfactory insulator up to this voltage. It would be dangerous to use it on voltages above 500 volts.

Insulators such as plastics contain tightly bound electrons which normally cannot be moved. However, at very high voltages these electrons can move and conduct electricity. Because of this, insulators are specified as suitable for particular voltages. The ESB uses long ceramic insulators to keep the high-voltage cables away from the metal pylons.

Static Electricity

Electric Charge

Electric charge (Q) is measured in coulombs.

A coulomb is the quantity of electric charge that passes when a current of one ampere flows for one second.

coulombs = amperes × seconds
Q = It

The gold leaf electroscope

The gold leaf electroscope is a simple instrument used to study electric charge. It has a glass-fronted case which is earthed. A metal disc is attached to a metal rod which passes through an insulating plug into the case. A gold leaf is attached to the metal rod.

The gold leaf electroscope is used to:
(a) detect small charges
(b) identify the type of charge (positive or negative)
(c) estimate the size of the charge
(d) distinguish between a conductor and an insulator.

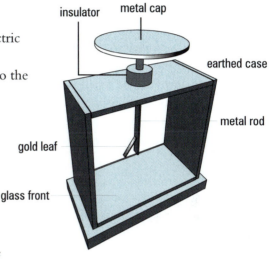

(a) Detecting small charges

Charge a polythene rod by friction. Touch it to the disc of the electroscope. The charges repel each other and spread out over the metal disc, rod and gold leaf. The gold leaf is very light, so the like charges repelling each other cause it to move out from the rod. The gold leaf opens.

(b) Identifying the type of charge (positive or negative)

Charge an electroscope positively. Bring, in turn, a positively charged, a negatively charged and a neutral material close to the electroscope. Observe the results. Repeat the test with a negatively charged electroscope. The results are as follows.

Charge on electroscope	Charge brought near disc	Effect on leaf divergence
+	+	Increase
−	−	Increase
+	−	Decrease
−	+	Decrease
+ or −	Uncharged body	Decrease

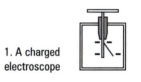

1. A charged electroscope

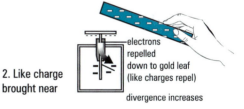

2. Like charge brought near

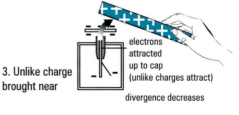

3. Unlike charge brought near

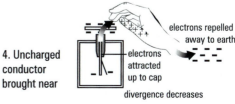

4. Uncharged conductor brought near

Physics Now!

CONCLUSION: The only true test of the sign of a charge is when you get an increase in the divergence of the leaf. This tells you that the sign of the test charge is the same as that on the electroscope.

(c) **ESTIMATING THE SIZE OF CHARGE**
The extent to which the leaf opens is **approximately** related to the size of the charge. This can be used to place charges in order of size.

(d) **DISTINGUISHING BETWEEN CONDUCTORS AND INSULATORS**
The human body is a conductor of electricity. If you touch an electrically charged body (e.g. an electroscope) with your bare hand, the charge will run through you into the earth. This is called earthing the electroscope.

Other substances can be tested as follows. Charge the electroscope. Touch the disc with the material you are testing. If the leaves collapse the electroscope has been earthed, so the substance is a conductor. An insulator causes little movement of the leaves.

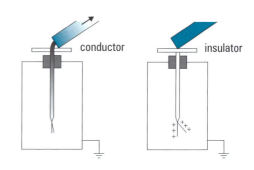

Charging by induction

Charges on an insulator cannot move, so to transfer charge onto an electroscope each part of the insulator must be brought into contact with the electroscope.

Charges produced on conductors are free to move and must be insulated from earth (and from other conductors) to prevent the charges from moving. In static electrical experiments conductors are mounted on insulating stands.

In charging by induction the charged rod never touches the electroscope. Instead, we use the fact that like charges repel to move the electrons around.

SEPARATING ELECTRIC CHARGES BY INDUCTION

Experiment 19.2

AIM: To separate electric charges by induction.
METHOD:
1. Place two uncharged metal spheres (on insulating stands) in contact.
2. Bring a negatively charged rod close to A. The charged rod drives electrons from sphere A to sphere B.
3. Separate the spheres, keeping the rod in position. Remove the rod.
4. Test each of the spheres for charge with an electroscope.

RESULT: Sphere A is positively charged; sphere B is negatively charged.

If you allow the two spheres to touch again they discharge each other, showing that the induced charges are equal and opposite.

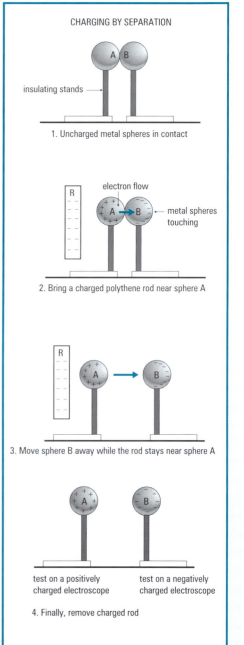

Static Electricity

INDUCTION CHARGING BY EARTHING

Experiment 19.3

AIM: To separate electric charges by induction and earthing.

METHOD:

1. Charge a polythene rod by friction.
2. Bring the charged rod close to the disc of an electroscope. The negatively charged rod repels electrons from the cap down to the leaves. The leaves open.
3. Earth the electroscope with your hand. This causes some electrons to be repelled to earth. The leaves collapse.
4. Remove your hand. The leaves stay collapsed. Removal of the earth connection, with the inducing charge in place, prevents further electron movement.
5. Remove the charged rod. The electroscope is now positively charged, as it has lost some electrons. The leaves open.

1. Start with an uncharged electroscope, and bring a charged rod near to its cap

2. Touch the cap with a finger, leave it for a moment, then remove the finger

3. Finally, remove the charged rod

The charge induced on an electroscope is opposite to that of the inducing charge.

ELECTROPHORUS

The electrophorus is a simple electrostatic induction machine based on the same principle.
The negatively charged polythene tile T induces a positive charge on the lower surface of the metal disc D and a negative charge on the upper surface. When the disc is earthed electrons flow to earth, leaving the disc positively charged.

1. Touch disc D with a finger

2. Remove disc D

DISTRIBUTION OF CHARGE ON A CONDUCTOR

The distribution of charge on a conductor can be found with a proof plane. The proof plane is touched to the conductor being tested and the charge is transferred to an electroscope. The electroscope gives a measure of the size of the charge at that point on the conductor.

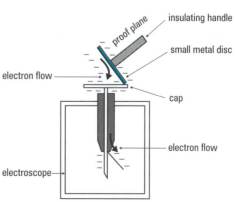

Proof plane transfers charge

Physics Now!

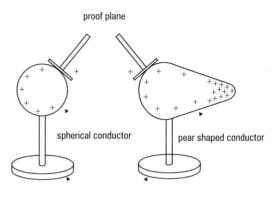

CONCLUSIONS:
Charge on a sphere is uniformly distributed.
Charge on a pear-shaped conductor is concentrated near the pointed end. The greater the curvature of the conductor (the more pointed it is), the greater is the charge density.

Experiment.19.4

AIM: to show that charge is found only on the outside of a charged conductor.

METHOD:
A cotton net on an insulating handle is used. The cotton is an adequate conductor for this experiment. The silk thread is used to hold the bottom of the net, as silk is a good insulator.
1. Charge the cotton net by induction.
2. Check with a proof plane that the charge is only on the outside.
3. Pull the silk thread so that the net turns inside out.
4. Check with a proof plane again.

RESULT: The charge is still found only on the outside. The forces between the charges cause them to move as far away from each other as possible. As the outside surface area is always greater than the inside, they can move further apart on the outside.

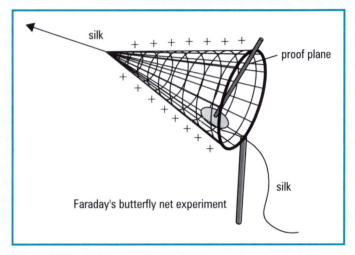

Faraday's butterfly net experiment

Charge is found only on the outside of a charged conductor.

POINT DISCHARGE

Experiment 19.5

AIM: To demonstrate point discharge.
1. Balance a metal windmill on a conducting pivot on the dome of a Van de Graaff electrostatic generator.
2. Charge the Van de Graaff generator.

RESULT: The windmill moves. If this is done in the dark, a glow is noticed at the points.
The high charge density at the points (e.g. a positive charge) attracts negative charges in the air (electrons and negative ions). Some of these are discharged at the point. The positive ions in the air are repelled and move away from the point.
The reaction of the windmill to this action causes it to spin.

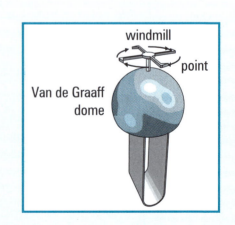

Static Electricity

1. Charge an electroscope by induction.
2. Hold the pointed end of a compass close to the disc.

Result: The electroscope is slowly discharged.

1. Connect a pointed conductor to a charged Van de Graaff generator.
2. Hold a candle flame very close to the point.

Result: The flame streams out, due to the ions moving away from the point.

If you bring the candle very close to the point, the flame will stream out in both directions. This shows the ions attracted towards the point (which are discharged) as well as those repelled.

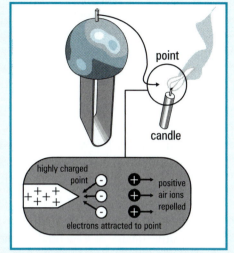

1. Hold a neon bulb by one of its leads.
2. Point the other lead towards the charged dome of a Van de Graaff generator.

Result: The neon bulb glows for an instant. This shows that static electricity is identical to current electricity and, given the opportunity, flows through you to earth.

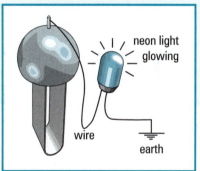

Lightning conductor

When lightning strikes a building, the enormous energy causes expansion and cracks the walls of the building. It can also cause fires. Lightning conductors protect buildings from these effects.

A lightning conductor uses point discharge to reduce the effects of electrical storms. It is an earthed conductor with several sharp points at the top fixed to the highest point of a building. When a negatively charged cloud passes over, it induces positive charges at the points and repels electrons to earth. The positive charges at the conductor points cause a downward flow of negative ions in the air and an upward flow of positive ions. The positive charge at the points neutralises the negative ions in the air, and the positive ions in the air reduce the electric charge on the cloud. The conductor also acts as a low-resistance path to the earth if lightning strikes.

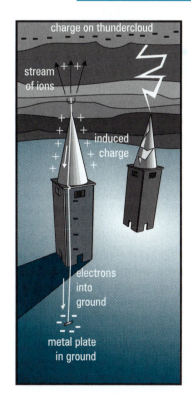

Van de Graaff electrostatic generator

The Van de Graaff generator can be charged to a very high voltage. This voltage depends on the size of the dome and the insulating pillars supporting it.

A smooth dome D is insulated from earth by tall pillars. The edges are curved to avoid point discharge. The rubber belt B moves on perspex pulleys/rollers. The metal comb A is connected to earth and the comb C is connected to the dome.

1. The perspex roller is positively charged by friction. This induces point action at comb A which sprays negative charge onto the belt.
2. The negative charge is carried by the belt to comb C, where it induces a positive charge at C and an equal negative charge on the dome.
3. The positive charge at C neutralises the negative charge on the belt. An increasing negative charge builds up on the dome.
4. The uncharged belt returns to A and the action continues.

Large Van de Graaff generators are used to accelerate charged particles in atomic research.

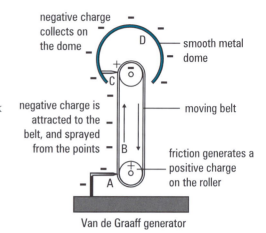
Van de Graaff generator

Static electricity causes problems

Have you noticed how dust seems to cling to your CDs, no matter how carefully you handle them? This is due to a static electrical charge on the CD. The charge attracts dust the way your biro attracts pieces of paper. This also happens when you clean glass with a duster. You produce a static charge on the glass which attracts dust.

TV screens attract dust in the same way. The electrons hitting the inside of the tube (to produce the picture) induce a static charge on the outside. You can feel this charge attract the hairs on your arm if you bring it close to the screen.

Static electricity (static cling) also builds up on clothes, particularly synthetics. This is caused by the layers of clothes rubbing against each other, particularly in clothes dryers. Workers in some chemical plants have to change into special clothes to avoid sparks produced by static electricity. Chemical additives in fabric conditioners reduce static effects in clothes.

Static electricity is a major problem in many industries. Carpet manufacturers often have problems of static build-up on machines. This causes a discharge spark similar to that produced by the Van de Graaff generator. Flash fires in textile industries are often caused by static discharge.

Static is also believed to cause mysterious explosions in grain silos. The charge built up in 'pumping' the grain gives a big spark discharge. This explodes a mixture of fine grain dust and air.

Jet and fuel tanker connected and earthed

Static Electricity

Pointed earthing conductors (to cause point discharge) are used to reduce this problem.

Refuelling aircraft means pumping large amounts of jet fuel into the tanks. The friction between the pumps and the fuel causes static charge to build up on the plane. Chemical additives are used to reduce the static, and the pumps and plane are connected and earthed.

Static electricity is noticed most when the air is very dry. Dry air stops the charges that have been separated from recombining. Static electricity is not as evident on a damp day, because the resistance of the air is reduced by the moisture and the static charge leaks off the surface.

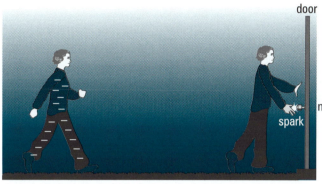

The build-up of charge is not noticed until we touch a conductor. Discharge then occurs.

The static charge built up when you rub your shoes on a carpet can reach a potential of 20,000 volts. You feel a shock when you are earthed by touching a metal object: this is the electric charge flowing through you. Even though the voltage is very big, this shock is not harmful because the current (charge flowing) is very small.

Summary

- A body becomes positively charged when it loses electrons.
- A body becomes negatively charged when it gains electrons.
- Conductors are substances through which electric charges can pass freely.
- Insulators are substances through which electric charges cannot pass.

	Current carriers
Solids	Electrons
Liquids	Positive and negative ions
Gases	Electrons and ions

- A coulomb is the quantity of electric charge that passes when a current of one ampere flows for one second.
- An electroscope is charged oppositely to the inducing charge.

Benjamin Franklin (USA) 1706–1790, an American scientist, inventor and writer, was prominent in founding the USA. Franklin showed that lightning was in fact a form of electricity with his famous kite experiment. He invented lightning rods to protect buildings. His later work included a theory of heat absorption, designing ships, tracking storm paths, and inventing bifocal lenses.

Short Questions

1. The unit of electric charge is _____.
2. A body may be given a charge by _____.
3. Indicate the charge (i) on the cap, (ii) on the leaves, of the electroscope in the diagram.
4. The function of the part labelled A in the diagram is _____.
5. What will happen to the leaves of the charged electroscope in the diagram when a conductor is brought into contact with the cap of the electroscope?
6. Give an everyday example of static charge.
7. When two bodies become charged by contact with each other, one loses _____ and becomes _____ charged, while the other gains _____ and becomes _____ charged.
8. The diagram shows a positively charged conductor. Indicate on the diagram how the charge would be distributed over the surface of the conductor.
9. In the diagram, metal spheres X (positively charged) and Y (uncharged) are close to each other and Y is touched with a finger. The finger is removed from Y. After this, sphere X is taken away. Is sphere Y now
   (A) positively charged
   (B) negatively charged
   (C) uncharged
   (D) negatively charged on the left side and positively charged on the right side
   (E) positively charged on the left side and negatively charged on the right side?
10. If an earthed copper plate is held near a fine stream of water falling from a tap, will the stream of water
    (A) curve towards the plate
    (B) curve away from the plate
    (C) be unaffected
    (D) split up into droplets
    (E) flow more slowly?

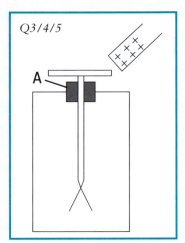

Q3/4/5

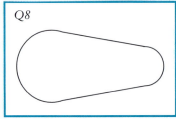

Q8

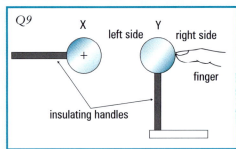

Q9

11. A piece of plastic is rubbed with a cloth and is then found to be negatively charged. The most likely explanation of this is that
    (A) cloths are always negatively charged
    (B) plastic is always negatively charged
    (C) the cloth rubs electrons off the plastic
    (D) positive ions are removed from the plastic
    (E) electrons are transferred from the cloth to the plastic.

12. In the diagram, two identical, uncharged metal spheres on insulated stands are in contact, when a negatively charged polythene rod is brought close to X. While the charged polythene rod is held stationary, spheres X and Y are separated. What are the charges on X and Y now?

    Charge on X   Charge on Y
    (A) Positive   Negative
    (B) Negative   Negative
    (C) Neutral   Neutral
    (D) Positive   Positive
    (E) Negative   Positive

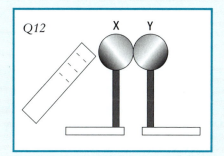

Long Questions

1. Explain the terms (i) conductor, (ii) insulator. Draw a labelled diagram of a Van de Graaff generator and explain the principle on which it is based. For what purpose is a Van de Graaff generator used?

2. In dry weather, when a driver touches the door while getting out of her car, she sometimes gets an electric shock as soon as her foot touches the ground.
   (a) Explain why this happens.
   (b) Why does it not happen in wet weather?
   (c) Some people fix a piece of fine chain to the car which drags on the road. How does this prevent shock?
   (d) Some people fix a piece of metal shaped as shown in the diagram under the car body. Even though it does not touch the road, it stops drivers from getting an electrical shock. How does it do this?

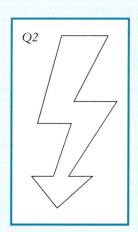

3. A manufacturer of nylon thread put heavy rubber mats under his spinning machines, which were made of metal, to deaden the noise. The following effects were subsequently noted.
   (a) The workers sometimes received an electrical shock when touching the machines. (There was no leak from the mains cable.)
   (b) Small bits of nylon fluff stuck to the thread, but this could be overcome by keeping the air in the workshop moist.
   State and explain the physical reasons for (a) and (b), and say how (a) could be overcome.

4. (a) Draw a labelled diagram showing the essential structural features of a gold leaf electroscope. Describe in detail how the electroscope could be charged by the method of induction. Explain how it could then be used
   (i) to determine whether another charged body had a charge of the same sign
   (ii) to show that a damp cotton thread is a much poorer insulator than one that is perfectly dry.
   (b) Explain why a dressing table mirror may become more dusty if wiped with cloth on a warm day.

5. Suppose you are supplied with a negatively charged rod and two identical and uncharged metal spheres, A and B, on insulating stands.
   (a) How, using the negatively charged rod, would you charge the two spheres equally so that A is negatively charged and B is positively charged?
   (b) How would you show experimentally, using any additional apparatus you may require, that this had in fact occurred?
   (c) Account for the production of the two equal charges in terms of the movement of electrons.

6. How would you establish the charge distribution on the surface of a charged conductor? A polystyrene ball is coated with aluminium paint and suspended by an insulating thread. When a charged rod is brought near, the ball is first attracted and then repelled. Why?

7. Explain how a lightning conductor reduces the charge at the base of a thundercloud.

8. Computer chips and other electronic equipment are damaged by high voltage. Technicians repairing electronic equipment touch a metal conductor before handling any part of the equipment. Why do you think they do this? Some technicians attach a metal strap to their wrist and connect it to a conductor (usually a metal pipe). What do you think is the purpose of the strap?

Electric Fields

CHAPTER 20

We have already seen that electric charges attract and repel each other. Coulomb measured the force between electric charges a distance apart. He found that the force between two charges Q_1 and Q_2 separated by a distance d is proportional to the product of the charges (Q_1 multiplied by Q_2) and inversely proportional to the square of the distance (d^2).

$$F \propto \frac{Q_1 \cdot Q_2}{d^2}$$

$$F = k \cdot \frac{Q_1 \cdot Q_2}{d^2}$$

In SI units, $k = \dfrac{1}{4\pi\varepsilon}$

$$F = \frac{Q_1 \cdot Q_2}{4\pi\varepsilon d^2}$$

ε is the permittivity of the material between the charges. Permittivity is a property that affects the force between the charges. If the material between the charges has a high permittivity, the force between the charges is small. If the permittivity is low, the force is big.

Coulomb's law: The force between two point charges is directly proportional to the product of the charges and inversely proportional to the square of the distance between them.

Coulomb's law is an example of an **inverse square law**, similar in mathematical form to Newton's law of gravitation.

Permittivity of a substance

ε_0 is the permittivity of free space or a vacuum. ε_r is the permittivity of a material relative to that of a vacuum: $\varepsilon_r = \dfrac{\varepsilon}{\varepsilon_0}$. It follows that the permittivity of a substance $\varepsilon = \varepsilon_r \cdot \varepsilon_0$.

The unit of permittivity is the farad per metre (F m^{-1}).

PROBLEM 1
Calculate the force a 2 µC charge exerts on a −2 µC charge when they are 0·01 m apart in a vacuum.

$$F = \frac{Q_1 \cdot Q_2}{4\pi\varepsilon d^2} = \frac{(2 \times 10^{-6}) \cdot (2 \times 10^{-6})}{4\pi \left(\dfrac{10^{-9}}{36\pi}\right)(0 \cdot 01)^2} \qquad \varepsilon_0 = \frac{10^{-9}}{36\pi}$$

$$= 360 \text{ N}$$

Charles Augustin Coulomb (France) 1736–1806 investigated the force between electric charges with a delicate torsion balance and discovered the inverse square law for electric forces (Coulomb's law). The unit of electric charge (the coulomb) is named after him.

Physics Now!

Problem 2

Point charges of 20 µC and 60 µC are separated by a 3 mm thick sheet of plastic. If each charge exerts a force of 200×10^3 newtons on the other, calculate the relative permittivity of the plastic.

$$F = \frac{Q_1 \cdot Q_2}{4\pi \varepsilon d^2}$$

$$\varepsilon = \frac{Q_1 \cdot Q_2}{4\pi d^2 F} = \frac{(20 \times 10^{-6})(60 \times 10^{-6})}{4\pi (3 \times 10^{-3})^2 \cdot (200 \times 10^3)} = \frac{1 \times 10^{-9}}{6\pi}$$

$$\varepsilon_r = \frac{\varepsilon}{\varepsilon_0} = \frac{1 \times 10^{-9}}{6\pi} \bigg/ \frac{10^{-9}}{36\pi}$$

$$\varepsilon_r = 6$$

Problem 3

Three point charges are arranged as shown in the diagram. What charge must be placed at C so that there is no net force on the charge at B?

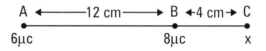

The force exerted on B by A must be balanced by the force exerted on B by C. By Coulomb's law, force is directly proportional to the product of the charges and inversely proportional to the square of the distance between them.

$$F_1 \propto \frac{(6\ \mu C)(8\ \mu C)}{12^2}$$

$$F_2 \propto \frac{(8\ \mu C)x}{4^2}$$

The forces are balanced, so $F_1 = F_2$.

$$\frac{(6\ \mu C)(8\ \mu C)}{12^2} = \frac{(8\ \mu C)x}{4^2}$$

$$x = \frac{2}{3}\ \mu C$$

Electric field

Experiment 20.1

AIM: To show the presence of an electric field.
METHOD:
1. Attach a polystyrene ball to a nylon thread.
2. Move the ball towards a charged Van de Graaff generator.

Result: As you get closer, the ball is pulled more and more from hanging vertically. The ball is uncharged, yet is affected by the Van de Graaff generator. This is because the space around the Van de Graaff generator is disturbed by the electric charge on it. We notice this effect on the polystyrene ball because it is so light.

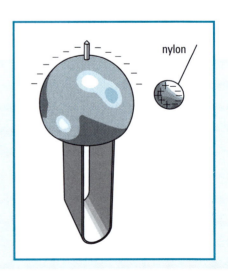

ELECTRIC FIELDS

The same effect can be seen when somebody with light hair stands near a Van de Graaff generator. Their hair stands out towards the Van de Graaff.

We call the space around a charge, that the charge disturbs, an electric field. Any charge placed in this field will be affected by the electric force of the field. This force is a vector, as it acts in a particular direction.

Electric field is the space around a charge in which the charge has an effect.

Experiment 20.2

AIM: To demonstrate electric field lines.

METHOD:

We demonstrate electric field lines with semolina in olive oil.
1. Connect two metal rods to leads from the dome and earth of a Van de Graaff generator.
2. Place the rods in a shallow dish of semolina in olive oil. Charge the Van de Graaff generator.

Result: The electric field pattern is indicated by the lines of semolina particles.

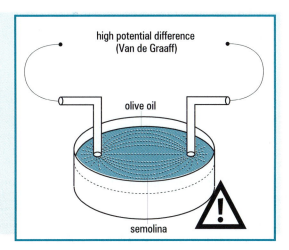

An electric field line is the line along which a positive charge will move when placed in the electric field. The electric field line gives the vector direction for the electric field.

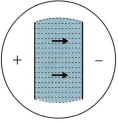
two parallel electrodes

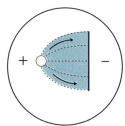
a straight electrode and a point electrode

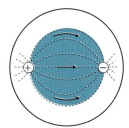
two point electrodes (unlike charges)

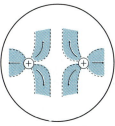
two point electrodes (like charges)

FIELD STRENGTH

The strength of the electric field at any point is measured by the force it exerts on a unit positive charge placed at that point. Electric field strength is a vector quantity.

Electric field strength at a point is the force per unit positive charge at that point.

Electric field strength $E = \frac{F}{Q}$.

The unit of electric field strength is the newton per coulomb (N C^{-1}) or the volt per metre (V m^{-1})

We can calculate the electric field strength at a point P a distance d from a charge Q as follows.

Take a unit point charge (1 coulomb) at P. The force between the charges is

$$F = \frac{Q.1}{4\pi\varepsilon d^2} \quad \text{(from Coulomb's law)}$$

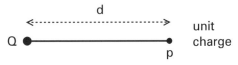

The electric field strength at P is the force on a unit charge at that point. As there is a charge of 1 unit there,

$$E = \frac{F}{1} = \frac{Q.1}{4\pi\varepsilon d^2} \div 1$$

$$= \frac{Q}{4\pi\varepsilon d^2}$$

PROBLEM 1

Calculate the electric field strength at a point where a 4 μC charge experiences a force of 0·04 newtons.

The electric field strength at a point is the force on a unit charge at that point.

$$E = \frac{F}{Q}$$

$$= \frac{0.04}{4 \times 10^{-6}}$$

$$= \frac{4 \times 10^{-2}}{4 \times 10^{-6}}$$

$$= 1 \times 10^4 \, \text{N C}^{-1}$$

PROBLEM 2

What is the electric field strength at a point 10 cm from a +2 μC point charge?

$$E = \frac{F}{Q}$$

The force between a unit charge and a +2 μC point charge is found by Coulomb's law:

$$F = \left(\frac{1}{4\pi\varepsilon}\right) \cdot \frac{Q.q}{d^2}, \text{ where } Q \text{ is 2 μC and } q \text{ is 1 C (unit charge)}$$

$$= \frac{1}{4\pi\left(\frac{10^{-9}}{36\pi}\right)} \cdot \frac{(2 \times 10^{-6}).1}{(0.1)^2}$$

$$= 18 \times 10^5 \, \text{N}$$

$$= 1.8 \times 10^6 \, \text{N}$$

$$E = \frac{F}{q} = \frac{1.8 \times 10^6}{1} = 1.8 \times 10^6 \, \text{N C}^{-1}$$

ELECTRIC FIELDS

Uses of electric fields

THE ELECTROSTATIC DUST PRECIPITATOR

Did you know that you have one of these in your home? Try cleaning the screen of your TV set with a white tissue. This dust is attracted to the screen in the same way that the electrostatic dust precipitator removes dust particles from smoke.

A very high voltage (50,000 V) electric field is set up between a central wire mesh and the earthed plates at the side. Dust is moved by this field to the plates, where it accumulates. The plates are struck regularly by a mechanical hammer and the ash falls into a bin.

SCREENING ELECTRONIC EQUIPMENT FROM ELECTRIC FIELDS

The electric field produced by the static electric charge on clothes, carpets and other surfaces can easily damage electronic equipment. Electronic equipment operates at low voltage. High voltage produced by the electric field of static charge destroys it. Computers have an earthed metal cage around the vulnerable parts to screen them from static discharge. Technicians working on computers earth themselves to discharge any static charges on their bodies before working on the circuit boards.

MAKING PHOTOCOPIES (XEROGRAPHY)

In a photocopier, the surface of a rotating drum is given a positive electric charge. Light is then reflected off the page you want to copy. The light discharges the parts of the drum corresponding to the white parts of the page. Negatively charged toner (fine black ink-dust) is attracted by the charge left in the parts corresponding to the black in the original page, and forms an image of it on the drum. Positively charged paper is moved over the drum and the toner image is transferred onto it. Hot rollers fuse (melt) the image onto the paper.
Laser printers work in the same way.

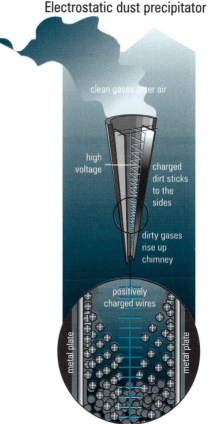

Electrostatic dust precipitator

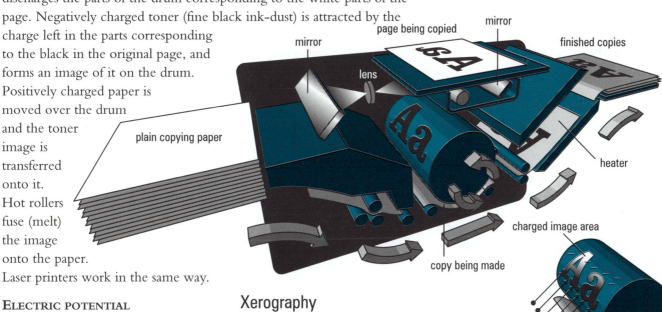

Xerography

ELECTRIC POTENTIAL

When you move a positive charge towards another positive charge, work must be done to overcome the force of repulsion between the charges. This energy is stored in the charges as potential energy. If you release the charge it will move. This releases the energy stored and lowers the potential energy of the charge.

Electric potential is a measure of the work done in moving a charge towards another charge. We usually want to know the difference in potential between two points.

The potential difference between two points is the work done in moving a charge of one coulomb from one point to the other.

Potential difference is measured in volts.

ZERO POTENTIAL

When two charges are an infinite distance apart, there is no force between them. If they are moved about at this distance, no work is done. We regard charges a great distance apart as being at zero potential. For practical purposes we take the earth as our zero potential. The potential of the earth (a very large spherical conductor) is not noticeably affected by charges moving towards or away from it.

A potential difference of one volt exists between two points if one joule of work is done in moving one coulomb between them.

$$V = \frac{W}{Q}$$

$$\text{volts} = \frac{\text{joules}}{\text{coulombs}}$$

Charge will move only when there is a potential difference between two points. Charge always moves towards the point at lower potential. Equipotentials are points at the same potential.

PROBLEM

2·5 µJ of energy is used to move a 0·5 µC charge between two points. Calculate the potential difference between the points.

$$V = \frac{W}{Q}$$

$$= \frac{(2·5 \times 10^{-6})}{(0·5 \times 10^{-6})}$$

$$= 5 \text{ volts}$$

PROBLEM

Calculate the work done in moving a 3 µC charge from a conductor at a potential of 20 kV to one at 60 kV.

$$V = \frac{W}{Q}$$

$$W = V . Q$$

The potential difference is

$$(60 - 20) \text{ kV} = 40 \text{ kV}$$

$$W = (40 \times 10^3) . (3 \times 10^{-6})$$

$$= 120 \times 10^{-3} \text{ J}$$

Electric Fields

Summary
- Coulomb's law: The force between two point charges is directly proportional to the product of the charges and inversely proportional to the square of the distance between them.
- An electric field is the space around a charge in which the charge has an effect.
- An electric field line is the line along which a positive charge will move when placed in an electric field.
- Electric field strength at a point is the force per unit positive charge at that point.
- A potential difference of one volt exists between two points if one joule of work is done in moving one coulomb of electric charge between them.

Short Questions
1. State Coulomb's law of force between electric charges.
2. An electric field line is _____.
3. Electric field strength is _____.
4. Electric potential is _____.
5. The unit of electric potential, the volt, is _____.
6. If you increase the permittivity of the material between two charges, the force will _____.
7. Electric fields can be demonstrated using _____ and _____.
8. The function of the metal case around the vulnerable parts of a computer is to _____.
9. Why is dust attracted to a photocopier or laser printer?
10. The joule per coulomb is also known as the _____.

Long Questions
*1. The diagram shows an arrangement of three collinear point charges. What charge must be placed at c so that there is no net force on the charge at b?

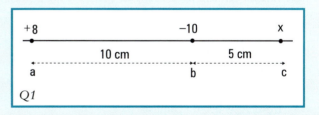

Q1

*2. The force between two isolated point charges 4 cm apart is 20 μN. What is the force between them when they are 2 cm apart?
*3. Calculate the electric field strength at a point where a 4 μC charge experiences a force of 0·04 newtons.
4. Calculate the work done in transferring a charge of 6C from one point to another when the potential difference between the points is 4 V.

*5. A spherical conductor of radius 3 cm has an electric field strength of 600 newtons per coulomb at its surface. Calculate the charge on the conductor.

*6. The distance between two charged spheres is halved and the charge on each sphere is doubled. Calculate the force on each of the charges, given that it was originally F newtons.

*7. A body of mass 10^{-10} kg, carrying a unit electric charge, shows an acceleration of 5 m s^{-2} when placed in an electric field. Calculate the electric field strength that produces this effect.

*8. Two equal small charges are 5 cm apart. They repel each other with a force of $2 \cdot 5 \times 10^{-6}$ N.
(a) What is the size of each charge?
(b) What would be the force between the charges at a distance of 10 cm?

9. Define electric field strength. Describe how an electric field pattern can be demonstrated in the laboratory.

10. What is an electric field? Describe a laboratory experiment to demonstrate the existence of an electric field.

*11. Point charges of 20 µC and 60 µC are on opposite sides of a sheet of mica (ε_r = 6) 3 mm thick. Find the force on either of the charges.
0·8 J of energy is expended in moving a 0·5 µC charge from one point to another. Calculate the potential difference between these two points.

12. Calculate the work done in moving a 3 µC charge from a conductor at a potential of 10 kV to one at 60 kV.

*13. A thundercloud is at a potential of 10^9 V. If a bolt of lightning transfers 40 C of electric charge, what is the energy of the bolt? If the lightning takes 1 millisecond to strike, what is the current flowing in the bolt?

14. Define electric field strength. Describe an experiment to demonstrate an electric field pattern.
Two point charges are situated at A and B, a distance of 35 cm apart in a vacuum. The charge at A is a positive charge of 16 µC and the field strength at X, a distance of 12 cm from A, is zero. Calculate:

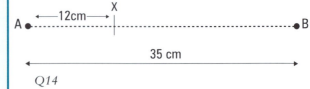

Q14

(i) The field strength at X due to the charge at A.
(ii) The charge at B.
(Permittivity of free space, ε_0 = 8.9 x 10^{-12} F m^{-1}.)

Simple Circuits

CHAPTER 21

Set up the apparatus as shown in the diagram. Close the switch. From this simple experiment we learn that electricity will flow only if there is a complete circuit. If you break the circuit, the flow of electricity stops: the bulb goes out. If you remove the battery but complete the circuit, the bulb also goes out.

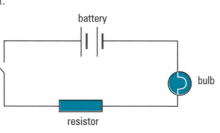

Luigi Galvani (Italy) 1737–1798 was a professor of anatomy who studied the effects of static electricity on animal muscles. He discovered the simple cell by using dissimilar metals in the dissection of frogs, but wrongly believed that the effect was due to animal electricity.

Electric current

An electric current is a flow of electric charge. Electric current is measured in a unit called the ampere. When one coulomb of electric charge moves through the circuit in one second, the current flow is one ampere. The ampere is a flow of charge of one coulomb per second.

amperes = coulombs/seconds

$$I = \frac{Q}{t}$$

Electromotive force (emf)

In the circuit shown above, the battery supplies the energy to drive the electricity around the circuit and light the bulb. The battery has an electromotive force (emf). This emf produces a potential difference across the circuit. Electric current flows because there is a potential difference (p.d.) across the circuit. The energy used to create this potential difference, and any other potential difference in the circuit, comes from the battery or other source of electrical energy. Only batteries, generators and other sources of electrical energy have emfs.

A voltage when applied to a circuit is called an emf

The battery or other source of emf supplies electrical energy to the circuit and creates the total potential difference across the circuit that causes the current to flow. In the above circuit there is a potential difference across the bulb. Current flows through the bulb which turns electrical energy into heat and light.

The electrical energy needed to move the current through the circuit comes from a dynamo or generator, a simple cell, battery or rechargeable battery, a semiconductor solar cell or a thermocouple. Each has its own strengths and weaknesses for particular applications. A dry cell is suitable for a calculator but would not work as a car battery while a car battery would be impractical for the calculator.

Alessandro Volta (Italy) 1745–1827 investigated "galvanism" and developed the first chemical cell. He joined a series of cells to form a battery. The unit of potential difference (the volt) is named after him.

PHYSICS NOW!

A potential difference of one volt exists between any two points when one joule of energy is expended in moving one coulomb between them.

Electricity will flow if there is a potential difference and a complete circuit.

PROBLEM 1

0·8 mJ of energy is used in moving a 0·5 µC charge from one point to another. Calculate the potential difference between these points.

$$V = \frac{W}{Q}$$

$$= \frac{(0·8 \times 10^{-3})}{(0·5 \times 10^{-6})}$$

$$= 1·6 \times 10^3 \text{ V}$$

PROBLEM 2

A total of 90 J of energy is used to move a charge of 15 C around a circuit in 3 seconds. Calculate the potential difference across the circuit and the current flowing.

$$V = \frac{W}{Q} = \frac{90}{15} = 6 \text{ V}$$

$$I = \frac{Q}{t} = \frac{15}{3} = 5 \text{ A}$$

The simple cell

Experiment 21.1

AIM: To make a simple electric cell.

1. Connect up the circuit as shown.
2. Place a strip of copper and a strip of zinc in a beaker of dilute hydrochloric acid (or copper sulphate solution). Read the voltage from the voltmeter. What do you notice happening to the voltage after a few seconds?
3. Repeat with the combinations of metals listed. Complete the table.

Metal A	Metal B	Voltage produced
Copper	Zinc	
Copper	Iron	
Copper	Lead	
Zinc	Iron	
Zinc	Lead	
Iron	Lead	

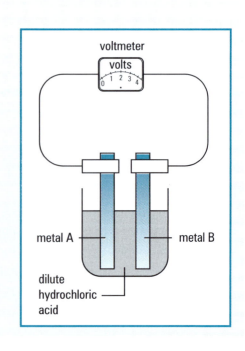

What do you notice? The greater the difference in reactivity of the two metals, the greater is the voltage produced. The metal strips are called electrodes, and the ionic solution between them is the electrolyte. The more reactive metal is always the negative electrode of the cell.

Any combination of two different electrodes in an electrolyte is a simple cell. The simple cell converts chemical energy into electricity.

Scientists are working to make new types of cell that give more electricity and are lighter and cheaper. They also have to ensure that batteries are safe and 'environment friendly'.

The dry cell

Dry cells are sometimes called zinc-carbon cells because these are the two electrodes used to make them. The dry cell has a voltage of 1·5 volts. A number of cells, called a battery, are joined in series to give bigger voltages: 3 V, 4·5 V, 6 V, etc.

Dry cells last well in radios and low-power devices. They are used up quickly in personal stereos and equipment with motors, because the motor takes a lot of energy. Alkaline cells are used in these. Mercury cells, silver cells and lithium cells are used in cameras, hearing aids and other special devices. All these cells are **primary cells** and convert chemical energy into electrical energy in a **non-reversible** way.

RECHARGEABLE CELLS

Rechargeable cells are better for many purposes. A car battery is a lead-acid accumulator: this means that the plates are made of lead and the electrolyte is sulphuric acid. The battery has an emf of over 12 V and consists of six lead-acid cells. These are **secondary cells**, which means they can be recharged many times. They supply the large current needed to start a car and are recharged by the dynamo (alternator) when the car engine is running. Car batteries last for many years. The car battery can be damaged by a short circuit that buckles the plates. Also, if it is left discharged the coating on the plates will harden and prevent recharge.

Nickel-cadmium cells have a voltage of 1·2 V and are often used to replace ordinary dry cells. They can be recharged up to 1,000 times in a special charging unit.

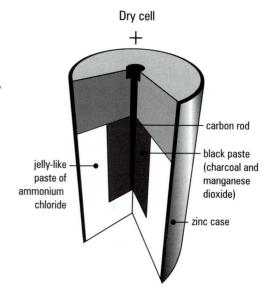

Cells and batteries convert chemical energy into electrical energy

PHYSICS NOW!

Resistance

Are all conductors the same? We can find out from the following experiment.

Experiment 21.2

AIM: To compare conductors.
1. Set up the circuit shown in the diagram.
2. Place the following substances between the clips and see how brightly the bulb lights. Copper wire, thin nichrome wire, a few strands of steel wool.

Result: With copper wire the bulb lights brightly. It barely glows with the nichrome wire, and the wire heats up. The strands of steel wool heat up and break.

Explanation: Electricity passes through the copper wire easily. It does not pass through the nichrome wire so easily: in other words, the nichrome wire has much greater resistance to electricity than copper wire has. The battery has to do a lot of work to drive the electricity through the nichrome. As a result, the battery uses up some of its energy, the electrical energy used turns to heat and the wire gets hot. The steel wool has a greater resistance, and gets so hot that it melts.

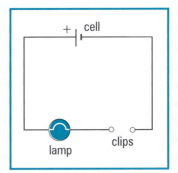

If energy is used in passing electricity through an object, that object has a resistance.

Mandatory experiment 21.3

AIM: To investigate the variations of current with potential difference for a metallic conductor.

METHOD:
1. Set up the apparatus as shown.
2. Set the variable resistor to give a small potential difference (voltage). Note the voltage and current.
3. Adjust the variable resistor to give a slightly larger voltage. Note the voltage and current again.
4. Repeat step 3 four or five times.
5. Draw a graph of voltage against current.

QUESTIONS:
1. What kind of graph did you get?
2. How could you use this graph to find the resistance of the resistor?
3. Why is it necessary to use a variable resistor?
4. How could you ensure that the temperature of the metallic conductor (wire) remains constant?
5. Identify two possible sources of error in this experiment.

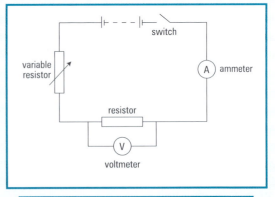

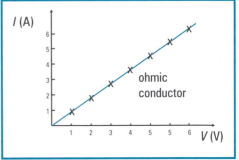

192

> Repeat experiment 21.3 with (i) a filament bulb, (ii) copper sulphate with copper electrodes and (iii) a semiconductor diode. Check that the diode is connected in 'forward bias'.

The ratio of the potential difference (p.d.) applied to the current flowing is constant for the metallic conductor. Resistance is defined as the direct relationship between p.d. and current for a conductor at a constant temperature. This is known as Ohm's law. Experiment 21.3 could be described as an experiment to verify Ohm's Law.

Ohm's law: At a constant temperature, the current passing through a metallic conductor is directly proportional to the potential difference across it.

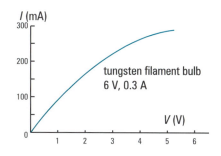

Resistance is the ratio of the potential difference across a conductor to the current flowing through it.

$$R = \frac{V}{I}$$

From this we define the unit of resistance, the ohm (Ω). The symbol is the Greek capital letter omega.

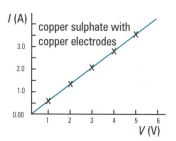

The ohm (Ω) is the resistance of a conductor when a potential difference of 1 volt across it produces a current flow of 1 amp through it.

$$\text{ohms} = \frac{\text{volts}}{\text{amperes}}$$

Not all conductors are ohmic (i.e. obey Ohm's law). Semiconductor diodes, thermistors and gases are not ohmic.

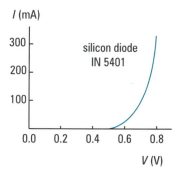

Conductor	Current carriers	Examples
Metals	Electrons	Copper, aluminium
Ionic solutions	Positive and negative ions	Salt water, copper sulphate solution
Gases	Electrons and ions	Fluorescent tube, neon lamp, sodium lamp
Vacuum	Electrons	Cathode ray tube, TV tube, photoelectric cell, X-ray tube
Semiconductors	Electrons and 'holes'	Diode, LED, photodiode, transistor

Physics Now!

Rheostat

A rheostat is connected to a circuit as shown in the diagram. By moving the sliding contact, the resistance through which the current flows can be increased or decreased. This controls the current flowing through the circuit. A rheostat is used in circuits where you want to limit the current. In many of the circuits used later in your course you will connect a large resistance in series with a sensitive galvanometer to protect it against too large a current. Light emitting diodes (LEDs) have resistors connected in series with them to limit the current passing through them to about 30 mA.

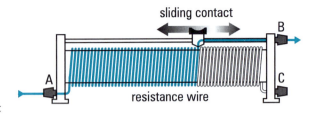

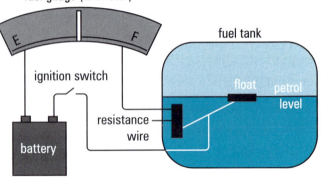

A fuel gauge uses a rheostat

Resistances in series and in parallel

There are some very simple rules for currents and potential differences in circuits.

1. The sum of the currents entering a point in a circuit equals the sum of the currents leaving it ($I = I_1 + I_2 + I_3$).
2. The emf of the circuit equals the sum of all the potential differences in the circuit ($E = V_1 + V_2 + V_3$).

RESISTANCES IN SERIES

The two resistors are connected in a line, so the same current I flows through both.

$V = V_1 + V_2$, but $V = IR$ (Ohm's law)

$IR = IR_1 + IR_2$

Dividing by I gives

$R = R_1 + R_2$

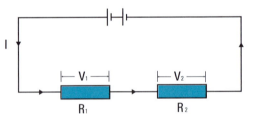

in series these two resistors have the same effect as a 6Ω resistor

PROBLEM

Two resistances of 2 Ω and 4 Ω are connected in series with a 6 V battery. Calculate the potential difference across each resistance.

$R = R_1 + R_2$

$R = 2 + 4 = 6\ \Omega$

$I = \dfrac{V}{R} = \dfrac{6}{6} = 1$ A

Potential difference across each resistor:

$V_1 = IR_1 = 1 \times 2 = 2$ V

$V_2 = IR_2 = 1 \times 4 = 4$ V

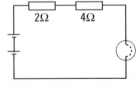

it is twice as difficult to get into a stadium if there are two turnstiles, one after the other

194

Simple Circuits

Resistances in parallel

The potential difference between two points is the same regardless of the path followed. The potential difference across each of the resistances from A to B is V.

$$I = I_1 + I_2$$

From Ohm's law,

$$I = \frac{V}{R}$$

$$\frac{V}{R} = \frac{V}{R_1} + \frac{V}{R_2}$$

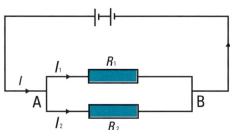

Dividing by V gives

$$\frac{1}{R} = \frac{1}{R_1} + \frac{1}{R_2}$$

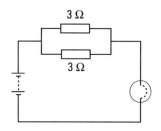

in parallel these two resistors have the same effect as a 1.5 Ω resistor

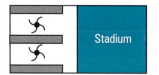

it is twice as easy to get into a stadium if there are two turnstiles, one beside the other

Problem

A battery of emf 4·5 V and resistance 2·1 Ω is connected to two resistances of 4 Ω and 6 Ω in parallel. Calculate (a) the current flowing through the battery and (b) the potential difference across the two resistors.

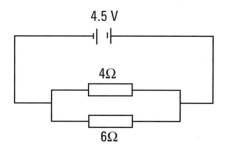

The two resistances in parallel:

$$\frac{1}{R} = \frac{1}{R_1} + \frac{1}{R_2}$$

$$\frac{1}{R} = \frac{1}{4} + \frac{1}{6} = \frac{5}{12}$$

$$R = \frac{12}{5} = 2·4 \ \Omega$$

This resistance is in series with the battery resistance

$$R = R_1 + R_2$$

$$R = 2·4 + 2·1 = 4·5 \ \Omega$$

$$I = \frac{V}{R} = \frac{4·5}{4·5} = 1 \ \text{A (answer (a))}$$

The potential difference across the two resistors:

$$V = IR = 1.2·4 = 2·4 \ \text{V (answer (b))}$$

Problem

A battery of emf 10 V is connected across three resistances arranged as shown in the diagram. Calculate (a) the total resistance in the circuit, (b) the current flowing through the 3 Ω resistance, (c) the voltage across the 3 Ω resistance, (d) the voltage across the 8 Ω resistance.

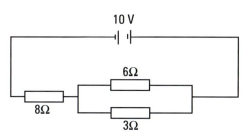

The 6 Ω and 3 Ω resistances are in parallel.

Physics Now!

$$\frac{1}{R} = \frac{1}{R_1} + \frac{1}{R_2}$$

$$\frac{1}{R} = \frac{1}{6} + \frac{1}{3} = \frac{3}{6}$$

$$R = \frac{6}{3} = 2\,\Omega$$

This equivalent resistance and the 8 Ω resistance are in series.

Total resistance in circuit: $R = R_1 + R_2$

$R = 2 + 8 = 10\,\Omega$ (a)

Total current flowing in circuit: $I = \frac{V}{R} = \frac{10}{10} = 1$ A

Potential difference across 8 Ω resistance: $V = IR = 1.8 = 8$ V (d)

The rest of the voltage is across the two resistances in parallel = 2 V

Voltage across the 3 Ω resistance = 2 V (c)

Current through the 3 Ω resistance: $I = \frac{V}{R} = \frac{2}{3} = \frac{2}{3}$ A (b)

Electricity in the home

The ESB supplies two cables to your home. One cable, the 'live', is maintained at 220 V relative to the other. The 'neutral' cable is earthed at the ESB sub-station and so is at earth (zero) potential. These cables are connected through the ESB meter, which measures the amount of electrical energy used in your house. They then pass through an isolating switch which can turn off all electric current in the house, and then into the fuse box. The fuse box contains either fuses or circuit breakers. The ESB supply is connected through the fuse box to the lighting circuits (for lights) and power circuits (for sockets).

RING MAIN CIRCUIT

In this case the live and neutral wires each form a ring or loop. A third loop is formed by the earth wire. When you plug a kettle into a socket, the live and neutral pins connect with the live and neutral wires so that current can flow from one wire to the other through the heating element of the kettle. No current flows in the earth wire, unless of course a fault develops. In a ring circuit there are two independent paths for the current to any point. This reduces the thickness of wire needed.

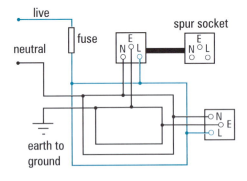

Ring circuit with spur

RADIAL CIRCUIT

The wires in a radial circuit go directly to the lighting points. Radial circuits are used for lighting circuits, as the currents flowing in these circuits are small.

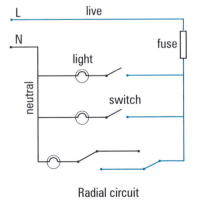

Radial circuit

Simple Circuits

Spur socket
A spur socket is an extra socket attached to one of the existing ring main sockets. Spur sockets should be avoided if possible, although they can sometimes be convenient. If you use them, remember the rule: one spur per socket, no more.

Switch
The live wire is always connected through the switch. This is essential for safety. If the live wire were connected directly to the appliance, the conducting parts of it would be at a potential of 220 V even with the switch in the 'off' position. This would give you a shock if you touched any conducting parts. The fuse is always on the live wire for the same reason.

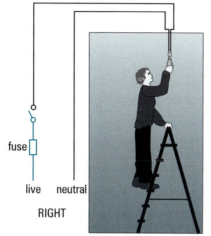
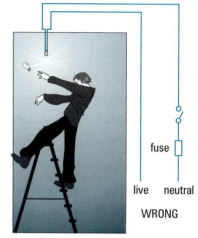

Fuse
A large current caused by an overload or fault in a circuit could (a) damage electrical equipment, and (b) overheat the house wiring and cause a fire. A fuse is a short length of wire of very low melting point. If a circuit becomes overloaded (too big a current), the fuse wire melts and breaks the circuit.

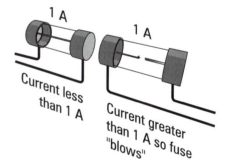

Miniature circuit breaker (MCB)
This circuit breaker is a mechanical alternative to a fuse. It cuts off the current when the current exceeds a particular value. The live wire is connected through a coil in the trip switch. The strength of the magnetic field in the coil depends on the current. When the current exceeds the set value, the magnetic field of the coil pulls the iron rod down and cuts off the current. MCBs can be reset.

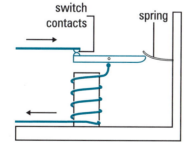
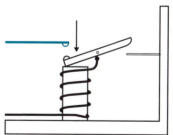

Circuit breaker. If the current in the coil is too big, the solenoid pulls the contacts open.

PHYSICS NOW!

EARTHING

Experiment 21.5

AIM: To demonstrate the effect of earthing.
The bulb and wire B represent you when you touch an electrical appliance: if the bulb lights up, you have just got a shock!

METHOD:
1. Disconnect the clip A from the calorimeter. Connect the clip B to the copper strip.
2. Touch the live wire to the side of the copper calorimeter. The bulb lights up.
3. Now connect the clip A (the earth) to the calorimeter. Touch the live wire to the calorimeter. The bulb doesn't light up: the fuse blows.

Safety note: This experiment must be done with a low voltage supply.

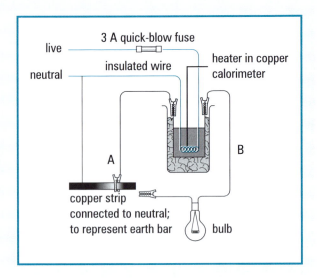

If you don't have an earth: When the live wire of a kettle touches the metal body, you will get a shock if you touch the kettle. Your body provides the path for the electricity to flow to earth.

When you have an earth: The metal parts of the kettle are connected by a third copper wire to a large metal plate buried in the ground. The case is at zero (earth) voltage and gives a low resistance path to earth. If the live wire or parts of the kettle touch the metal case, a large current will flow to earth and so blow the fuse. This protects you from getting a shock if you touch the metal case. It is absolutely essential to have a proper earth connection.

BONDING

Bathrooms and kitchens are particularly hazardous places for electricity. A good earth connection and effective circuit breakers are essential if a fault develops. Bonding ensures that there is always an unbroken low-resistance path for the current to flow to earth. This is done by connecting all the metal objects in a bathroom (pipes, metal parts of shower and of bath) to a good earth.

Where there is a poor earth connection the circuit breakers will not work fast enough to prevent a shock.

DOUBLE-INSULATED APPLIANCES

Some electrical appliances, such as hairdryers, do not have an earth connection. All live connections to these appliances are insulated, and all metal parts that could become live if there were a fault are also insulated.

What should happen

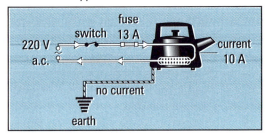

What can happen

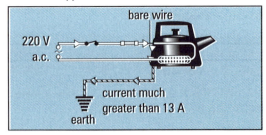

198

Simple Circuits

RESIDUAL CURRENT DEVICE (RCD)
The RCD is a trip switch that cuts off the current very quickly when a fault in an appliance causes a small current to flow to earth. The earth is connected through a coil in the trip switch.

When an appliance is operating correctly, no current flows to earth so that the current in the live wire is the same as the current in the neutral wire. In an RCD these currents flow through two opposed electromagnets which are balanced as long as the two currents are the same.

If a fault develops a current flows to earth. The current in the neutral is now less than the current in the live. The electromagnets are no longer balanced, so the switch is tripped. This cuts off the current to the faulty appliance. A typical RCD is tripped by an earth current of 30 mA.

RCD plugs should be used for electric hedgecutters, lawnmowers and power tools.

PLUGS
Plugs should be wired as shown in the diagram, with undamaged insulation on all wires. The flex should be firmly clamped in place in the plug.

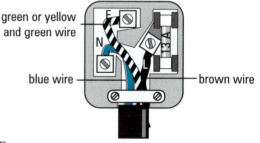

MAINS TESTER
A mains tester is a metal screwdriver encased in transparent plastic. A neon bulb is connected to the screwdriver. Above this a large resistance limits the current. The metal cap provides the connection to earth. When you touch the mains tester to a live wire, a tiny current flows through your body to earth: the current is so small that you do not feel it. The potential difference across the neon bulb causes it to light. The mains is at 220 V; your body is at earth or zero potential.

Safety

You have already seen that fuses, switches, earthing, bonding and RCDs can help to improve the electrical safety of your home. The kitchen and the bathroom are the two danger spots for electrical safety: water and electricity are a fatal combination. Water reduces your skin's resistance, so that any shock you get is likely to be fatal.

You can help to make your home safer as follows.
1. Keep all mains appliances out of the bathroom.
2. Use fuses of the correct rating.
3. Replace damaged or frayed flex: don't repair it.
4. Don't join cables together.
5. Don't have more than one appliance plugged into a socket: avoid adaptors.
6. Use an RCD with electrical tools used in the garden.

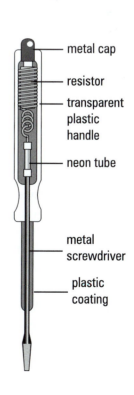

PHYSICS NOW!

Summary

- An electric current is a flow of electric charge.
- A potential difference of one volt exists between two points when one joule of energy is expended in moving one coulomb of electric charge between them.
- Electricity will flow if there is a potential difference and a complete circuit.
- Any combination of two different electrodes in an electrolyte is a simple cell.
- Ohm's law: At a constant temperature, the current passing through a metallic conductor is directly proportional to the potential difference across it.
- Resistance is the ratio of the potential difference across a conductor to the current flowing through it.
- The ohm is the resistance of a conductor such that a potential difference of one volt across it produces a current flow of one ampere through it.
- Resistances in series: $R = R_1 + R_2$
- Resistances in parallel: $\dfrac{1}{R} = \dfrac{1}{R_1} + \dfrac{1}{R_2}$
- If energy is used in passing electricity through an object, the object has a resistance.

SHORT QUESTIONS

1. One advantage of lead-acid batteries over dry-cell batteries for use in a car is that (A) topping up with distilled water restores the voltage, (B) they have the right voltage, (C) they have a larger emf, (D) it does not matter if they are treated roughly, (E) they can give a larger current.
2. The unit of electric current is the (A) watt, (B) volt, (C) ampere, (D) ohm, (E) coulomb.
3. The rate at which electrical charge flows in a circuit is measured in (A) volts, (B) ohms, (C) amperes, (D) coulombs, (E) watts.
4. Metals allow electric currents to flow through them easily because they (A) have more atoms, (B) have heavier atoms, (C) have free electrons, (D) are good conductors of heat, (E) have high densities.
5. The volt is the unit of (A) energy, (B) power, (C) electric current, (D) electric charge, (E) potential difference.
6. Which of the following instruments is used to measure an electric current? (A) voltmeter, (B) electrometer, (C) ohmmeter, (D) ammeter, (E) micrometer.

7. In the circuit shown, the switch S is open. When the switch is closed the ammeter reading changes from (A) $\frac{1}{2}$ A to 1 A, (B) 1 A to $\frac{1}{2}$ A, (C) 1 A to 2 A, (D) 1 A to 3 A, (E) 2 A to 1 A.

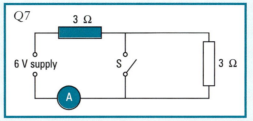

8. The current in the conductor YZ will be (A) 2 amperes, (B) 3 amperes, (C) 7 amperes, (D) 8 amperes, (E) 10 amperes.

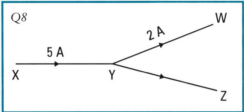

9. Electric charge is measured in (A) amperes, (B) volts, (C) joules, (D) watts, (E) coulombs.

10. Ohm's law states that, provided the temperature of a metallic conductor is constant, (A) its resistance is proportional to the current through it, (B) the current through it is constant, (C) the current through it is proportional to the potential difference across it, (D) the current through it is inversely proportional to the potential difference across it, (E) the potential difference across it is proportional to its resistance.

11. A volt can be defined as (A) a coulomb per second, (B) a joule per second, (C) an ampere per coulomb, (D) a coulomb per joule, (E) a joule per coulomb.

12. In the circuits shown (A to E), all the cells are identical and all the lamps are identical. In which circuit will the lamp marked L be brightest?

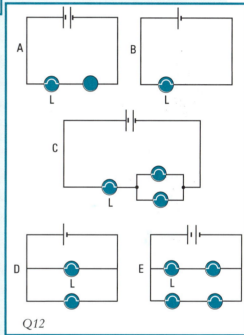

13. A simple voltaic cell was made by dipping a copper plate and a zinc plate into dilute sulphuric acid. The zinc plate was removed and replaced by another plate X, but no emf was obtained. Which of the following substances was the plate X made of, assuming that all the connections were still good? (A) carbon, (B) copper, (C) iron, (D) lead, (E) steel.

14. Resistance can be calculated from the expression:
    (A) potential difference/current,
    (B) potential difference × current,
    (C) current/potential difference,
    (D) (potential difference)^2/current,
    (E) (current)^2/potential difference.

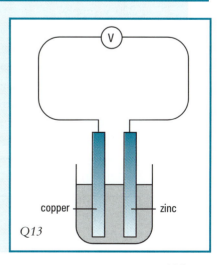

201

15. Which of the graphs in the diagram shows the current-voltage relationship for an ohmic conductor?
16. You will get an electric shock if you touch a _____ wire.
17. Double insulation, fuses and RCDs are all _____.
18. A short piece of _____ with a _____ melting point is used as a _____.
19. What is the effective resistance of the three resistors shown?
    (A) $\frac{1}{6}$ Ω
    (B) $\frac{2}{3}$ Ω
    (C) $\frac{3}{2}$ Ω
    (D) 2 Ω
    (E) 6 Ω

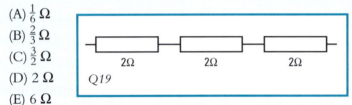
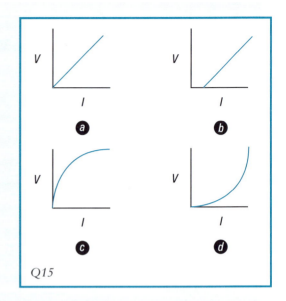

20. What is the effective resistance of the arrangement of resistors shown? (A) 1 Ω (B) 2 Ω (C) $3\frac{2}{3}$ Ω (D) $4\frac{1}{2}$ Ω (E) 9 Ω
21. The emf of a simple cell depends on: (A) The material of the electrodes; (B) The current being drawn from the cell; (C) The internal resistance of the cell; (D) The mass of the electrodes; (E) The volume of the electrolyte.

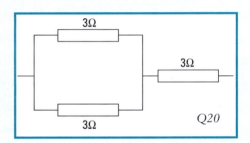

Long Questions
1. State Ohm's law. The diagram shows an arrangement of three resistors, each of value 12 ohms. Calculate the resistance of the single resistor that could be used to replace this arrangement.
2. What is the resistance of a 12 V heater with a current of 2 A?
3. Calculate (i) the current flowing through each resistor, (ii) the potential difference across each resistor, in the circuit shown in the diagram.
4. What current flows in a 20 W resistor connected to a 220 V supply?
5. A battery of emf 4·5 V and resistance 0·5 ohms is connected to a 2 ohm and a 3 ohm resistance in parallel. Calculate the current flowing through each and the potential difference across the battery.
6. The following table shows the variation of current with potential difference for a resistor. Graph the data and deduce whether or not this resistor is ohmic.

V	0	0·5	0·75	0·9	1·0	1·2
I	0	0·1	0·2	0·3	0·4	0·5

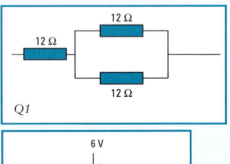
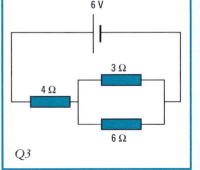

202

7. (a) Explain why certain domestic electrical appliances require an earth connection, and describe simply how this is achieved. Name one such electrical appliance.
   (b) A current of 3 A flows through an appliance when it is connected to the mains supply. State the rating of the fuse that would be most suitable for protecting the appliance. Explain why the fuse you have chosen is suitable.
8. What is the function of a fuse in a household circuit? Which of the following fuses would be suitable for a lighting circuit: 6 A, 16 A, 30 A? Draw a sketch of a household lighting circuit that contains two light bulbs, labelling the switches and the live wires.
9. Fuses and RCDs (residual current devices) are both used to cut off the current in a faulty circuit. Explain, with reasons, which you would use in a circuit for (i) an electric lawnmower and (ii) a lighting circuit.
10. A black box has two terminals. The current flowing through the box is measured for different potential differences across it.

Potential difference (V)	0	2	4	6	8	10	12
Current (A)	0	1·0	1·5	1·9	2·2	2·5	2·8

   (i) Graph these results.
   (ii) Does the conductor in the black box obey Ohm's law?
   (iii) Suggest, with reasons, what is in the box.
   (iv) What is the resistance when the voltage is (a) 5 V, (b) 10 V?
11. (a) State Ohm's law. State two factors on which the resistance of a metallic conductor depends.
   Calculate: (i) the total resistance in the circuit shown in the diagram; (ii) the current passing through the ammeter. (Take the resistance of the battery and ammeter as zero.)

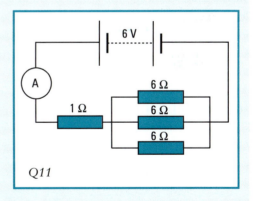

Q11

12. The wiring diagram of a domestic electric fire is shown.
   (i) Explain the purpose of wire E in this diagram.
   (ii) Why is it important, when connecting this appliance to a 3-pin fused plug, that the wire L is connected to the live pin of the plug and the wire N to the neutral pin, rather than the other way around?
   (iii) State clearly the standard colour of the insulation on each of the wires L, N and E.
   Give *one* difference between the type of wire used in lighting circuits (i.e. for light switches and bulbs) and that used in power circuits (i.e. for wall sockets etc.) in a house.

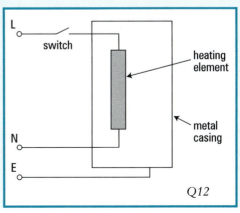

Q12

Magnetism and Magnetic Fields

CHAPTER 22

Most people know that a magnet attracts certain metals. If you put a bar magnet into a box of nails you will find that most nails stick to the two ends (the poles).

A magnet is a piece of iron, cobalt or nickel (or an alloy of these) that can attract other pieces of the same metals.

Hang a magnet from a non-metal stand and wait for it to stop swinging. It will stop with one end pointing north. Mark this end with an N. Swing the magnet slightly. When it stops the same end will be pointing north.

This end is called the north pole of the magnet. The other end is called the south pole.

When a magnet is free to swing it will settle in a north-south direction.

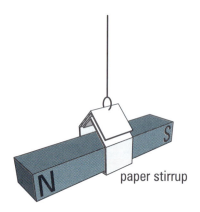
paper stirrup

A compass
Almost 2000 years ago the Chinese found that a piece of special iron ore (lodestone) suspended from a wooden pole would always come to rest pointing in the same direction. They used this as a primitive compass. A simple modern compass contains a magnetic needle which does the same thing.

compass

Forces between magnets
1. Move the two north poles close together. They push apart.
2. Move the two south poles close together. They push apart.
3. Bring a north pole close to a south pole. They move together.

Conclusion:

Like magnetic poles repel. Unlike magnetic poles attract.

Magnetic fields
If a small nail is placed too far away from a magnet, the magnet cannot move it. The magnet has an effect only within a certain space: its magnetic field.

Magnetic field: The space within which a magnetic force has an effect.

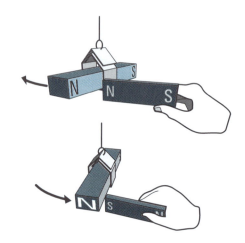

204

Magnetism and Magnetic Fields

Experiment 22.1

AIM: To plot the magnetic field round a bar magnet.

METHOD:
1. Place a bar magnet on a sheet of paper and draw its outline.
2. Place a small plotting compass close to the north pole of the magnet.
3. Place a dot in front of the needle.
4. Move the compass until the dot is behind the needle.
5. Put another dot in front of the needle.
6. Continue in this way to produce a magnetic field map.

The field lines show the direction of the magnetic force.

You could also show the magnetic field pattern as follows.
1. Place a piece of paper over the magnet.
2. Sprinkle iron filings thinly onto the paper.

Result: You will get the pattern shown in the diagram.

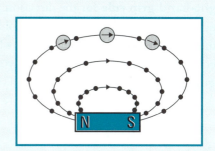

Examine your magnetic field map. You will find that the magnetic field lines seem to be coming from two points just inside each end. These points are the magnetic poles.

A magnetic field line is the path along which a north pole would move if it were free to do so.

A magnetic field line has both strength and direction at any point and so is a vector.

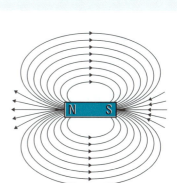

Magnetic effect of an electric current

When an electric current flows through a conductor, it has a magnetic effect.

Experiment 22.2

AIM: To demonstrate the magnetic effect of an electric current.

METHOD:
1. Close the switch. The compass needle is deflected.
2. Open the switch and change the direction of the current, by turning the battery round.

You will find that the compass needle behaves as if a bar magnet were near it.

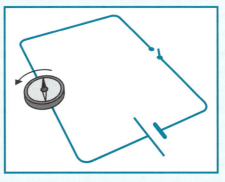

Hans Christian Oersted (Denmark) 1777–1851 discovered that there is a magnetic field around a current-carrying conductor. This discovery opened the way for the development of motors and current-measuring meters.

An electric current has a magnetic effect.

Physics Now!

Right-hand grip rule for the direction of the magnetic field around a straight current carrying conductor: Hold your right hand with your thumb pointing along the direction in which the current flows. The direction in which your fingers point (your grip) is the direction of the magnetic field lines.

Experiment 22.3

AIM: To map the magnetic field patterns of (a) a straight conductor, (b) a loop, and (c) a solenoid.

(a) **METHOD** for a straight conductor
1. Place the plotting compass on the cardboard. Close the switch. Put a mark at the tip and one at the tail of the compass needle.
2. Move the compass so that the tail of the compass points to the previous position of the tip.

Continue until the field pattern is established.

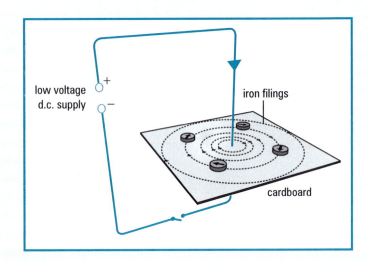

(b) **METHOD** for a loop
Repeat the procedure given in (a). The loop should contain 5–10 turns of wire. We find that the magnetic field in the centre of the coil is uniform, i.e. all the field lines are parallel.

(c) **METHOD** for a solenoid Repeat the procedure given in (a). As you can see from the diagram, the magnetic field round a solenoid is the same as the field round a bar magnet.

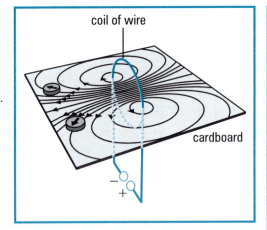

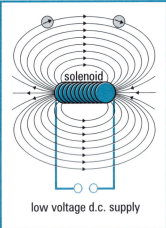

Experiment 22.4

AIM: To show that a current-carrying loop is a magnetic dipole.
METHOD:
1. Set up a loop of wire as in experiment 22.3(b). Pass a current through the loop.
2. Hang a magnet in a paper stirrup from a wooden stand.
3. Bring the magnet close to the loop. You should be able to

identify which side of the loop is behaving as a north pole
and which as a south pole.
4. If you cover the coil with a black cloth it is impossible
to tell whether a magnet or a current-carrying loop is
under the cloth.

Magnetic flux

Just as we think of electric flux as spreading out from an electric charge, we also have the concept of magnetic flux spreading out from a magnet (or the magnetic field produced by a conductor carrying a current). The total magnetic flux depends on the strength of the magnet that produces the flux. Magnetic flux (Φ) is measured in webers (Wb).

The flux spreads out through the magnetic field. Close to the magnet the magnetic flux is more concentrated. We usually need to know the strength of the magnetic field in one particular place: we need to know the **magnetic flux density**.

Magnetic flux density (B) is the magnetic flux per unit area at right angles to the direction of the magnetic field lines.

The unit of magnetic flux density is the tesla (T) or weber per square metre (Wb m^{-2}). Magnetic flux density is a vector. The direction of the magnetic flux density is the direction of the field lines through the area.

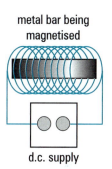

Making magnets

The most efficient way to make a magnet is to place a steel bar inside a solenoid (long coil of wire) and pass a large direct current through the wire. Modern magnets are steel alloys such as alnico, alcomax and ticonal. These contain iron, nickel, cobalt and aluminium in various proportions and produce very powerful magnets.

The earth's magnetism

The earth behaves as though a giant magnet were buried in it, with one pole close to the North Pole and the other close to the South Pole. This has a magnetic field which surrounds the earth and extends out into space. However, this picture is simplified, as the earth's magnetic field is changing slowly and is known to have reversed polarity a number of times.

The source of the earth's magnetic field cannot be permanently magnetised materials, as the earth is too hot for such materials to retain their magnetism. Neither can permanently magnetised materials move about rapidly enough to cause the known changes in the direction, strength and pattern of the earth's magnetic field.

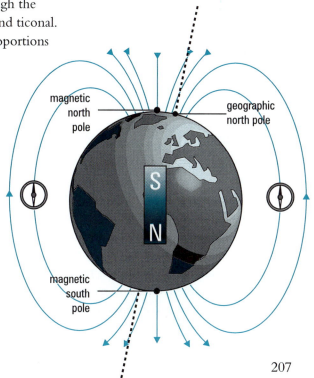

The earth's core is believed to be fluid and contains mainly iron and nickel. The flow of these generate electric currents which in turn induce a magnetic field. This theory suggests that the gravitational energy released by heavy matter sinking drives this flow. This gives a self-sustaining dynamo where the flow through the magnetic field induces an electric current which induces a magnetic field.

Magnetic field maps of the earth do not show straight lines going from north to south. The direction of these lines varies from place to place, and is rarely in line with the geographic meridian (north–south axis).

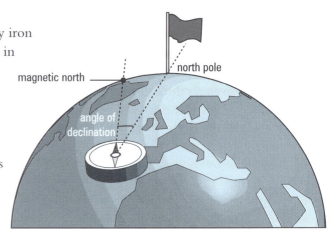

It is obvious from the diagram of the earth's magnetic field that the magnetic field lines are parallel to the ground at the equator and perpendicular to the ground at the poles. Between the equator and the poles the magnetic field lines make an angle of less than 90° with the earth (the horizontal).

The earth's magnetic flux is changing slowly with time. Exact navigation by magnetic compass depends on knowing the variations in the earth's magnetic field.

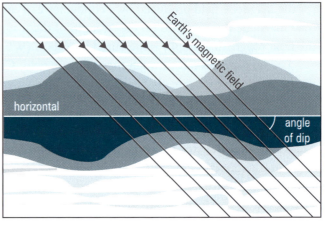

Demagnetising

Heating or hammering a magnet will destroy its magnetism. So will storing it without keepers. Often we want to demagnetise an object that has become magnetic by induction through being in contact with strong magnets. We demagnetise by passing alternating current (a.c.) through a solenoid containing the object and then slowly withdrawing the object.

Storing magnets

Magnets can lose their magnetism if they are not stored properly, as shown in the diagram. The two keepers along with the magnets form a closed system, and the magnetism is preserved.

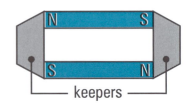

Magnetic tapes

Audio and video tapes are widely used for storing information (music, films, etc.). The plastic tape is coated with iron oxide particles. The recorder converts the information into electric pulses. The pulses magnetise the iron oxide particles into a pattern that represents the information. When the tape is replayed the pattern is converted back to electric pulses, which are then converted to sound (and pictures).

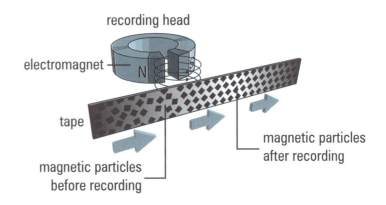

Uses of magnets

Magnets are used as catches on cupboard doors. Magnetic seals are used on fridge doors. Magnets are also used in electric motors, loudspeakers and dynamos. Electromagnets are used on cranes in scrapyards, in relays and in electric doorbells.

Summary

- A freely suspended magnet will settle in a north-south direction.
- Like magnetic poles repel; unlike magnetic poles attract.
- Iron, nickel, cobalt and steel can be magnetised.
- The space within which a magnet has an effect is called its magnetic field.
- A magnetic line of force is the path along which a north pole would move if it were free to do so.
- The right-hand grip rule for the direction of the magnetic field around a current-carrying conductor: Hold your right hand with your thumb pointing along the direction in which the current flows. The direction in which your fingers point (your grip) is the direction of the magnetic field lines.
- The right-hand grip rule for the direction of the magnetic field in the centre of a current-carrying loop or a solenoid: Point the fingers (grip) of your right hand along the direction in which the current flows through the coil or solenoid. Your thumb now points in the direction of the magnetic field.

Electromagnets are particularly useful because the magnetic field can be switched off

Short Questions

1. A freely suspended magnet comes to rest pointing _____.
2. Like magnetic poles _____; unlike magnetic poles _____.
3. The three elements _____ and some of their alloys can be magnetised.
4. What is a magnetic field line? _____
5. The space within which a magnet has an effect is called _____.
6. The core of an electromagnet is usually made of _____. Steel would not be suitable for use in the core of an electromagnet because _____.
7. If you have a music system, why should you not store cassette tapes near the speakers?
8. Which of the following is a magnetic material?
   (A) manganese, (B) brass, (C) magnesium, (D) iron, (E) copper.
9. A temporary magnet should be made from
   (A) copper, (B) steel, (C) tin, (D) aluminium, (E) iron.

10. In some cases a piece of metal can be permanently magnetised by placing it in a solenoid through which a current is passed. A permanent magnet will be obtained if (A) steel is used and direct current in the solenoid, (B) soft iron is used and alternating current in the solenoid, (C) copper is used and direct current in the solenoid, (D) soft iron is used and direct current in the solenoid, (E) copper is used and alternating current in the solenoid.

11. The diagrams represent wires carrying electric currents. In which of the following do the dotted lines correctly represent the shape of the magnetic field surrounding the wires? (A) 1 only, (B) 2 only, (C) 1 and 2 only, (D) 2 and 3 only, (E) all three.

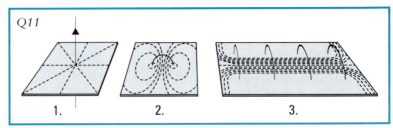

12. A bar of metal M is suspected of being a permanent magnet. Which of the following tests best show whether or not it is one? (A) Suspend M freely and make it swing. It always comes to rest in the N–S direction.
(B) Suspend M freely and make it swing. It always comes to rest in the E–W direction.
(C) Suspend M freely and make it swing. Each time it comes to rest in a different direction.
(D) Bring one end of M near another magnet. Attraction occurs. (E) Bring one end of M near a bar of copper. No attraction occurs.

13. The magnetic field pattern shown in the diagram is produced by bringing together (A) N pole and S pole, (B) N pole and N pole, (C) S pole and S pole, (D) S pole and N pole, (E) S pole and an unmagnetised iron bar.

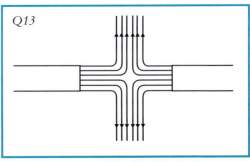

14. The diagram shows two soft iron nails on the end of a magnet. Which of the following statements about the arrangement is most likely to be correct?
(A) The free ends of the nails are N poles.
(B) The free ends of the nails are attracting one another.
(C) The nails have become permanently magnetised.
(D) The nails are induced temporary magnets.
(E) The nails will hang like this only from the S pole of the magnet.

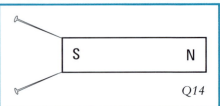

Long Questions

1. The diagram shows the magnetic field pattern of a bar magnet.
   (a) Which pole, A or B, is the north pole of the magnet?
   (b) How might the magnetic field pattern be demonstrated in the laboratory?
   (c) In what way might a magnetic field pattern be produced other than by using a magnet?

2. You are given three metal bars A, B and C, which have been painted black and look exactly alike. One of them is a magnet, another is made of steel but is not magnetised and the third one is made of copper. Describe how, using a bar magnet, you can identify each of the metal bars.

3. The diagram shows the apparatus required to make an electromagnet. Identify the items labelled A and B. Explain how the items could be used to make an electromagnet.

4. Steel car bodies are often repaired using a plastic resin filler. How could you tell if a car has been repaired in this way?

Measuring Resistances

CHAPTER 23

An ohmmeter uses Ohm's law to measure resistance. A cell of known emf is connected to an ammeter. The leads X and Y are connected across the unknown resistance R. The current passing through R is measured by the ammeter.

From Ohm's law, $R = \frac{V}{I}$. The emf of the cell is taken as V: by measuring I we get a value for R.

When the scale on the ammeter is calibrated to give a direct reading of the resistance, the instrument is known as an ohmmeter. The ohmmeter is not a very accurate way of measuring resistances. However, for many purposes it is convenient and adequate.

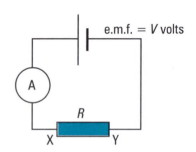

Resistance of a metallic conductor

What factors determine the resistance of a metallic conductor? The following experiments investigate how resistance varies with length, cross-sectional area and temperature of a conductor.

Experiment 23.1

AIM: To investigate how resistance varies with length.

METHOD:
1. Measure the resistance of 1 metre of wire with an ohmmeter (40 s.w.g. iron wire is suitable for this experiment).
2. Repeat with 2 m, 3 m, 4 m and 5 m of the same material.
3. Draw a graph of R against l. The graph is a straight line through the origin.

Conclusion: R is proportional to l.

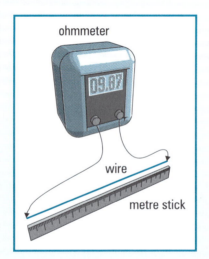

Georg Simon Ohm (Germany) 1789–1854 investigated current flow through various conductors and discovered the relationship between potential difference and current flow through a metal conductor (Ohm's law). The unit of resistance (the ohm) is named after him.

Experiment 23.2

AIM: To investigate how resistance varies with cross-sectional area.

METHOD:
1. Measure the resistance of 1 metre of 40 s.w.g. iron wire with an ohmmeter.
2. Repeat with 1 m of (i) 38 s.w.g., (ii) 36 s.w.g., (iii) 34 s.w.g., (v) 32 s.w.g. iron wire.
3. Measure the diameter of each wire using a micrometer screw gauge. The diameter is measured at a number of points along each length and the average value is taken.
4. Calculate the cross-sectional area (A) of each wire.
5. Draw a graph of R against $\frac{1}{A}$. The graph is a straight line through the origin.

Conclusion: R is inversely proportional to A.

From these two experiments we conclude that:

$$R \propto \frac{l}{A}$$

$$R = \frac{kl}{A}$$

The constant k depends on the material of the wire and is called the **resistivity (ρ)** of the metal.

$$R = \frac{\rho l}{A}$$

Rearranging: $\rho = \frac{RA}{l}$

Unit of resistivity: ohm metre = Ω m

PROBLEM

A piece of wire has a length of 68·5 cm. The diameter of the wire is 0·20 mm and its resistance is 26·4 Ω. Calculate the resistivity of the material of the wire.

$$\rho = \frac{RA}{l}$$

$$= \frac{(26\cdot4)\pi(0\cdot10 \times 10^{-3})^2}{68\cdot5 \times 10^{-2}}$$

$$= 1\cdot21 \times 10^{-6} \ \Omega \text{ m}$$

PROBLEM

The resistance of a length of wire is 19 Ω. Its diameter is 2 mm and the resistivity of the material of the wire is 1×10^{-6} Ω m. Calculate the length of the wire.

$$l = \frac{RA}{\rho} = \frac{(19)\pi(1\cdot0 \times 10^{-3})^2}{1 \times 10^{-6}} = 59.69 \text{ m}$$

PHYSICS NOW!

Mandatory experiment 23.3

AIM: To measure the resistivity of the material of a wire.

METHOD:
1. Connect the wire to a digital ohmmeter. Measure the exact length of nichrome wire between the terminals.
2. Measure the resistance of the wire with the ohmmeter.
3. Check the micrometer for zero error. Measure the diameter of the wire at a number of places with the micrometer screw gauge. Take the average of these as the diameter. Calculate the cross-sectional area of the wire. Assume that it is perfectly circular ($A = \pi r^2$).
4. Calculate the resistivity of the material from the formula:
$\rho = R\frac{A}{l}$

QUESTIONS
1. Why did you measure the diameter at a number of places?
2. Which measurement do you think was least accurate?

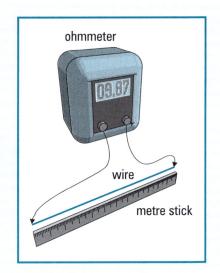

Resistance varies with temperature

The resistance of a material varies with temperature. For most metals the resistance increases with temperature. For semiconductors such as silicon and germanium, the resistance decreases with temperature. The resistance of alloys such as magnanin does not vary appreciably with temperature.

Mandatory experiment 23.4

AIM: To investigate how the resistance of a metallic conductor varies with temperature.

METHOD:
1. Set up the apparatus as shown.
2. Heat the water slowly to raise the temperature to about 90°C.
3. Measure the resistance of the wire with the digital ohmmeter.
4. Note the temperature.
5. Measure the resistance at temperature intervals of 10°C as the temperature of the wire resistor falls. Note the temperature.
6. Plot a graph of R against θ. Estimate from this graph what value the resistance has at 0°C.

QUESTION
Why is it better to measure the resistance and temperature as the temperature falls?

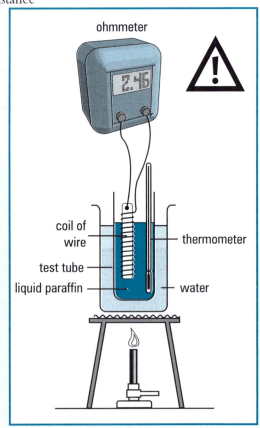

Measuring Resistances

The resistance of a metallic conductor varies directly with temperature

Thermistors

A thermistor is a semiconductor device whose resistance changes greatly with a change in temperature. Thermistors are usually metal oxides of copper, nickel or cobalt. The resistance changes from about 400 Ω at room temperature to about 40 Ω when hot.

Thermistors are used as temperature sensors and thermometers. Thermistors are also connected in series with high powered light bulbs to protect them against the large currents that flow when they are switched on. This is because the resistance of a bulb is low when it is cold. The resistance of the bulb increases as it heats up, while the thermistor resistance decreases.

Thermistors made of barium titanate differ from other types in that their resistance increases when the temperature rises. They are used to protect electric circuits and motors from overheating.

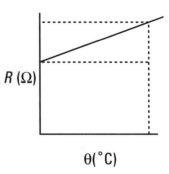

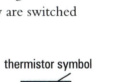
thermistor symbol

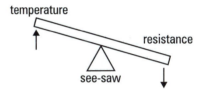
see-saw

A thermistor is a semiconductor device whose resistance changes greatly with temperature.

Mandatory experiment 23.5

AIM: To investigate how the resistance of a thermistor varies with temperature.

Method:
1. Set up the apparatus as shown.
2. Heat the water slowly to raise the temperature to about 90°C.
3. Measure the resistance of the thermistor with the digital ohmmeter.
4. Note the temperature.
5. Measure the resistance at temperature intervals of 10°C as the temperature of the thermistor falls. Note the temperature of the water each time.
6. Plot a graph of R against θ. You can now find the temperature by measuring the resistance of the thermistor. From the graph you can find the temperature that corresponds to this resistance.

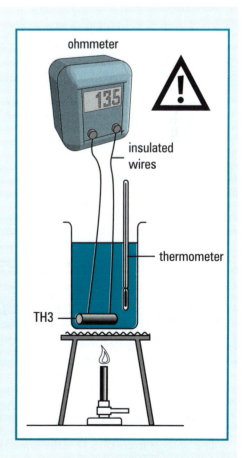

Questions
Thermistors are used as heat sensors: how do you think this is done? List two possible sources of error in this experiment.

215

PHYSICS NOW!

Light-dependent resistor (LDR)

A light-dependent resistor (LDR) is a semiconductor device whose resistance changes with the amount of light falling on it. This is because the light 'frees' some electrons in the cadmium sulphide (CdS) semiconductor. This allows a greater current to flow (it reduces its resistance). The resistance of the CdS light-dependent resistor is about 10 MΩ in the dark and falls to about 1 kΩ in normal daylight. In intense light it falls to about 100 Ω.

CdS light-dependent resistors are used in many camera lightmeters as they are sensitive even at low light intensities. They are also used in circuits that automatically switch on (or off) lights, light sensors, burglar alarms, etc.

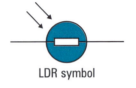
LDR symbol

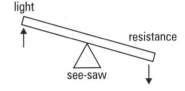
see-saw

A light-dependent resistor is a semiconductor whose resistance changes with the amount of light falling on it.

Experiment 23.6

AIM: To demonstrate that the resistance of an LDR varies with the light.

METHOD:
1. Set up the circuit as shown in the diagram.
2. Cover the LDR with your finger and switch on the circuit. The bulb does not light.
3. Remove your finger. Does the bulb light?
4. Bring a desk lamp close to the LDR. Does the bulb light now?

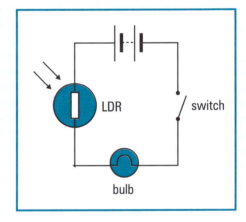

Wheatstone bridge

We use a Wheatstone bridge circuit when we need to measure resistance accurately. This is a method of measuring resistance by comparing an unknown resistance with a known standard resistance. It is done by balancing a network of four resistors so that no current flows through the galvanometer from one arm of the bridge to the other. This means that the accuracy of the galvanometer does not matter: it is used only to indicate whether current is flowing or not.

When the Wheatstone bridge is balanced, no current flows through the galvanometer. This means that there is no potential difference between B and C. B is at the same potential as C.

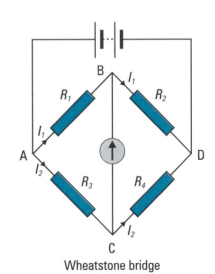
Wheatstone bridge

The voltage from A to B is the same as the voltage from A to C.

$\therefore I_1 R_1 = I_2 R_3$

The voltage from B to D is the same as the voltage from C to D.

$\therefore I_1 R_2 = I_2 R_4$

Dividing, we get

$$\frac{I_1 R_1}{I_1 R_2} = \frac{I_2 R_3}{I_2 R_4}$$

$$\frac{R_1}{R_2} = \frac{R_3}{R_4}$$

The ratio of resistances R_1 and R_2 is usually a power of ten (10, 100, etc.). R_3 is a variable resistance which can be set at known values. R_4 is the resistance being measured.

PROBLEM
A Wheatstone bridge circuit is balanced when $R_1 = 1\ \Omega$, $R_2 = 1000\ \Omega$ and $R_3 = 694\ \Omega$. What is the resistance of the fourth resistor?

$$\frac{R_1}{R_2} = \frac{R_3}{R_4}$$

$$\frac{1}{1000} = \frac{694}{X}$$

$X = 694{,}000 = 694\ k\Omega$

PROBLEM
In a Wheatstone bridge circuit $R_1 = 1000\ \Omega$, $R_2 = 1\ \Omega$, $R_3 = 248\ \Omega$ and $R_4 = 0{\cdot}5\ \Omega$. Is the bridge balanced?

$$\frac{R_1}{R_2} = \frac{R_3}{R_4}$$

$$\frac{1000}{1} = \frac{248}{X}$$

$1000X = 248$
$X = 0{\cdot}248\ \Omega$
$X \neq R_4$
The bridge is not balanced.

Uses of the Wheatstone bridge

When a Wheatstone bridge circuit is unbalanced, the current flowing through the galvanometer depends on how out-of-balance the bridge is.

STRAIN GAUGES
Engineers replace R_3 and R_4 in a Wheatstone bridge with strain gauges. The strain gauge consists of a length of fine resistance wire. Any strain increases the length of the wire (and decreases its cross-sectional area), and so increases its resistance. Any increase in current indicates a difference in strain between the two locations of the gauge.

*Charles Wheatstone
(England) 1802–1875
invented the electric telegraph
and developed the rheostat
and the Wheatstone bridge.
He also invented the
concertina.*

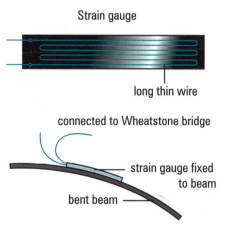

PHYSICS NOW!

FIRE ALARM

A pair of resistances can also be replaced by thermistors. The Wheatstone bridge remains balanced with normal fluctuations in temperature that affect both. A fire affects the thermistor nearer the fire far more than the other. This unbalances the Wheatstone bridge and sets off an alarm.

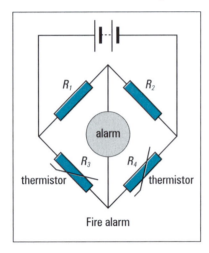

Fire alarm

THERMOSTAT

The Wheatstone bridge circuit can also be used to maintain a steady temperature in an oven. Resistor R_4 is set to a value that corresponds to a particular oven temperature. The circuit is now unbalanced and the potential difference across the bridge switches on the heating element. When R_3 reaches the set temperature ($R_4 = R_3$), there is no p.d. across the bridge and the element switches off.

FAIL SAFE DEVICE

A balanced Wheatstone bridge can be used as a fail safe device. When thermistor R_3 is hot (the pilot flame is on in a boiler), the bridge is balanced. If the pilot flame goes out the thermistor goes cold, its resistance increases and the bridge is now unbalanced. The p.d. across the bridge operates a solenoid and shuts off the fuel.

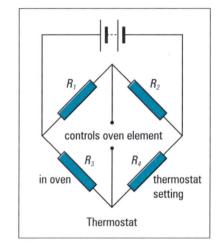

Thermostat

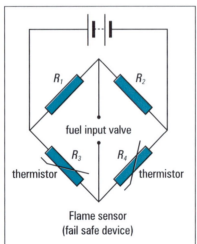

Flame sensor
(fail safe device)

Measuring Resistances

METRE BRIDGE

The metre bridge is a variation of the Wheatstone Bridge. A metre length of uniform resistance wire is divided into two resistances R_1 and R_2 by the slider which makes contact with the wire.

Since the resistance is uniform R_1 is proportional to the length l_1 and R_2 is proportional to l_2.

Applying the equation for the Wheatstone Bridge.

$$\frac{R_1}{R_2} = \frac{R_3}{R_4}$$

but

$$\frac{R_1}{R_2} = \frac{l_1}{l_2}$$

so that $R_4 = \left(\dfrac{l_2}{l_1}\right) R_3$

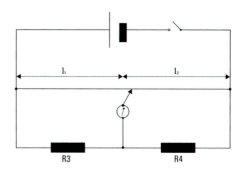

The metre bridge is most sensitive when resistance R_3 is adjusted to get a balance near the centre of the wire.

The metre bridge can measure resistances more accurately than an ohmmeter.

Potential divider

The voltage of our power supply is usually fixed at 220 V in the household, at 12 V in the car and at 3 V in a small radio. The voltage required to operate different pieces of equipment is often very different from the supply voltage. The different components inside the equipment may also need different voltages. One way in which we can get a variety of different voltages from a single voltage supply is by using a potential divider.

A potential divider is connected to a circuit as shown in the diagram. When a 12 V supply is connected across the two resistors, the same current flows through each resistor. The potential difference (voltage) across each resistor is proportional to its resistance (I is the same in both cases). The potential difference is therefore divided in the same proportion as the two resistors ($V = I.R$).

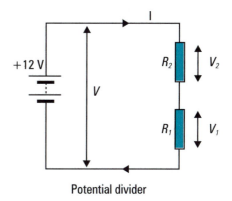

Potential divider

PROBLEM

Calculate the potential difference (voltage) across each of the resistors shown in the diagram. The resistors are in series.

Total resistance $= 3 + 6 = 9\ \Omega$

Current flowing through the circuit:
$I = \dfrac{V}{R} = \dfrac{12}{9} = \dfrac{4}{3}$ A

p.d. across 3 resistor: $V = IR = \dfrac{4}{3} \times 3 = 4$ V

p.d. across 6 resistor: $V = IR = \dfrac{4}{3} \times 6 = 8$ V

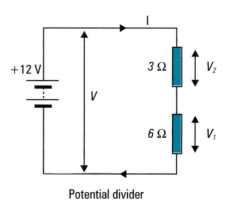

Potential divider

Clearly the supply voltage was divided between the two resistors in proportion to their resistances.

Physics Now!

When the supply voltage is connected across a resistor with a sliding contact between the two terminals, the voltage can be altered easily by moving the sliding contact. The greater voltage is across the larger resistance. This type of potentiometer (potential divider) is often used to adjust voltages in electronic equipment.

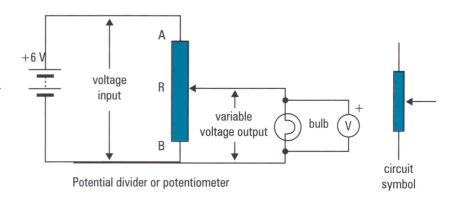

Potential divider or potentiometer · circuit symbol

Although the rheostat and the potential divider look alike, and frequently the same device can be connected to one circuit as a rheostat and to another circuit as a potential divider, it is important to realise that the principle of operation is not the same.

Summary

- The resistance of a metallic conductor varies directly with temperature.
- A thermistor is a semiconductor device whose resistance changes greatly with temperature.
- The resistance of a thermistor falls sharply with increasing temperature.
- A light-dependent resistor is a semiconductor whose resistance changes with the amount of light falling on it.

Short Questions

1. The resistance of a metallic conductor _____ temperature.
2. The resistance of a thermistor _____ with increasing temperature.
3. Resistivity is _____.
4. The resistance of a piece of uniform copper wire is
    (A) proportional to its length and to its diameter
    (B) proportional to its length and to its diameter squared
    (C) proportional to its length and inversely proportional to its diameter squared
    (D) proportional to its length and inversely proportional to its diameter
    (E) proportional to its length and inversely proportional to the square root of its diameter.
5. A potentiometer is used to give a variable _____ supply.
6. The voltage of a cell when no current is flowing is _____.

7. The resistance of a uniform wire is proportional to _____ and inversely proportional to _____.
8. A piece of wire has a resistance of 2 Ω. What is the resistance of a piece of wire of the same material, four times the length and half the diameter of the first?
9. You are given some 1 Ω, 2 Ω and 3 Ω resistors and a 12 V supply. How would you connect the resistors to give a 5 V supply for an electronic circuit?
10. What happens to the resistance of an LDR as the light falling on it increases in intensity?

Long Questions

1. In an experiment to measure the resistivity of nichrome, the following readings were obtained for a wire sample.

   Resistance of wire (Ω):   6

   Length of wire (cm):   78·4

   Micrometer readings (mm): 0·45   0·44   0·46   0·44   0·43

   (a) If the reading on the micrometer when it was fully closed was 0.02 mm, calculate the average diameter of the wire.
   (b) Give two precautions that should have been taken when measuring the length of the wire.
   (c) Use the data above to calculate the resistivity of nichrome.
   (d) How can you tell from the data above that the resistance measurement is the least precise?
   (e) Why should the current be kept low when measuring the resistance of the wire?

2. In an experiment to investigate the variation of the resistance of a metallic conductor with temperature, the resistance of a coil of wire was measured at a number of different temperatures.
   (a) Draw a circuit diagram for the experiment, labelling each component.
   (b) How can the temperature of the metallic conductor be varied in the experiment?
   (c) Sketch the type of graph you would expect to obtain from the experiment.

3. The following is part of a student's report of an experiment to measure the resistivity of nichrome.
   'The length and resistance of the wire were measured. The diameter of the wire was found at different points along its length.'

(i) Name the instrument which would have been used to measure the diameter of the wire.

(ii) Give the steps involved in finding the length of the wire.

(iii) The four values obtained for the diameter of the wire were: 1.8×10^{-4} m; 1.9×10^{-4} m; 1.7×10^{-4} m; 2.0×10^{-4} m. From these values calculate an average value for the diameter of the wire.

(iv) The length of the wire, l, was found to be 1.26 m and the resistance of the wire, R, was found to be 52.4 Ω. Use the equation $R = \frac{\rho l}{A}$ to calculate a value for the resistivity of nichrome.

4. Which of the following graphs is of a conductor that conforms with Ohm's law?

5. Two wires are made of the same metal. A is 20 times as long as B and has one-third of the cross-sectional area. If the resistance of B is 1 ohm, calculate the resistance of A.

6. A transatlantic cable 3,000 km long consists of seven strands of copper wire, each of cross-sectional area 2 mm². Calculate the resistance of the cable. (Resistivity of copper is 1.7×10^{-8} Ω m.)

7. Calculate the resistance of a wire of length 60 m, diameter 2 mm and resistivity 1.0×10^{-6} Ω m.

8. The following table shows how the resistance of a wire varied with temperature.

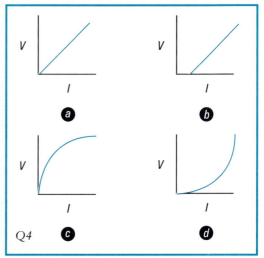

Q4

Temperature (°C)	12	22	32	42	52	62	72	82
Resistance (Ω)	3·8	4·1	4·4	4·8	5·0	5·3	5·7	6·0

(a) Graph the resistance against the temperature.

(b) Use the graph to estimate the resistance of the wire at 20°C.

(c) What is the temperature of the wire when the ohmmeter reading is 4·2 Ω?

9. The resistance of a wire is 0·80 ohms. Its length is 21 cm and its diameter is 4 mm. Calculate the resistivity of the material.

10. PVC has a resistivity of the order of 10^{13} Ω m. What is the resistance of a PVC rod of length 20 cm and radius 10 mm?

11. The apparatus shown in the diagram was used in an experiment to investigate how the resistance of a length of wire varied with temperature.

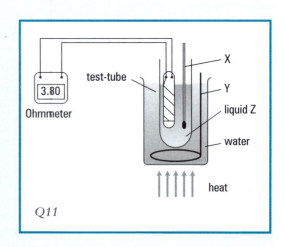

Q11

(i) Name the part labelled X. What is measured with X?
(ii) Name the part labelled Y.
(iii) Name a liquid which could be used as the liquid Z.
(iv) The table below shows how the resistance of the wire varied with temperature.

Temperature in °C	20	40	60	80	100
Resistance in ohms	3.5	4.3	5.0	5.9	6.8

Use the data in the table to draw a graph of resistance against temperature.
Use the graph to estimate the temperature of the wire when the reading on the ohmmeter is as shown in the diagram.

12. A 10 Ω resistor consists of a piece of wire of uniform cross-sectional area and of length 65 cm. If the resistivity of the material of the wire is $1\cdot3 \times 10^{-6}$ Ω m, what is the diameter of the wire?

The Heating and Chemical Effects of an Electric Current

CHAPTER 24

Heating effect

We know that electricity has a heating effect from our everyday experience of toasters, cookers, hair dryers, electric fires and electric kettles. Most electrical appliances produce some heat. Computers, hi-fi systems and light bulbs all heat up when they are on.

In 1841, Joule investigated the heating effect of an electric current. He found that the heat produced in a fixed time for a given resistance is proportional to the current squared:

$H \propto I^2$

Joule's law: The heat produced in a fixed time for a given resistance is proportional to the current squared.

Joule also experimented with different resistances (he used different lengths of similar wire), and found that the heat produced in a given time for a fixed current is proportional to the resistance

$H \propto R$

Joule also found that the heat produced by a fixed current in a given heating coil is proportional to the time that the current flows.

$H \propto t$

Combining all three results gives: heat produced equals current squared by resistance by time

$H = I^2Rt$

We could have derived this equation from our definition of the volt.

$\frac{W}{Q} = V \Rightarrow W = Q.V$

but $Q = It$ and $V = IR$

Substituting, $W = It.IR = I^2Rt$

The work done in this case shows as heat.

James Prescott Joule (England) 1818–1889 experimented with heating effects of mechanical and electrical changes. He investigated heating effects of currents flowing through various resistors, and established the relationship known as Joule's law. The unit of energy (the joule) is named after him.

THE HEATING AND CHEMICAL EFFECTS OF AN ELECTRIC CURRENT

Power

The energy produced or consumed per second is known as the power. The unit of power is the watt (W).

$$\text{power} = \frac{\text{energy}}{\text{seconds}}$$

$$\frac{J}{t} = \frac{I^2 Rt}{t} = I^2 R = V.I$$

watts = volts × amps

$$P = V.I$$

PROBLEM

A heating element is rated at 25 W and has a resistance of 100 Ω. What is the maximum current that can safely be passed through this heater? What is the voltage across the resistance?

$$P = V.I = I^2 R$$
$$I^2 = \frac{P}{R} = \frac{25}{100} = \frac{1}{4}$$
$$I = \frac{1}{2} \text{ A}$$
$$V = I.R = \frac{1}{2}.100 = 50 \text{ V}$$

PROBLEM

The supply cables to a cooker can safely carry 60 A. The cooker is rated as 12 kW at 220 V. Can the cables carry the current safely when fully switched on?

$$P = V.I$$
$$12{,}000 = 220 I$$
$$I = \frac{12{,}000}{220} = 54 \cdot 5 \text{ A}$$

The cables can carry this current safely.

PROBLEM

An electric kettle holds 1 kg of water when full. It is rated as 1200 W at 220 V. How long does the full kettle take to come to the boil if the tap water is at 20°C? (The boiling point of water is 100°C and its specific heat capacity is 4,200 J kg^{-1} K^{-1}.)

electrical energy = VIt = $P.t$

heat = $m.c.\Delta\theta$ = electrical energy

$$P.t = m.c.\Delta\theta$$
$$1200 t = (1)(4{,}200)(80)$$
$$t = 280 \text{ s}$$

PHYSICS NOW!

Mandatory experiment 24.1
AIM: To verify Joule's law.
METHOD:
1. Set up the apparatus as shown in the diagram.
2. Add enough water to cover the heating element in the calorimeter. Note the temperature of the water.
3. Pass a current of 0·5 A through the heating coil. Keep the current constant by adjusting the rheostat.
4. Note the temperature rise after 5 minutes.
5. Repeat by passing the currents of 1 A, 1·5 A, 2 A, 2·5 A, 3 A successively through the heating coil for 5 minutes. Note the temperature rise for each current.
   The heat energy produced is the mass multiplied by specific heat capacity by rise in temperature ($H = m.c.\Delta\theta$). As the mass and specific heat capacity are constant, $H \propto \Delta\theta$.
6. Draw a graph of the temperature rise $\Delta\theta$ against I^2 (the square of the current). The result is a straight line through the origin.

Conclusion: The heat produced in a given time for a fixed resistance is proportional to the current squared.

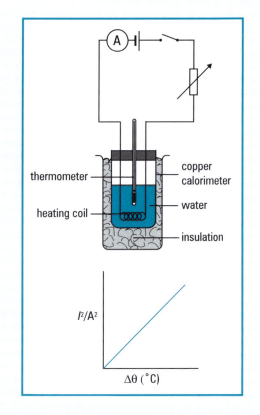

QUESTIONS
1. Why is it not necessary to know the mass of the water used?
2. Why would the current flowing change?
3. Give two possible sources of error in this experiment.

Why does the ESB transfer energy at a high voltage?

Electrical energy can be transferred from one place to another in either of two ways:
(a) at high voltage and consequently low current
(b) at low voltage and high current.

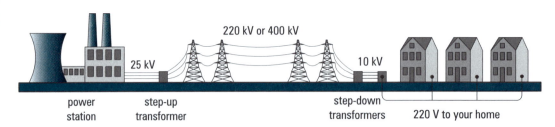

national grid system

The transmission lines have the same resistance either way.
   Why, then, does the ESB transfer electrical energy at high voltage? Heat loss due to current flowing through the cables, by Joule's law, depends on the current squared and the resistance. The resistance is constant, so the heat loss depends on the square of the current. To minimise heat loss it makes sense to keep the current low. This can be done only by transmission at high voltage. The ESB high-tension

(high-voltage) transmission lines are 400 kV, 220 kV, 110 kV, 38 kV and 10 kV. The higher voltages are used for long distances.

The kilowatt hour

A one kilowatt electric heater uses 1,000 joules each second. It is clear from this that the joule is a fairly small unit. The unit used by the ESB to measure the amount of electrical energy you use is the kilowatt hour. A one kilowatt appliance left on for one hour uses one kilowatt hour of electrical energy.

kilowatt hours = kilowatts × hours

Problem

How much does it cost to run a 2 kW electric fire for three hours if one unit (kilowatt hour) costs 8·0p?

kilowatt hours = kilowatts × hours
2 kilowatts × 3 hours = 6 kilowatt hours
6 units @ 8·0p = 48p

Problem

You are going away on holidays and think of leaving on a 25 W light. If you are away for 7 days, how much will this cost if one unit costs 8·0p?

$25 \text{ W} = \frac{25}{1000} = 0·025 \text{ kW}$
0·025 kilowatts × (7 × 24) hours = 4·2 kilowatt hours
4·2 units @ 8·0p = 33·6p

Chemical effect: electrolysis

We know that electricity can flow through salt solutions. The electric current is carried through the solution by the movement of ions. All metal salts have positive metal ions; the other part of the salt is the negative ion, e.g. sulphate ions, chloride ions, hydroxyl ions. Hydrogen ions are positive.

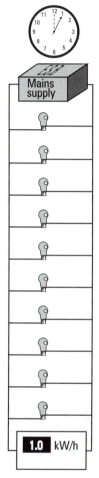

ten 100 watt light bulbs (one kilowatt) lighting for one hour use one kilowatt/hour (or unit) of electrical energy

Substance in solution	Positive ion	Negative ion
Copper sulphate	Copper [Cu^{2+}]	Sulphate [SO_4^{2-}]
Sodium chloride	Sodium [Na^+]	Chloride [Cl^-]
Potassium hydroxide	Potassium [K^+]	Hydroxyl [OH^-]
Water	Hydrogen [H^+]	Hydroxyl [OH^-]

The breaking up of a substance in solution to free positive and negative ions is called **dissociation**.

An electrolyte is a substance that, molten or in solution, conducts electricity by the movement of ions.

Physics Now!

Electrolysis is the process of causing chemical changes by passing an electric current through an electrolyte.

Experiment 24.2

AIM: To demonstrate electrolysis.

METHOD:
1. Clean a piece of steel with emery paper. Wash with methylated spirits to remove any grease. Rinse in distilled water.
2. Place the steel in a solution of copper sulphate. Connect to the negative pole of the battery.
3. Place a copper plate in solution. Connect to the positive pole of the battery.
4. Pass a current of 0·5 A through the circuit for about 15 minutes.
5. Examine the steel.

Result: The steel has a coating of copper on it.

6. Now connect the steel to the positive pole of the battery and the copper to the negative pole. Pass the same current for the same time.

Result: The copper plating on the steel has been removed.

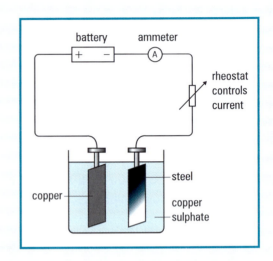

Copper is plated onto the steel surface only when it is connected to the negative pole of the battery. This is true of all other metals also. The metal plate connected to the negative pole of the battery is the **cathode**. The plate connected to the positive pole is the **anode**. Any arrangement of cathode, anode and electrolyte is known as a **voltameter**.

The maximum current suitable for the electrolysis experiment can be calculated by multiplying the surface area of the cathode by $\frac{1}{50}$. A current of about half the maximum value is usually used. A bigger current than this would produce a soft spongy copper that would not stick to the steel.

COMMERCIAL USES OF ELECTROLYSIS

1. **Electrolytic refining of metals.** Electrolytically produced copper is purer than copper smelted in the normal reduction process. Sodium, aluminium and other metals are produced by electrolysis of molten salts of the metal.
2. **Electroplating.** This improves the appearance of base (cheaper) metals, e.g. silver plating of cutlery. It also helps prevent corrosion, e.g. chromium plating of steel parts of cars.
3. Electrolysis is used to make thin metal printing plates.

Electrolytes obey Ohm's law when precautions are taken to exclude any back emfs.

The Heating and Chemical Effects of an Electric Current

CuSO₄ with copper electrodes: This obeys Ohm's law as the copper ions discharged at the cathode are immediately replaced by copper ions entering the solution at the anode.

CuSO₄ with inert (platinum) electrodes: This does not obey Ohm's law, as oxygen is produced at the anode. The oxygen and the platinum electrode produce a 'back emf' which must be overcome before current will flow.

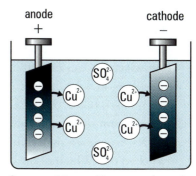

Copper sulphate with copper electrodes

Summary
- Joule's law: The heat produced in a fixed time for a given resistance is proportional to the current squared.
- Power: The energy produced or consumed per second.
- watts = volts × amperes
- Electricity is transmitted at high voltage to reduce energy losses due to heat.
- Kilowatt hours equal kilowatts multiplied by hours.
- An electrolyte is a substance that when molten or in solution conducts electricity by the movement of ions.
- Electrolysis is the process of causing a chemical reaction by passing an electric current through an electrolyte.

Short Questions
1. State Joule's law.
   _____
2. A kilowatt hour is _____.
3. Power is measured in _____.
4. Electricity is transmitted at _____ voltage to reduce _____ losses.
5. An electric oven is rated at 12,000 W for use on a 240 V supply. Select from the following ratings the minimum current rating of supply cable for the oven to operate safely.
   (A) 15 A, (B) 30 A, (C) 45 A, (D) 60 A, (E) 120 A.
6. A car headlamp bulb is marked 12 V, 48 W.
   This indicates that when
   (A) a voltage of 12 V is applied, a current of $\frac{1}{4}$ A flows
   (B) a power of 48 W is developed, the resistance is 4 ohms
   (C) a voltage of 12 V is applied, the resistance is 4 ohms
   (D) a voltage of 12 V is applied, energy is used at a rate of 48 J s^{-1}
   (E) a current of $\frac{1}{4}$ A flows, 48 W of power is used.
7. An electric heater is rated 2,000 W, 240 V and is run from a three-pin plug fitted with a fuse. The most suitable fuse rating is: (A) 1 A, (B) 2 A, (C) 5 A, (D) 7 A, (E) 10 A.
8. The cost of running a 3 kW heater and a 200 W lamp for 2 hours at 4p per unit is: (A) 25·6p, (B) 75p, (C) 200p, (D) 400p, (E) 600p.

229

9. When a current of 3 A flows for 2 seconds from one point to another in an electric circuit, 24 joules of energy is changed from electrical to some other form. What is the potential difference, in volts, between the two points in the circuit?
(A) 3, (B) 4, (C) 6, (D) 8, (E) 12.

10. The diagram shows a circuit containing two equal resistors, R_1 and R_2, which are switched on at S for a short time and then switched off. Which of the following statements is correct?
(A) Neither resistor heats up.
(B) No heat is generated in R_2 because the current is all used in heating R_1.
(C) The heat generated in R_1 is greater than that in R_2, because the current gets there first.
(D) The heat generated in each resistor is the same.
(E) The heat generated in R_2 is greater than that in R_1, because the current is stopped more easily in the second resistor.

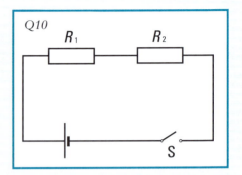

11. What is an electrolyte?
12. Electrolysis is _____.
13. When a current is passed through copper (II) sulphate solution, using copper electrodes, copper is
(A) removed from the anode and deposited on the cathode
(B) removed from the cathode and deposited as sludge
(C) removed from the cathode and deposited on the anode
(D) removed from the solution and deposited as sludge
(E) removed from the solution and deposited on both the anode and the cathode.
14. A fine coating of silver is put on cutlery by _____.
15. A constant current of 4.0 A flows through a 5Ω resistor for 1.5 minutes. The heat produced in the resistor is:
(A) 30 J (B) 120 J (C) 150 J (D) 1800 J (E) 7200 J
16. The relationship $P \div I^2$ is an expression for the _____ in a resistor.
17. The current flowing in the filament of a light bulb when it is first switched on is greater than it is a short time later. Explain.
18. When transmitting electrical energy through metal cables, why is it more economical to use high voltages?

Long Questions
1. Joule's law was verified experimentally by passing a current I through a heating coil in a calorimeter containing water and determining the rise in temperature for a series of values of I. The time for which the current flowed in each case was 3 minutes. The following results were obtained.

I (A)	0·5	1·0	1·5	2·0	2·5	3·0	3·5
Δθ (°C)	1·0	4·0	6·4	14·0	21·6	29·4	40·0

(a) Draw a suitable graph and explain how this verifies Joule's law.

(b) How would the accuracy of the experiment have been affected if the current flowed for a shorter time in each case?

(c) Given that the mass of water in the calorimeter was 80 g in each case and assuming that all the electrical energy supplied was absorbed by the water as heat, use the graph to determine the resistance of the heating coil. (Specific heat capacity of water = $4·18 \times 10^3$ J kg^{-1} K^{-1}.)

2. A cell of emf 5 volts passes a steady current of 0·1 amps for 40 minutes. What energy is stored in the cell?

3. A 10 ohm resistor dissipates (loses) 22·5 watts as heat. Calculate (a) the current, (b) the potential difference across the resistor.

4. An 8 kilowatt electric cooker is connected to a 220 volt mains. Calculate the maximum current flowing through the supply cables.

5. A 50 ohm resistor can safely pass a current of 0·1 amp. Calculate the power rating of the resistor.

6. A bulb is marked 100 watts, 240 volts. This bulb lasts longer when operated at 220 volts. Suggest a reason for this.

7. An electric heater is rated at 6 kilowatts at 220 volts. Calculate the mass of water that can be raised from 10°C to 100°C in five minutes.

8. A 550 watt toaster passes a current of 5 amps. What is the resistance of the heating element?

9. A circuit consists of a battery of emf 6·0 V and a resistor of resistance 8 Ω. If 80% of the work done by the battery appears as heat in the resistor, what is the potential difference across the resistor? Calculate (i) the current flowing in the circuit, and (ii) the rate at which heat is produced in the resistor.

10. Explain why it is more economical to transmit electrical energy at high voltages. Why is a.c. more suitable for this purpose than d.c?

    Discuss the safety features that are included in domestic circuits.

11. How do you think an electric blanket works? What type of wire would you expect to find in a blanket? Safety instructions warn against allowing any folds in the blanket. Why is this?

12. Factories producing aluminium are usually sited close to a power station. What reason connected with the production process can you give for this? Name two other metals that are refined in the same way as aluminium.

The Force on a Current-carrying Conductor in a Magnetic Field

CHAPTER 25

You have shown that a conductor carrying a current produces a magnetic field around it. You also know that magnets can attract and repel each other. Can a magnet affect a current-carrying conductor? The following experiment will give you the answer.

Experiment 25.1

AIM: to demonstrate that there is a force on a current-carrying conductor in a magnetic field.

METHOD:
1. Place two thick copper rails horizontally, about 4 cm apart. Lightly rub with emery paper to ensure a good connection.
2. Place a short strip of light copper wire, about 5 cm long, on the horizontal rails.
3. Put the horseshoe magnet over the wires, so that the wire is at right angles to the magnetic field.
4. Pass a current of 5 A through the wire. Note the direction in which the wire moves.
5. Reverse the direction of the current and repeat.
6. Reverse the direction of the magnetic field (turn the magnet the other way) and repeat.

Conclusions: (i) A current-carrying conductor in a magnetic field experiences a force; (ii) the direction of this force depends on the direction of the current and the direction of the magnetic field.

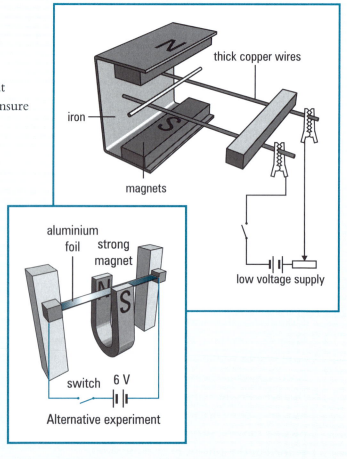

Alternative experiment

The Force on a Current-carrying Conductor in a Magnetic Field

Left-hand motor rule: Put the forefinger, thumb and centre finger of your left hand at right angles to each other. Point your **F**orefinger along the direction of the magnetic **F**ield and your **C**entre finger along the direction of the **C**urrent. Your **T**humb points in the direction of the **T**hrust (force).

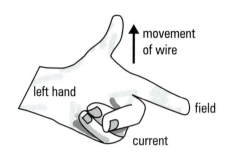

We can explain the force on a current-carrying conductor in a magnetic field as being caused by the interaction of the magnetic field of the magnet and the magnetic field caused by the current. Experiments can be conducted to measure this force using
  (i) different currents through the conductor
  (ii) conductors of different lengths
  (iii) magnets of different strengths.
These experiments show that:

$$F \propto I$$
$$F \propto l$$
$$F \propto B$$

Combining these, we get $F \propto IlB$. Using SI units (newton, ampere, metre and tesla), we get the equation

$F = IlB$

where I is the current, l is the length of the conductor in the magnetic field and B is the magnetic flux density through the conductor at right angles.

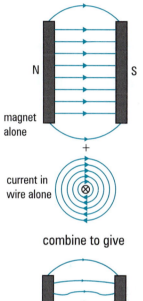

Problem
A current of 1 A flows through a wire 0·10 m long at right angles to a magnetic field of magnetic flux density 0·25 tesla. What is the force on the wire?

$$F = IlB$$
$$= (1)(0·10)(0·25) = 0·025 \text{ N}$$

Problem
A straight horizontal wire of length 0·20 m carrying a current of 10 A is perpendicular to a magnetic field of flux density 0·60 T. What force is acting on the wire?

$$F = IlB$$
$$= (10)(0·20)(0·60)$$
$$= 1·2 \text{ N}$$

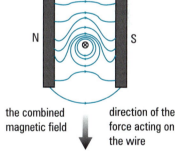

Problem
A current flowing through a conductor at right angles to a magnetic field experiences a force of 1·5 N. If the wire is 20 cm long and carries a current of 5 A, what is the strength of the magnetic field?

$$F = IlB$$
$$B = \frac{F}{Il} = \frac{1·5}{(0.20)(5)} = 1·5 \text{ T}$$

Physics Now!

Moving-coil loudspeakers, electric motors and moving-coil meters all work on the principle that **there is a force on a current-carrying conductor in a magnetic field**. They all have coils of wire carrying current in a magnetic field.

Conductor not perpendicular to magnetic field
It is only the component of the magnetic field perpendicular to the current that produces a force on the conductor. This component is $B \sin \theta$, where θ is the angle between the conductor and the magnetic field lines.

When the magnetic field lines lie along the direction of the conductor, $\theta = 0$, so $B \sin \theta = 0$. There is no force on the conductor. When the magnetic field is perpendicular to the conductor, $\theta = 90°$, so $B \sin \theta = B$. The force on the conductor is at its maximum.

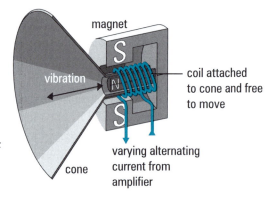

Magnetic flux density
The force on a current-carrying conductor in a magnetic field can be used to measure the strength of the magnetic field: the magnetic flux density.

$$F = IlB$$

so that the magnetic flux density $B = \frac{F}{Il}$ (the force acting per unit current length).

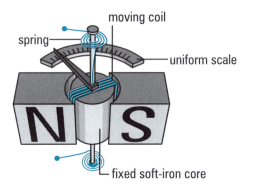

The magnetic flux density (B) is one tesla when a current of one ampere flowing through a conductor of length one metre in a magnetic field produces a force of one newton.

Force on a moving charge in a magnetic field
The force on a conductor in a magnetic field is

$$F = IlB$$

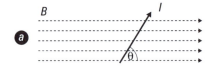

The current flowing through the conductor is made up of n individual charges of q coulombs moving with an average velocity of v m s^{-1}. The total charge $Q = nq$.

$$F = IlB, \quad \text{but } I = \frac{Q}{t} \text{ where } Q \text{ is the total charge}$$

$$F = \frac{QlB}{t}, \text{ but } Q = nq$$

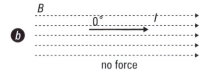

$$F = \frac{nqlB}{t}, \text{ but } \frac{l}{t} = v, \text{ the average velocity of the charges}$$

$$F = nqvB$$

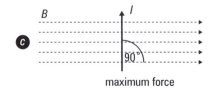

This is the force on n charges; the force on a single charge $F = qvB$.

Problem
An electron, charge $1 \cdot 6 \times 10^{-19}$ C, is travelling at a velocity of 5×10^5 m s^{-1} at right angles to a magnetic field of flux density 3 T. What is the force on the electron?

The Force on a Current-carrying Conductor in a Magnetic Field

$$F = qvB$$
$$= (1{\cdot}6 \times 10^{-19})(5 \times 10^5)(3)$$
$$= 24 \times 10^{-14}$$
$$= 2{\cdot}4 \times 10^{-13} \text{ N}$$

FORCES BETWEEN CURRENTS

Experiment 25.2

AIM: To show that there are forces between electric currents.

METHOD:
1. Set up strips of aluminium foil (cooking foil) as shown.
2. Connect the power supply to the ends of the foil. The timber pieces keep the strips taut until the current is switched on.

Result: When they are connected as shown in (a), the current flows in the same direction through both conductors. The conductors are attracted towards each other. When they are connected as shown in (b), the current flows in opposite directions through the conductors. The conductors repel each other.

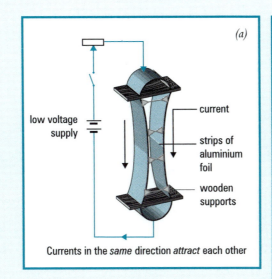

Currents in the *same* direction *attract* each other

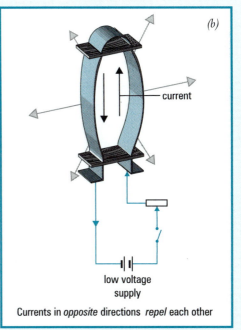

Currents in *opposite* directions *repel* each other

The unit of electric current (the ampere) is defined in terms of the force between currents.

> **The ampere is the constant current that, if maintained in two infinitely long conductors of negligible cross-section one metre apart in a vacuum, would produce between the conductors a force of 2×10^{-7} newtons per metre of length.**

Andre Marie Ampere (France) 1775–1836 investigated forces between currents and developed a meter to measure current. He was the first to distinguish between current and potential difference, and also investigated magnetic fields produced by currents. The unit of current (the ampere) is named after him.

Summary
- A current-carrying conductor in a magnetic field experiences a force.
- The magnetic flux density (*B*) is one tesla when a current of one ampere flowing through a conductor of length one metre in a magnetic field produces a force of one newton.

235

PHYSICS NOW!

- Magnetic flux density (B) is the magnetic flux per unit area at right angles to the direction of the magnetic field lines.
- The ampere is the constant current that, if maintained in two infinitely long conductors of negligible cross-section one metre apart in a vacuum, would produce between the conductors a force of 2×10^{-7} newtons per metre length.
- $F = IlB$ for a conductor
- $F = qvB$ for a moving charge

SHORT QUESTIONS

1. On what basic principle does the moving coil galvanometer depend?
2. Name one other device that is based on the same principle.
*3. Give an expression for the force on a charge q travelling at a speed v in a uniform magnetic field of flux density B.
4. When is there no force on a conductor in a magnetic field?
5. Give an expression for the force on a current-carrying conductor in a magnetic field.
6. Name two devices that are based on the principle that a current-carrying conductor in a magnetic field experiences a force.
7. A straight horizontal wire of length 0·20 m carries a current of 10 A in a magnetic field of flux density 6·0 tesla. The force acting on the wire is (A) 1·2 N, (B) 2 N, (C) 6 N, (D) 12 N, (E) 120 N.
8. The wire in the diagram carries a current in the direction shown. The direction of the force on the wire is (A) into paper, (B) out of paper, (C) non-existent, (D) from S to N, (E) from N to S.
*9. The ampere is

_____.

10. One tesla is the magnetic flux density when

_____.

LONG QUESTIONS

1. Describe an experiment to show that a current-carrying conductor in a magnetic field experiences a force. How can you show the factors that determine the direction of this force?
2. A piece of wire 0·20 m long experiences a force of 2×10^{-3} N when carrying a current of 10 A in a magnetic field. What is the magnetic flux density?

The Force on a Current-carrying Conductor in a Magnetic Field

★3. A piece of wire 0·20 m long experiences a force of 1×10^{-3} N when carrying a current in a magnetic field of magnetic flux density 0·5 tesla. What current is flowing through the wire? The diagram shows a rectangular loop of wire which is free to rotate about an axis parallel to its longer sides. The plane of the loop is parallel to a uniform magnetic field of magnetic flux density B. The dimensions of the loop are 20 cm by 15 cm and the direction of B is perpendicular to the longer sides. The magnitude of B is 0.44 T and a current of 2.6 A flows around the loop. Calculate: (i) the magnitude of the force acting on one of the longer sides of the loop; (ii) the moment of the force about the axis.
Explain why the moment of the force decreases as the loop turns through 90° about the axis from the position shown.

4. Electric motors are used in many domestic and DIY appliances. Describe how these motor-driven devices have changed the way in which people live. List the devices in your home naming the device and its use.

5. Loudspeakers are based on the principle that a current-carrying conductor in a magnetic field experiences a force. What common household devices contain loudspeakers. Are devices containing loudspeakers as common as those containing motors? The invention of the loudspeaker has led to the development of a number of entertainment industries. List the developments made possible by loudspeakers.

6. The diagram shows a loudspeaker.
(i) Name the parts labelled A, B, C.
(ii) Explain how the loudspeaker produces sound when a changing current is passed through B.

7. Give an expression for the force on a current-carrying conductor in a magnetic field.
Outline an experiment to demonstrate that a current-carrying conductor in a magnetic field experiences a force.
The diagram shows a straight horizontal wire of length 0.8 m carrying a current of 5.0 A. The wire is placed at right angles to a horizontal magnetic field of flux density 0.60 tesla. Calculate the force on the wire.

8. An electric motor operates on the principle that a current-carrying conductor in a magnetic field experiences force. Describe an experiment to demonstrate this principle.
Name another device which operates on the same principle as the electric motor.

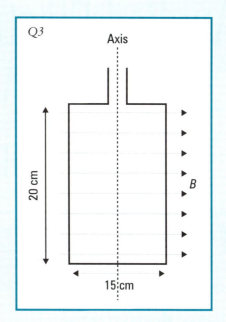

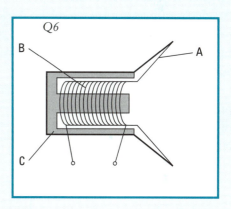

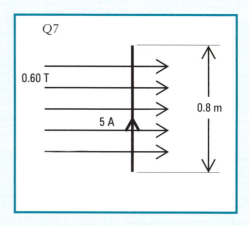

Applied Electricity: Current and Magnetic Fields (Option 2)

CHAPTER 26

The magnetic effect of an electric current and the force on a conductor in a magnetic field have both produced many practical devices. When you examine the electrical appliances in your home, you will find that these applications of electricity are used in many of them.

Electromagnetic relay

An electromagnetic relay is a solenoid (electromagnet) that is used to switch another circuit not connected to the solenoid. Electromagnetic relays are used in electronic devices, cars and other machines.

When a current flows through a solenoid, the magnetic field produced attracts a pivoted piece of iron. This switches another circuit on.

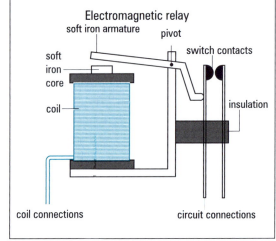

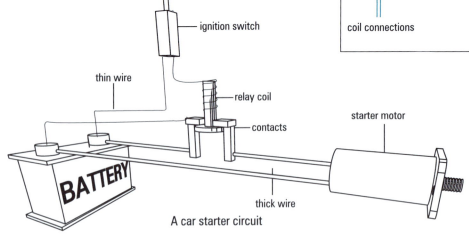

A car starter circuit

In a car, a low-current circuit is turned on by the ignition key. This operates an electromagnetic relay to switch on the large-current circuit to the starter motor. Lights and heated windows in a car are also switched on using electromagnetic relays.

An electromagnetic relay is a device that enables a small current in one circuit to switch on (or off) a large current in an adjoining circuit.

Applied Electricity: Current and Magnetic Fields (Option 2)

Simple d.c. motor

The d.c. motor consists of a rectangular coil of wire wound on a frame of laminated soft iron. This is mounted on a shaft so that it can rotate between the concave pole faces of a magnet. The ends of the coil are connected to a copper split-ring commutator. This is attached to the coil and rotates with it.

Two fixed carbon brushes press lightly against the commutator. When these are connected to a battery, current flows through the coil and the coil rotates.

When the coil is in the horizontal position, the current is switched on. By the left-hand motor rule, side **ab** experiences an upward force and side **cd** a downward force. The torque turns the motor and the coil rotates to the vertical.

Couple (torque) is the product of the force and the perpendicular distance between the forces ($T = Fd$).

The brushes now touch the gap in the commutator: no current flows. The momentum of the coil carries it beyond the vertical. The commutator now changes contact from one brush to the other. Side **ab** is now on the right-hand side with a downward force; side **cd** is on the left with an upward force. So the motor rotates continuously in one direction.

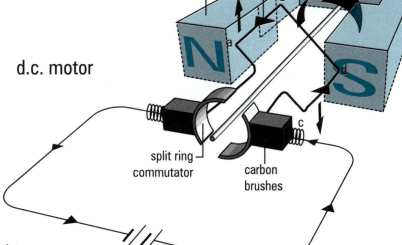

d.c. motor

Radial magnetic field

To ensure that the couple on the coil is at a maximum at all times, we arrange to have the plane of the coil always lying along the direction of the magnetic field lines. This is done by using a radial magnetic field.

A soft iron cylinder placed between the concave pole pieces produces a uniform radial field. A coil pivoted about the centre will lie along the direction of the field lines in all positions.

Problem

An electric motor consists of 1,000 turns of wire around a rectangular frame 10 cm long and 2 cm wide. The frame lies in a magnetic field of strength 5×10^{-3} T. Calculate the torque on the coil when a current of 0.1 A flows through the coil.

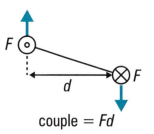

couple = Fd

F = IlB for one turn
F = 0.1 x 0.1 x 5 x 10^{-3} = 5 x 10^{-5} N

For 1,000 turns the force is 1000 x 5 x 10⁻⁵ = 5 x 10⁻² N

The torque T = F x d = 5 x 10⁻² x .02 Nm
= 0.1 x 10⁻² Nm
= 1.0 x 10⁻³ Nm

Motors and 'back' emf

Experiment 26.1
AIM: To show that motors produce a 'back' emf.
METHOD:
1. Connect a simple motor to a flywheel. Switch on the current.
2. When the flywheel is spinning freely, switch off the current and connect the motor to a light bulb.

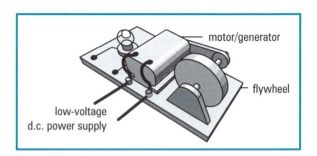

Result: The light bulb lights up until the flywheel stops. This shows that the coil of the motor generates an emf when it turns. This emf acts in a direction opposite to that of the battery which supplies current to the motor. It is known as a 'back' emf as its effect is to slow down the motor.

This back emf of the motor depends on
(a) the magnetic flux density B
(b) the length of conductor cutting through the magnetic field
(c) the speed of the motor.

As the magnetic flux density and the length of the conductor in the motor are fixed, the back emf (E) depends on the speed of revolution of the motor.

AN ELECTRIC MOTOR REGULATES ITS SPEED ACCORDING TO THE LOAD ON IT
When a load is applied to a motor, the speed decreases. This reduces the back emf. So the current flowing through the motor increases and gives a greater torque.

If the load on a motor is reduced, the speed of the motor increases. This increases the back emf. The current flowing through the motor decreases, and the motor slows down. This process regulates the motor speed according to the load on the motor. Simple d.c. motors are used in tape recorders, video recorders, automatic cameras and starter motors in cars.

Applied Electricity: Current and Magnetic Fields (Option 2)

Loudspeakers

A varying current at the same frequency as the sound is passed through a free-moving coil attached to the paper cone. The coil is in a magnetic field and experiences a force that moves it backwards and forwards at the frequency applied. This moves the cone at the same frequency, sets the air vibrating and produces the sound. Loudspeakers for low frequencies have big cones (45 cm diameter); high-frequency speakers have small cones (4–5 cm diameter).

The principle of a moving coil loudspeaker is that a current-carrying conductor in a magnetic field experiences a force that moves a cone at the frequency of the current.

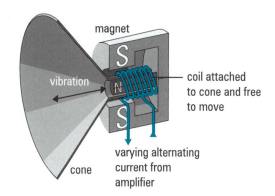

Moving coil meters

A galvanometer is made of a coil of fine wire wound on an aluminium frame. The coil is pivoted on bearings and carries a pointer. A fixed soft iron cylinder and a magnet with concave pole faces produce a radial magnetic field. The current to and from the coil goes through hairsprings.

When current flows through the coil, it produces a couple that turns it. The hairsprings produce an opposing couple when turned. This opposing couple depends on the spring used and the angle (θ) through which it is turned.

The couple produced by the coil is $F.d = nIlB.d$ (but $l.d = A$, the area of the coil).

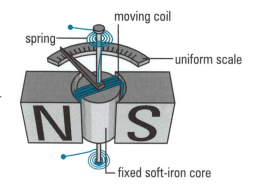

The couple produced by the coil $T_1 = nIAB$.
The opposing couple due to the spring $T_2 = k\theta$.

When the pointer is at rest

$T_1 = T_2$
$nIAB = k\theta$

As n, B, A and k are constants

$\theta \propto I$

The principle of the moving coil galvanometer is that a current-carrying conductor in a magnetic field experiences a force.

Sensitivity of the galvanometer

A sensitive meter produces a large angular deflection (θ) for a small current (I). $\frac{\theta}{I}$ should be big.

$$\frac{\theta}{I} = \frac{nAB}{k}$$

A sensitive galvanometer is made by using: (a) a strong magnet (B is large); (b) a coil of many turns (n is large); (c) a coil of large area (A is large); (d) a weak spring (k is small).

PHYSICS NOW!

DAMPING
The coil of the galvanometer is wound on an aluminium frame to 'damp' the movement of the coil and bring the pointer quickly to rest. The frame produces a back emf when it cuts through the magnetic field and slows down the coil.

To convert a galvanometer to an ammeter, voltmeter or ohmmeter

The basic construction of the moving coil ammeter, voltmeter and ohmmeter is the same: each is a modified galvanometer. We shall now see how to convert the galvanometer into each of these meters.

AMMETER
A galvanometer is converted to an ammeter by connecting a small resistance in parallel with it.

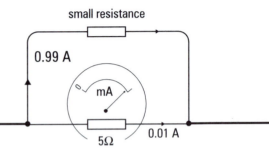

To convert a galvanometer to an ammeter

A galvanometer can safely pass only a few milliamperes (mA). We convert it to an ammeter by connecting a small resistance in parallel. This is a 'shunt' resistance, R_s. The shunt resistance is much smaller than the resistance of the galvanometer R_g, and so allows the current to flow through it more readily than through the galvanometer. We choose a resistance that allows a simple fraction (e.g. one-tenth) of the current through the meter. The current is then 10 times the reading on the galvanometer. The scale on the galvanometer is usually changed to read this value.

PROBLEM
A galvanometer has a resistance of 5 Ω and gives a full-scale deflection with a current of 10 mA. What resistance must be connected in parallel to enable the galvanometer to measure currents of up to 1 A?

10 mA is the maximum current that can pass through the galvanometer. 990 mA must pass through the parallel resistor: the shunt resistance. The voltage across each resistance is the same:

$(10 \times 10^{-3})(5) = (990 \times 10^{-3})(R)$

$R = 0.05$ Ω

When you place an ammeter in a circuit, you add a resistance – the resistance of the ammeter – to the circuit. This added resistance causes a decrease in the current. The current you measure is not exactly the one you set out to measure. To reduce this problem, the resistance of the ammeter should be as small as possible. In theory, the resistance of the ammeter should be zero. It would not alter the circuit in that case, and the ammeter would measure the true current. In practice, the resistance of the ammeter is as small as possible.

Applied Electricity: Current and Magnetic Fields (Option 2)

Voltmeter

A galvanometer is converted to a voltmeter by connecting a large resistance in series.

A galvanometer is a current-measuring device. However, we can adapt it to measure voltage by connecting a large resistance in series with it. The voltage (by Ohm's law) equals the current measured by the galvanometer multiplied by the resistance.

A voltage of even 0·1 V would damage a galvanometer. A very large resistance of several hundred ohms is connected in series with the galvanometer. This limits the current flowing through the galvanometer. The value of the series resistance is chosen so that the voltage across it is a known simple multiplier of the voltage across the galvanometer resistance. The voltage across the galvanometer ($V = IR$) is indicated by the current reading, as the resistance is constant. The scale is usually changed to give a direct reading of the full voltage.

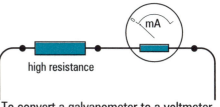

To convert a galvanometer to a voltmeter

Problem

A galvanometer has a resistance of 5 Ω and gives a full-scale deflection with a current of 10 mA. What resistance must be connected in series to enable the galvanometer to measure a voltage of 5 V?

10 mA is the maximum current that can pass through the galvanometer.
5 V is the maximum voltage you want to measure

The total resistance $R = \dfrac{V}{I} = \dfrac{5}{10 \times 10^{-3}} = 500\ \Omega$

The galvanometer has a resistance of 5 Ω, so the series resistor must supply the other 495 Ω

Series resistance = 495 Ω

You want to measure the potential difference across the resistor R. This voltage is IR (from Ohm's law, $V = IR$).

You alter the voltage reading if you alter the current flowing through the resistance. To reduce this effect, the voltmeter should have a very large resistance. In this way only a tiny current will flow through the voltmeter, and the effect on the potential difference across the resistance will be small.

In theory, the resistance of the voltmeter should be infinitely large and so allow no current through the voltmeter. In practice it as large as possible.

Limitations of moving coil meters

The moving coil galvanometer cannot measure alternating current (a.c.). Only small currents can be measured directly because of the fine wire in the coil.

The moving iron type of meter is more robust, and can measure both a.c. and d.c. currents. Two pieces of iron are mounted inside a coil. One piece is fixed and cannot move;

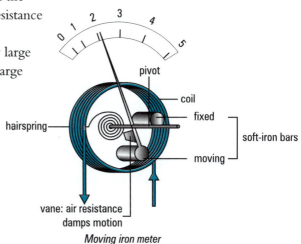

Moving iron meter

243

PHYSICS NOW!

the other piece is attached to the pointer and can move. When current flows through the coil both pieces are magnetised in the same way. The like poles repel each other and the moving iron moves until balanced by the spring.

OHMMETER

A galvanometer is converted to an ohmmeter by connecting a dry cell (1·5 V) in series with a resistor R_s. The series resistor is necessary to ensure that too big a current does not flow through the galvanometer. There is also an adjusting resistor R_a which allows you to compensate for changes in the emf of the battery as it ages.

PROCEDURE

1. Touch the two leads together: the resistance between the leads should now be zero. Adjust resistor R_a until the scale reads zero ohms.
2. Connect the leads to the unknown resistance R_x. Read the resistance from the scale. The scale is not linear and the ohmmeter is not an accurate instrument, often having an error of 10%.

Ohmmeters are used:
(a) to test a circuit for continuity – to ensure that there are no breaks in the circuit
(b) to get approximate values of resistances.

Summary

- An electromagnetic relay is a device that enables a small current in one circuit to switch on (or off) a large current in an adjoining circuit.
- The principle of the moving coil loudspeaker is that a current-carrying conductor in a magnetic field experiences a force.
- The principle of the moving coil galvanometer is that a current-carrying conductor in a magnetic field experiences a force.
- A galvanometer is converted to an ammeter by connecting a small resistance parallel to it.
- A galvanometer is converted to a voltmeter by connecting a large resistance in series with it.

Conversion to:	ammeter	voltmeter
The resistor has:	very low resistance	very high resistance
The resistor is connected:	in parallel with the galvanometer	in series with the galvanometer
	low R	high R
Symbol	A	V

SHORT QUESTIONS

1. What is the basic principle of an electromagnetic relay? Give one application of the electromagnetic relay.
2. The diagram shows a simple d.c. motor.
   (a) Identify the part A.
   (b) What is the function of A?
   (c) What happens to the coil B when the circuit is switched on?
   (d) Why is the coil B usually wound on an iron core?
   (e) Name an appliance that uses an electric motor.

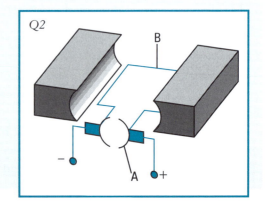

3. The purpose of the commutator in a simple d.c. motor is to (A) provide an a.c. output from the motor (B) reverse the direction of the current in the coil twice in each revolution (C) reverse the direction of rotation of the armature twice in each revolution (D) reverse the polarity of the magnet twice in each revolution (E) stop the armature from getting overheated.

4. The moving-coil loudspeaker has a permanent magnet. What happens to the cone of the loudspeaker on passing a varying current through the coil?

5. The diagram shows the basic structure of a moving coil galvanometer. Name the parts labelled A, B and C.

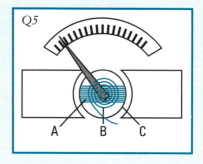

6. How can a galvanometer be converted to an ammeter?

7. Why does a charged particle, travelling at right angles to a magnetic field of uniform magnetic flux density, follow a circular path?

8. To convert a galvanometer into an ammeter:
   (A) a low resistance is connected in parallel
   (B) a low resistance is connected in series
   (C) the terminals are shorted
   (D) a high resistance is connected in series
   (E) a high resistance is connected in parallel.

9. The purpose of a moving coil meter is to
   (A) measure the value of a direct current
   (B) measure the peak value of an alternating current
   (C) convert alternating current into direct current
   (D) convert direct current into alternating current
   (E) increase the value of an alternating current.

10. A moving coil meter has a full-scale deflection of 1 mA and an internal resistance of 1 ohm. In order to adapt this meter up to 1 A, a resistor is connected in parallel with the meter. What is the resistance of this parallel resistor? (A) $\frac{1}{999}$, (B) $\frac{1}{99}$, (C) $\frac{1}{9}$, (D) 99, (E) 999.

11. A stream of positively charged particles is projected between two magnetic poles as shown in the diagram. Under the influence of the magnetic field the particles will
    (A) accelerate without change of direction
    (B) be deflected towards the north pole
    (C) be deflected towards the south pole
    (D) be deflected into the plane of the paper
    (E) be deflected out of the plane of the paper.

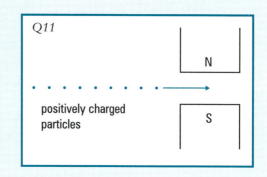

12. An electromagnetic relay is based on the principle that
    (A) a current in a magnetic field experiences a force

(B) a changing current in a solenoid experiences a force
(C) a changing current in a solenoid induces an emf
(D) a current in a solenoid produces a magnetic field
(E) a current in a magnetic field induces an emf

Long Questions

1. The diagram shows a coil free to rotate about the axis shown between the poles of a strong magnet. What will happen to the coil (a) when a current is passed through the coil; (b) when the same current is passed through the coil but the poles are interchanged?

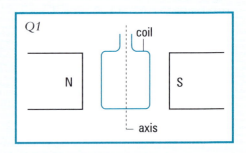

2. Describe an experiment to show that a current-carrying conductor in a magnetic field experiences a force. Draw a labelled diagram of a simple d.c. motor and explain how it works.

3. Describe, using a diagram, the structure and operation of a moving coil loudspeaker.

4. The plane of a rectangular coil of 500 turns lies perpendicular to a magnetic field of 3×10^{-3} T. The coil is 16 cm long and 5 cm wide. Calculate the maximum torque on the coil when it carries a current of 0.125 amps.

5. A rectangular coil of 50 turns of wire is 5 cm long and 2 cm wide. It lies in a radial magnetic field of 0.3 T. The torque on the coil is 7.2×10^{-3} newton metres. Calculate the current flowing through the coil.

6. On what principle is the moving coil galvanometer based? Show by means of a circuit diagram how a galvanometer can be converted to (i) an ammeter, (ii) a voltmeter.

7. (a) Name the parts A to E of the moving coil galvanometer shown in the diagram.
   (b) Describe how this galvanometer works.
   (c) State two ways in which it could be made more sensitive to the current passing through it.

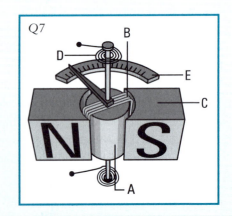

8. A galvanometer has a resistance of 100 Ω and gives a full-scale deflection for a current of 50 μA. Calculate the resistance required in order to convert it to (i) an ammeter reading up to 1 mA, (ii) a voltmeter reading up to 0.5 V.

9. Describe an experiment to show the magnetic field due to a current in a solenoid. The diagram shows an electromagnetic relay in a circuit with a battery and an electric motor, M. Explain why the motor is switched on when the terminals of the coil are connected to a battery or power supply. Why does the coil of the relay have an iron core?

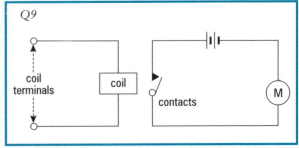

10. State the principle on which the moving-coil galvanometer is based and name one other device which is based on the same principle. Use a circuit diagram to show how a resistor may be used to convert a galvanometer to (a) an ammeter, (b) a voltmeter. Comment on the size of the resistance of the resistor in each case. A galvanometer coil consists of 18 m of copper wire. The wire is of uniform circular cross-section and has a diameter of 0.085 mm. The resistivity of copper is 1.7×10^{-8} Ω m. Calculate the resistance of the coil.

Given that the full scale deflection of the galvanometer is 2 mA calculate:

(i) the maximum voltage which should be applied between its terminals;

(ii) the resistance of the resistor required to convert the galvanometer to a voltmeter of full-scale deflection 10 V.

Electromagnetic Induction

CHAPTER 27

Electricity is usually produced by use of a generator or a dynamo. The dynamo on your bicycle and the large generators used by the ESB both operate on the same physical principle. The following experiments show how electricity can be generated.

Experiment 27.1
AIM: To demonstrate electromagnetic induction.
METHOD:
1. Push the magnet into the coil. The meter shows current flowing through the coil.
2. Pull the magnet out again. The meter shows current flowing in the opposite direction.
3. Hold the magnet stationary. Move the coil onto the magnet. The meter shows current flowing through the coil.
4. Pull the coil off the magnet. The meter shows current flowing in the opposite direction.

Conclusion: Relative movement between the magnet and the coil causes an electric current to flow in the coil. It does not matter whether the coil is stationary and the magnet moves or vice versa.

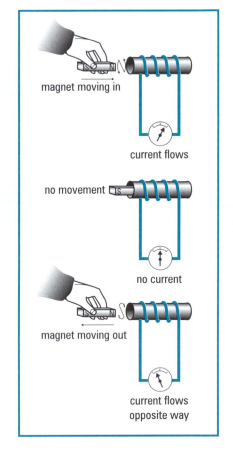

Electromagnetic induction means that an emf is induced whenever the magnetic flux cutting a conductor changes.

If you repeat these experiments using the magnetic field of a solenoid carrying a current instead of a bar magnet, you will get the same results. Electromagnetic induction takes place whenever a magnetic field moves through a conductor, or vice versa.

Repeat the above experiment using magnets of different strengths. A simple way of comparing the strengths of bar magnets is to see how many iron nails they can lift.

You will find that the greater the magnetic flux density, the greater is the emf produced.

$E \propto B$

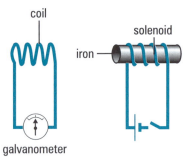

248

Electromagnetic Induction

Now use coils with different numbers of turns. You will find that the greater the number of turns, the greater is the emf produced.

$E \propto N$

Now connect the leads of a bicycle dynamo to a voltmeter. Raise the back wheels of the bicycle off the ground and turn the pedal, starting in the lowest gear and increasing the speed steadily. Note the reading of the voltmeter. Move through the gears and measure the voltage each time. You will find that the greater the speed of revolution, the greater is the emf.

$E \propto v$

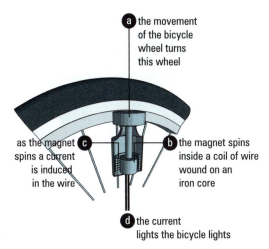

These results combine to give Faraday's law of electromagnetic induction.

Faraday's law: Whenever there is a change in the magnetic flux linking a circuit, an emf is induced whose strength is proportional to the rate of change of flux linking the circuit.

Experiment 27.2

AIM: To find the direction of the current induced in a circuit.

METHOD:
1. Connect a coil to a galvanometer.
2. Place a magnet on an electronic balance (which should measure to 0·01g).
3. Move the coil down over the magnet (make sure that the coil does not touch the magnet). Note that the balance shows a slight increase in the weight of the magnet.
4. Pull the coil up from the magnet. The balance shows a decrease in weight.

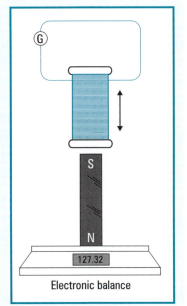

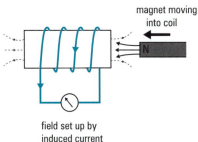

Magnet repelled by field of coil

This can be explained as follows. The emf induced in the coil produces a current flow. This creates a magnetic field which opposes the change (the movement) that caused it.

When we move the coil down, current flows in a way that pushes the magnet down. It opposes the change causing it.

When we move the coil up, current flows in a way that produces a magnetic field which attracts the magnet; this opposes the change causing it.

This is known as Lenz's law of electromagnetic induction.

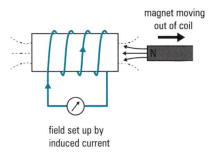

Magnet attracted by field of coil

Lenz's law: The direction of the induced emf is always such as to oppose the change causing it.

PHYSICS NOW!

Alternate Experiment to demonstrate Lenz's Law

1. Drop a non-magnetic cylinder through a copper tube. Note the transit time.
2. Drop a similar magnetic cylinder through the same tube. Again note the transit time.

Result: The transit time for the magnetic cylinder is greater.

Explanation: The movement of the magnetic cylinder induced an electric current in the copper tube in a way that opposes the change causing it — the movement of the magnetic cylinder. This slows the cylinder — hence the slower transit time.

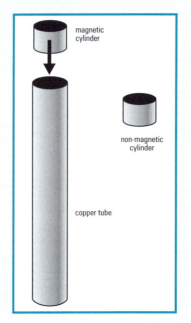

Michael Faraday (England) 1791–1867 was probably the greatest inventor of the 19th century. He investigated static electricity, developed the electric motor, investigated electrolysis and stated the laws of electrolysis. He also discovered electromagnetic induction, which allowed the development of the electricity generator and consequently the ESB! A unit of electric charge (faraday) and the unit of capacitance (farad) are named after him.

ELECTROMAGNETIC INDUCTION IS A CONVERSION OF MECHANICAL ENERGY INTO ELECTRICAL ENERGY

Lenz's law is a result of the law of conservation of energy. When electricity is generated, some other form of energy, usually mechanical, is converted into the electrical energy. Electromagnetic induction is simply the conversion of mechanical energy into electrical energy. If the magnet moving through the coil is to do work then it must experience a force. This means that the direction of the induced emf must always oppose the change causing it.

Magnetic flux density (B) is the magnetic flux (Φ) per unit area (A) at right angles to the direction of the magnetic field lines

$$B = \frac{\phi}{A}$$
$$\Rightarrow \phi = B.A.$$

The unit of magnetic flux (the weber) is defined by electromagnetic induction.

The weber (Wb) is the magnetic flux that, linking a circuit of one turn, produces in it an emf of one volt as the flux is reduced to zero at a uniform rate in one second.

Faraday's law can be stated mathematically as

$$E = -\frac{d\phi}{dt}$$

where E is the emf induced, and $\frac{d\phi}{dt}$ is the instantaneous rate of change of magnetic flux with time (the negative sign is due to Lenz's law). Where there is more than one turn of conductor in the circuit,

$$E = -N\frac{d\phi}{dt}$$

where N is the number of turns.

As we proved earlier,

$E \propto B$
$E \propto N$
$E \propto v$

E is also proportional to l, the length of conductor in the magnetic field, so

$E = -NBlv$

Right-hand (generator) rule: Put the forefinger, thumb and centre finger of your right hand at right angles to each other. Point your **F**orefinger along the direction of the magnetic **F**ield and your **T**humb along the direction of the **T**hrust (movement). Your **C**entre finger now points in the direction of the induced **C**urrent.

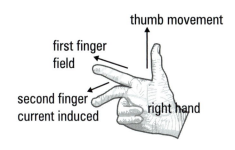

If you connect the leads of your bicycle dynamo to an oscilloscope, the change in the voltage (and current) can be seen. The oscilloscope shows that the change follows the pattern of the graph of the sine of an angle.

The emf generated by a rotating coil is an alternating emf which varies with the sine of the angle of rotation. This explains the sine wave pattern of the emf seen on the oscilloscope.

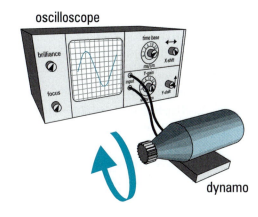

PEAK VALUES

You saw on the oscilloscope that the value of an a.c. voltage is changing constantly. At one instant the voltage is zero; a fraction of a second later it reaches its maximum value. The maximum value is shown by the height of the peak on the graph. This is called the peak value. The peak value is reached for two instants in each turn: once in the positive direction and once in the negative direction.

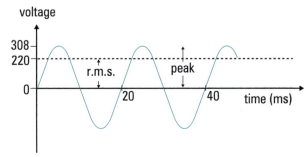

ROOT MEAN SQUARE VALUE

It is difficult to deal in a simple way with something that is constantly changing. The ESB voltage supply to your house is a.c. and is constantly changing. How then can we say that the ESB supply is 220 V?

If we averaged the voltage, as shown in the graph in the diagram, we would get 0 V as our answer. All the positive values (above the line) would cancel out the negative ones (below the line). This isn't much help!

The way we deal with a problem like this is to square all the values first. All values, positive and negative, are positive when squared. We then get the average or mean value. Finally, we get the square root of this mean. The square root reverses the squaring at the first step. The value we get in this way is called the root mean square (r.m.s.) value.

The peak value of the voltage, V_0, is $\sqrt{2}$ times the root mean square value.

$V_{rms} = \dfrac{V_0}{\sqrt{2}}$

PHYSICS NOW!

As the current is directly related to the voltage,

$$I_{rms} = \frac{I_0}{\sqrt{2}}$$

PROBLEM

The ESB voltage is 220 V (r.m.s. value). What is the peak value of the ESB voltage to your house?

peak value = $\sqrt{2}(220)$ = 308 V

TRANSFORMERS CHANGE A.C. VOLTAGES

Experiment 27.3

AIM: To show the action of a transformer.

(A)
1. Wind ten turns of insulated wire on a C-shaped laminated soft-iron frame, A.
2. Wind 20 turns of wire on a similar frame, B.
3. Connect A to a 1 V a.c. supply. Connect B to a 3 V bulb.
4. Bring the two frames together slowly. Measure the voltages with an a.c. voltmeter.

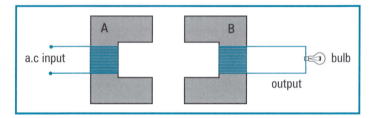

Result: The bulb lights when the two frames are held tightly together. The magnetic flux from the coil on frame A is linking the coil on frame B, through the laminated soft-iron. If you slide a sheet of paper between the two frames, the bulb goes out. This is because the flux is not closely linked in this case.

(B)
1. Connect coil B to the 1 V a.c. supply and coil A to the bulb.
2. Clamp the two frames together.
3. The bulb does not light.
4. Connect coil A to the 1 V a.c. again and coil B to the bulb. The bulb lights again.
5. Measure the voltages with an a.c. voltmeter.

(C)
1. Replace coil B with 30 turns of insulated wire.
2. Connect coil A to the 1 V a.c. and coil B to the bulb.
3. The bulb light is brighter than before when the frames are clamped together.
4. Measure the voltages again.

Conclusion: The ratio of the number of turns of wire in coil B to that in coil A is the same as the ratio of the voltage across B to the voltage across A.

$$\frac{V_A}{V_B} = \frac{N_A}{N_B}$$

252

How a transformer works

A transformer is used to change the voltage of a.c. supplies. It is constructed of separate primary and secondary coils of insulated wire on a laminated soft-iron frame. The resistance of the coils is kept low to prevent power losses.

When an alternating voltage V_I is applied across the primary coil N_p it produces an alternating magnetic flux through the primary coil and soft-iron core. This flux cuts through the secondary coil N_s and induces an emf V_o in it.

$$\frac{V_I}{V_o} = \frac{N_p}{N_s}$$

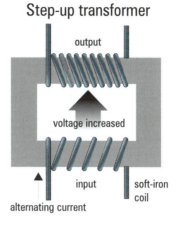

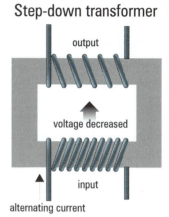

The ratio of secondary turns to primary turns determines whether the transformer is 'step-up' or 'step-down'.

PROBLEM

A transformer has a primary coil of 200 turns and a secondary coil of 20 turns. The primary coil is connected to a 20 V a.c. supply. What emf is induced in the secondary coil? Is this a step-up or a step-down transformer?

$$\frac{V_I}{V_o} = \frac{N_p}{N_s}$$

$$\frac{20}{V_o} = \frac{200}{20}$$

$$V_o = 2\text{ V}$$

It is a step-down transformer.

PROBLEM

The coil in the problem above is connected the wrong way round and the 20 turns are connected to the 20 V supply. What emf is induced in the other coil?

20 turns are acting as the primary coil, 200 turns as the secondary.

$$\frac{V_I}{V_o} = \frac{N_p}{N_s}$$

$$\frac{20}{V_o} = \frac{20}{200}$$

$$V_o = 200\text{ V}$$

This is a dangerous voltage, particularly since the expected voltage (as shown above) is only 2 V!

PHYSICS NOW!

Uses of transformers

We have already seen that the ESB 'steps up' voltage for transmission of energy and then 'steps down' the voltage to supply electrical energy to homes, offices and factories. Many of the transformers used for this are big oil-cooled transformers.

Transformers are used in TV sets to step up voltage for the tube and also to step down voltage for the electronic circuits. In fact, transformers are used whenever an appliance needs a voltage different from the mains voltage.

Mutual induction

Magnetic fields can be moved without any physical movement of a solenoid by increasing or decreasing the current through the solenoid.

Experiment 27.4

AIM: To demonstrate electromagnetic induction due to a change in a magnetic field.

1. Set up the circuit shown in the diagram. There is no electrical connection between coil A and coil B.
2. Close the switch on the primary circuit. The galvanometer shows a small current flowing through coil B.
3. Open the switch on the primary circuit. The current now flows in the opposite direction through coil B.
4. When a steady current flows in coil A, there is no induced current in coil B. An emf is induced only while the current (and magnetic field) is actually changing.

When current flows through coil A, a magnetic flux builds up through the iron core, coil A and coil B. This induces an emf in the secondary coil (coil B) which causes a deflection of the galvanometer. A steady current causes no change in the magnetic flux, and so no emf is induced. When the circuit is switched off the magnetic flux collapses and induces an emf in the secondary coil which deflects the galvanometer in the opposite direction.

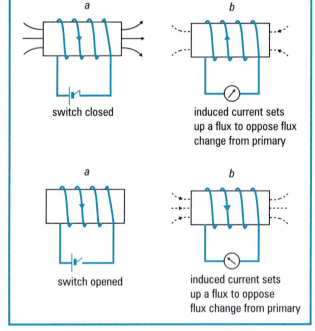

When an emf is generated in the secondary coil by a change in the magnetic field produced by the primary coil, this is **mutual induction.**

254

Electromagnetic Induction

Self-induction

Experiment 27.5
AIM: To demonstrate that an emf is produced when the current in a coil is switched off.
1. Set up the circuit shown. The electromagnet should have a large number of turns of wire in its coil.
2. Pass a current through the electromagnet to give a magnetic flux around and through the coil.
3. Switch off the current: the magnetic flux collapses through the coil. This induces a big emf across the coil and lights up the neon bulb connected across it. This emf is big because (a) there are a large number of turns in the electromagnet coil, (b) the magnetic flux collapses rapidly when the current is switched off.
4. Connect the battery directly to the neon bulb. The neon bulb does not light. This shows that the emf of the battery is not big enough to light the bulb.

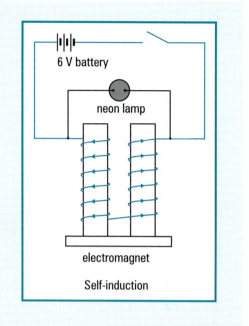

Self-induction

When an emf is generated in a coil by a change in the magnetic field of the same coil, this is **self-induction**.

Experiment 27.5 shows that the self-induced emf can be very big. This causes problems when currents are switched in circuits with large coils. Special precautions must be taken in these circuits to protect equipment from damaging voltages.

Inductors and a.c.
We have already shown the effects of self-induction and mutual induction with direct current. We know that an emf is generated in a coil only while the current is changing. Any coil of wire will produce these effects. Coils that show these effects are inductors. It is important to realise that many resistances are in the form of a coil of wire, e.g. the element of an electric fire and the coil in an electromagnetic relay. These coils have an inductance.

Experiment 27.6
AIM: To investigate the effect of inductors on a.c.
1. Connect a coil of wire with a large number of turns in series to a light bulb and a low-voltage a.c. supply.
2. Close the switch K. The bulb lights.
3. Push some iron wires into the coil. This increases the inductance of the coil. The bulb goes dim.
4. Remove the iron wires. The bulb lights brightly again.

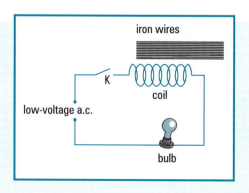

255

Physics Now!

Can you see how this could be used to dim lights and control stage lights?

This effect is due to a back emf induced in the inductance (coil) which opposes the applied emf.

The greater the inductance of the coil, the smaller is the current passed by an inductor when connected to a.c.

Summary

- Electromagnetic induction means that an emf is induced whenever the magnetic flux cutting a conductor changes.
- Faraday's law: Whenever there is a change in the magnetic flux linking a circuit, an emf is induced whose strength is proportional to the rate of change of flux linking the circuit.
- Lenz's law: The direction of the induced emf is always such as to oppose the change causing it.
- Right-hand (generator) rule: Put the forefinger, thumb and centre finger of your right hand at right angles to each other. Point your **F**orefinger along the direction of the magnetic **F**ield and your **T**humb along the direction of the **T**hrust (movement). Your **C**entre finger now points in the direction of the induced **C**urrent.
- Mutual induction: where an emf is generated in the secondary coil by a change in the magnetic field produced by the primary coil.
- Self-induction: where an emf is generated in a coil by a change in the magnetic field of the same coil.
- A transformer can step up or step down the voltage of an a.c. (alternating current) supply.
- The greater the inductance of the coil, the smaller is the current passed by an inductor when connected to a.c.

Short Questions

1. What is meant by electromagnetic induction?
2. State Lenz's law of electromagnetic induction.
3. Electrical energy is transmitted at high voltages in the ESB grid system because
   (A) the power-station generator rotates at high speed
   (B) some factories need high voltages
   (C) it is easier to generate high voltages
   (D) energy losses in the cables are lower at high voltages
   (E) the resistance of the cables is lower at high voltages.
4. The diagram shows a coil connected to a sensitive centre-reading galvanometer with a magnet near by. Which of the following statements is true?
   (A) The meter pointer moves when the magnet is moving towards the coil but not when it is moving away from the coil.

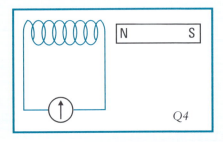

Q4

(B) The meter pointer moves if the magnet is moved quickly towards the coil.
(C) The meter pointer does not move if the coil is moved towards the stationary magnet.
(D) The biggest movement of the meter pointer is obtained when the magnet is stationary in the coil.
(E) The movement of the meter pointer is in the same direction regardless of the direction in which the magnet is moving.

5. What is meant by mutual induction?
6. When an a.c. voltage of 200 V was applied to the primary coil of a transformer, the voltage across the secondary coil was 20 V. If the primary coil contained 1000 turns, the secondary coil contained (A) 100 turns, (B) 4,000 turns, (C) 250 turns, (D) 10,000 turns, (E) 10 turns.
7. A 400 V a.c. electrical device has a primary coil of 4,000 turns and a secondary coil of 200 turns. The most likely description of this device is (A) 2:1 step-down transformer, (B) 10:1 step-down transformer, (C) 10:1 step-up transformer, (D) 20:1 step-down transformer, (E) 20:1 step-up transformer.
8. A mains transformer working on 240 V has 4,000 turns on the primary coil and 100 turns on the secondary. Assuming no power loss, the secondary output will be (A) 6 V, (B) 12 V, (C) 24 V, (D) 960 V, (E) 1,440 V.
9. A transformer for a model electric railway is operated from the 240 V mains supply and delivers 12 V to the railway. If the secondary coil in the transformer has 1,000 turns, the number of turns required in the primary is (A) 50, (B) 500, (C) 1,000, (D) 2,000, (E) 20,000.
10. Which of the following is associated only with direct current? (A) electric lamp, (B) electroplating, (C) electroscope, (D) slip-ring dynamo, (E) magnetic field?
11. What is meant by self-induction?
12. A transformer has 800 turns of wire in the primary coil and 100 turns in the secondary coil. Calculate the voltage in the secondary coil if the primary coil is connected to an a.c. power supply of 220 V.
13. A transformer coil is designed to be used on a 220 V a.c. supply. What is likely to happen if the transformer is accidentally connected to a 220 V d.c. supply?
14. An induction coil was invented by _____, working at Maynooth College in the _____ century.
15. A transformer may be used to (A) increase or decrease a.c. voltages, (B) switch a circuit, (C) generate a.c., (D) store charge, (E) generate d.c.

LONG QUESTIONS

1. Outline a laboratory experiment to show the presence of a magnetic field. What is meant by electromagnetic induction? State one of the laws of electromagnetic induction.

2. (a) State (i) Faraday's law of electromagnetic induction, (ii) Lenz's law. Describe an experiment to illustrate one of these laws.

   (b) A square coil of side l contains N turns of wire of total resistance R. It is travelling in a direction parallel to the side EH, as shown in the diagram, when it enters a magnetic field which is perpendicular to the plane of the coil and is of uniform magnetic flux density B. Given that the two terminals of the coil are connected together, explain why the coil slows down as it is entering the field.

   (c) Use Faraday's law to show that the emf induced in the coil in (b) at any instant while it is entering the field is given by $E = -NBlv$, where v is the speed of the coil at that instant. Hence, derive an expression in terms of v for (i) the current in the coil, (ii) the force on the coil.

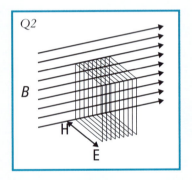

3. In a sensitive experiment to measure the acceleration due to gravity by free fall, a ball-bearing is dropped from a height h and the time it takes to fall is measured accurately. The experiment is repeated with the ball-bearing falling through a solenoid carrying a current. State, with reasons, whether you would expect the time for the ballbearing to fall to be (a) the same as before, (b) greater than before or (c) less than before.

*4. The magnetic flux through a coil of 100 turns of wire changes from 0·40 webers to zero in 0·1 seconds. Calculate the average emf induced in the coil.

5. Complete the following table.

N_p	N_s	V_I	V_o
100	12	48	
300	100	12	
1,600	200	220	
2,400	100		10
	2,000	8	32

6. State the laws of electromagnetic induction.
   A coil of wire (P) is connected to a battery as shown in the diagram. A second coil (S) is connected to a galvanometer (G). The two coils are linked by a soft iron core.

What happens to the galvanometer when the switch, K, is (i) closed and then (ii) opened? Explain. What changes should be made in the arrangement shown in the diagram in order to use it to obtain high voltage a.c. from a low voltage a.c. source? What is the name given to the new arrangement?

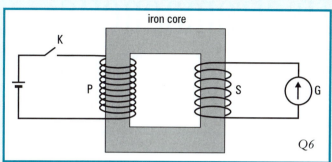

*7. State Lenz's law of electromagnetic induction and describe an experiment to illustrate the law. The diagram shows a coil connected in series with a lamp L and a 12 V a.c. power supply. The lamp lights when the power supply is switched on. Explain why the brightness of the lamp will decrease if an iron core is placed in the coil.

The resistance of the lamp in the circuit in the diagram is 60 Ω. If the resistance of the rest of the circuit is negligible calculate the electromotive force (emf) induced in the coil when the current flowing through the lamp is 80 mA.

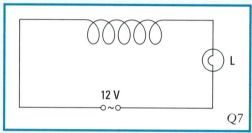

8. State Faraday's law of electromagnetic induction. Describe an experiment to illustrate this law. Explain the principles involved in each of the following:
(i) A coil with an iron core has a higher effective resistance to a.c. than it does to d.c.
(ii) A galvanometer coil is wound on an aluminium former to slow the motion of the coil.

*9. State Faraday's law of electromagnetic induction and describe an experiment to illustrate this law. A coil consists of 200 turns of wire of total resistance 400Ω and is connected to an a.c. supply. Over a certain time period of 1 ms (1 x 10^{-3}s) the flux threading each turn of the coil increases by 4.0 x 10^{-4} Wb. Calculate:
(i) The average induced emf over the 1 ms period;
(ii) The average current in the coil if the average applied voltage over the 1 ms period is 100 V.

Electromagnetic Induction (Option 2)

CHAPTER 28

The induction coil

Cars use 12 V direct current to power the lights, rear-screen heater, radio and other appliances. This voltage couldn't possibly produce a spark in the plugs. The induction coil invented at Maynooth in 1836 by Nicholas Callan gives the spark needed. The induction coil consists of a primary coil with a make-and-break switch and a secondary coil.

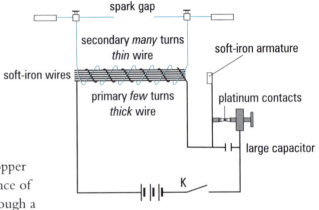

Induction coil

PRIMARY COIL

The primary coil has comparatively few turns of thick copper wire, wound round a core of soft iron wires. The resistance of the primary coil is low. It is connected to the battery through a make-and-break switch, and a capacitor is connected across the contacts of the switch.

SECONDARY COIL

The secondary coil consists of many thousands of turns of thin wire wound on top of (but insulated from) the primary coil. The secondary coil is connected to an adjustable spark gap.

HOW THE INDUCTION COIL WORKS

When K is closed, current flows through the primary coil and a magnetic flux builds up slowly. This flux cuts through the secondary coil. The core is now magnetised and attracts the armature, breaking the circuit. The magnetic flux through the primary coil now collapses (the circuit is broken). It also cuts through the secondary coil and induces an emf. The emf induced in the secondary coil is very big and can produce sparks several centimetres long between the points.

The emf $E = -N\frac{d\phi}{dt}$ and depends on

(a) N, the number of turns in the secondary coil

(b) $\frac{d\phi}{dt}$, the rate at which the magnetic flux collapses.
This depends on the rise and fall of current in the primary circuit.

The rise and fall of current in the primary circuit depends on the inductance of the coil (L) and the resistance in the circuit (R). The inductance of the coil depends on the number of turns of wire in it and the material in the core: both of these are fixed and do not change. The

Nicholas Callan (Ireland) 1799–1864 worked in Maynooth College. He developed large electromagnets and a battery, experimented with electromagnetic induction and invented an induction coil.

260

total resistance of the circuit does change, as follows. When the primary circuit is made, the resistance of the circuit is small, so that $\frac{L}{R}$ is large and the 'rise' time is large. The current rises slowly through the primary and induces a relatively small emf in the secondary (and a self-induced back emf in the primary).

When the primary circuit is broken, the very large resistance of the contact gap makes R big. $\frac{L}{R}$ is small and so the 'fall' time is short. The current falls rapidly and induces a large emf in the secondary (and a self-induced emf in the primary).

WHAT DOES THE CAPACITOR DO?
The self-induced back emf in the primary coil when the circuit is broken causes sparking at the gap. This melts the metal contacts and causes them to stick. A large capacitor connected across the gap (in parallel with the gap) prevents this. The back emf charges the capacitor. This takes the energy from the circuit so sparking is stopped.

Uses of the induction coil

CAR
An induction coil is used in the ignition system of a car. The 12 V car battery (or generator when the car is running) is connected to the primary circuit of the coil through a contact breaker: the 'points'.

When the points open, an emf of several thousand volts is induced across the secondary. A rotating connector, the distributor, sends this high voltage to the spark plugs in the correct order. The big voltage makes a spark across the gap in the spark plug and ignites the petrol and air mixture.

The metal body of the car acts as the return wire for most circuits.

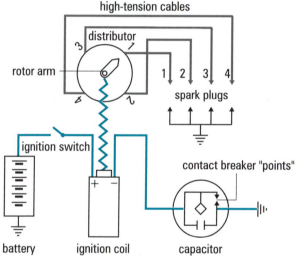

ELECTRIC FENCE
The electric fence is another use of the induction coil. The coil provides a short pulse of high-voltage current to the wire. A cow earths the wire when it touches it and gets a harmless shock. This prevents cattle from straying from their pasture.

The a.c. generator
The a.c. generator has a coil of wire (armature) wound on a laminated soft-iron core. The magnetic pole pieces are concave and fit closely round the armature. Slip rings are attached to the armature and rotate with it. Carbon brushes press against the slip rings and connect the generator to the outside circuit.

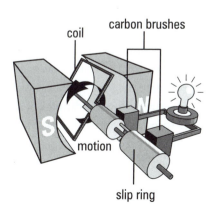

261

Experiment 28.1

AIM: To demonstrate the operation of an a.c. generator.

1. Connect an a.c. generator to a galvanometer. Turn the armature slowly and note the deflection of the galvanometer.
2. When the coil is in the vertical position no field lines are cut: the induced emf is zero.
3. As it moves to the horizontal the number of field lines cut increases to a maximum, and the induced emf reaches a maximum.

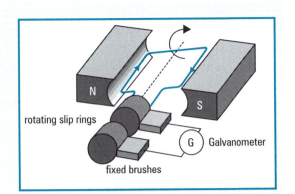

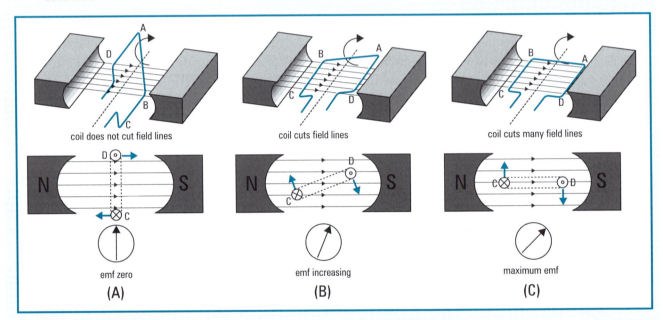

4. As the coil rotates to the vertical the induced emf again decreases to zero. As the coil continues to turn the emf increases again (but in the opposite direction), goes to a maximum and decreases to zero.

For a single coil, steps 2-4 happen every full revolution.

The emf from a generator is increased by (a) using a strong magnet (or electromagnet), (b) using a laminated soft-iron core to produce a large magnetic flux density, (c) using a large number of turns of wire in the armature, (d) increasing the speed of rotation. As a generator is turned, the induced current flowing through it produces a motor force. This opposes the turning motion. The work done against this force is converted into electrical energy.

Electromagnetic Induction (Option 2)

Induction effects in metals

When a motor or dynamo moves, the soft-iron core of the armature cuts through the magnetic flux. This induces an emf in the core and causes currents (called eddy currents) to flow. If the core is made of one piece the induced currents flow through the resistance of the core material and produce much heat. ($H = I^2Rt$). This effect is prevented by making the core out of sheets, or laminations, of soft iron that are electrically insulated from each other. The current induced in each separate lamina is small and so the heat loss due to eddy currents is small.

Efficiency of transformers

If the transformer is 100% efficient,

Power of primary (input) circuit = power of secondary (output) circuit
$$V_I . I_I = V_o . I_o$$

An efficient transformer has
1. low-resistance coils to reduce heating losses
2. closely wound primary and secondary coils to ensure that all the magnetic flux links the coils
3. a laminated core to (a) produce total linkage of magnetic flux, (b) reduce eddy current losses.
4. a core of soft magnetic material to ensure small energy losses in bringing about the constant changes in the magnetic field.

Most transformers have efficiencies in excess of 99%.

Some practical uses of induction effects

INDUCTION FURNACE

High-frequency a.c. produces a rapidly changing magnetic flux through the metal in the crucible. Eddy currents are induced in the metal that produce heat and melt the metal.

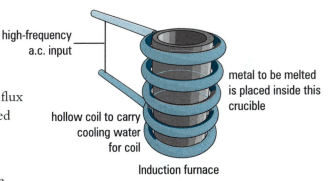

Induction furnace

DAMPING

(a) Moving coil meters: the coil is wound on a metal frame. When it moves, eddy currents in the frame oppose the motion of the coil.
(b) Balances: a piece of non-magnetic metal (copper or aluminium) is attached to the balance. This is suspended between the poles of a horseshoe magnet. As the balance oscillates, eddy currents in the metal oppose the motion and cause it to come to rest quickly.

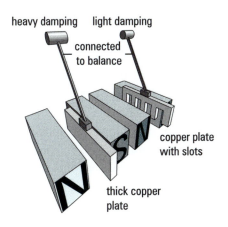

263

PHYSICS NOW!

The induction motor

The following experiment demonstrates the principle of the induction motor in a simple way.

Experiment 28.2

AIM: To demonstrate the principle of the induction motor.

METHOD:
1. Set up a thick copper disc pivoted at its centre so that it can spin freely.
2. Attach a strong magnet to a variable-speed power drill.
3. Gradually increase the speed of rotation of the magnet.

Result: The copper disc turns with the magnet and increases in speed with it. Note that there is no physical connection between the magnet and the disc: the only thing linking the two is the magnetic flux.

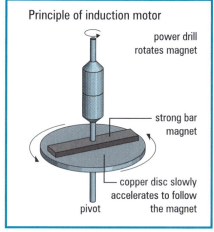

Principle of induction motor

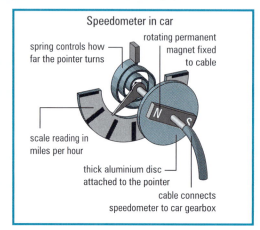

Speedometer in car

The rotating magnet induces a current in the copper disc. The disc begins to rotate in the same direction as the magnet and so reduces the relative motion between disc and magnet (the induced current opposes the change causing it). This is the basis of the induction motor. (This principle is also used in the speedometer. The magnet is driven by the car's transmission; the torque of the disc is proportional to the speed of rotation of the magnet and the car. The torque is opposed by hairsprings.)

The simple induction motor consists of a fixed stator and a rotor that moves, mounted on a free-moving axle. The rotor consists of a cylinder of copper with a core of iron. This is mounted on a shaft and is free to rotate. Around the rotor is fitted a stator. The stator consists of two electromagnets set at right angles to each other and around the rotor. The electromagnets are connected to the same a.c. supply, but one of them is connected through a capacitor. This has the effect of making the voltage across one electromagnet lag behind the voltage of the other by 90°. The magnetic field produced by the two electromagnets appears to rotate around the rotor for each complete cycle of the a.c.: in effect, a rotating magnetic flux sweeping round the stator. The rotor attempts to eliminate the relative motion between itself and the rotating magnetic flux by rotating in the same direction. This induces the rotor to spin at the same rate.

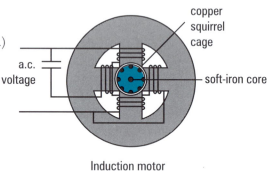

Induction motor

It is important to realise that no electric current is supplied to the rotor. This means that there are no brushes or commutators or slip rings in the induction motor. The only electrical connections are the fixed connections to the stator. Since induction motors are a.c. machines, they can be connected directly to the mains supply.

There is an iron core in the rotor to ensure that the magnetic flux links the copper cylinder tightly. This link can be made even closer by embedding copper rods in the iron; the rods are connected at each end to make a single conducting unit. This is called a squirrel cage.

The principle of the induction motor is based on Lenz's law: a rotating magnetic field induces a free-moving conductor to rotate at the same speed.

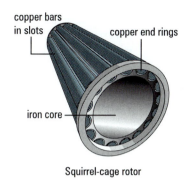

Squirrel-cage rotor

Summary

- The induction coil consists of a primary coil with a make-and-break switch and a secondary coil.
- The a.c. generator has slip rings.
- Most transformers have efficiencies in excess of 99%.
- The induction motor uses a rotating magnetic field to produce movement in the rotor.

Short Questions

1. Name the principal parts of an a.c. generator.
2. (a) What causes eddy currents in the core of a transformer?
   (b) How is the effect of these currents reduced?
3. An _____ is used to produce the spark in the engine of a car.
4. Which of the following will not increase the voltage produced by a generator?
   (A) Using a stronger magnetic field,
   (B) using thicker wire for the coil,
   (C) using a soft-iron core inside the coil,
   (D) increasing the number of turns on the coil,
   (E) increasing the speed of rotation.
5. Which of the following would work only on a d.c. supply and not on an a.c. supply of suitable voltage?
   (A) a filament lamp,
   (B) an electric iron,
   (C) an electric water heater,
   (D) an electroplating machine,
   (E) a fluorescent lamp.
6. A multi-turn coil is rotated in a magnetic field. Which of the following sets of changes would produce the greatest increase in the induced voltage?

	Strength of magnetic field	Number of turns on coil	Speed of rotation of coil
(A)	increase	increase	increase
(B)	increase	decrease	increase
(C)	increase	increase	decrease
(D)	decrease	decrease	decrease
(E)	decrease	increase	increase

7. A voltage will be _____ in a wire if the wire moves through a _____ field.
8. Induced _____ tend to oppose the motion causing them.
9. When the current in a coil of wire is switched off, a spark is sometimes seen at the switch. What is the cause of this?
10. A mechanic tells you that your car will not start because the contacts have stuck together. What part of the spark coil circuit (other than the contacts) is likely to be broken?
11. When a magnet is moved over a sheet of aluminium, the sheet of aluminium will tend to follow the magnet. Name a device that is based on the principle illustrated by this phenomenon.

LONG QUESTIONS
1. An induction coil is shown in the diagram.
   (a) State the principle on which the induction coil is based.
   (b) Why is the core usually laminated?
   (c) State one difference between the primary and secondary coils.
   (d) What is the purpose of the capacitor, C?
   (e) What is meant by back emf?
   (f) Name the Irish scientist who invented an induction coil.

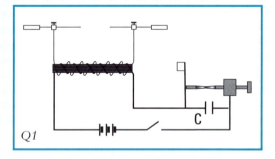
Q1

2. The diagram shows a transformer in which the primary coil is connected to a cell and a switch and the secondary coil is connected to a centre-zero galvanometer.
   (a) What is observed when (i) the switch is closed, (ii) the switch remains closed so that a steady current flows through the primary coil, (iii) the switch is opened?
   (b) The cell in the diagram is replaced by an a.c. supply, and the galvanometer is replaced by a filament lamp. What is observed when (i) the switch is closed, (ii) the switch remains closed, (iii) the switch is now opened?
   (c) Give three ways in which the brightness of the lamp in this transformer circuit could be increased.
   (d) You are given a transformer designed to operate a 12 V train set from the 240 V mains. You find that the secondary

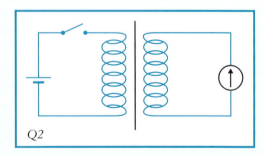
Q2

coil of the transformer is damaged. How many turns will you need to wind on a new secondary coil if you find the primary coil has 1,500 turns?

(d) Explain why the national grid uses step-up transformers at the power station and step-down transformers at the consumer end.

3. Diagram (A) represents a transformer with a primary coil of 400 turns and a secondary coil of 200 turns.
   (a) If the primary coil is connected to the 240 V a.c. mains, what will be the secondary voltage?
   (b) Explain carefully how the transformer works.
   (c) Calculate the efficiency of the transformer if the primary current is 3 A and the secondary current is 5 A.
   (d) Give reasons why you would expect this efficiency to be less than 100%.
   (e) The secondary coil is removed and a small coil connected to a low-voltage lamp is placed as shown in diagram (B). Explain the following observations: (i) the lamp lights, (ii) if the coil is moved upwards the lamp gets dimmer, (iii) if a soft-iron rod is now placed through the coil the lamp brightens again, (iv) the lamp will not light if a d.c. supply is used instead of an a.c. one.

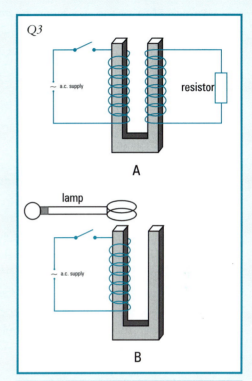

Q3

4. (a) Outline a laboratory experiment to show the presence of a magnetic field. What is meant by electromagnetic induction? State one of the laws of electromagnetic induction.
   (b) The diagram shows an induction coil.
   (i) For what purpose is an induction coil used?
   (ii) Name the parts of the coil labelled A, B, C.
   (iii) Indicate what happens at D in the diagram.

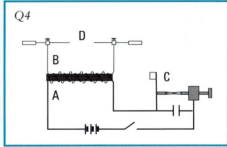

Q4

5. Describe the structure and the principle of operation of a simple a.c. generator. Sketch a graph to show how the voltage generated by the a.c. generator varies with time.

6. The $\frac{\text{primary}}{\text{secondary}}$ turns ratio in a transformer is 10:1.
   The power input to the primary is 100 watts. If a current of 2 amps flows in the secondary coil, calculate
   (a) the current flowing in the primary coil
   (b) the potential difference across the primary coil
   (c) the potential difference across the secondary coil.

7. An input of 200 kilowatts to a transformer produces an output of 50 A at 3 kV. Calculate the efficiency of the transformer.

8. A transformer with an input of 12 volts can have an output of 120 volts. Explain how this does not contradict the principle of conservation of energy.

9. (a) Explain the principles underlying the operation of an induction motor.
   (b) The diagram shows a coil with an iron core connected to a lamp and an a.c. power supply. Explain why the lamp would light more brightly if the a.c. supply were replaced with a d.c supply.

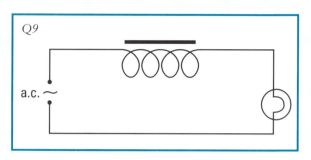

10. Explain the basic physical principles in each of the following.
    (i) When a magnet is moved past a sheet of aluminium, the aluminium tends to follow the magnet.
    (ii) The efficiency of a transformer is improved by laminating the core.

11. 10 kW of electrical power is transmitted through a cable of resistance 3 Ω.
    (a) Calculate the current flowing through the cable when it is transmitted at (i) 220 V and (ii) 400,000 V.
    (b) Calculate the power loss due to the heating effect of the current in (i) and (ii) of (a).

12. What is meant by electromagnetic induction? The diagram shows a simple a.c. generator. Explain how it works. Suggest an alteration that could be made in order to convert the generator into one that would generate a higher voltage.

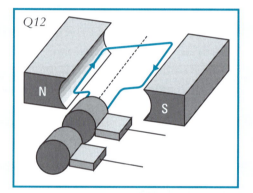

13. What is meant by electromagnetic induction? State *one* of the laws of electromagnetic induction. The diagram shows a simple a.c. generator. The main parts are labelled A, B, C, D.
    (i) Name each of the parts labelled.
    (ii) Give the functions of any *three* of the parts labelled.
    (iii) Sketch a graph showing how the voltage generated by the a.c. generator varies with time. State *one* energy conversion which occurs in an a.c. generator.

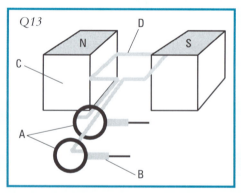

14. The induction coil is based on electromagnetic induction.
    (i) State the purpose for which an induction coil is used.
    (ii) Coil A is connected to the battery. Name coil A.
    (iii) Coil B is connected to D. Name coil B.
    (iv) Name part C.
    (v) What happens at D when the induction coil is working?
    Name another device which is based on electromagnetic induction.

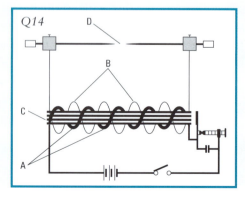

Capacitors and Capacitance

CHAPTER 29

Capacitors are used in radios and television sets, in electronic equipment and in camera flash guns.

Experiment 29.1

AIM: To demonstrate that a capacitor stores a small quantity of electric charge.

METHOD:
Connect a large capacitor, an electric bell and a battery through a two-way (single-pole double-throw) switch as shown in the circuit.
1. Move the switch to position A. Nothing seems to happen.
2. Move the switch to position B. The bell sounds.

Conclusion: The bell is not connected to the battery, so the only possible source of the electrical energy is the capacitor.

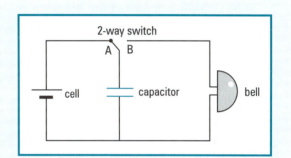

A capacitor is a device for storing a small quantity of electric charge.

We can see where the currents are flowing if we connect two galvanometers in the circuit as shown.

Experiment 29.2

AIM: To show the flow of current in charging and discharging a capacitor.

METHOD:
1. Move the switch to position A; galvanometer G_1 shows a current flowing for an instant. This current obviously came from the battery.
2. Move the switch to position B; galvanometer G_2 shows a current. This could not have come from the battery since the battery is not connected to this circuit. The current through G_2 must have come from the capacitor.

Conclusion: When the capacitor is connected to a battery, the current flows to the capacitor for a very short time. Once the capacitor is charged to the same voltage as the battery there is no difference in potential between them, and no more current flows.

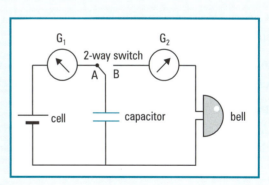

How much electric charge can a capacitor hold? We find out by doing the following experiments.

Experiment 29.3

AIM: To verify that the charge on a capacitor is directly proportional to the voltage applied.

METHOD:

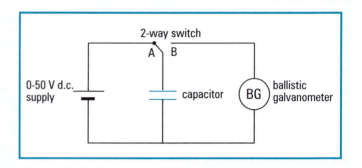

1. Connect a capacitor to a variable 0–50 V d.c. voltage supply.
2. Connect a ballistic galvanometer (BG) to the capacitor through a two-way switch. The first deflection or kick of the BG gives a measure of the charge stored in the capacitor.
3. Charge the capacitor to a voltage of 10 V.
4. Discharge it through the BG. Note the deflection of the BG.
5. Charge successively to voltages of 20 V, 30 V, 40 V and 50 V; each time discharge through the BG and note the deflection.
6. Draw a graph of the potential difference (voltage) against the charge (the deflection of the BG). The result is a straight-line graph through the origin.

Conclusion: The charge on a capacitor is directly proportional to the voltage applied. The ratio $\frac{Q}{V}$ is a constant and is the capacitance of a capacitor. The capacitance is a measure of the charge the capacitor can store for a given voltage.

Capacitance is the ratio of the charge on a capacitor to the potential difference applied across it.

$$C = \frac{Q}{V}$$

Capacitance is measured in farads (F). Practical capacitors have capacitance in the microfarad (µF) range.

A capacitor has a capacitance of one farad when the ratio of charge to potential difference on it is one coulomb per volt

PROBLEM

A parallel plate capacitor is charged to a voltage of 50 V. The charge on the capacitor is 2×10^{-5} C. What is the capacitance of the capacitor?

$$C = \frac{Q}{V}$$
$$= \frac{2 \times 10^{-5}}{50 V}$$
$$= 0\cdot 4 \times 10^{-6} \text{ F or } 0\cdot 4 \text{ µF}$$

PROBLEM
A 20 µF capacitor has a charge of $1{\cdot}6 \times 10^{-4}$ C. What is the voltage across the capacitor?

$$C = \frac{Q}{V}$$

$$V = \frac{1{\cdot}6 \times 10^{-4}}{(20 \times 10^{-6})}$$

$$= 8 \text{ V}$$

PROBLEM
A 1 µF capacitor is charged to a voltage of 10 V. What is the charge on each of the plates?

$$C = \frac{Q}{V}$$

$$Q = CV = 1 \times 10^{-6} \times 10 \text{ coulombs}$$

$$= 10^{-5} \text{ coulombs}$$

Parallel plate capacitor
The simplest form of capacitor consists of a pair of metal plates separated by a thin sheet of insulating material. The insulating material is known as the dielectric.

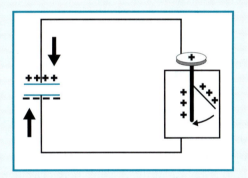

Experiment 29.4
AIM: To verify that the capacitance of a parallel plate capacitor depends: (A) inversely on the distance between the plates, (B) directly on the common area and (C) directly on the permittivity of the medium.

METHOD FOR (A):
1. Connect one plate of the capacitor to the disc of an electroscope.
2. Connect the other plate to the case (earth terminal) of the electroscope.
3. Charge the capacitor. The leaves of the electroscope diverge; the divergence gives a measure of the potential difference across the capacitor.
4. Move the plates closer to each other. The divergence of the leaves decreases. This means that the voltage across the capacitor has decreased. The distance between the plates is directly proportional to the voltage.

$$d \propto V, \text{ but } C \propto \frac{1}{V}$$

$$C \propto \frac{1}{d}$$

Method for (b):

1. Move the plates sideways, keeping them parallel to each other. The area of each plate directly opposite the other plate (called the common area) is now smaller. The divergence of the leaves increases.
2. Move the plates back, increasing the common area. The divergence of the leaves decreases. The greater the common area of the plates, the smaller is the divergence of the leaves. The common area of the plates is inversely proportional to the voltage.

$A \propto \frac{1}{V}$, but $C \propto \frac{1}{V}$

$C \propto A$

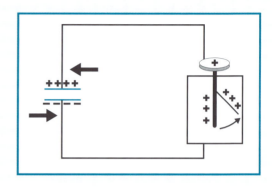

Method for (c):

1. Put a block of plastic between the plates. The plastic has a permittivity about five times greater than that of air (or a vacuum). The divergence of the leaves decreases.
2. Repeat with a number of materials of different permittivities. The greater the permittivity, the smaller is the divergence of the leaves. The permittivity of the material between the plates is inversely proportional to the voltage.

$\varepsilon \propto \frac{1}{V}$ but $C \propto \frac{1}{V}$

$C \propto \varepsilon$

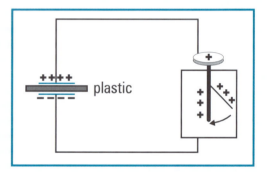

Combining all three results of experiment 29.4 gives

$$C \propto \frac{A\varepsilon}{d}$$

The capacitance of a parallel plate capacitor depends on
(i) the common area of the plates A
(ii) the permittivity of the material between the plates ε
(iii) the inverse of the distance between the plates d.

Problem

A pair of metal plates 0.5 m² in area are 0.1 mm apart. Calculate the capacitance when the medium between the plates is air (permittivity of air $\varepsilon = 8.9 \times 10^{-12}$ F m⁻¹).

$$C = \frac{A\varepsilon}{d}$$

$$= \frac{0.5 \times 8.9 \times 10^{-12}}{0.1 \times 10^{-3}}$$

$$= 44.5 \times 10^{-9} \text{ F}$$

PROBLEM

The capacitance of a parallel plate capacitor is 1·5 µF. The common area of the plates is 0·2 m². The material between the plates has a relative permittivity of 5. Calculate the distance between the plates (permittivity of a vacuum $\varepsilon_0 = 8.9 \times 10^{-12}$ F m⁻¹).

$$C = \frac{A\varepsilon}{d} \quad (\varepsilon = \varepsilon_r . \varepsilon_0)$$

$$d = \frac{A\varepsilon}{C}$$

$$= \frac{(0.2)5(8.9 \times 10^{-12})}{1.5 \times 10^{-6}}$$

$$= 5.9 \times 10^{-6} \text{ m}$$

Energy stored in a capacitor

We know that a capacitor stores electrical energy, because we used this energy to sound a bell (or light a bulb). A large capacitor charged to 6 V can be used to light a 6 V bulb for a few minutes, sound an electric buzzer for 10 minutes or operate a small electric motor.

The energy stored in the capacitor is the work done by the battery to charge the capacitor.

$$W = \tfrac{1}{2} \cdot CV^2$$

PROBLEM

The capacitance of a capacitor is 2·2 µF. When the potential difference between the plates is 10 V, what energy is stored in the capacitor?

$$W = \tfrac{1}{2} CV^2$$

$$= \tfrac{1}{2} (2.2 \times 10^{-6}) \times 10^2$$

$$= 1.1 \times 10^{-4} \text{ J}$$

PROBLEM

A capacitor has a capacitance of 4·7 µF. What is the charge on the plates if the energy stored is 0·52 mJ?

$$W = \tfrac{1}{2} CV^2$$

$$V^2 = \frac{2W}{C} = \frac{2(0.52 \times 10^{-3})}{(4.7 \times 10^{-6})}$$

$$= 0.22 \times 10^3$$

$$V = 15 \text{ V}$$

$$Q = CV = 4.7 \times 10^{-6} . 15 = 70.5 \times 10^{-6} \text{ C}$$

$$= 70.5 \text{ µC}$$

PHYSICS NOW!

CAPACITORS DO NOT CONDUCT IN A d.c. CIRCUIT

When you connect a capacitor to a battery (d.c.), the current flows to the capacitor for a very short time. The electrons flow on to one plate and off the other plate. This produces a potential difference across the capacitor. Once the capacitor is charged to the same voltage as the battery, there is no difference in potential between them and no more current flows.

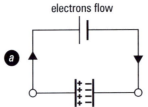
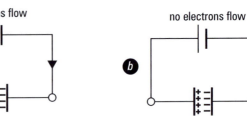
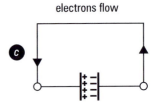

There is no continuous flow of current in a capacitor circuit with d.c.

CURRENT FLOWS IN A CAPACITOR CIRCUIT WITH a.c.

Experiment 29.5

AIM: To investigate the factors that affect current flows in a capacitor circuit with a.c.

METHOD:
1. Connect a 100 µF capacitor and a bulb in series with an a.c. source.
2. Switch on the a.c. The bulb lights.
3. Replace the capacitor with a 200 µF capacitor. The bulb lights more brightly.

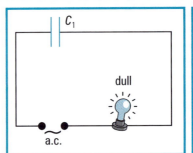
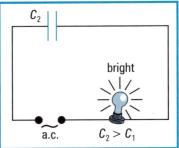

The larger the capacitance, the greater is the current flow with a.c.

4. Connect a 100 µF capacitor and a bulb in series to a variable-frequency a.c. source.
5. Switch on the a.c. The bulb lights.
6. Increase the frequency of the a.c. source. The bulb lights more brightly.

The greater the frequency, the greater is the current flow with a.c.

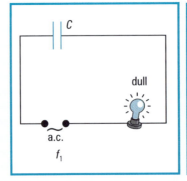
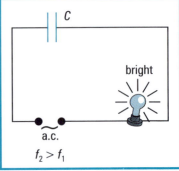

When you connect a capacitor to an a.c. supply, electrons flow on to one plate and off the other. But the polarity of the applied a.c. potential difference changes and so the electrons now flow around the circuit in the opposite direction. This happens continuously: this is a flow of electricity.

Capacitors are used in many circuits

Flash gun
1. Switch on the unit with K_1. The battery charges the capacitor through the large resistance in about 10 seconds.
2. The camera shutter closes switch K_2. This completes the flash tube circuit and sets off the flash.

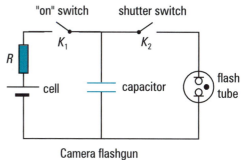
Camera flashgun

Capacitors as filters
Car circuits sometimes contain both a.c. and d.c. The a.c. causes interference in radio reception and must be removed. If a capacitor is connected across the circuit it will pass a.c. to earth and leave pure d.c.

Capacitors are also used to filter high-frequency a.c from low-frequency a.c. in hi-fi sound systems. The size of the capacitor determines the frequency that is filtered out.

Capacitors are used to tune radios
A circuit containing a capacitor and a coil of wire is used to tune in to a particular radio frequency. The exact frequency is determined by changing the value of a variable capacitor.

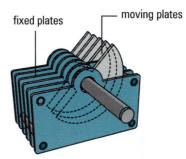
Variable or tuning capacitor

Capacitors smooth rectified a.c.
When alternating current is rectified using diodes, the d.c. is not steady. Its value varies considerably and is of little use in many circuits. Rectified d.c. is smoothed by connecting it to a capacitor and a coil (inductor). The inductor resists any current change in the circuit; the capacitor acts as a reservoir of charge to smooth out the circuit.

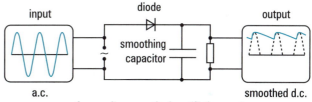
A capacitor smoothed rectified current

Summary
- A capacitor is a device for storing a small quantity of electric charge.
- Capacitance is the ratio of the charge on a capacitor to the potential difference applied across it.
- A capacitor has a capacitance of one farad when the ratio of charge to potential difference on it is one coulomb per volt.
- There is no continuous flow of current in a capacitor circuit with d.c.
- In an a.c. circuit, the current flow is directly proportional to the capacitance and to the frequency of the a.c.

Short Questions
1. A capacitor is a device that _____.
2. Capacitance is the ratio of _____ to _____.
3. The unit of capacitance (the farad) is _____.

*4. The capacitance of a capacitor is 2·2 µF. When the potential difference between its plates is 10 V, the energy stored in it is
(A) $1·1 \times 10^{-8}$ J, (B) $1·1 \times 10^{-5}$ J, (C) $2·2 \times 10^{-5}$ J, (D) $1·1 \times 10^{-4}$ J, (E) $2·2 \times 10^{-4}$ J.

*5. When a capacitor of capacitance 10 µF holds a charge of 40 µC, the energy stored in the capacitor is (A) 8,000 µJ, (B) 400 µJ, (C) 200 µJ, (D) 80 µJ, (E) 4 µJ.

*6. $\dfrac{A\varepsilon}{d}$ is an expression for _____.

7. Define the unit of charge, the coulomb.

*8. The energy stored in a parallel plate capacitor is
(A) proportional to the capacitance and to the potential difference between the plates
(B) proportional to the capacitance and to the potential difference between the plates squared
(C) proportional to the capacitance squared and to the potential difference between the plates
(D) proportional to the capacitance squared and inversely proportional to the potential difference between the plates
(E) proportional to the capacitance squared and inversely proportional to the potential difference between the plates squared.

*9. Which of the following would cause the capacitance of a parallel plate capacitor to be doubled, assuming that the dielectric is the same in each case?
(A) Doubling the distance between the plates while keeping their common area constant.
(B) Doubling the common area of the plates and doubling the distance between them.
(C) Keeping the common area of the plates constant while reducing the distance between them by a factor of four.
(D) Increasing the common area of the plates by a factor of four while keeping the distance between them constant.
(E) Keeping the common area of the plates constant while halving the distance between them.

*10. Write down an expression for the energy stored in a charged capacitor.

11. A capacitor holds a charge of 10 µC on each plate when charged to a potential difference of 9 V. Calculate the capacitance of the capacitor.

12. X and Y are two plates of a charged capacitor as shown in the diagram. If the distance between the plates is increased what effect will this have on the reading on the voltmeter V?

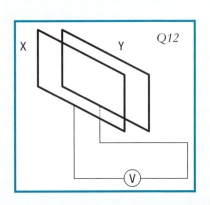

Long Questions

★1. What is meant by (i) potential difference, (ii) capacitance? Describe an experiment to show that the capacitance of a parallel plate capacitor depends on the distance between the its plates.

2. What is the capacitance of a capacitor with a charge of 6 μC and a potential difference of 6 V? Give one common use of a capacitor in an electric circuit.

★3. Describe an experiment to show how the capacitance of a pair of parallel plates varies with their common area.

4. One plate of a parallel plate capacitor is earthed and the other is raised to a potential of 200 kV. If the capacitance of the capacitor is 1 μF, calculate the charge placed on the capacitor.

5. Calculate the potential difference required to place a charge of 200 μC on a 100 μF capacitor.

★6. Calculate the potential difference to which a 10 μF capacitor must be charged to store $3 \cdot 125 \times 10^{-3}$ J of energy.

★7. While a heart attack patient is being revived, a defibrillator containing a 20 μF capacitor is charged to 600 V and then discharged across the chest of the patient. The charge is passed in 2·5 ms. Calculate the total charge passed and the average current of the discharge.

★8. Capacitors with a very large capacitance are used as temporary back-up power supplies for electronic equipment. One such capacitor has a capacitance of 1 F and is charged to 5 V. How long will this act as a back-up for equipment with a minimum power requirement of 5 mW?

★9. (a) Define capacitance. How might it be demonstrated experimentally that a charged capacitor stores energy?
(b) A capacitor has a capacitance of 4·7 μF. What is the charge on the plates when the energy stored is 0·52 mJ ?

★10. An electronic flash gun on a camera has a 50 μF capacitor. It has an average power of 10 kW for 2 ms. Calculate the voltage the capacitor is charged to and the charge it carries.

11. A capacitor has a capacitance of 1,000 μF. What is the charge on the capacitor when the potential difference between its plates is 50 V? Give a use which is made of capacitors.

12. Define capacitance. State the factors on which the capacitance of a parallel-plate capacitor depends. Explain the principles involved in each of the following.
(i) A capacitor connected in series in a circuit conducts a.c. but not d.c.
(ii) When the plates of a charged capacitor are joined together a spark may be seen.

Semiconductors

CHAPTER 30

Diodes, transistors, thermistors, light-dependent resistors (LDRs), light-emitting diodes (LEDs) and integrated circuits are some of the practical electronic components made from semiconductors.

Conductors, insulators and semiconductors

Conductors have loosely bound electrons in their outer electron orbits. These are free to move through the metal. Once a small voltage is applied the electrons move: electricity flows. Conductors have a low resistance.

Insulators have very tightly bound electrons. These electrons require a great amount of energy to free them for conduction. Insulators do not conduct electricity unless a very big voltage is applied across them. Insulators have a high resistance.

Semiconductors have a resistance between conductors and insulators. Their electrons are not free to move but do not need a great amount of energy to free them for conduction. Silicon and germanium are the two principal materials used as semiconductors. They are used in the crystalline state. Metal oxides such as copper(I) oxide are also used in semiconductor devices.

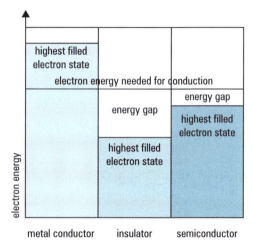

Semiconductors are substances with outer electrons that are not free to move but require little energy to free them for conduction.

Intrinsic conduction

Silicon and germanium have a valency of four. When silicon forms a crystal, each silicon atom forms four covalent bonds with four other silicon atoms. The silicon used must be extremely pure to ensure that the crystal formed is perfect.

Most electrons in silicon are held tightly in the crystal structure. At room temperature some electrons will have greater energy than others and will move away from their position in the crystal. When a small voltage is applied across the crystal, these electrons move and a current flows through the crystal. This **intrinsic** current is very small.

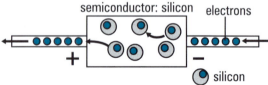

The intrinsic current depends on the temperature of the semiconductor. A rise in temperature frees more electrons in the crystal and so leads to an increase in the intrinsic current. This effect is so great in germanium that the increase in intrinsic current with rising temperature produces a heating effect. This heating effect produces a further increase in current and sets up a continuous cycle that can ultimately destroy the semiconductor. This effect is known as **thermal runaway**.

278

Thermal runaway limits the temperature at which germanium semiconductors can be used. Silicon does not suffer this effect to the same degree, and is more widely used as a semiconductor.

Intrinsic conduction is the movement of charges through a pure semiconductor. The intrinsic current is very small and depends on the temperature of the semiconductor.

Extrinsic conduction

The electrical properties of silicon and germanium crystals are significantly changed when small amounts of phosphorus, arsenic, aluminium or indium are added to them. These elements have atoms of roughly the same size as silicon (or germanium) so that they fit into the crystal structure. Only one in every ten thousand million atoms of silicon is replaced by an atom of one of these elements. This is sufficient to alter the behaviour of the semiconductor markedly, and is known as doping.

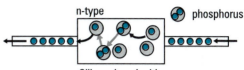
Silicon doped with phosphorus provides electrons for current flow

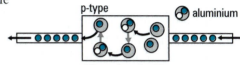
Silicon doped with aluminium provides "holes" for current flow

Doping is the addition of a small amount of another element to a pure semiconductor to increase its conductivity.

Extrinsic conduction is the movement of charges through a doped semiconductor.

n-type semiconductor

Silicon has a valency of four, phosphorus has a valency of five; so when an atom of silicon is replaced by an atom of phosphorus in the crystal structure there is an extra or spare electron that is not used in bonding the crystal. When a voltage is applied to the crystal these free electrons move and a current flows through the crystal. The silicon now contains a supply of free electrons as current carriers. Silicon doped with phosphorus is called an n-type semiconductor.

silicon atom

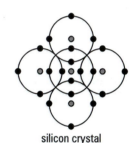
silicon crystal

The semiconductor is n-type only because it contains a supply of electrons that are free to move through the crystal: it is not electrically charged.

phosphorus atom

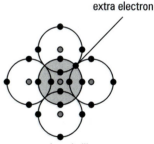
n-type doped silicon

n-type semiconductor: a semiconductor in which electrons are the majority carriers.

p-type semiconductor

Silicon has a valency of four, aluminium has a valency of three; so when a silicon atom is replaced by an aluminium atom the structure lacks one electron. This makes a vacancy or 'hole' available to an electron. An electron can move across this type of semiconductor by going from vacant space to vacant space: from hole to hole. This movement of electrons in one direction creates the impression of a movement of positive charge in the opposite direction. Since this type

aluminium atom

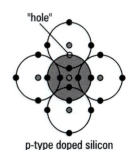
p-type doped silicon

of semiconductor contains a supply of holes which are regarded as positive current carriers, it is called a p-type semiconductor.

p-type semiconductor: a semiconductor in which holes are the majority carriers.

Movement of holes

The movement of 'positive charge' or holes in p-type semiconductors is caused by the movement of electrons in the opposite direction. This can be illustrated very simply as follows.

Set up five chairs in a line. Four students sit on the chairs, leaving the chair at one end vacant. If the student beside the vacant chair moves on to it, her chair is now vacant: the vacancy moved. If this process is repeated in turn by each student, the vacancy moves from one side to the other!

If we regard the students as the electrons and the chairs as the holes or vacant positions, it is clear that movement of electrons in one direction causes movement of holes in the opposite direction.

It is important to realise that it is the electrons which actually move in n-type and p-type semiconductors.

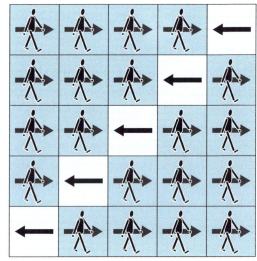

"Hole" or empty space moves in opposite direction to the way you move

In n-type semiconductors electrons are the main conductors of electricity, and are known as majority carriers. There are also a few holes in n-type material. These contribute in a small way to the conduction of electricity, and are known as minority carriers.

In p-type semiconductors, the movement of holes is the main conduction process. In p-type semiconductors, holes are the majority carriers. p-type material also contains a small number of free electrons. These contribute a little to the conduction of electricity in p-type material, and are known as minority carriers.

	Majority carriers	Minority carriers
n-type	electrons	holes
p-type	holes	electrons

The diode is a p–n junction

The simplest application of p-type and n-type semiconductors is in the p–n junction diode. This is formed from a single piece of silicon crystal that is doped by a p-type element on one side and an n-type element on the other. The junction of the p-type and n-type materials forms the diode.

diode symbol

Experiment 30.1

AIM: To show the flow of current across a p–n junction.
METHOD:
1. Connect a diode, a bulb and a battery in series as shown in the diagram.
2. The bulb lights, showing that current flows.
3. Reverse the direction of the diode. Close the switch. The bulb does not light: current does not flow.

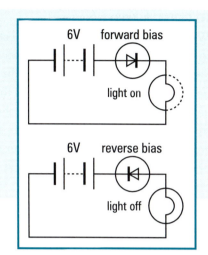

The way that we connect a diode in a circuit determines whether or not current will flow. Current flows when the diode is connected in one way; current does not flow when it is connected in the opposite way.

Unbiased junction

A p–n junction with no voltage applied across it is said to be unbiased.

In an unbiased junction some electrons from the n-type material diffuse across the junction into the p-type material. This produces a small region of negative charge on the p side of the junction. Also, holes from the p-type material diffuse across into the n-type material and produce a small region of positive charge on the n side of the junction. This tiny region acts as a barrier to any further movement of current carriers. It is known as the 'barrier' or 'depletion layer'.

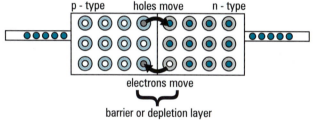

Depletion layer: A p–n junction area that has few charges available for conduction and so acts as a barrier to the movement of charges.

Forward-biased junction

When a battery is connected across a p–n junction with the positive terminal of the battery connected to the p-type side and the negative terminal connected to the n-type side, the junction is said to be forward-biased. The electrons in the n-type are repelled by the negative terminal and attracted across the junction to the positive terminal. The holes of the p-type behave like positive electric charge, and are repelled by the positive terminal and attracted across the junction to the negative terminal. This produces a flow of electrons in one direction and of positive holes in the opposite direction, so that current flows through the junction when it is forward-biased. A small voltage (0·6 V for a silicon diode and 0·1 V for a germanium diode) must be applied before any current will flow in a forward-biased junction. This voltage is required to overcome the barrier or depletion layer.

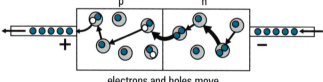

REVERSE-BIASED JUNCTION

When the positive terminal of the battery is connected to the n-type material and the negative terminal is connected to the p-type material, the junction is said to be reverse-biased. The electrons in the n-type material are attracted by the positive terminal of the battery away from the p–n junction. The holes in the p-type material are attracted away from the junction by the negative terminal of the battery. This leaves a region at the junction that contains no current carriers.

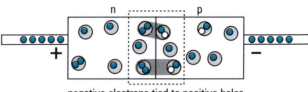

negative electrons tied to positive holes when n-type is positive ~no current flows

A reverse-biased p–n junction conducts only a tiny current. This current is due to the minority carriers present in both p-type and n-type materials.

Rectification

Current flows through a diode only when it is forward-biased. An alternating (a.c.) voltage is constantly changing. Over a cycle it changes from positive to negative to positive again. When a.c. is connected to diode the diode is forward-biased only when the a.c. voltage is positive and current flows through the diode. When the a.c. is negative the diode is reverse-biased and current does not flow. When the a.c. is positive again the diode is once more forward-biased and current again flows through the diode.

The current flows in one direction only and so is direct current. This process is called **rectification** — the diode is acting as a rectifier.
A rectifier changes a.c. to d.c.

Experiment

AIM: To show rectification.
1. Set up the apparatus as shown in the diagram.
2. Connect a low voltage a.c. supply to the diode circuit.
3. The oscilloscope shows the rectified voltage.

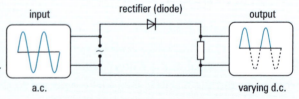

LEDs and photodiodes

Two special types of diode are the LED and the photodiode.

The LED (light-emitting diode) is used as an indicator light in electronic devices. It gives off light when electricity passes through the p–n junction.

The photodiode is used to detect light or to complete a circuit when light falls on it. The photodiode conducts more electricity when light falls on the p–n junction.

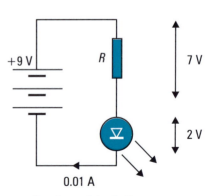

A series resistor limits the current through the LED to a safe value

Semiconductors

Summary

- Semiconductors are substances with outer electrons that are not free to move but require little energy to free them for conduction.
- Intrinsic conduction is the movement of charges through a pure semiconductor.
- The intrinsic current is very small and depends on the temperature of the semiconductor.
- Thermal runaway limits the temperature at which germanium semiconductors can be used.
- Doping is the addition of a small amount of another element to a pure semiconductor to increase its conductivity.
- Extrinsic conduction is the movement of charges through a doped semiconductor.
- In n-type semiconductors, electrons are the main carriers (majority carriers) of electricity.
- In p-type semiconductors, the movement of holes is the main conduction process: holes are the majority carriers of electricity.
- A depletion layer is a p–n junction area that has few charges available for conduction and so acts as a barrier to the movement of charges.
- A diode is a p–n junction that conducts electricity freely in one direction only.
- Integrated circuits (ICs) are thin slices of semiconductor with circuits containing many thousands of transistors, diodes, capacitors and resistors constructed on them.

Short Questions

1. What is a semiconductor?
2. An intrinsic semiconductor can be made into an extrinsic semiconductor by _____.
3. What is a p–n junction?
4. When will current flow across a p–n junction?
5. State one use of a p–n junction.
6. Using the axes provided in the diagram, sketch a graph showing how the resistance of a piece of semiconductor material varies with its temperature.
7. Identify which of the following are insulators, conductors and semiconductors: aluminium, germanium, glass, gold, graphite, porcelain, silicon.
8. Changing a.c. to d.c. is called _____.
9. In __type semiconductors, electrons are the majority carriers.
10. An ohmmeter is connected to a light dependent resistor (LDR) as shown in the diagram. What is observed as the intensity of the light falling on the LDR is increased?

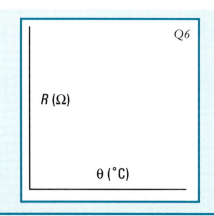

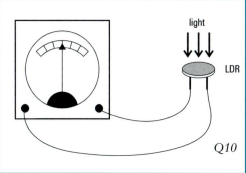

Long Questions

1. When a p-type region and an n-type region are formed in the same silicon crystal, a depletion layer is formed. Explain the underlined terms.

2. What is a semiconductor? Explain the terms intrinsic conduction, doping. The diagram represents a junction diode. Describe what happens when a potential difference is applied across the junction (i) when A is positive with respect to B, (ii) when A is negative with respect to B.

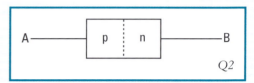
Q2

3. Which, if either, of the two bulbs L₁ and L₂ lights up in each of the circuits in the diagram?

4. Explain how the circuit in the diagram can be used to protect a delicate moving coil meter from being connected with the wrong polarity.

5. The diagram shows a circuit that may be used in an experiment to investigate the variation of voltage with current for a semiconductor diode. Describe how you would perform the experiment and sketch the graph you would expect to obtain.

6. Explain the term semiconductor. The diagram shows a lamp which is connected to X and a 6 volt battery. Name and give the function of X. Sketch the structure of X. Is the lamp lighting? Explain your answer. What is observed to happen when the switch S is closed? Explain your answer.

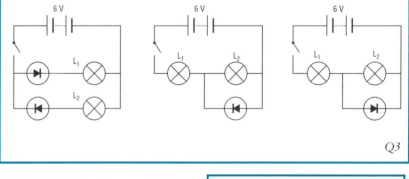
Q3

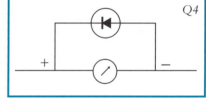
Q4

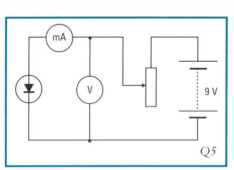
Q5

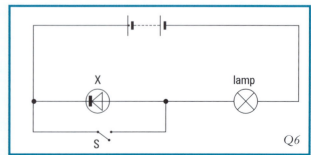
Q6

Applied Electricity: Semiconductors (Option 2)

CHAPTER 31

Applications of the diode: rectification

THE DIODE IS A HALF-WAVE RECTIFIER

Experiment 31.1
AIM: To show half-wave rectification with a diode.

METHOD:
1. Set up the circuit as shown in the diagram.
2. Connect the low-voltage a.c. supply to the diode.
3. Connect the cathode ray oscilloscope across the resistor.
4. The oscilloscope shows that the output across the resistor is only half of the applied a.c. voltage. The output is flowing in one direction only, and is direct current (d.c.). This is known as half-wave rectification.

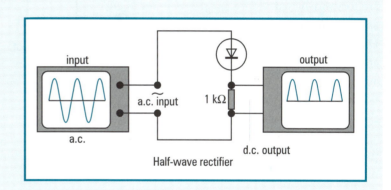

We have already seen that current flows through a diode only when it is forward-biased, i.e. when the p-type material is connected to the positive terminal of the supply voltage.

The polarity of the a.c. voltage is constantly changing. Over a single cycle it changes from positive to negative to positive again. When this is connected to the p-type material of a p–n diode, the diode is forward-biased only when the a.c. voltage is positive. Current flows through the diode when the a.c. voltage is positive. When the a.c. voltage is negative, the diode is reverse-biased and so current does not flow through it. When the a.c. voltage is positive again, the diode is once more forward-biased and current flows through it.

This gives an output where only half of every wave of the a.c. cycle produces a flow of current: half-wave rectification. The output flows in one direction only, and so is direct current. It is varying d.c. and contains only half of the energy of the input.

A rectifier changes a.c. to d.c.

BRIDGE RECTIFIER: FULL-WAVE RECTIFICATION

A bridge rectifier or full-wave rectifier is an arrangement of four diodes which allows a flow of current for the complete a.c. cycle.

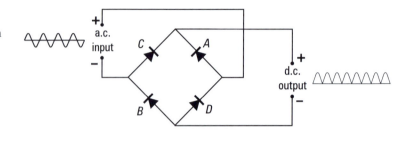

In the first stage of an a.c. cycle, diodes A and B are forward-biased and current flows. Diodes C and D are in reverse bias and do not allow a current flow.

In the second stage of the cycle, diodes C and D are forward-biased and current flows. Diodes A and B are in reverse bias and no current flows. In this way the complete a.c. wave is rectified.

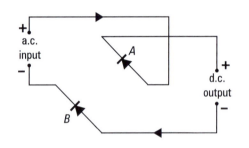
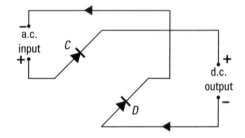

The addition of a smoothing circuit of an inductance and a capacitor converts the varying d.c. output to smooth d.c.

Light-emitting diode (LED)

When current flows through a silicon semiconductor, the energy lost in the semiconductor is emitted as heat. In other semiconductors, such as gallium arsenide, gallium phosphide and gallium arsenide phosphide, the energy is given off as visible light. The semiconductor must be very thin for the light to be seen. The light is usually red or green.

The LED must be forward-biased, because light is emitted only when current flows through the LED. The maximum current an LED can safely pass is very small (about 50 mA), and the forward voltage is about 2·0 V. A series resistor is required to keep the current below the maximum value.

USES OF LEDs

LEDs are used as current on/off indicators, as the numerical display in calculators and as part of an optical switch.

Applied Electricity: Semiconductors (Option 2)

On/off indicator
The LED is forward-biased in the circuit. A suitable series-'limiting' resistor is included. When the circuit is 'on' (i.e. the voltage is applied), current flows through the LED, which emits light and indicates that the circuit is 'on'. When the circuit is off the LED does not light.

Optical display
The calculator display is made from seven-segment LED assemblies: each assembly has seven LEDs arranged as shown in the diagram. When a forward-bias voltage is applied to a segment, it lights up. Different combinations of seven segments produce all the numerals from 0 to 9. Other displays can be made to produce the letters of the alphabet.

LEDs are better than ordinary filament-type bulbs for these displays because of their small size and because a very small current is required to operate them, they have a long life and they operate at a high speed.

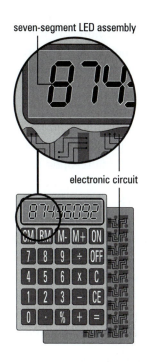

Photodiode
When energy falls on a semiconductor it produces more current carriers (electrons or 'holes'), and consequently its resistance falls. The energy can be heat, light, infrared radiation, microwaves, X-rays or gamma rays. This effect is greatest when the energy falls on a thin slice of the semiconductor.

The photodiode is a p–n junction with a 'window' that exposes the junction to light. It sometimes has a small plastic lens that focuses the light on the junction.

The photodiode is operated in reverse bias
A tiny 'leakage' current flows when the junction is not exposed to light. When light energy falls on the junction, electrons and 'holes' are produced in the semiconductor. This increases the leakage current in proportion to the intensity of the light falling on it.

Optical switch
This consists of an LED and a photodiode (or a phototransistor, which is more sensitive) mounted in a single package. The LED emits light when current flows through it. The light falls on the photodiode. Current flows through the photodiode and completes that circuit. Optical switches have many applications. They are used as:
(a) safety guards in machines
(b) end-of-tape indicators in tape recorders
(c) out-of-paper machine controls in printing machines
(d) smoke alarms.

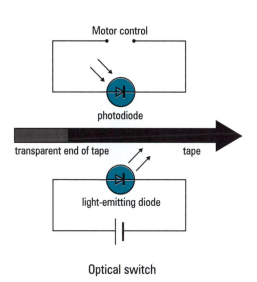

Optical switch

Fibre-optic receiver
Fibre-optic cables are rapidly replacing metal conductor cables for carrying telephone, television and data (computer) messages from one place to another. A fibre-optic cable would typically carry 100 fibre pairs

with each fibre pair carrying the equivalent of 50,000 telephone connections. The fibres are made of ultra-pure glass. The fibres are smaller than metal cables and are not affected by magnetic and electric fields and do not corrode. Fibre-optic cables are usually 30–50 km in length.

An electrical signal is converted by a LED or laser into a series of light pulses and these are sent through the fibre. At the other end the light pulses reach a photo-transistor and are converted back into an electrical signal — this is a fibre-optic receiver.

Transistors

The transistor was developed in 1947 by Bardeen, Brattain and Shockley at Bell Laboratories in the USA. Transistors are used to amplify (magnify) an electrical signal and as electronic switches. They are widely used in electronic equipment, both individually and in integrated circuits. Integrated circuits are semiconductor 'chips' that contain thousands of transistors in a single 'thumbnail-size' slice of silicon. They are used in all types of computers and electronic controls.

BIPOLAR TRANSISTOR

The npn bipolar transistor is a 'sandwich' of a thin slice of p-type material between two much thicker slices of n-type material. Transistors are usually made in a number of steps from a single piece of semiconductor. The thin centre slice of material is known as the **base**; the other two slices are the **emitter** and the **collector**. The emitter is usually more heavily 'doped' than the other two parts.

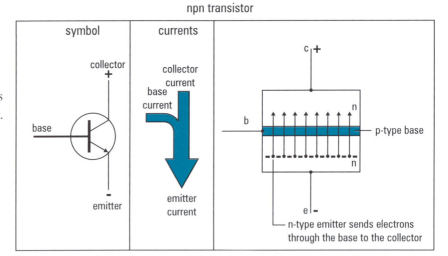

Clearly, there are two p–n junctions in this transistor (which is why it is called a bipolar transistor). The operation of the transistor depends on what happens at these two junctions.
The transistor operates with:
(a) the emitter–base junction forward-biased
(b) the base–collector junction reverse-biased.

HOW THE TRANSISTOR WORKS

We have already seen that no current flows in a forward-biased p–n junction until the voltage across it is about 0·6 V (for silicon semiconductors). Once the voltage is greater than 0·6 V, current flows. The forward bias on the emitter-base junction means that electrons flow from the emitter into the base. Since the base is very thin, the electrons do not have to go very far to be attracted by the positive voltage on the collector. In this way most of the electrons flowing from the emitter reach the collector (even though the base–collector junction is negatively biased). About 99% of the electrons flowing from the emitter to the base reach the collector. The remainder form the base current. **The emitter current equals the sum of the collector current and the base current.** A very thin base region allows more emitter electrons through to the collector than a thick base region would. A thin base region also allows the transistor to act faster, since the electrons have a shorter distance to travel. Once the emitter–base voltage (base voltage) falls below 0·6 V, the current is cut off. Clearly, the transistor can be switched on and off by the base voltage

The base voltage controls the base current I_b, which in turn controls the collector current I_c.
$I_e = I_c + I_b$
$I_c = kI_b$, where k is the amplification factor or 'gain' of the transistor.

SWITCHING ACTION OF THE TRANSISTOR

The switching action of the transistor is demonstrated in the circuit in the diagram, which is used to switch a bulb on when it gets dark. This circuit uses a light-dependent resistor (a cadmium sulphide (CdS) photoresistor).

Experiment 31.2

AIM: To demonstrate the switching action of the transistor.
1. The two resistors R and the LDR act as a potential divider for the supply voltage. The supply voltage is divided in the ratio of the two resistances.
2. When it is bright, the resistance of the LDR is about 100 Ω and R is 4·7 kΩ. Most of the voltage is across R. The voltage across the LDR is the emitter–base voltage of the transistor, and is too small to switch 'on' the transistor.
3. When it gets dark, the resistance of the LDR is about 2·5 kΩ. The voltage across the LDR (the emitter–base voltage of the transistor) is now greater than 0·6 V and switches 'on' the transistor. The collector current lights the bulb. The light intensity at which the transistor switches can be set by altering the value of R.
4. If you swap around the LDR and R, the potential divider is effectively reversed. The circuit now operates to switch a light on by day and off by night.

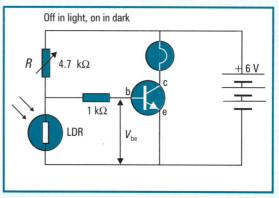

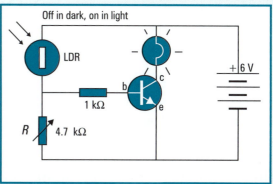

PHYSICS NOW!

THE REASON FOR A REVERSE-BIASED DIODE IN RELAY CIRCUITS

A reverse-biased diode is used in transistor circuits that contain electromagnetic relays. This is because of the self-inductance of the relay coil. When the relay is switched on (or off), a high back emf is induced across the coil. This would destroy the transistor. The diode offers a low-resistance path to the resultant current and protects the transistor.

TEMPERATURE SENSOR OR FIRE ALARM

This circuit can be made using a thermistor (temperature-dependent resistor) and a resistor R. The thermistor and R act as a potential divider. When the thermistor gets hot (resistance low), the emitter–base voltage is sufficient to switch on the transistor. This can be used to set off a fire alarm. If you swap around the thermistor and R, the circuit will operate when the thermistor is cold and switch off when it gets hot.

It is important to connect a transistor with the correct biasing. The emitter–base junction is always positively biased and the base–collector junction is always negatively biased. Incorrect battery connections will damage the transistor.

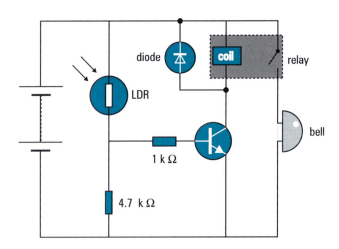

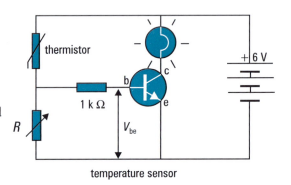

temperature sensor

PNP TRANSISTORS

A pnp transistor is similar in construction and operation to an npn transistor. In the pnp transistor a thin slice of n-type semiconductor is sandwiched between pieces of p-type material. Holes form the current carriers from emitter, through base, to collector. The emitter–base junction is forward-biased and the base–collector junction is reverse-biased.

npn transistors are faster then pnp and can operate at higher frequencies. This is because electron movement is faster than hole movement.

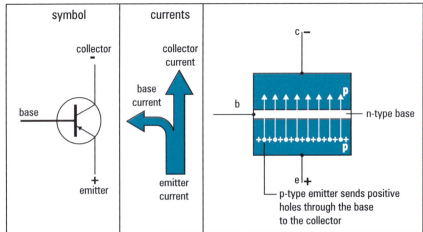

The transistor is a voltage amplifier

We use the transistor as a voltage amplifier to produce an enlarged copy of an alternating voltage input.

Applied Electricity: Semiconductors (Option 2)

Experiment 31.3

AIM: To demonstrate the action of a transistor as a voltage amplifier.

METHOD:
1. Set up the circuit shown.
2. When no input voltage V_i is applied, the output voltage V_o should be about half the supply voltage. This allows the maximum voltage swing when an alternating voltage signal is applied to the input. This can be set by adjusting the values of R_b and R_L.
3. An a.c. signal V_i is applied to the input circuit from a signal generator. The voltage of this signal is very small. The peak voltage (amplitude) of the signal can be measured using an oscilloscope.
4. The peak voltage of the output V_o is measured with the oscilloscope.
5. The output voltage V_o is an enlarged copy of the input voltage V_i.

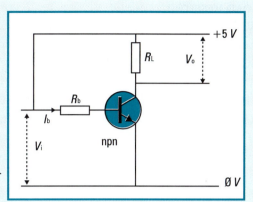

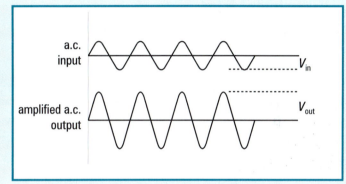

Explanation

The input voltage V_i adds to or takes from the base–emitter voltage V_b. This causes the base current I_b to increase and decrease in step with the applied input, and controls the much larger collector current I_c. This current flows through the load resistor R_L and causes a voltage drop across it (by Ohm's law this voltage is $I_c \times R_L$).

When V_i adds to V_b, I_b increases. This causes a much greater increase in I_c. The voltage produced by this current across R_L is large. The output voltage V is large.

When V_i takes from V_b, I_b is reduced. This causes a much greater reduction in I_c. The voltage produced by this current across R_L is small. The output voltage taken across this resistor is small.

Bias resistor

In practical transistor circuits, just one power supply is provided. The transistor is connected so that the base–emitter junction is forward-biased and the base–collector circuit is reverse-biased. This is done by connecting a base bias resistor R_b in circuit. The action of the bias resistor can be explained in terms of either current or voltage.

The bias resistor is a large series resistor which limits the base current I_b to a safe value. It is also a resistor across which most of the supply voltage is dropped, leaving only a small safe voltage to forward-bias the emitter–base circuit.

PHYSICS NOW!

LOAD RESISTOR
We have seen the purpose of the load resistor R_L in the explanation of the transistor as a voltage amplifier. The voltage across this resistor (by Ohm's law, $V = I_c \times R_L$) is the output voltage.

The transistor is a voltage inverter
A voltage inverter always gives an output voltage that is the opposite of the input voltage. We use the same basic circuit as in the voltage amplifier, but take the output across the transistor.

Experiment 31.4
AIM: To demonstrate the action of a transistor as a voltage inverter.

METHOD:
1. Set up the circuit shown.
2. When no input voltage V_i is applied, the output voltage V_o should be about half the supply voltage. This allows the maximum voltage swing when an alternating voltage signal is applied to the input. This can be set by adjusting the values of R_b and R_L.
3. An a.c. signal V_i is applied to the input circuit from a signal generator. The voltage of this signal is very small. The peak voltage (amplitude) of the signal can be measured using an oscilloscope.
4. The peak voltage of the output V_o is measured with the oscilloscope.
5. When the input voltage V_i is small, the output voltage V_o is big. When the input voltage is big, the output voltage is small. Clearly the transistor inverted the signal (turned it upside-down) as well as amplifying it.

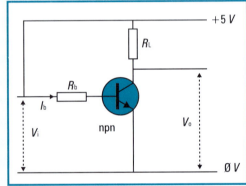

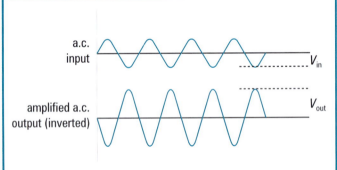

The action of a transistor as either a voltage amplifier or a voltage inverter depends on whether the output is taken across a load resistor or across the transistor.

Logic gates
A logic gate is a device that gives an output signal only when certain conditions are met in the input signal. The following examples show the basic principles of logic gates.

Applied Electricity: Semiconductors (Option 2)

AND

In this circuit the bulb represents the output. It will light only when both switch A and switch B are pressed at the same time. This type of circuit is called an **AND** gate.

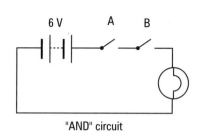

"AND" circuit

An AND gate is a circuit where there is an output only when BOTH inputs are ON.

Input A	Input B	Output
Off	Off	Off
On	Off	Off
Off	On	Off
On	On	On

OR

In this circuit the bulb will light when either switch A or switch B is pressed. This type of circuit is called an OR gate.

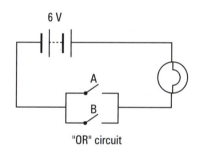

"OR" circuit

An OR gate is a circuit where there is an output when EITHER input is ON.

Input A	Input B	Output
Off	Off	Off
On	Off	On
Off	On	On
On	On	On

All the sorting, processing, control and other functions in digital computers are carried out by semiconductor logic gates built into the integrated circuits.

In logic tables a low input, 0 V or close to 0 V, is represented by 0. A high input, in the above case 6 V, is represented by 1. Inputs and outputs are regarded as 0 or 1 ('off' or 'on'). This is why quantities are represented by binary code in digital computers. The **AND** gate is represented by the following truth table.

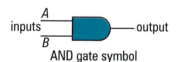

AND gate symbol

AND truth table

inputs A	B	output
0	0	0
1	0	0
0	1	0
1	1	1

If we represent a low input or output by 0 and a high input or output by 1, we get the following truth table for the OR gate.

OR gate symbol

OR truth table

inputs A B	output
0 0	0
1 0	1
0 1	1
1 1	1

A NOT gate is a circuit where there is an output only when the input is OFF.

The **NOT** gate functions by giving a low or 0 V output when the input is high (6 V), and a high output (6 V) when the input is low (0 V). A **NOT** gate contains only a single input.

The transistor as a voltage inverter acts as a NOT gate: When the input is high, the output is low; when the input is low, the output is high.

Input voltage	Output voltage
low	high
high	low

The truth table for the **NOT** function is as follows.

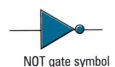

NOT gate symbol

NOT truth table

inputs	output
0	1
1	0

AND, **OR** and **NOT** gates are in practice made as integrated circuits (ICs) with connections for input, power supply and output. The following experiments can be conducted using an appropriately connected IC gate.

George Boole (England) 1815–1864 was appointed Professor of Mathematics at Queen's College, Cork (now UCC) in 1849 even though he didn't have a degree. He taught there for the rest of his life. Boole approached mathematical logic in a new way by reducing it to simple algebra. His two-valued (binary) algebra has wide applications in the logic circuits of computers.

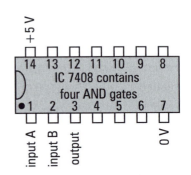

Experiment 31.5

AIM: To establish truth tables for **AND**, **OR** and **NOT** gates.

APPARATUS: **AND**, **OR** and **NOT** circuits as shown in the circuit diagrams. An LED is used to indicate the output state.

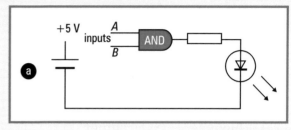

METHOD: AND

1. Connect up the circuit as shown in the circuit diagram. Check that circuit is correct before connecting to the battery.
2. Apply a 0 V input to A and a 0 V input to B by connecting to the ground (0 V) line (minus of battery). Note whether the LED is 'on' or 'off'.
3. Apply a 5 V input to A by connecting A to the 5 V line (plus of battery). Apply a 0 V input to B. Again note the state of the LED.
4. Apply a 0 V input to A and a 5 V input to B. Note the state of the LED.
5. Apply a 5 V input to A and a 5 V input to B. Again note the state of the LED.
6. Complete the truth table for the **AND** circuit. An 'on' input is recorded as '1'; an 'off' input as '0'. The output is taken as the state of the bulb: 'on' or 'off'.

Input A	Input B	AND output
0	0	
1	0	
0	1	
1	1	

METHOD: OR

1. Connect up the circuit as shown in the diagram.
2. Apply inputs to A and B in the same order as for **AND** above.
3. Note the state of the LED after each set of inputs.
4. Complete the truth table for the **OR** circuit.

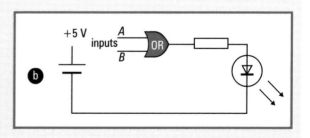

Input A	Input B	OR output
0	0	
1	0	
0	1	
1	1	

METHOD: NOT
1. Set up the circuit as shown.
2. Apply a 0 V input to the circuit. Note the state of the LED.
3. Apply a 5 V input to the circuit. Again note the state of the LED.
4. Complete the truth table for the **NOT** circuit.

Input	NOT output
0	
1	

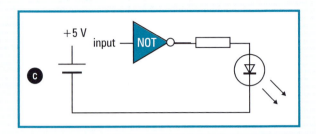

C

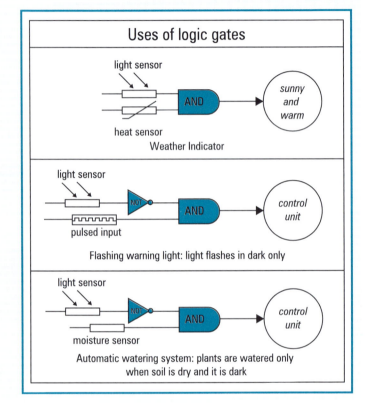

Uses of logic gates

Weather Indicator

Flashing warning light: light flashes in dark only

Automatic watering system: plants are watered only when soil is dry and it is dark

Summary

◆ A rectifier changes a.c. to d.c.
◆ A light-emitting diode emits light when current flows through it.
◆ Photodiode: The current flowing through a p–n junction operated in reverse bias increases when light falls on the junction.
◆ The base voltage controls the base current in a transistor, which in turn controls the collector current.
◆ A reverse-biased diode is used in relay circuits because of the self-induction of the coil of the relay. The diode offers a low-resistance path to the resultant current.
◆ The action of a transistor as either a voltage amplifier or a voltage inverter depends on whether the output is taken across a load resistor or across the transistor.

Applied Electricity: Semiconductors (Option 2)

- **AND** gate: A circuit where there is an output only when **BOTH** inputs are **ON**.
- **OR** gate: A circuit where there is an output when **EITHER** input is **ON**.
- **NOT** gate: A circuit where there is an output only when the input is **OFF**.
- **AND**, **OR** and **NOT** gates are in practice made as integrated circuits (ICs) with connections for inputs, power supply and output.

Short Questions

1. The process of converting alternating current to direct current is known as (A) declination, (B) modulation, (C) oscillation, (D) radiation, (E) rectification.
2. A diode is often used to (A) reduce current, (B) change d.c. into a.c., (C) reduce voltage, (D) change a.c. into d.c., (E) increase current.
3. A reverse-biased diode is used in relay circuits because _____.
4. The diagram shows three semiconductor devices. Name the devices labelled A, B and C. Give one application for each device.

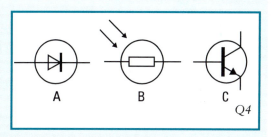

5. In a photodiode, the number of free charge carriers is increased by _____.
6. Why should a light-emitting diode (LED) always have a resistor connected in series with it?
7. The current flowing through a _____ diode is proportional to the _____ of the light.
8. Give two differences between an LED and a photodiode.
9. The diagram shows a simple rectifier circuit using a diode. When an oscilloscope was placed across the resistor and suitably adjusted, which of the traces A to E in the diagram would you expect to see on the screen?

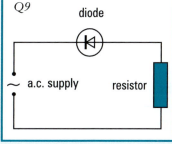
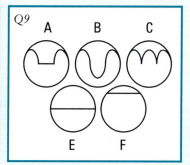

10. An AND gate has two inputs, A and B. In what circumstances will the output of the gate be 'high'?
11. (a) A circuit where there is an output only when BOTH inputs are ON is _____ gate.
    (b) A circuit where there is an output when EITHER input is ON is _____ gate.
    (c) A circuit where there is an output only when the input is OFF is _____ gate.

12. An LED is connected in series with a resistor and a 6 V battery. Calculate the minimum resistance of the resistor given that the maximum safe current for the LED is 10 mA and the potential difference across the LED is 1·7 V when this current flows.
13. An AND gate has two inputs, A and B. Under what circumstances will the output of the gate be 'high'?
14. The resistance of a _____ depends on the intensity of the light falling on it.
15. The resistor connected to a LED (A) controls the battery voltage, (B) increases the voltage across the LED, (C) changes the colour of the light (D) keeps the current through the LED to a safe value, (E) increases the current through the LED.
16. Match up each item in list A with one item in list B

A	B
Heater	Changes electricity to light
LED	Resistance changes with temperature
LDR	Changes electricity to heat
Relay	Current changes with light
Thermistor	Changes electricity to movement
Photodiode	Resistance changes with light

17. A NOT gate gives a _____ output when the input is low.
18. Which of the following pairs of values gives the resistance of an LDR?

Dark	Bright
(A) 1 kΩ	10 MΩ
(B) 100 Ω	10 MΩ
(C) 10 MΩ	100 Ω
(D) 1 kΩ	1 kΩ
(E) 10 MΩ	100 kΩ

Applied Electricity: Semiconductors (Option 2)

Long Questions

1. The points X and Y on the circuit shown in the diagram were connected to the terminals of an a.c. generator. What is the function of the diode (A) in this circuit? Sketch the graph you would expect to see on an oscilloscope connected across R.

   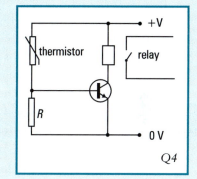
   Q1

2. An npn transistor consists of two layers of n-type semiconductor with a thin layer of p-type semiconductor between. Give the circuit symbol for an npn transistor and label the base, collector and emitter.

3. The diagram shows a temperature-controlled switch based on an npn bipolar transistor. T is a semiconductor thermistor.
   (a) Explain why the light-emitting diode (LED) comes on when the thermistor is warmed.
   (b) Explain the function of each of the resistors R_1 and R_2.

   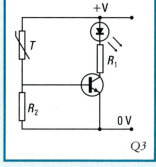
   Q3

4. (a) Describe the basic structure of an npn transistor. What is (i) a thermistor, (ii) an LDR?
   (b) The diagram shows a circuit that was used to switch a relay. State why the relay switches when the thermistor is heated beyond a certain temperature.

5. Under what lighting conditions would you expect the lamp L in the diagram to light? Explain your answer.

6. Draw two circuits to show how an 'on' LED could be used to indicate that the output from a circuit is (i) 'on', (ii) 'off'.

7. An LED lights when a current of 15 mA flows and the voltage across it (V_F) is 2·4 V. Calculate the value of the series resistor needed when a 6 V battery is connected to this LED.

8. A gas boiler has a logic gate to ensure that the pilot flame is alight before the gas valve is switched 'on' to supply gas to the boiler. If the thermostat applies a 'high' signal when the room temperature drops below the selected value and the pilot flame sensor applies a 'high' signal when the flame is 'on', what type of logic gate is used in this control system? Explain how this works.

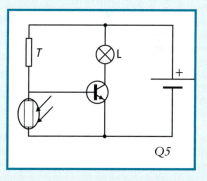
Q4

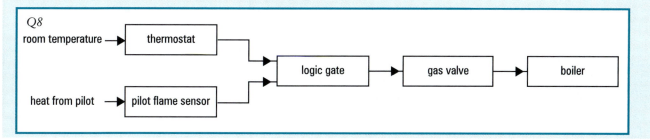
Q5

Q8

299

9. The thermistor in the circuit in the diagram is heated.
   (a) Does its resistance increase or decrease?
   (b) What happens to the reading on the voltmeter as the thermistor is heated?
   (c) Will the bell ring when the thermistor is hot or when it is cold? Why?
   (d) Give one practical use for this circuit.

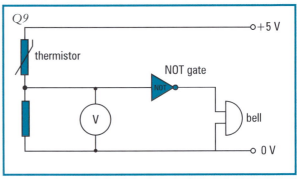

10. A washing machine must have water up to a particular level, be at a certain temperature and have its door closed before the motor works. What types of sensors and logic gates would you use to do this? Draw a simple diagram, showing the gates and the sensors, to illustrate your answer.

11. A central heating boiler has a control system that shuts off a solenoid valve when the boiler temperature is too high or when the flame goes out. The flame sensor is high when hot and the temperature sensor is high when hot.
    (a) What type of logic gate is in this system?
    (b) What type of sensors are used?
    (c) What additional type of logic gate must be connected to the flame sensor for the control unit to work?
    (d) Why is this not needed on the boiler temperature control?

12. A certain logic gate has two inputs, A and B, and one output. Part of the truth table for the gate is shown in the table. State the name of this gate and give its symbol. Copy the table and complete the last two lines of the truth table. Draw a diagram of a circuit which might have been used in an experiment to verify the truth table. Label the input and output terminals and give the steps involved in carrying out the experiment. Explain how the output of the gate might have been detected.

A	B	Output
1	1	1
1	0	1

13. The diagram shows a light controlled switch. While light falls on the CdS cell the light-emitting diode (LED) is off. While the CdS cell is in darkness the LED is on. Explain why the LED comes on when no light falls on the CdS cell and give one use of this type of circuit.

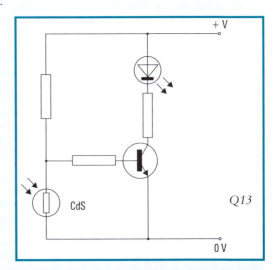

The Electron

CHAPTER 32

The electron was discovered as a result of experiments into the conduction of electricity through gases. Gas does not usually conduct electricity, but when a high voltage is used the gas ionises (breaks into ions) and conducts electricity.

Scientists found that when the gas pressure was reduced almost to a vacuum, the glass walls of the tube fluoresced. They thought this was caused by 'cathode rays'. The fluorescence happens with all gases and with all types of metal electrode. This suggests that the 'cathode rays' are part of all substances.

We now know that 'cathode rays' are in fact electrons. The electrons are produced at the cathode when positive ions (produced by ionisation of the gas) hit the cathode with a lot of energy. This releases many electrons.

ELECTRONS HAVE A NEGATIVE CHARGE

In 1895, J. B. Perrin showed that cathode rays have a negative electric charge by an experiment similar to the following one.

1. Connect up the circuit as shown in the diagram.
2. Connect the 'can' of the Perrin tube to the cap of the electroscope.
3. Move the magnet close to the tube until the electron beam is deflected into the 'can'. The leaves of the electroscope diverge: it is charged.
4. Test the charge on the electroscope.

Result: It has a negative charge.

Jean Baptiste Perrin (France) 1870–1942 was the first to show that cathode rays consist of negatively charged particles. He was awarded the Nobel Prize for physics in 1926.

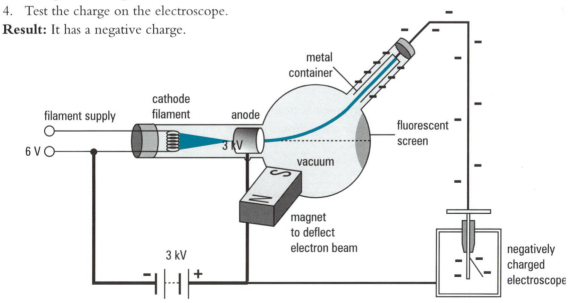

301

Physics Now!

All electrons have the same mass and charge

In 1897 J. J. Thomson experimented with a narrow beam of electrons. He found that electrons are deflected by a magnetic field in a way that shows they are a beam of negative charge. He also deflected electrons with an electric field.

The electron beam was deflected by a fixed amount by a magnetic field (and by the electric field). This means that electrons all have the same mass and carry the same amount of negative charge. If the beam contained particles of different masses and charge we would expect the electron beam to be deflected by different amounts and to split into a number of parts.

Joseph John Thomson (England) 1856–1940 experimented with effects in a gas discharge tube. He also investigated 'cathode rays' and discovered that these were negative charges (electrons), and measured the charge-to-mass ratio of the electron (cathode rays). He was awarded the Nobel Prize for physics in 1906.

Experiments show that cathode rays:
1. cause fluorescence
2. blacken photographic plates
3. travel in straight lines
4. are deflected by magnetic and electric fields in a direction that shows them to be negative
5. cause a heating effect when they strike a small target
6. can pass through a thin metal foil
7. produce X-rays when they strike a heavy metal target
8. have a nature that is independent of the metal used in the cathode.

Conclusion: Cathode rays are negatively charged particles: electrons.

The idea that there was a natural unit of electricity in each atom was suggested in 1891 by Irishman George Johnstone Stoney. Stoney named the unit an 'electron'.

Energy of an electron

An electron has a negative charge. An electric field accelerates an electron and gives it kinetic energy. The amount of energy depends on the strength of the electric field (the voltage across the cathode ray tube).

An electron accelerated across a potential difference of 1 volt has an energy of 1.6×10^{-19} J. A more convenient way of describing this is to say that the energy gained by the electron accelerated across a potential difference of 1 volt is **one electron-volt or 1 eV.** When the voltage is 1,000 V the energy is **1 keV**. An **MeV** is 10^6 **eV** and a **GeV** is 10^9 **eV**.

The Electron

CHARGE-TO-MASS RATIO OF THE ELECTRON

Thomson measured the ratio of the electric charge of the electron to the mass of the electron in 1897, as follows.

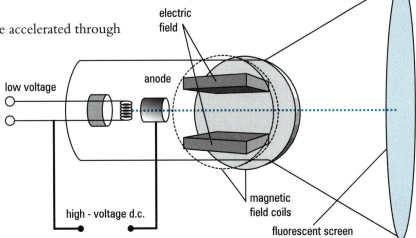

1. Electrons produced by a hot cathode are accelerated through the hollow cylindrical anode and strike the centre of a fluorescent screen.
2. The magnetic field is switched on. This deflects the beam away from the centre of the screen.
3. The electric field between the two plates is switched on and adjusted until the electron beam returns to its original position at the centre of the screen.
4. When the beam is restored to its original position these two forces equal each other.

Thomson calculated a value of $\frac{e}{m}$ from this experiment.
He found that the specific charge (charge-to-mass ratio) of the electron did not vary.

An electron is a particle found in all matter which carries the fundamental unit of negative charge.

THE CHARGE OF THE ELECTRON

The charge of the electron was measured accurately by Robert Millikan in 1909. This followed a less accurate measurement by Thomson in 1898.

The smallest charge measured by Millikan was 1.6×10^{-19} C, and every other charge measured was a whole-number multiple of this charge. He concluded from this and from other evidence that the charge of the electron is 1.6×10^{-19} C.

The Millikan oil drop experiment demonstrates conclusively that the electron has an indivisible quantity of electric charge.

Robert Millikan (USA) 1868–1953 verified experimentally Einstein's photoelectric law. He carried out an experiment now known as Millikan's oil drop experiment, and found the unit of electric charge. He was awarded the Nobel Prize for physics in 1923.

The mass of the electron

The value of $\frac{e}{m}$ is 1.76×10^{11} C kg^{-1} from Thomson's experiment. The charge of the electron is 1.6×10^{-19} C (from Millikan). We can calculate the mass of the electron from these values:

$$\frac{e}{m} = 1.76 \times 10^{11}$$

$$e = 1.6 \times 10^{-19}$$

$$\Rightarrow m = 9.09 \times 10^{-31} \text{ kg}$$

The mass of the hydrogen atom

We can estimate the mass of the hydrogen atom as follows.
A mole of any substance is its molecular mass in grams. 1 mole of hydrogen has a mass of 2 g or 2×10^{-3} kg.

The number of molecules in a mole of any substance is 6.023×10^{23}, and is called Avogadro's number.

$$\text{mass of 1 molecule of hydrogen} = \frac{2 \times 10^{-3}}{(6.023 \times 10^{23})} \text{ kg}$$

One molecule of hydrogen contains 2 atoms.

$$\text{mass of 1 atom of hydrogen} = \frac{1 \times 10^{-3}}{(6.023 \times 10^{23})} \text{ kg} = 1.66 \times 10^{-27} \text{ kg}$$

This shows that an atom of hydrogen is about 2,000 times the mass of the electron.

PROBLEM

An electron beam in a cathode ray tube carries a current of 10 mA. Calculate the number of electrons crossing the tube each second.

$10 \text{ mA} = 10 \times 10^{-3} \text{ C s}^{-1}$

$1 \text{ e} = 1.6 \times 10^{-19} \text{ C}$

$$\text{number of electrons} = \frac{10 \times 10^{-3}}{1.6 \times 10^{-19}} = 6.25 \times 10^{16}$$

Thermionic emission

Thermionic emission is the emission of electrons from a hot metal surface.

We can show thermionic emission by the following experiment.

Experiment 32.1

AIM: To demonstrate thermionic emission.

METHOD:
1. Connect up the circuit as shown in the diagram. Pass a small current through the metal filament.
2. Connect A to the positive pole of the high-voltage d.c. supply.
3. Increase the voltage across CA from 0 to 300 V in 50 V steps. Note the current reading on the milliammeter (0–2.5 mA) for each voltage.
4. Draw a graph of the voltage against the current. The current does not go above a certain maximum value

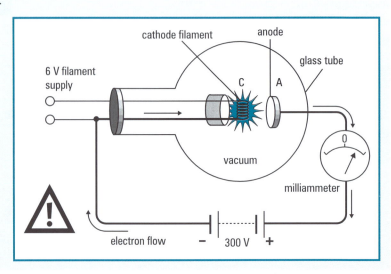

The Electron

regardless of the voltage applied. This is known as the 'saturation' current for that temperature.

5. Pass a bigger current through the filament. The metal glows more brightly. The cathode is now at a higher temperature.
6. Repeat steps 3 and 4. The new saturation current is greater than before.
7. Connect A to the negative pole of the d.c. supply. Increase the voltage from 0 to 300 V. The milliammeter registers no current flow even when the voltage is big.

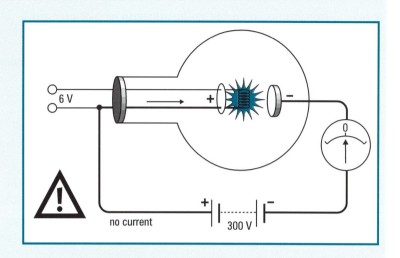

Explanation: The hot filament transfers energy to the cathode. Some electrons near the surface of the metal gain enough energy to leave the metal. These electrons form a 'cloud' of electrons above the metal. The negative charge repels any more electrons and stops them from leaving the metal surface.

When the anode is at a positive potential these free electrons move from the cathode to the anode, current flows and more electrons are freed from the surface. If the anode is at a negative potential it repels electrons and no current flows. Electrons flow in one direction only through the thermionic vacuum tube.

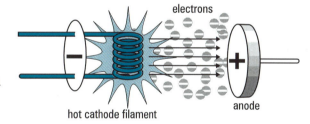

Explanation of graph

A to B: A small current flows between the anode and cathode due to some of the free electrons reaching the anode.

B to C: As the voltage increases the free electrons are moved across to the anode by the electric field. Increasing the voltage moves more electrons across.

C to D: A voltage is reached where each electron is moved over to the anode as soon as it is freed by the hot cathode. Increasing the voltage does not produce an increase in current. This maximum current is known as the saturation current.

E to F: Increasing the temperature of the cathode produces more electrons, and this gives a higher saturation current.

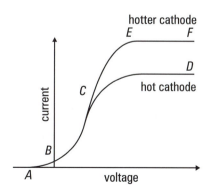

Work function

The minimum amount of energy necessary to release an electron from the surface of a metal is the **work function**. The work function depends on the metal surface used. Temperatures of about 2,000°C are required with cathodes of tungsten or platinum. Thermionic emission takes place at 800°C from tungsten coated with strontium or barium oxides. These cathodes have lower work functions than tungsten.

The work function is the minimum amount of energy needed to release an electron from the surface of a metal.

In thermionic emission:
1. electrons are emitted from the surface of a hot metal
2. the higher the temperature of the metal, the more electrons are emitted
3. electrons are accelerated across the vacuum tube only when the anode A is at a positive potential
4. the greater the positive potential of A, the greater is the current up to a limit (the saturation current).

How the cathode ray tube produces a picture

A hot cathode produces a beam of electrons by thermionic emission. The electron beam is accelerated towards the anode by a high positive voltage. The tube is a vacuum tube so that nothing can get in the way of the electrons. When the electron beam strikes the phosphorescent screen coating it gives a spot of light.

THE NEED FOR A FOCUSING SYSTEM

A beam of electrons is a beam of negatively charged particles. The electrons repel each other and spread out. This produces a blurred spot on the screen. A system of focusing anodes is used to correct this problem.

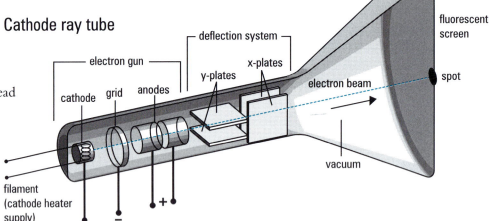

BEAM DEFLECTION

An electron beam can be deflected by an electric field or by a magnetic field. Two fields, at right angles to each other, are used in a cathode ray oscilloscope to deflect the electron spot in vertical and horizontal directions.

ELECTRIC FIELD DEFLECTION

The electric field deflection plates are mounted inside the cathode ray tube close to the neck of the tube. The horizontal plates (X-plates) deflect the beam in the horizontal direction. The vertical plates (Y-plates) deflect it in the vertical direction.

MAGNETIC FIELD DEFLECTION

The magnetic field deflection coils are fitted around the outside neck of the cathode ray tube. Magnetic field coils in the horizontal position deflect the beam in a vertical direction. Magnetic field coils in the vertical position deflect the beam in a horizontal direction. This is easily understood if you think of the beam as a current flowing through a magnetic field and apply the left-hand motor rule.

Uses of thermionic emission

Cathode ray tubes are used to produce a picture on a phosphor screen in televisions, oscilloscopes and computer monitors.

ELECTROCARDIOGRAPH (ECG) AND ELECTROENCEPHALOGRAPH (EEG)

A cathode ray oscilloscope is used to display the signal trace in an electrocardiograph (ECG). An ECG monitors the electrical activity of the heart muscle with electrodes attached to the body. Doctors can diagnose heart disease from the print-out of an ECG machine.

The electrical activity of the brain can be measured with an electroencephalograph (EEG) attached to electrodes on the head. EEGs are used to help diagnose strokes, epilepsy and brain tumours.

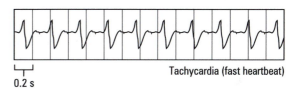

OSCILLOSCOPE

An oscilloscope is a cathode ray tube used to measure a.c. frequencies and voltages. Vertical and horizontal plates deflect the electron beam. A voltage across the Y-plates produces a deflection of the beam proportional to the voltage. A voltage is applied to the X-plates that deflects the beam steadily across the screen and then jumps back rapidly. This is the time-base circuit and can be varied from microseconds to about 10 seconds. A combination of the two deflections produces the oscilloscope trace.

TELEVISION

A television set is a cathode ray tube. An electron beam sweeps across the screen, flies back very quickly (so fast you don't even see it) and sweeps across again lower down. This takes place 625 times as the beam moves down the screen, and is repeated 25 times a second. The television signal varies the strength of the beam and changes the brightness on the screen. The fluorescence of the screen persists for a short time so that a complete picture is produced by the beam moving down the screen.

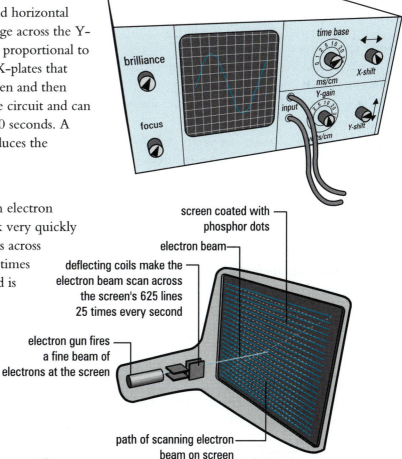

Physics Now!

Colour television

The screen is made of carefully placed lines of three different phosphors. These produce red or green or blue light when struck by an electron beam. Three electron guns produce electron beams: one for each colour phosphor. Each electron beam is aligned so that it will pass through a set of holes in a metal screen and strike only its own colour phosphors. Combinations of the three primary colours produced by the phosphors give all other colours.

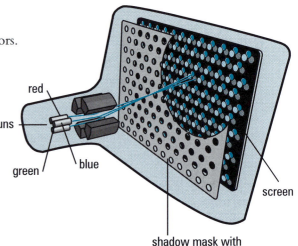

Colour television

Summary

- Cathode rays are composed of electrons.
- Cathode rays: travel in straight lines, cause fluorescence, blacken photographic plates, are deflected by magnetic and electric fields, cause heating when they strike a target, can pass through thin metal foil and can produce X-rays.
- An electron is a particle that carries the fundamental unit of negative charge and is found in all matter.
- Thermionic emission is the emission of electrons from a hot metal surface.
- The work function is the minimum amount of energy needed to release an electron from the surface of a metal.

Short Questions

1. The force needed to deflect a beam of electrons may be produced by _____ or _____.
2. Which of the following is not a correct statement about cathode rays?
   (A) They are deflected by an electric field.
   (B) They are deflected by a magnetic field.
   (C) They travel in straight lines.
   (D) They are streams of electrons.
   (E) They have a positive charge.
3. In a cathode ray tube a beam of cathode rays is most likely to cross the tube if
   (A) the filament is heated and the anode voltage is switched off
   (B) the filament is heated and the anode is negative with respect to the cathode
   (C) the filament is switched off and the anode is negative with respect to the cathode
   (D) the filament is heated and the anode is positive with respect to the cathode
   (E) the filament is switched off and the anode is positive with respect to the cathode.

The Electron

4. The diagram illustrates a cathode ray tube. Name the five parts indicated by the letters A to E.
   (A) _____
   (B) _____
   (C) _____
   (D) _____
   (E) _____
   Which part is used to detect the cathode rays?

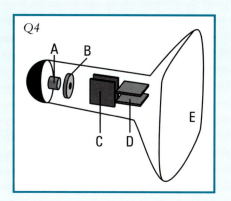

5. (a) What type of beam is produced in a cathode ray tube?
   (b) Where is the beam produced?
   (c) What causes the beam to move?
   (d) What happens when the beam hits the screen?
   (e) Name one everyday application of a cathode ray tube.
6. (a) How is the beam of electrons deflected in a TV tube?
   (b) How many horizontal lines are formed on the screen?
   (c) Why is the screen scanned 25 times each second?
   (d) What three colours are emitted by phosphors in a colour TV?
7. Give two properties of electrons.
8. What is meant by thermionic emission?
9. Give one application of thermionic emission.
10. Give two methods by which a beam of electrons can be deflected.
★11. What is the kinetic energy, in joules, of an electron which has been accelerated from rest through a potential difference of 2000 V (charge on electron, $e = 1.6 \times 10^{-19}$ C)?
12. When a current flows through a gas the charge carriers are electrons and _____.
13. When electrons are emitted from a hot metal surface the process is known as _____.
14. What is the purpose of the grid in a cathode ray tube?
15. Millikan's oil-drop experiment was designed to measure
    (A) The speed of an electron
    (B) The mass of an electron
    (C) The charge of an electron
    (D) The charge to mass ratio for an electron
    (E) The force on an electron.

Long Questions

★1. A cathode ray tube has a beam current of I amps. Show that the number of electrons striking the anode per second is given by $n = I/e$ where e is the electronic charge.

★2. Sketch the path of an electron in (a) a uniform magnetic field, (b) a uniform electric field, and (c) a composition of a uniform electric field and a uniform magnetic field.

Physics Now!

3. Describe how a beam of electrons can be produced using a cathode ray tube and state two ways in which the beam can be deflected.

4. State two properties of electrons. Outline, with the aid of a labelled diagram, the production of electrons in a cathode ray tube.

5. Compare electrons and protons under the headings 'mass' and 'charge'. State one everyday application of a beam of electrons.

6. What are cathode rays? State briefly how it may be shown experimentally that cathode rays are charged and indicate how the sign of the charge may be identified.
The diagram shows a diagram of a cathode ray tube. State how cathode rays are produced in the tube and explain what happens when they strike the screen. Identify the parts of the tube labelled X and Y and give their functions.

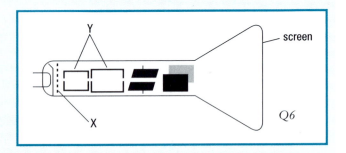

Photoelectric Emission and X-rays

CHAPTER 33

The photoelectric effect is the emission of electrons from the surface of a metal when electromagnetic radiation of suitable frequency falls on it.

Experiment 33.1
AIM: To demonstrate photoelectric emission.
1. Clean the surface of a zinc plate with fine emery paper.
   Attach the plate to the cap of an electroscope.
2. Charge the electroscope with a negative charge.
3. Shine an ultraviolet (UV) lamp on the zinc plate.
4. The leaf slowly falls, indicating that the zinc plate and the electroscope have lost their charge.
5. Charge the electroscope with a positive charge.
6. Shine the UV light on the zinc plate.
7. The deflection of the leaf does not change.
8. Clean the surface of a zinc plate with fine emery paper. Attach the plate to the cap of an electroscope.
9. Charge the electroscope with a negative charge.
10. Shine light from (i) a filament bulb, (ii) an infra-red light on the zinc plate.
11. The deflection of the leaf does not change.

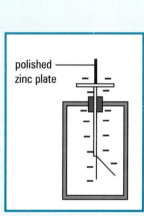
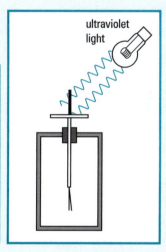

Experiments similar to the above were performed by Hallwachs in 1888. He concluded that negative charges are emitted by the zinc plate when UV light shines on it. When the plate is negatively charged, the charges are repelled from it and the electroscope loses its charge. When the plate is positively charged, it attracts back the negative charge and so no charge is lost.

Hallwachs' experiments were the result of a discovery by Hertz in 1887. Hertz found that the distance a spark could jump across a gap was increased if ultraviolet light fell on the gap.

In 1899 Thomson measured the charge-to-mass ratio of the negative charges released in photoelectric emission. He found that they were identical to cathode rays or electrons. As the electrons are freed from the metal by light, we refer to them as 'photoelectrons'.

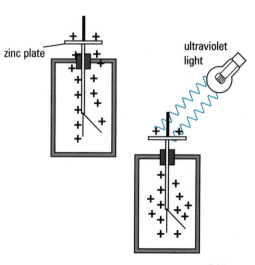

Physics Now!

In 1902 Lenard carried out a series of experiments on the photoelectric effect and discovered that:

1. electrons are emitted when light of suitable frequency falls on a metal surface
2. below a certain frequency of light (the threshold frequency), no electrons are emitted regardless of the intensity of the light
3. the number of electrons emitted depends on the intensity of the light
4. the energy of the electrons emitted depends on the frequency of the light.

Photoelectric effect: The emission of electrons from the surface of a metal when electromagnetic radiation of suitable frequency falls on it.

The threshold frequency is the minimum frequency necessary to cause photoelectric emission.

Photoelectric emission and the wave theory of light

Photoelectric emission caused many problems with the wave theory of light. The wave theory was accepted from 1801, when Young showed that light has wave properties. Light was seen as a continuous wave spreading out from the source. A wave has energy spread evenly over the entire wavefront and gives up its energy right across the wavefront.

When light falls on a zinc surface, all the electrons on the surface of the zinc should share this energy (according to the wave theory) and eventually get enough to leave the surface. A wave would take about 900 seconds to give electrons enough energy to escape. Electrons are in fact emitted after about 10^{-9} seconds.

Another problem was that the wave theory predicted that an intense beam of light would release electrons regardless of the frequency. Wave theory could not explain why photoelectron emission did not happen with light below the threshold frequency.

Planck's quantum theory

Planck put forward his theory in 1900. He said that light (and other electromagnetic energy) is emitted and absorbed in small 'packets' (quanta). Each quantum contains a definite amount of energy which depends only on the frequency of the light.

The quantum of energy is given by the equation $E = hf$, where h is a constant (Planck's constant).

PROBLEM

Calculate the number of photons emitted per second by a 100 W bulb if the wavelength emitted is 600 nm (a quantum of light energy is called a photon). Assume that 10% of the energy of the bulb is emitted as light.

Philipp Lenard (Hungary/Germany) 1862–1947 discovered the characteristics of the photoelectric effect. This was the basis for Einstein's photon theory of light. Lenard was awarded the 1905 Nobel Prize for physics.

Max Planck (Germany) 1858–1947 developed the quantum theory of light, which states that light is emitted in small energy packets called quanta. The constant of proportionality in the relationship between the energy of a quantum and the frequency of the radiation is called Planck's constant. Planck was awarded the Nobel Prize for physics in 1918.

energy of one photon $E = hf = \dfrac{hc}{\lambda}$

$= (6.6 \times 10^{-34}) \cdot \dfrac{(3 \times 10^8)}{600 \times 10^{-9}}$

$= 0.33 \times 10^{-17}$ J

10% of 100 W = 10 W = 10 J s^{-1}

number of photons per second $n = \dfrac{10}{(0.33 \times 10^{-17})}$

$= 3.03 \times 10^{18}$ photons

Einstein's photoelectric law

Planck's quantum theory was developed further by Einstein in 1905 and used to explain the photoelectric effect. Einstein proposed that
1. each photon travels closely concentrated in space
2. in photoelectric emission a photon gives up all its energy to one electron.

A photon is a quantum of light energy whose energy is given by Planck's equation: $E = hf$

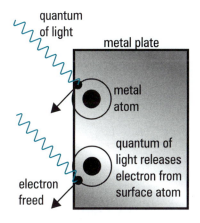

The minimum energy a photon needs to remove an electron from the surface of a metal is the work function Φ. If a photon doesn't have this energy it cannot cause photoelectric emission.

The work function is the minimum amount of energy needed to release an electron from the surface of a metal.

When a photon whose energy hf is greater than the work function Φ gives its energy to an electron, Φ is used by the electron to leave the metal. The remainder of the photon energy ($hf - \Phi$) is the maximum amount of kinetic energy the electron can have. This is Einstein's photoelectric law:

$hf = \Phi + \tfrac{1}{2} mv^2_{max}$

A photon has wave properties in that its energy depends on the frequency. It also has particle properties by being closely confined in space and interacting with matter as a single unit.

Threshold frequency

When a photon has just enough energy to release an electron from the surface of a metal, the frequency is called the threshold frequency f_0.

$\Phi = hf_0$

$f_0 = \dfrac{\Phi}{h}$

The threshold frequency is the minimum frequency needed to cause photoelectric emission.

PROBLEM

Calculate the energy of a 900 nm photon.

$$E = hf = \frac{hc}{\lambda} = (6 \cdot 6 \times 10^{-34}) \cdot \frac{(3 \cdot 0 \times 10^{8})}{(900 \times 10^{-9})} = 2 \cdot 2 \times 10^{-19} \text{ J}$$

PROBLEM

A metal has a work function of 1·0 eV. Calculate the maximum kinetic energy of electrons emitted when this metal is illuminated by light of wavelength 900 nm.

energy of 900 nm photon = $2 \cdot 2 \times 10^{-19}$ J (from above)

work function = 1·0 eV = $1 \cdot 0 \times 1 \cdot 6 \times 10^{-19}$ J = $1 \cdot 6 \times 10^{-19}$ J

Einstein's photoelectric law:

$$\tfrac{1}{2} m v^{2}_{max} = hf - \Phi$$

$$= (2 \cdot 2 \times 10^{-19}) - (1 \cdot 6 \times 10^{-19})$$

$$= 0 \cdot 6 \times 10^{-19} \text{ J}$$

Photocell

A photocell is a vacuum tube with a concave cathode made from a material that emits photoelectrons easily. Photoelectrons are emitted when light above the threshold frequency falls on it. The concave cathode focuses the electrons on a thin wire anode. The thin anode does not block light.

When the anode is at a positive potential, the electrons move across to the anode. The vacuum tube ensures that nothing gets in the way of the electrons. The intensity of the light controls the number of photoelectrons emitted.

VARIATION OF PHOTOELECTRIC CURRENT WITH THE INTENSITY OF LIGHT

In measuring the variation in photoelectric current with the intensity of a monochromatic light source, we assume that light intensity follows an inverse square law. This means that as we double the distance of a surface from a light source, the intensity of light falling on it drops to one quarter of the previous value. In mathematical terms, intensity $I \propto 1/d^2$.

Experiment 33.2

AIM: To demonstrate that photoelectric current varies with the intensity of a monochromatic light source.

METHOD:

1. Set the photocell at a distance d from the light source.
2. Adjust the voltage between the anode and cathode to give a maximum current reading. Read the photoelectric current I.
3. Increase the distance d and read I. Repeat for a number of distances.
4. Draw a graph of I against $1/d^2$. This is the same as a graph of photoelectric current against intensity of light.

The straight-line graph through the origin shows that photoelectric current varies directly with the light intensity. The light must be of greater frequency than the threshold frequency, and the voltage must be big enough to move all the electrons as they are emitted by photoelectric emission.

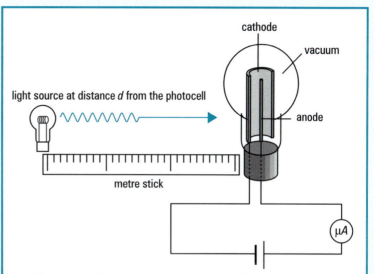

Uses of a photocell

Photocells have been used in burglar alarms, smoke alarms, automatic doors, safety switches on cutting machinery, laboratory light meters, optical soundtrack in film and control sensors in central heating boilers. Solid state photodiodes, photoresistors, light-dependent resistors (LDRs) and phototransistors have replaced the photocell in many of these uses.

X-rays

Roentgen discovered X-rays in 1895 while working with cathode rays. He found fluorescence in a chemical (barium platinocyanide) at a distance of about 2 m from a cathode ray tube. He covered the tube with black paper and found that the fluorescence could not have been caused by visible light. Roentgen knew from experimental evidence that cathode rays cannot travel through 2 m of air. He concluded that the fluorescence was caused by an unknown type of radiation: 'X-rays'. Roentgen continued his experiments on X-rays over many years.

Wilhelm Roentgen (Germany) 1845–1923
discovered X-rays while working on cathode rays. He investigated the nature of X-rays and developed a type of X-ray machine. Roentgen was the first recipient of the Nobel Prize for physics (in 1901).

X-rays were found to have the following properties. They:
1. are produced when fast electrons strike a solid body
2. produce fluorescence
3. blacken photographic emulsions (Roentgen took the first radiograph, of his wife's hand)
4. cannot be deflected by electric and magnetic fields
5. travel in straight lines and cannot be reflected or refracted easily
6. cause ionisation of the air
7. are diffracted by thin crystals
8. penetrate most substances
9. are absorbed by substances depending on the thickness and the density of the substance
10. are electromagnetic radiation of extremely short wavelength.

In 1912 Friedrich, Knipping and von Laue used a diffraction technique to measure the wavelengths of X-rays. They found that X-rays have wavelengths from 10^{-9} to 10^{-15} m.

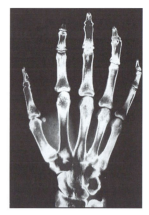

X-rays are used to diagnose breaks and other problems in bones and joints.

X-rays are electromagnetic radiation of extremely short wavelength.

Hot-cathode X-ray tube

Modern X-ray tubes are hot-cathode vacuum tubes. One type of hot-cathode tube was developed by William D. Coolidge in 1913.

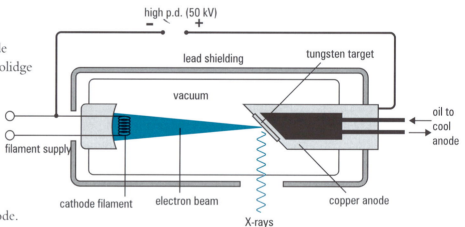

1. The hot-cathode X-ray tube has a hot cathode which produces electrons by thermionic emission.
2. A vacuum ensures that nothing slows the electrons.
3. A tungsten target is set into the anode.
4. The high voltage (>50 kV) across the tube accelerates the electrons.
5. The high-energy electrons hit the tungsten target in the anode and produce X-rays.
6. Only 1% of the electrons produce X-rays.
7. About 99% of the electrons produce heat in the anode. The heat produced is dissipated by cooling fins or cooling liquids circulated through the anode.
8. A lead shield with a small window ensures that X-rays are emitted in one direction.

INTENSITY OF THE X-RAY BEAM

The greater the number of electrons that hit the target, the more X-rays are produced. The number of electrons produced depends on the temperature of the cathode.

X-ray intensity depends on the temperature of the cathode.

PENETRATING POWER OF THE X-RAY BEAM
The greater the kinetic energy of the electrons that hit the target, the more penetrating are the X-rays produced. The kinetic energy of the electrons depends on the voltage across the tube.

X-ray penetrating power depends on the voltage across the tube.

How X-rays are produced
We know that light is emitted when an electron falls from an electron orbit, or energy level, to a lower one. The greater the energy drop, the shorter is the wavelength of light emitted. If the energy drop is great enough the electromagnetic radiation emitted is X-rays.

X-rays are emitted when an electron falls from an outer electron orbit (high energy level) to an inner orbit (lower energy). This happens when a fast electron knocks an electron out of an inner orbit. An electron from an outer orbit falls into this vacant place. The energy given off is an X-ray.

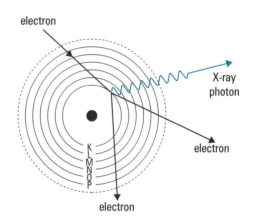

X-ray production is the inverse process of photoelectric emission. In photoelectric emission, photon energy frees an electron. In X-ray emission, the electron energy produces an X-ray photon.

PROBLEM
Calculate the wavelength of the X-ray photons emitted when electrons accelerated across a tube at a potential of 50 kV strike a tungsten target.

Energy of the electrons: $eV = (1·6 \times 10^{-19})(50 \times 10^3) = 80 \times 10^{-16}$ J

Energy of photon produced: $E = hf$

$$f = \frac{E}{h} = \frac{(80 \times 10^{-16})}{(6·6 \times 10^{-34})} = 1·212 \times 10^{19} \text{ Hz}$$

$$\lambda = \frac{c}{f} = \frac{(3 \times 10^8)}{(1·212 \times 10^{19})} = 2·475 \times 10^{-11} \text{ m}$$

Detection of X-rays
X-rays are detected by fluorescence in some materials: barium platinocyanide, glass, rock salt, fluorescent calcium salts. X-rays are also detected by a blackening of photographic film. This is used to take X-rays of broken bones and internal organs.

Uses of X-rays
X-RAYS IN MEDICINE
Bones are denser than flesh and show up on an X-ray photograph. X-rays are used to diagnose and locate breaks in bones. Modern techniques have reduced the amount of X-rays used. CAT scans are images from a

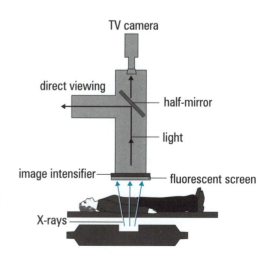

number of X-ray 'slices' through the body. The information is used by a computer to build a picture of the internal organs.

Very penetrating X-rays are used in X-ray therapy for cancer. These rays are focused on cancerous cells and destroy them.

X-RAYS IN INDUSTRY

X-rays are used to check welds in pressure vessels and in aircraft bodies, and to detect cracks in machinery under stress. X-rays are used in security checks of baggage in airports.

X-RAYS IN RESEARCH

Research scientists use X-ray diffraction to discover the structure of crystals and large molecules.

HARMFUL EFFECTS OF X-RAYS

X-rays have the same harmful effects as other ionising radiation (from radioactive substances). Repeated exposure to X-rays seriously damages your cells and may even cause cancer. Radiographers (operators of X-ray tubes) take special care to protect themselves from these effects. The lead shielding around the X-ray tube is not enough to protect them from all the X-rays they are exposed to in their work. They also wear lead-lined aprons and stand behind lead-glass screens to prevent radiation damage, and wear special film badges that show how much radiation they have absorbed.

Does this mean that it is dangerous to have your arm X-rayed if you break it? Of course not! You are exposed to just one small dose of X-rays, which doesn't harm you. You would suffer far more damage if you didn't have your arm properly set!

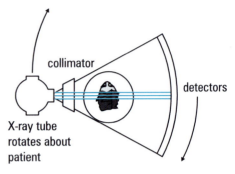

CAT scanner

Summary

- Photoelectric effect: the emission of electrons from the surface of a metal when electromagnetic radiation of suitable frequency falls on it.
- Photon: a packet of electromagnetic (light) energy whose energy is given by Planck's equation ($E = hf$).
- The work function is the minimum amount of energy needed to release an electron from the surface of a metal.
- The threshold frequency is the minimum frequency needed to cause photoelectric emission.
- Einstein's photoelectric equation: $hf = \Phi + \frac{1}{2}mv^2_{max}$
- X-rays are produced when fast electrons strike a solid metal target.
- X-rays are electromagnetic radiation of extremely short wavelength.
- X-rays cause ionisation of the air and other materials.
- X-rays penetrate most materials.

PHOTOELECTRIC EMISSION AND X-RAYS

SHORT QUESTIONS

Note:
Charge on electron, $e = 1.6 \times 10^{-19}$ C;
Planck's constant, $h = 6.6 \times 10^{-34}$ J s;
Speed of light in a vacuum, $c = 3 \times 10^{8}$ m s^{-1}.

1. What is a photon? When does light incident on a metal surface cause electrons to be emitted? The energy of a photon is proportional to _____. The constant of proportionality is known as _____.

2. The photoelectric effect is
   (A) the emission of electrons from a heated metal
   (B) the deflection of electrons in an electric field
   (C) the bombarding of a metal with electrons
   (D) the deflection of electrons in a magnetic field
   (E) the emission of electrons from a metal when light falls on its surface.

3. The photoelectric effect was discovered by _____ in 1888 and explained by _____ in 1905.

4. Which of the following has **no** effect on the maximum kinetic energy of the electrons emitted from a metal by photoelectric emission?
   (A) The nature of the metal.
   (B) The work function of the metal.
   (C) The frequency of the light.
   (D) The brightness of the light.
   (E) The wavelength of the light.

5. What is the photoelectric effect?

6. Give an expression for the energy of a photon in terms of the **wavelength** of the light.

★7. (a) What is the work function of a metal for which the threshold frequency is 5.0×10^{14} Hz?
   (b) What are X-rays?
   (c) What happens when the cathode of the X-ray tube is heated?
   (d) What causes the electrons to be accelerated in an X-ray tube?
   (e) Why are cooling fins needed?
   (f) Why is shielding necessary in an X-ray tube?
   (g) Name one application of X-rays.

8. What happens when high-speed electrons collide with a metal target?

9. Which of the following is not a correct statement about X-rays?
   (A) They are a stream of particles of small mass.
   (B) They can cause damage to body issue.
   (C) They pass easily through sheets of cardboard.

(D) They are formed when fast-moving electrons are stopped.
(E) They are a form of electromagnetic radiation.

10. Before switching on the X-ray machine, the operator usually walks behind a safety screen. The patient being photographed is exposed to the rays.
    (a) What material is the safety screen likely to contain?
    (b) Is the patient at risk from the X-rays she receives?
    (c) What would be the risk to the operator if there were no safety screen?
11. X-rays are produced when _____ electrons strike a _____ target.
12. X-rays were discovered by _____ towards the end of the _____ century.
13. Give two uses of X-rays.
14. What is the energy of an X-ray photon of wavelength 2.2×10^{-10} m?
15. In 1921 Albert Einstein won the Nobel Prize in Physics for his work on the photoelectric effect. What is the photoelectric effect?
16. Give the equation used by Einstein to explain the photoelectric effect.
17. What is meant by the work function of a metal?
18. Calculate the energy of a photon of frequency 1.6×10^{15} Hz. (The Planck constant, $h = 6.6 \times 10^{-34}$ J s.)

Long Questions

⋆1. (a) What is the photoelectric effect?
    (b) Give an expression for Einstein's photoelectric law.
    (c) Light of wavelength 4.6×10^{-7} m falls on a metal which has a work function of 2·3 eV. Calculate the maximum kinetic energy of the emitted electrons.

⋆2. Read the following extract and then answer the questions below. 'The explanation of the photoelectric effect was the major work cited in the award to Albert Einstein of the Nobel Prize in physics . . . Einstein's theory, proposed in 1905, played a major role in the development of atomic physics. The theory was based on a daring proposal. Not only were most of the experimental details still unknown in 1905, but the key point of Einstein's explanation was contrary to the classical ideas of the time.' (*The Project Physics Course*, Holt, Rinehart and Winston, New York.)
    (a) What is the photoelectric effect?
    (b) Give Einstein's explanation of the photoelectric effect.
    (c) How was Einstein's explanation 'contrary to the classical ideas of the time'?

(d) Outline an experimental procedure for the demonstration of the photoelectric effect.

⋆3. A 50 watt sodium lamp emits 10% of its energy at a wavelength of 593 nm. Calculate the number of light quanta emitted per second.

⋆4. The threshold wavelength for photoelectric emission for magnesium is 3.4×10^{-7} m. Calculate the work function. Light of wavelength 3.0×10^{-7} m is shone on magnesium. Calculate the maximum energy of the emitted photoelectrons.

⋆5. (a) Give two properties of the electron. A photoelectric cell is a device that is sensitive to light. Describe the structure of the photocell and explain what happens when light falls on the device. Describe an experiment to show how the current in a photoelectric cell depends on the intensity of the light falling on it.
(b) When light of frequency 4.6×10^{16} Hz falls on a certain photoelectric cell, the photo current is found to be 0·12 mA. Assuming that each of the incident photons causes an electron to be emitted and that all the emitted electrons cross the cell, calculate (i) the number of photons striking the cathode per second, (ii) the light energy falling on the cathode per second.

6. The diagram shows an X-ray tube. (a) Name the parts labelled E, F and G. (b) What material is used for the target? (c) Why is this material suitable? (d) Out of which window, H or I, are the rays emitted? (e) What is the reason for the fins? (f) Give two uses of X-rays. (g) Explain how a beam of electrons can be used in the production of X-rays. (h) Give two precautions that should be taken in the use of X-rays.

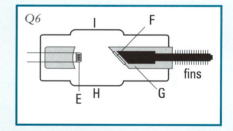

⋆7. The following is an extract from a report of a famous discovery that was made towards the end of the nineteenth century. Read the passage carefully and answer the questions that follow it. 'The most striking feature of this phenomenon is the fact that an active agent here passes through a black cardboard envelope which is opaque to the visible and ultraviolet rays of the sun or of the electric arc; an agent, too, which has the power of producing active fluorescence. The active agent proceeds from the spot where, according to the data obtained by different investigators, the cathode rays strike the glass wall.' (Adapted from *Source Book in Physics*, Harvard University Press.)
(a) What name was given to the 'active agent'?
(b) What physicist discovered this phenomenon?
(c) In what way does the 'active agent' differ from the 'visible and ultraviolet rays of the sun'?

(d) What are cathode rays? Explain how a beam of cathode rays can be produced.

*8. Calculate the minimum wavelength of X-rays produced by (a) a 20 kV and (b) a 40 kV tube.

*9. 99% of the energy of an X-ray tube operating at 20 kV is dissipated as heat. The tube current is 1 mA. How much energy per second falls on a photographic plate if the object being radiographed transmits 10% of the X-rays?

*10. (a) What is the energy of an X-ray photon of wavelength 2.2×10^{-10} m?
(b) Give an expression for Einstein's photoelectric law.
(c) Light of wavelength 4.6×10^{-7} m falls on a metal which has a work function of 2·3 eV. Calculate the maximum kinetic energy of the emitted electrons.

11. Give one difference between X-rays and cathode rays. Describe how X-rays are produced in an X-ray tube. Give two uses of X-rays.

12. (a) Give two properties of electrons.
(b)(i) Name the process by which the electrons are produced at the cathode in the diagram. (ii) Why does the target in the diagram get hot when the X-ray tube is in operation? (iii) What is the function of the high voltage supply? (iv) Give one use of X-rays. (v) Name another piece of apparatus which uses a beam of electrons.

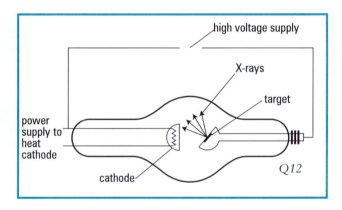

Radioactivity

CHAPTER 34

The discovery of radioactivity

Uranium salts phosphoresce after exposure to sunlight. Phosphorescence means that a glow of light is given off: the energy is stored from the sunlight.

Between 1896 and 1899, Becquerel investigated the possibility that fluorescent and phosphorescent substances could naturally emit X-rays. He experimented with uranium salts and placed them on photographic plates wrapped in black paper. He found that the photographic plates were blackened: some form of penetrating radiation must have caused this.

Becquerel then varied the exposure of the salts to sunlight and found that this had no effect. He later tried uranium salts, which do not phosphoresce, and found that these also blackened the photographic plate. Becquerel concluded that it couldn't be phosphorescence that produced the penetrating radiation.

Experiments by the Curies and others led to the discovery and chemical separation of substances that produce penetrating radiation naturally. Polonium was one of the first radioactive elements found. This was named after Poland, the birthplace of Marie Curie. Thorium and radium are two other radioactive elements that were identified.

Antoine Henri Becquerel (France) 1852–1908 discovered radioactivity while working on fluorescence in uranium salts. He established that radiation comes from all salts of uranium and that different types of radiation exist. The unit of radioactive decay (becquerel) is named after him. He shared the 1903 Nobel Prize for physics with the Curies.

Three kinds of radiation

Rutherford experimented on the penetration of the radiation. He showed that some of the radiation could be stopped by a sheet of paper. He called this alpha (α) radiation. He found a ray that was 100 times more penetrating: beta (β) radiation.

Other experiments showed that α and β radiation was deflected by electric and magnetic fields. α radiation is deflected in a way that shows it to have a positive electric charge. The deflection of β radiation shows that it has a negative electric charge.

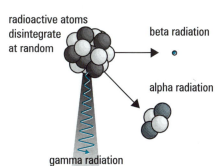

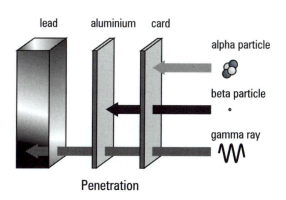

Penetration

Physics Now!

Pierre Curie found that some of the radiation was not deflected by either electric or magnetic fields. Other experiments showed that this radiation was extremely penetrating but had little ionising effect, and so was difficult to detect. It was, in fact, like very penetrating X-rays. This radiation is gamma (γ) rays.

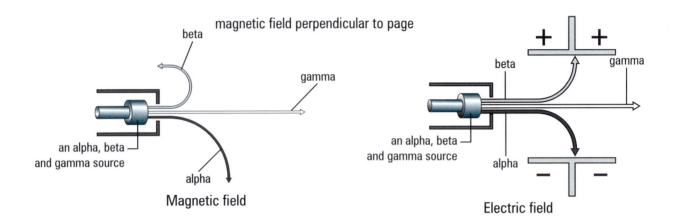

Natural radioactivity is the spontaneous disintegration of the nucleus with the emission of alpha, beta or gamma radiation.

Penetration by α, β and γ radiation

We can investigate the penetrating power of alpha, beta and gamma radiation with low-energy radioactive sources.

Experiment 34.1

AIM: To show the penetration of α, β and γ radiation.

METHOD: (α radiation)

1. Connect the Geiger-Müller (G-M) tube to the ratemeter (a counter could be used). The G-M tube should have a thin window.
2. Take the reading due to the radiation of the surrounding area (i.e. 'background radiation') on the ratemeter.
3. Place the alpha source in front of the G-M tube. Take the reading of the ratemeter.
4. Slowly move the alpha source away from the G-M tube. Where the reading is the same as the background count, the alpha radiation is not reaching the G-M tube. This is the range of alpha particles in air.
5. Place the source in front of the G-M tube. Note the reading on the ratemeter. Place a thin sheet of paper between the source and the window. If the reading is not the same as the

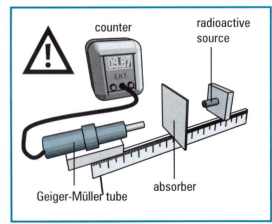

background reading, add further sheets of paper. The penetrating power is related to the thickness of paper the alpha particles can pass through or the distance they can travel through air.

β radiation
1. Repeat steps 1–4 above to get the range of beta radiation in air.
2. Place a thin aluminium sheet of known thickness between the G-M tube and the source. Place the source about 2 cm from the window. Take the reading of the ratemeter.
3. Add further sheets of aluminium and note the ratemeter reading until it is the same as the background reading.

γ radiation
1. Set up the apparatus as in the diagram. Position the gamma source about 10 cm in front of the G-M tube.
2. Place a lead sheet of known thickness in front of the G-M tube. Note the ratemeter reading.
3. Add further lead sheets of increasing thickness and note the ratemeter reading each time.
4. Graph the ratemeter reading against the thickness of the lead.

Conclusion: Alpha radiation is the least penetrating. It is stopped by 5 cm of air or a thin sheet of paper or foil. Beta radiation is more penetrating, and can penetrate 500 cm of air. Gamma radiation is the most penetrating of these radiations, and can pass through considerable thicknesses of material.

Ionisation by α, β and γ radiation

Many of the experiments done by Becquerel, Curie and Rutherford used electroscopes to detect and measure radioactivity. This is because the radiation has an ionising effect and discharges a charged electroscope. We can show the ionising powers of the three types of radiation with an electroscope.

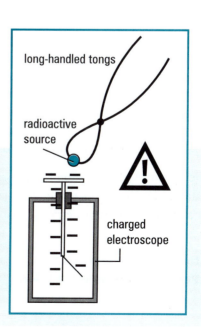

Experiment 34.2

AIM: To show the ionising powers of alpha, beta and gamma radiation.

METHOD:

The time taken for the electroscope to discharge without any source of radiation present is first measured.

Alpha radiation
1. Charge an electroscope by induction.

2. Hold an alpha radiation source (use a long-handled tongs) 1 cm above the electroscope.
The electroscope loses its charge quickly.

Beta radiation
Repeat the above procedure using a beta radiation source.
The electroscope loses its charge more slowly than with α.

Gamma radiation
Repeat the procedure using a gamma radiation source. The time taken to discharge the electroscope is much longer than with either α or β.

The radiation emitted causes ionisation of the air, which discharges the electroscope. As alpha radiation discharges the electroscope fast, beta radiation is slower and gamma radiation is very slow, we conclude that alpha radiation is the most ionising, beta radiation is less ionising and gamma radiation is the least ionising of the three.

A DIFFUSION CLOUD CHAMBER SHOWS IONISATION AND PENETRATION
A simple experiment with a diffusion-type cloud chamber can show both ionisation and penetration in a visible way.

The cloud chamber shows up the radiation by forming a vapour trail along the ions formed when the radiation moves through the cloud chamber. The more ionising the radiation, the thicker the vapour trail will be. The more penetrating the radiation, the further the trail will go.

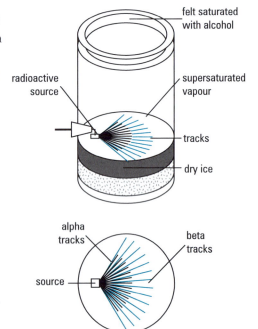

1. Place some solid carbon dioxide (dry ice) in the bottom compartment of the diffusion cloud chamber.
2. Soak the felt ring with alcohol (methylated spirit).
3. Place the radioactive source in the cloud chamber. Put on the transparent cover.

Result: The alpha vapour trail is thick but does not go very far. If you put a thin sheet of foil in front of the source, the alpha radiation is stopped. The beta vapour trail is thin, but extends further than the alpha. Gamma radiation produces no visible trail.

Conclusion: Alpha radiation is the most ionising of the three types of radiation, but does not penetrate very far. Beta radiation is less ionising than alpha but is more penetrating. Gamma radiation is less ionising than beta but is the most penetrating of the three.

Ionising power: α > β > γ
Penetrating power: γ > β > α

RADIOACTIVITY

Alpha particles are helium nuclei

Experiments carried out in 1908 and 1909 by Rutherford, Geiger and Royds proved that α radiation is identical to helium nuclei and has a positive electric charge of 3.1×10^{-19} per particle, or double the electron charge.

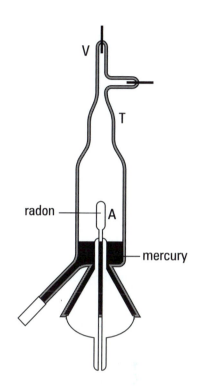

1. The α-emitting radon gas was put in thin-walled tube A.
2. The surrounding tube T was evacuated.
3. After some days, any gas produced in T was compressed into the discharge tube V by raising the mercury level in T. A discharge was then passed through the gas and the spectrum was examined.
4. The spectrum was found to be that of helium.
5. To confirm that the helium gas could not pass through the walls of A, the experiment was repeated with helium gas in tube A. No helium was found in T.

Conclusion: α particles emitted by radon pass through the thin walls, are neutralised by picking up electrons and so form helium atoms.

PROPERTIES OF ALPHA PARTICLES

Alpha particles
1. cause fluorescence
2. blacken photographic plates
3. are strongly ionising, producing 10,000 pairs of ions per cm of air travelled
4. have weak penetration: are stopped by paper or 5 cm of air
5. have an electric charge of +2 (or $+3.2 \times 10^{-19}$ C)
6. have an atomic mass of 4 a.m.u.
7. have velocities ranging from 0.5% to 1% of the speed of light
8. are identical to doubly ionised helium atoms.

An α particle is a combination of two protons and two neutrons ejected from the nucleus.

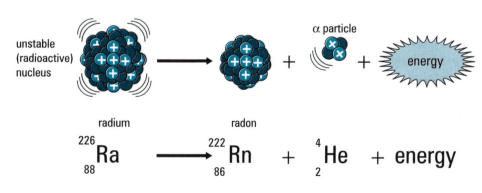

The emission of an α particle from the nucleus takes two protons and two neutrons from the nucleus. This leaves a nucleus with an atomic number of two less and an atomic mass of four less.

In writing nuclear reactions, we show the α particle as $^{4}_{2}He$:

$$^{228}_{90}Th \rightarrow \, ^{224}_{88}Ra + \, ^{4}_{2}He$$

PHYSICS NOW!

Beta particles are high-speed electrons

The deflection of β particles in electric and magnetic fields shows that they have a negative electric charge. Measurements made by Bucharer in 1909 showed that the β particles have velocities ranging from 30% to 70% of the speed of light. This range of velocities made it difficult to measure the charge-to-mass ratio of the β particles. The value of $\frac{e}{m}$ found varied with the velocity of the particle.

If we assume that the electric charge of the β particle is constant, the variation of $\frac{e}{m}$ must be due to a variation in mass. The experimental results suggest that the mass varies with velocity. In his special theory of relativity in 1905, Einstein stated that mass varies with velocity. When this is taken into account, the $\frac{e}{m}$ value of the β particles is the same as that of an electron.

Conclusion: β particles are high-speed electrons emitted by the nucleus.

PROPERTIES OF BETA PARTICLES

Beta particles
1. cause fluorescence
2. blacken photographic plates
3. are moderately ionising, producing about 100 pairs of ions per cm of air travelled
4. are moderately penetrating: are stopped by about 500 cm of air
5. have an electric charge of -1 ($-1 \cdot 6 \times 10^{-19}$ C)
6. have the same mass (when at rest) as the electron
7. have velocities ranging from 30% to 70% of the speed of light
8. are high-speed electrons originating in the nucleus.

A β particle is a high-speed electron ejected by the decay in the nucleus of a neutron into a proton.

Some nuclei contain too many neutrons to be stable. A neutron in one of these nuclei turns into a proton and an electron. The electron is emitted from the nucleus: this is the β particle. The proton remains in the nucleus. This gives a nucleus containing one proton more: the atomic number goes up by one. The mass of the electron is tiny so that the atomic mass is the same:

$$^{212}_{82}\text{Pb} \rightarrow {}^{212}_{83}\text{Bi} + \beta$$

As the sum of the atomic numbers and of the mass numbers on each side must be equal, the β particle is written as $^{0}_{-1}$e:

$$^{212}_{82}\text{Pb} \rightarrow {}^{212}_{83}\text{Bi} + {}^{0}_{-1}\text{e}$$

β particles are emitted by the nucleus because it would take an enormous amount of energy to confine an electron in the small space of the nucleus.

Marie Curie (Poland/France) 1867–1934 investigated radioactive ores with her husband, the chemist Pierre Curie, and discovered the radioactive elements polonium and radium. She established that there are three different types of natural radioactivity: α, β and γ radiation. She shared the 1903 Nobel Prize for physics and was awarded the Nobel Prize for chemistry in 1911: she is the only Nobel laureate in both physics and chemistry. Her daughter Irene Joliot-Curie was awarded the Nobel Prize for chemistry in 1935.

Gamma rays are electromagnetic radiation of extremely short wavelength

Experiments show that γ rays are not deflected by magnetic or electric fields, and are very penetrating. Early investigators of γ rays thought that they were X-rays. In fact the wavelengths of many γ rays overlap those of X-rays, but γ rays can have wavelengths much shorter than X-rays.

When a nucleus emits a γ ray photon, the structure of the nucleus does not change. γ rays remove excess energy from the nucleus, and often occur along with α and β emission from radioactive substances.

$$^{238}_{92}U + ^{1}_{0}n \rightarrow ^{239}_{92}U + \gamma$$

PROPERTIES OF GAMMA RAYS

Gamma rays
1. cause slight fluorescence
2. blacken photographic plates
3. are only weakly ionising
4. are very penetrating, passing through a considerable thickness of material
5. have no electric charge: are not deflected by electric or magnetic fields
6. have zero mass
7. have the same velocity as light
8. can be diffracted
9. produce a photoelectric effect
10. are shown by measurements to have shorter wavelengths than X-rays.

γ rays are high-energy photons of extremely short wavelength emitted by the nucleus.

	Atomic number	Atomic mass
α particles	decrease by 2	decrease by 4
β particles	increase by 1	no change

PROBLEM

How many α particles and β particles are emitted in the following radioactive decay?

$$^{235}_{92}U \rightarrow ^{207}_{82}Pb$$

Mass change is 235 − 207 = 28
Number of α particles = $\frac{28}{4}$ = 7
Seven α particles decrease the atomic number by 14 (7 × 2)
Atomic number should be = 92 − 14 = 78

Physics Now!

Atomic number is in fact 82 = increased by 4 = four β particles emitted.

Answer: Seven α particles and four β particles.

How to detect radiation

Radiation given off by a radioactive substance cannot normally be detected by any of our senses. The first scientists to experiment with radioactivity used electroscopes and fluorescent substances as detectors. These simple techniques still form the basis of many detectors, and have been developed into sensitive instruments. Photographic plates are still used also, and are seen in the film badges worn by doctors and nurses in X-ray and radiation treatment units in hospitals.

Geiger-Müller tube

The principle of the G-M tube is that radiation ionises the gas in the tube and produces an electric current.

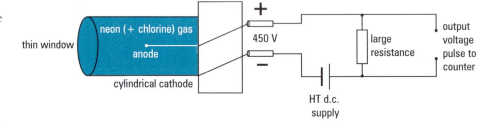

The Geiger-Müller tube consists of a central thin wire anode and a cylindrical cathode maintained at a potential difference of 500 V. The tube contains a monatomic gas (neon) at low pressure.

Operation

1. The electric field near the anode is very strong. Radiation ionises neon into electrons and positive neon ions. These are accelerated in the electric field.
2. The electrons have a small mass and are accelerated most. They collide with neon atoms and cause further ionisation: more electrons and positive ions.
3. The new electrons are also accelerated and cause further ionisation. In this way a large number of electrons are produced. This is called an avalanche.
4. The current flows through the large resistance R and produces a voltage pulse which is detected by the counter. The size of the voltage pulse is not related to the energy of the radiation.

Electrons that do not have enough energy to ionise the atoms can 'excite' them. These atoms emit this energy as photons. Photons are not affected by electric fields and so move in all directions. The photon energy is absorbed by other excited atoms to produce ionisation, so the avalanche spreads through the tube.

The positive ions produced by the radiation and by the avalanche effect move towards the cathode. They are slower than the electrons (why?) and reach it after the electron pulse. They release electrons from the cathode by bombardment. These electrons would produce a further avalanche and the process would continue, preventing the tube from

RADIOACTIVITY

detecting more radiation. The avalanche is stopped by 'quenching' and the tube is made ready to count the next incoming particles.

A Geiger-Müller tube and electronic counter is called a Geiger counter.

Methods of quenching
1. The voltage across the tube is removed electronically for a brief time (400 μs) following a count. The ions can recombine in this time. During this 400 μs the G-M tube cannot detect radiation passing through it. This is called the dead time of the counter.
2. By use of a quenching agent
   (a) Organic quenching (ethyl alcohol, 10% by volume). Ethyl alcohol absorbs photons, undergoes irreversible chemical changes and stops the discharge. The life of the tube is limited, and it must be operated at 1–2 kV.
   (b) Halogen quenching (chlorine, 0·1% by volume). The chlorine molecules absorb photons and split into individual atoms. These atoms eventually recombine when they lose their excess energy as heat. This process happens easily with halogens but cannot happen with a monatomic gas, so neon or argon is chosen as the tube gas. These tubes have a long life and operate at a voltage of 400–500 V.

SOLID-STATE DETECTOR

Diodes, transistors and other semiconductors are affected by light and heat energy. The energy of α, β or γ radiation can also affect them. Silicon or germanium chips are now used in solid-state radiation detectors.

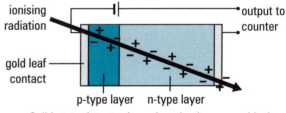

Solid state detector (p–n junction in reverse bias)

A solid-state detector consists of a diode: a p–n junction with gold electrodes at each end. A voltage is connected across the junction in reverse bias. No current flows through the diode now.

When radiation passes through the diode it 'knocks out' electrons and produces more charge carriers. These are sufficient to make the diode conduct electricity, and a pulse of electricity flows. The size of this pulse is proportional to the energy of the radiation that caused it.

A solid-state detector is a p–n junction in reverse bias.

The number of pulses gives a count of the number of radioactive particles or radiation passing through the diode. The solid-state detector can detect very low-energy particles and can also distinguish between different types of radiation.

Summary
- Natural radioactivity is the spontaneous disintegration of the nucleus with the emission of alpha, beta or gamma radiation.

PHYSICS NOW!

	Nature	Charge	Ionising power	Penetrating power
α particle	two protons and two neutrons (helium nucleus)	+2	good	poor
β particle	high-speed electron	−1	medium	medium
γ ray	electromagnetic radiation of very short wavelength ($<10^{-15}$ m)	0	poor	good

- Principle of the Geiger-Müller tube: Radiation ionises the gas in the tube. A strong electric field accelerates electrons and gives rise to an 'avalanche' effect of further ionisation that produces a large number of electrons. This current produces a voltage pulse across a resistor, which is detected by the counter.
- Principle of the solid-state detector: Radiation striking a reverse-biased p–n junction causes a current to flow.

SHORT QUESTIONS

1. When $^{238}_{92}$U decays to $^{226}_{88}$Ra, the number of α particles emitted is _____ and the number of β particles emitted is _____.
2. Name two types of radiation that are emitted from radioactive isotopes.
3. In decreasing order of penetrating power, the three kinds of nuclear radiation are:
   (A) alpha, beta, gamma
   (B) beta, alpha, gamma
   (C) gamma, beta, alpha
   (D) gamma, alpha, beta
   (E) alpha, gamma, beta.
4. Which of the following statements is correct?
   (A) α particles and γ rays are deflected in magnetic fields.
   (B) γ rays and β particles are deflected in electric fields.
   (C) α particles and β particles are charged.
   (D) β particles and γ rays travel at the speed of light.
   (E) γ rays and α particles travel at the speed of light.

5. Alpha particles are
   (A) strongly ionising and penetrate far in air
   (B) weakly ionising and penetrate far in air
   (C) not affected by magnetic and electric fields
   (D) weakly ionising and do not penetrate far in air
   (E) strongly ionising and do not penetrate far in air.
6. In increasing order of ionising effect, the three kinds of nuclear radiation are:
   (A) alpha, beta, gamma
   (B) beta, gamma, alpha
   (C) beta, alpha, gamma
   (D) gamma, alpha, beta
   (E) gamma, beta, alpha.
7. The radiation with the greatest ability to pass through a steel plate 1 cm thick is (A) ultraviolet, (B) infra-red, (C) visible light, (D) radar, (E) gamma.
8. When a $^{228}_{90}$Th nucleus undergoes radioactive decay by the emission of an alpha particle, the new nucleus formed is _____.
9. An alpha particle consists of (A) 2 protons and 2 electrons, (B) 4 protons, (C) 2 protons and 2 neutrons, (D) 4 neutrons, (E) 2 neutrons and 2 electrons.
10. Certain atoms emit gamma radiation because
    (A) they have a large nucleon number
    (B) their nuclei emit electrons
    (C) their nuclei contain protons and neutrons
    (D) their nuclei are unstable
    (E) their nuclei are at a high temperature.
11. The following equation represents parts of a radioactive series.
    $$^{238}_{92}U \rightarrow {}^{234}_{90}Th \rightarrow X \rightarrow {}^{234}_{92}U \rightarrow {}^{230}_{90}Th$$
    What is substance X, and what radiation is emitted by $^{234}_{90}$Th to produce X?
    (A) $^{234}_{91}$Pa + γ, (B) $^{230}_{90}$Th + β, (C) $^{230}_{90}$Th + γ, (D) $^{234}_{91}$Pa + β, (E) $^{234}_{91}$Pa + α.
12. Which of the following is not a correct statement about gamma rays?
    (A) They are a form of electromagnetic radiation.
    (B) They penetrate metals better than beta particles.
    (C) They have very short wavelengths.
    (D) They have very high frequencies.
    (E) They travel very slowly compared to light waves.
13. A radioactive source emits one type of radiation only. On investigation it is found that the radiation will penetrate quite well through 1 mm of aluminium, but will not penetrate 1 cm

of lead. The radiation is probably (A) beta radiation, (B) alpha particles, (C) cathode rays, (D) infrared rays, (E) gamma rays.

14. The radiation from a source is strongly deflected by a magnetic field into a circular path. It also produces a small current in an ionisation chamber. What type of radiation is the source emitting?

15. The nature of α particles was established by _____ working in Cambridge in the early years of the _____ century.

16. In a process of decay, a radioactive nucleus emits a total of 2 α particles and 3 β particles. As a result:
    (A) the atomic number decreases by one and the mass number decreases by eight
    (B) the atomic number increases by one and the mass number decreases by four
    (C) the atomic number increases by one and the mass number decreases by one
    (D) the atomic number decreases by five and the mass number decreases by four
    (E) the atomic number decreases by four and the mass number decreases by five.

LONG QUESTIONS

1. Sketch the type of trace found in a cloud chamber from (a) alpha radiation, (b) beta radiation. Explain the difference between the traces in terms of ionising effect and penetration.

2. Complete the following nuclear reactions.
    (a) $^{238}_{92}U + ^1_0n \rightarrow \quad + \gamma$
    (b) $^{63}_{29}Cu + ^1_0n \rightarrow \quad + 2^1_0n$
    (c) $^{27}_{13}Al + ^1_0n \rightarrow \quad + ^4_2He$
    (d) $^{53}_{24}Cr + ^4_2He \rightarrow \quad + ^1_1H$
    (e) $^{27}_{13}Al + ^1_0n \rightarrow \quad + ^1_1H$
    (f) $^{23}_{12}Mg + ^1_1H \rightarrow \quad + ^1_0n$
    (g) $^9_4Be + ^4_2He \rightarrow \quad + ^1_0n$

3. Identify the processes shown in diagrams (i)–(v) from this list: (a) beta emission, (b) photoelectric emission, (c) X-rays, (d) gamma radiation, (e) fluorescence.

4. $^{225}_{89}Ac$ undergoes three successive alpha decays. What is the resulting nucleus?

5. Complete the following:
    (a) $^{214}_{84}Po \rightarrow \quad + ^4_2He$
    (b) $^{214}_{83}Bi \rightarrow \quad + \beta$
    (c) $^{13}_6C \rightarrow \quad + ^1_1H$

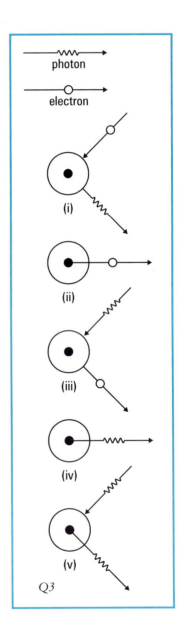

Q3

(d) $^{239}_{92}U \rightarrow \quad + \beta \rightarrow \quad + \beta$

(e) $^{98}_{79}Au \rightarrow \quad + \beta$

(f) $^{63}_{29}Cu \rightarrow \quad + \beta$

(g) $^{32}_{15}P \rightarrow \quad + \beta$

6. Calculate the number of α decays and β decays in each of the following.

   (a) $^{232}_{90}Th \rightarrow {}^{208}_{82}Pb$

   (b) $^{237}_{93}Np \rightarrow {}^{209}_{83}Bi$

   (c) $^{238}_{92}U \rightarrow {}^{206}_{82}Pb$

   (d) $^{235}_{92}U \rightarrow {}^{207}_{82}Pb$

7. $^{239}_{92}U$ decays to element X by emitting 6 α particles and 8 β particles. What is X?

8. A source S of radioactivity is placed in front of a detector of radiation. When a thin sheet of aluminium is placed in front of the source, no radiation is detected.
   (i) Name one type of radiation detector.
   Outline how it operates.
   (ii) Name the type of radiation emitted by S.
   (iii) In what material is S usually stored? Why?

9. What is an alpha-particle?
   Give two properties of alpha-particles emitted by a radioactive source.
   Name a device which may be used for detecting alpha-particles and outline its principle of operation.

The Structure of the Atom

CHAPTER 35

The nucleus

Once Thomson had shown that the electron was a negatively charged particle, scientists began to look for a positively charged particle. They believed it had to exist because atoms and molecules are normally electrically neutral. Positive rays were discovered in a similar way to cathode rays. They were shown to be positive by the way they were deflected in a magnetic field. Thomson found that the positive rays had a far greater mass than the electron.

Scientists knew nothing about the way the positive and negative particles were arranged in the atom. Thomson suggested that the positive and negative charges were scattered uniformly through the atom: Thomson's 'plum-pudding' model.

Rutherford's gold foil experiment

In 1909 Geiger and Marsden carried out the following experiment.

A thin sheet of metal foil was placed in the path of a beam of alpha particles. The angles at which the alpha particles were deflected were measured by observing where the particles struck a zinc sulphide screen. The screen gave a small flash of light when struck by an alpha particle.

Results

1. Most particles were not deflected at all or were deflected at very small angles.
2. About 1 in every 8,000 particles was deflected through a much greater angle, and some were reflected back in the direction they had come from.

The 'plum-pudding' model of the atom predicted that alpha particles would be scattered through very small angles only. It could not explain the large scattering angles or the reflection of particles.

Rutherford explained the experimental results by putting forward a model of the atom that has all the positive charge concentrated in a very small volume: the nucleus. The alpha particles are scattered through small angles when they pass through the atom at a distance from the nucleus. As the particles come closer to the nucleus, the force of repulsion between the positive charge of the nucleus and the positive charge of the alpha particle increases, and the particle is deflected through a greater angle. If a particle approaches the nucleus 'head-on' it is scattered back in the direction from which it came.

Ernest Rutherford (New Zealand/Britain) 1871–1937 established the nature of α radiation. He proposed the nuclear model of the atom as a result of experiments suggested by him and performed by his students Geiger and Marsden, now known as the Rutherford gold foil experiment. He was awarded the Nobel Prize for chemistry in 1908.

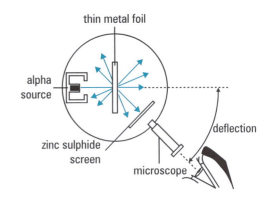

336

The Structure of the Atom

From these experiments we get our present understanding of the atom as made of a nucleus (a dense small core of positively charged mass) surrounded by a vast area containing a number of negative charges of very small mass.

The nucleus has a radius of the order of 10^{-15} m. The size of the atom – the space occupied by the electrons – is much greater. The radius of the atom is of the order of 10^{-10} m. If you picture the nucleus as a football, the atom is the size of the stadium!

The nucleus has a radius of the order of 10^{-15} m.
The atom has a radius of the order of 10^{-10} m.

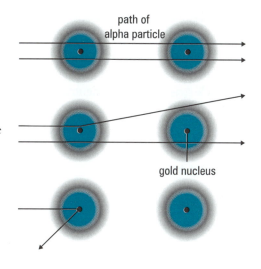

RUTHERFORD DISCOVERS THE PROTON

Rutherford discovered the proton in 1919 by the following experiment.

1. An α particle source was placed in a nitrogen-filled chamber. A metal foil was placed in front of the fluorescent screen to prevent α particles from reaching it.
2. Radiation was detected, showing that particles were emitted that could penetrate the foil. The radiation could not be α particles.
3. Deflection of the radiation by a magnetic field showed that it was positively charged.
4. Traces of oxygen were found in the chamber.

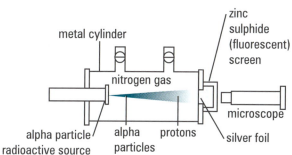

From this and other evidence, Rutherford proved that an alpha particle bombarded the nitrogen nucleus and changed (transmuted) it to oxygen, and that a proton was given off in the nuclear reaction:

$$^4_2He + {}^{14}_{7}N \rightarrow {}^{17}_{8}O + {}^{1}_{1}H$$

CHADWICK DISCOVERS THE NEUTRON

Scientists believed that an electrically neutral particle existed long before the neutron was discovered by Chadwick in 1932, because the mass of the protons did not account for all the mass of the nucleus. No other charged particle was found in the nucleus, so they expected to find a neutral particle: the neutron.

1. Chadwick bombarded a beryllium target with alpha particles. He found what he thought were high-energy gamma rays. These rays were not deflected by electric or magnetic fields and so did not have an electric charge.

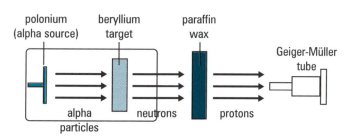

2. When he put a wax block in the path of these rays, protons were emitted from the wax.

3. He measured the velocities of the protons.

From calculations applying the conservation of momentum to the collision, Chadwick concluded that the radiation was due to a particle with a mass close to that of the proton but with no electric charge: the neutron.

$$^9_4\text{Be} + {}^4_2\text{He} \rightarrow {}^{12}_6\text{C} + {}^1_0\text{n}$$

Scientists now had a clearer picture of the nucleus as composed of protons and neutrons.

Atomic number

X-ray measurements taken by Moseley in 1913 showed that the positive charge on the nucleus is equal to the atomic number times the charge of the electron. This means that the number of protons in the nucleus is given by the atomic number, Z. The atomic number also gives the number of electrons in a neutral atom.

The atomic number of an element is found in the periodic table.

Atomic number of an element (Z): The number of protons in the nucleus of an atom of the element. Also, the number of electrons around the nucleus of a neutral atom of the element.

ISOTOPES

When Boltwood was experimenting with radioactive substances in 1906, he thought he found a new element, which he called ionium. The substance was chemically identical to thorium but had different radioactive behaviour. A great number of other 'new elements' were found around that time, but most of them were chemically identical to known elements.

Soddy suggested that these substances were not new elements but were atoms of the same element with different atomic masses. He called these atoms 'isotopes'.

A MASS SPECTROMETER SEPARATES ISOTOPES

A mass spectrometer separates substances of different mass by first ionising them (to give them an electric charge) and then accelerating them into a strong magnetic field. The smaller the mass, the smaller is the radius of the circular paths. This separates the different masses. Thomson used a mass spectrometer to separate two types of neon: one with an atomic mass of 20, the other with an atomic mass of 22. The chemical atomic mass of neon is 20·2, so he concluded that the isotope of mass 20 is the more abundant one. Many other experiments showed that most elements have isotopes.

Clearly, the mass of the atom is made up of the separate masses of the protons, neutrons and electrons. The number of protons (and electrons) is given by the atomic number of the element. The different atomic masses in isotopes must then be due to different numbers of neutrons in the nucleus.

James Chadwick (England) 1891–1974 discovered the neutron as a result of experiments in 1932 using alpha particles to bombard light elements. He won the Nobel Prize for physics in 1935.

The most common isotope of carbon is used as the standard to compare the masses of different isotopes. An atom of this isotope of carbon is taken as having a mass of 12 atomic mass units.

Relative atomic mass: The mass of an atom in atomic mass units, where the mass of the carbon-12 isotope is taken as having a mass of 12 units.

Mass number (A) is the whole number nearest the relative atomic mass of an atom. It gives the number of protons and neutrons in the nucleus.

Isotopes: Atoms of the same atomic number (of the same element – same number of protons) but with a different atomic mass (different number of neutrons).

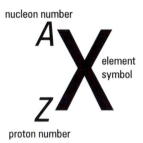

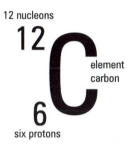

Spectroscopy

Bunsen and Kirchhoff discovered that no two elements emit the same spectrum. This fact is used as a tool to analyse substances by heating them and studying the spectrum produced. The lines seen in the spectrum enable scientists to identify the elements present. Tiny quantities of a substance (as little as 10^{-10} g) can be analysed in this way.

Emission spectra

If you heat some sodium chloride in a Bunsen flame, its atoms become excited and it emits yellow light which is the same as the light given out by sodium street lamps. This is called an emission spectrum.

An emission spectrum is a spectrum given out by a substance when its atoms are excited.

If you examine this light with a spectrometer, you will see that it consists of a number of distinct lines: a **line** spectrum. Line spectra are emitted by substances in a monatomic gas state.

If you examine the spectrum emitted by a filament lamp you will see a **continuous** spectrum. A continuous spectrum is emitted by a hot solid or liquid.

Lasers

A laser tube produces a beam of light in which all the waves are of the same frequency and in phase. As a result of constructive interference, a beam of high-energy light is produced. This narrow beam can be controlled with great precision.

The Bohr model of the atom

How can an electron keep moving around the nucleus if it has a negative charge and the nucleus has a positive charge? Wouldn't you expect it to be attracted to the nucleus?

Problems like these led scientists to question the way they thought about atoms. Niels Bohr used the experiments in spectroscopy to develop

Niels Bohr (Denmark) 1885–1962 *proposed a model of the atom that explained emission spectra and a model of the nucleus that explained fission. He was awarded the Nobel Prize for physics in 1922. His son, Aage Niels Bohr, shared the Nobel Prize for physics in 1975.*

Physics Now!

a model for the structure of the atom to explain how spectra are produced. The Bohr model is based on two basic ideas.

1. Electrons can exist only in certain definite orbits, or energy levels, around the nucleus. As long as they are in these orbits, they do not lose energy.
2. When an electron jumps from one energy level to another, it emits its excess energy in a photon. Planck's equation gives the frequency of the photon: $E_2 - E_1 = hf$.

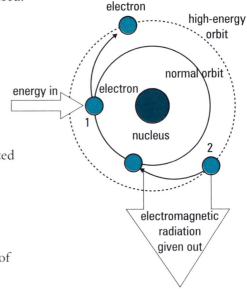

Line spectra are explained by the Bohr model as the wavelengths emitted when an electron jumps from one energy level to another. As each element has its own unique set of energy jumps, the line spectrum of each element is unique.

Problem

An electron jumps from an electron energy level of 0·0045 eV to one of 0·0030 eV. Calculate the frequency of the emitted photon.

$$E_2 - E_1 = hf$$

$$E_2 - E_1 = 0\cdot0045 - 0\cdot0030 \text{ eV} = 0\cdot0015 \times 1\cdot6 \times 10^{-19} \text{ J} = 2\cdot4 \times 10^{-22} \text{ J}$$

$$f = \frac{E_2 - E_1}{h} = \frac{(2\cdot4 \times 10^{-22})}{(6\cdot6 \times 10^{-34})}$$

$$= 0\cdot36 \times 10^{12} \text{ Hz} = 3\cdot6 \times 10^{11} \text{ Hz}$$

Summary

- Atomic number of an element (Z): The number of protons in the nucleus of the atom of the element. Also, the number of electrons around the nucleus of a neutral atom.
- Relative atomic mass: The mass of the atom in atomic mass units, where the mass of the carbon–12 isotope is taken as 12.
- Isotope: Atoms of the same atomic number but with different atomic masses. Isotopes have the same number of protons but different numbers of neutrons.
- Mass number (A): The whole number nearest the relative atomic mass of an element. It equals the number of protons and neutrons in the nucleus.

Short Questions

1. The atomic number of a nucleus is Z and its mass number is A. In the nucleus there are
   (A) Z neutrons and A protons
   (B) A neutrons and Z protons
   (C) Z neutrons and Z − A protons
   (D) A − Z neutrons and A protons
   (E) A − Z neutrons and Z protons.

2. Which of the following is the order of magnitude of the radius of the nucleus? (A) 10^{-10} m, (B) 10^{-15} m, (C) 10^{-19} m, (D) 10^{-27} m, (E) 10^{-31} m.

3. The scattering experiments of alpha particles by gold foil suggest that
   (A) alpha particles travel very quickly
   (B) gold is more dense than alpha particles
   (C) gold atoms are negatively charged
   (D) gold atoms have very dense nuclei
   (E) atomic nuclei contain positive and uncharged particles.

4. A neutron has (A) no electric charge, (B) a double positive charge, (C) a single negative charge.

5. In all atoms except hydrogen you would expect to find:
   (A) protons and electrons in orbit round a neutron
   (B) protons and neutrons in the nucleus and orbiting electrons
   (C) electrons and protons in the nucleus and orbiting neutrons
   (D) electrons and neutrons in orbit and protons in the nucleus
   (E) electrons and neutrons in the nucleus and orbiting protons.

6. The nucleus of the atom of a certain element contains 5 protons and 6 neutrons. Its mass number is (A) 5, (B) 6, (C) 11, (D) 12, (E) 17.

7. Which of the following particles constitutes the nucleus of a hydrogen atom? (A) alpha particle, (B) electron, (C) ion, (D) neutron, (E) proton.

8. The diagram represents an atom of beryllium. The correct way to write the formula for this element is (A) $^{4}_{5}Be$, (B) $^{9}_{4}Be$, (C) $^{5}_{4}Be$, (D) $^{4}_{9}Be$, (E) $^{9}_{5}Be$.

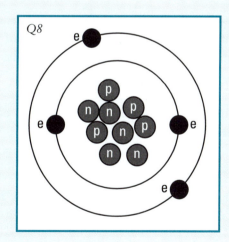

Q8

9. Isotopes of an element have
   (A) the same number of neutrons
   (B) the same number of protons
   (C) the same physical properties
   (D) different numbers of protons
   (E) different numbers of electrons.

10. An atom of tin has an atomic number of 50 and a mass number of 112. Which of the following is an isotope of tin?
    (A) $^{112}_{51}X$, (B) $^{114}_{50}X$, (C) $^{112}_{49}X$, (D) $^{112}_{62}X$, (E) $^{51}_{112}X$.

Radioactive Decay

CHAPTER 36

Experiments with radioactive substances show that the emission of radiation is a random process. Experiments also show that the rate at which a substance gives off radiation cannot be changed by temperature, pressure or any other physical or chemical means. This means that the emission of radiation is a spontaneous process. The rate at which radiation is emitted is the rate of radioactive decay. The rate at which radioactive particles are emitted in a given time period shows that the process is random. However, the average number of particles emitted over a number of successive time periods shows a pattern. This shows that the rate at which radiation is emitted from a given substance depends only on the amount of the substance present (the number of atoms of the radioactive substance).

Law of radioactive decay: The rate of radioactive decay depends only on the number of atoms of a radioactive substance present.

In other words, the rate of radioactive decay is directly proportional to the number of radioactive atoms present. Mathematically:

Rate of decay = $-\lambda N$

λ is the decay constant. N is the number of atoms in the sample.

The rate of decay is the number of nuclear disintegrations occurring per second.

The becquerel (Bq) is a rate of decay of one disintegration per second.

Half-life

The time it takes for half the radioactive atoms in a substance to decay is constant and is known as the half-life ($T_{\frac{1}{2}}$). The half-life is a characteristic of a radioactive substance. Half-lives range from fractions of a second to many millions of years.

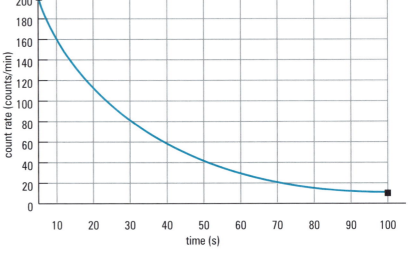

Graph of activity of radioactive sample

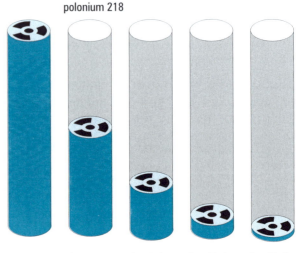

radon 222   after 4 days   after 8 days   after 12 days   after 16 days

Half-life

342

The half-life is the time taken for half the atoms of a radioactive substance to decay.

HALF-LIFE AND DECAY CONSTANT

Clearly, a substance with a short half-life decays very fast and so must have a big decay constant. A substance with a long half-life decays very slowly and so must have a small decay constant.

We conclude that decay constant and half-life are inversely related.

$$T_{\frac{1}{2}} = \frac{\ln 2}{\lambda}$$

$$T_{\frac{1}{2}} = \frac{0.693}{\lambda}$$

PROBLEM

A radioactive substance has a half-life of 2.4 days. Calculate the time taken for a radioactive sample to decay to one-sixteenth of the original activity.

One half-life	→	$\frac{1}{2}$ activity
Two half-lives	→	$\frac{1}{4}$ activity
Three half-lives	→	$\frac{1}{8}$ activity
Four half-lives	→	$\frac{1}{16}$ activity

Four half-lives = 4 × 2.4 days = 9.6 days

PROBLEM

The decay constant for a particular radioactive isotope is $3.5 \times 10^4 \text{ s}^{-1}$. Calculate its half-life. Comment on the result.

$$T_{\frac{1}{2}} = \frac{0.693}{\lambda}$$

$$= \frac{0.693}{3.5 \times 10^4}$$

$$= 0.198 \times 10^{-4}$$

$$= 1.98 \times 10^{-5} \text{ s}$$

The decay constant is very big, so the half-life must be very short.

Nuclear reactions

1. **Conservation of electric charge:** This requires that the sum of the atomic numbers of the initial nuclei equal the sum of the atomic numbers of the resultant nuclei.
2. **Conservation of mass–energy:** Energy is conserved in any individual reaction, provided that mass is taken as a form of energy according to the equation $E = mc^2$.
3. **Conservation of momentum:** The momentum before the reaction equals the momentum after.

The total number of nucleons (protons + neutrons) also remains unchanged. This rule is a result of the study of nuclear reactions, and is not a general physical law.

Summary

- Law of radioactive decay: The rate of decay is proportional to the number of atoms of the radioactive substance present.
- A becquerel (Bq) is a rate of decay of one disintegration per second.
- Half-life: The time taken for half the atoms of a radioactive substance to disintegrate. The half-life is a constant and is related only to the decay constant.

Short Questions

1. What is meant by the half-life of a radioactive isotope?
*2. A radioactive substance has a half-life of 1 minute. How long does it take for the activity of a sample of this substance to fall to one-sixteenth of its original value? (A) 2 minutes, (B) 3 minutes, (C) 4 minutes, (D) 8 minutes, (E) 16 minutes.
*3. Ra-288 has a half-life of 12 days. If a mass of M kg of this isotope is initially present, the amount remaining after 48 days will be (A) M kg, (B) $\frac{1}{2}M$ kg, (C) $\frac{1}{4}M$ kg (D) $\frac{1}{8}M$ kg, (E) $\frac{1}{16}M$ kg.
*4. If the half-life of a radioactive gas is 2 minutes, after 8 minutes the activity will have fallen to a fraction of its initial value. This fraction is (A) $\frac{1}{2}$, (B) $\frac{1}{6}$, (C) $\frac{1}{8}$, (D) $\frac{1}{16}$, (E) $\frac{1}{32}$.
*5. Thorium has a half-life of 24 days. How many days would it take 8 g thorium to disintegrate to 1 g? (A) 3, (B) 24, (C) 72, (D) 96, (E) 192.
*6. (a) The graph in the diagram was plotted from readings taken with a radioactive source at daily intervals. The half-life of the source is: (A) 1·0 days, (B) 1·5 days, (C) 2·0 days, (D) 2·5 days, (E) 3·0 days.
   (b) The count rate will have fallen to 160 counts per minute after (A) 5·0 days, (B) 6·5 days, (C) 7·0 days, (D) 7·5 days, (E) 8·0 days.
*7. The decay constant for a particular radioactive isotope is 9.8×10^{-3} s^{-1}. The half-life, in seconds, is (A) 6.8×10^{-3}, (B) 3.3×10^{-2}, (C) 1.4×10^{-2}, (D) 31, (E) 71.
*8. One-sixteenth of a sample of a certain radioactive isotope remains after 4 years. Calculate the half-life of the radioactive isotope.
*9. A radioactive isotope has a half-life of 3 days. What fraction of the sample of the isotope will remain after 9 days?
*10. An alpha-emitting radioactive isotope has a half-life of 11·2 days and decays to form radon-219. Write down the name,

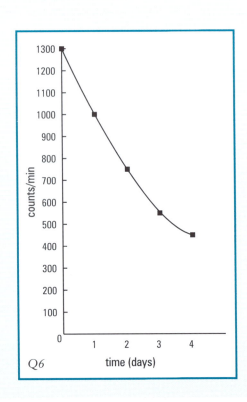

Q6

atomic number and mass number of the radioactive isotope. Calculate the decay constant for this isotope.

LONG QUESTIONS

⋆1. $^{25}_{11}$Na is an isotope of sodium. It is radioactive and has a half-life of one minute.
Explain the underlined terms. What fraction of the sample of $^{25}_{11}$Na remains after 3 minutes?

The following table shows the results of an experiment to measure the radiation from a particular radioactive source over a period of time. Allowance has been made for the background count.

Time (seconds)	10	20	30	40	50	60	70	80	90	100	110	120	130	140	150
Counts per second	50	38	34	32	28	25	22	19	16	14	13	11	10	8	7

Show how the half-life of this radioactive substance can be calculated, starting at (i) 50 counts per second, (ii) 28 counts per second.

⋆2. Sodium-24 has a half-life of 14 hours. What fraction of a sample of sodium-24 will have decayed after 42 hours?

3. (a) A radioactive nucleus has a half-life of 1,000 years. Explain what is meant by this.
(b) Gamma radiation may be emitted from a radioactive nucleus. Give two ways in which this type of radiation differs from alpha and beta emission.
(c) Describe three precautions that should be taken when using or transporting radioactive materials.
(d) What are isotopes?
(e) Give examples of two uses to which radioactive isotopes may be put.

⋆4. The graph in the diagram shows how the activity of a sample of bismuth-210 varies with time. From the graph, find the half-life of bismuth-210.

⋆5. $^{3}_{1}$H has a half-life of 12·5 years, undergoing β decay. What fraction of a sample is left undecayed after 50 years?

⋆6. The half-life of Na-24 is 14 hours. How long will it take 93·75% of a sample to undergo radioactive decay?

⋆7. $^{222}_{86}$Rn → α + X   (T$_{\frac{1}{2}}$ = 3·8 days)
What new isotope is produced by this disintegration?

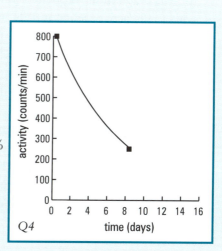
Q4

How much of the initial sample is left after (a) 3·8 days, (b) 11·4 days?

★8. An experiment to measure the half-life of a radioactive isotope gave the following readings. The background radiation was two counts per second.

N (per second)	210	164	106	80	52	40	26	18	12
t (seconds)	0	30	60	90	120	150	180	210	240

Graph these data, and estimate from the graph the half-life of this isotope.

★9. 1·0 mg of carbon from a piece of living material gives a count of 100 counts per minute due to the presence of C-14. A piece of ancient wood (also 1·0 mg) gives 25 counts per minute. Calculate the age of the ancient wood ($T_{\frac{1}{2}}$ for C-14 = 5,700 years).

★10. (a) A Geiger-Müller tube attached to a ratemeter is placed on a bench in the laboratory. Over three consecutive minutes the ratemeter reads 11, 9 and 16 counts per minute. When a radioactive source is placed near the Geiger-Müller tube, the counts over three consecutive minutes are 1,310, 1,270 and 1,296 per minute. When a piece of thick paper is placed between the source and the tube, the counts are 1,250, 1,242 and 1,236 per minute. When the paper is replaced by a sheet of aluminium 2 mm thick, the counts are 13, 12 and 11 per minute.
(i) Why is there a reading when no source is present?
(ii) Why do the three readings in any one group differ?
(iii) What can be deduced about the nature of the emission? Give reasons for your answer.
(b) The graph in the diagram is plotted from readings taken with a radioactive source at daily intervals. Use the graph to deduce the half-life of the source. Hence give the count rate after five days, and the time when the count is 160 per minute. Would you expect the mass of the source to have changed significantly after 4 days? (Give a reason for your answer.)

11. (a) State the law of radioactive decay and explain what is meant by the half-life of a radioactive isotope.
(b) 'Radioactivity was discovered by Becquerel in 1896.'
(i) What is meant by the term 'radioactivity'?
(ii) How did Becquerel make this discovery?

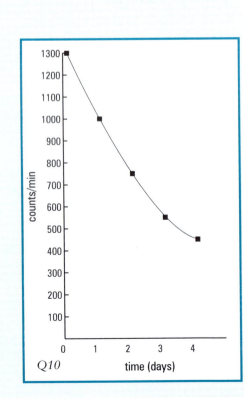

Q10

★12. A uranium ore was discovered by Marie and Pierre Curie early in the twentieth century to contain the two <u>radioactive isotopes</u>, radium and polonium. Explain the underlined words.

Radium-226 decays to polonium-218 in two stages, with the same particle emitted in each stage. Name this particle and give an equation for the process.

Outline an experiment to demonstrate the ionising effect of the particles emitted.

Given that the half-life of radium-226 is very much greater than the half-life of polonium-218 explain why you would expect to find much more radium-226 than polonium-218 in a sample of the uranium ore.

If a sample of radium contains 2.6×10^{21} radium-226 nuclei and is emitting 3.5×10^{10} particles per second calculate (i) the decay constant, (ii) the half-life, of radium-226.

★13. State the law of radioactive decay.

A sample of a certain substance contains 2.5×10^{21} radioactive nuclei. If the nuclei are decaying at a rate of 3.4×10^{10} per second calculate the half-life of the substance.

★14. What is meant by the term radioactivity?

Polonium-218 is radioactive with a half-life of 3.1 minutes and emits α-particles. Give an equation to represent the decay of Po-218 and name the element produced in the reaction. (Refer to the Periodic Table of the elements in the Mathematics Tables, p. 44.)

Calculate the decay constant for Po-218.

A sample of Po-218 has a mass of 3.5 μg. Calculate the number of α-particles emitted per second from the sample.
(1 mol of Po-218 = 218g; Avogadro's constant, $N_A = 6.0 \times 10^{23}$ mol^{-1}.)

15. 'Some <u>nuclei</u> are <u>radioactive</u>. They disintegrate into smaller nuclei and emit various types of radiation. The <u>half-life</u> of a radioactive substance may be a tiny fraction of a second or many billions of years.' Explain the underlined terms. Name three types of radiation that may be emitted by radioactive nuclei. Of the three, state which type of radiation is the most ionising and which is the most penetrating.

Uses of Radioisotopes and Radiation Hazards

CHAPTER 37

All the radioactive substances mentioned so far are found in nature: substances such as uranium, radium and thorium. They produce natural radioactivity. Relatively few naturally occurring atoms are radioactive. Many radioactive atoms that once existed have by now emitted radiation and become non-radioactive.

Man-made radioactive isotopes

Radioactive substances can be made by bombarding non-radioactive isotopes with charged particles or neutrons. These particles are incorporated into the nucleus, which becomes unstable and emits radiation.

Radioisotopes are made in nuclear reactors and in nuclear research laboratories. The radioactivity of these substances is called artificial radioactivity. The term 'artificial' only distinguishes the way in which the isotopes were made: in all other ways they are similar to naturally radioactive substances.

Most radioactive isotopes are produced in nuclear reactors, because nuclear reactors produce large numbers of neutrons. A non-radioactive isotope is placed in the core of the reactor. The neutrons bombard the atoms of the isotope. Some neutrons penetrate and become part of the nucleus. The atoms affected in this way are now radioactive. Radioactive isotopes have many uses in medicine, agriculture, research and industry.

Artificial radioactivity: Radioactivity produced by bombarding non-radioactive isotopes with charged particles or neutrons.

Medical uses of radioisotopes

Gamma ray imaging

Gamma rays are used like X-rays to produce photographic images of the inside of the body.

Developments of gamma ray imaging are PET (positron emission tomography) scans and SPECT (single photon emission computerised tomography) scans. Radiation from a radioisotope injected into the body is detected by sensors outside. A computer-generated image of the organ being examined is built up from radiation emitted from the radioisotopes. Both these methods are more sensitive than X-rays.

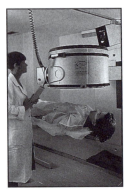

Gamma ray cameras are used in medicine to take pictures of the inside of the body.

RADIATION TREATMENT OF CANCER

Radioisotopes are used to kill cancerous cells. The most common radioisotope used for this purpose is the gamma emitter cobalt-60. The radiation 'dose' (the amount of radiation the body is exposed to) is carefully calculated by the doctor, to prevent serious damage to healthy cells.

In some cases a tiny pellet of radioisotope such as gold-198, with a half-life of 2·5 days, is placed directly into the cancerous growth.

Iodine-131 is used in the treatment of disorders of the thyroid gland. This is very effective because the radioactive iodine collects in the thyroid gland. Iodine-131 is a beta emitter and so its radiation is localised in the gland. Because of this the radiation has little effect on the rest of the body.

In a combination of biological and radiation techniques, specially produced antibodies containing radioisotopes are used to target particular cells in the body. This reduces damage to other cells.

STERILISATION OF MATERIALS USED IN HOSPITALS

High levels of gamma radiation kill all living matter. In this way bacteria and other living organisms can be destroyed without the use of heat or chemicals. Syringes, scalpels, bandages and dressings as well as heat-sensitive medicines can be sterilised by gamma radiation. These can be prepacked in airtight plastic containers before sterilisation, since the gamma rays easily penetrate plastic. The plastic keeps the materials sterile after treatment.

It is important to realise that exposing substances to γ radiation does not make them radioactive.

MEDICAL RADIOISOTOPE TRACERS

Radioisotopes produce radiation which can be detected wherever they go. This has given doctors and scientists a means of monitoring from outside the body the path followed by a radioisotope inside a body.

Injections into the bloodstream of salt containing the radioisotope sodium-24 enable doctors to chart the flow of blood through the body. This helps them diagnose heart disease and circulatory problems. It is also used to check that blood is flowing in skin grafts. If a blood supply does not develop in the new skin, the skin-graft has failed.

ENERGY SOURCE

A plutonium-238 radioisotope is used to generate electricity to power heart pacemakers.

Industrial uses of radioisotopes

SMOKE DETECTORS

Americium-241 emits α particles that strongly ionise the air in the small gap in the electronic circuit. This allows a current to flow. Smoke particles stick to the ions and reduce the flow of current. This sets off the alarm.

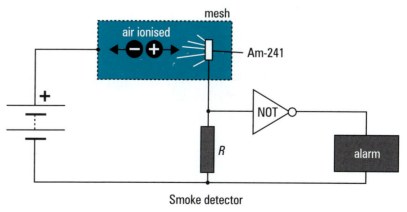

Smoke detector

Physics Now!

Energy sources

Radioactive isotopes release energy when they give off radiation. This energy is converted to light when the radiation strikes certain materials. This principle is used in luminous emergency signs: they require no external power supply.

The heat given off by radioisotopes such as strontium-90 is converted to electricity by a thermopile and used to power small radio transmitters and flashing warning beacons at sea. Radioisotope generators also power satellites.

Gamma ray photography

Gamma ray photography is similar to X-ray photography, but the gamma rays are more penetrating than X-rays and don't need electric power. The radioisotope source can be carried about. It can be used in awkward confined spaces and in conditions where X-rays cannot be used. Cobalt-60 and iridium-192 are used as sources of gamma rays. Gamma ray photography is used to check jet engines, aircraft frames and pipelines.

A disadvantage is that, unlike X-rays, you cannot turn the gamma rays off. Gamma ray sources must be stored in lead-lined containers, and operators must be shielded from the gamma rays when they are in use.

Checking the thickness of materials

Thick sheets of material allow less radiation through than thin sheets. This fact is used to check the thickness of materials produced in continuous sheets, and to adjust the rollers automatically to keep the thickness constant.

A radioisotope is placed on one side of the material and a radiation detector on the other side. The reading on the detector is inversely proportional to thickness of the material. This reading can be connected through a feedback system to adjust the gap between the rollers.

A similar system is used to check that packets are full. An empty packet allows more radiation through than a full packet. A certain level is set for a full packet. Any reading above this indicates that the packet is not full and should be rejected.

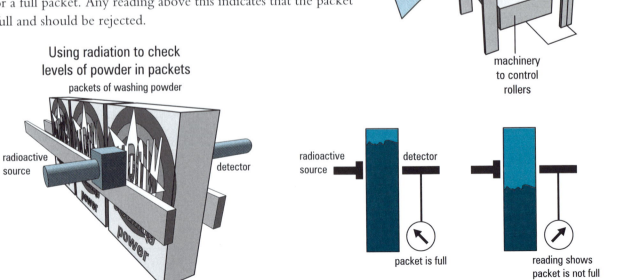

Uses of Radioisotopes and Radiation Hazards

Radioisotope tracers
Radioisotope tracers are used to check pipes for leaks. A small quantity of a short-lived isotope is added to the liquid or gas in a pipe. The area around the pipe is then checked for radiation. A radiation level above normal would pinpoint a leak.

Checking that a mixing process is complete
Small quantities of radioisotopes are added to mixtures such as fertilisers, foodstuffs and vitamins. A constant level of radiation in a number of samples indicates that the components are properly mixed. The radioisotopes chosen have such a short half-life that the radiation level in the mixture could not be detected after a few hours.

Zinc-65 added to mud in rivers is used in studies of silting in rivers and harbours.

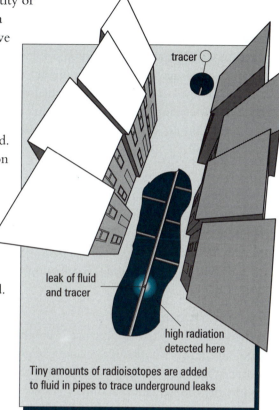

Tiny amounts of radioisotopes are added to fluid in pipes to trace underground leaks

Agricultural uses of radioisotopes

Food irradiation
Micro-organisms (bacteria and fungi), insects and parasites spoil food. The radioisotope cobalt-60 emits gamma rays that kills them. Very high levels of γ radiation are used to sterilise foods.

Fresh fruit treated with radiation will keep for a much longer time than untreated fruit. One disadvantage is that irradiation can change the appearance and flavour of meat, seafood and fresh fruit and vegetables.

Agricultural research
The radioisotope phosphorus-32 (in a phosphate fertiliser) is used in agricultural research to monitor the intake of phosphates by plants.

Making insects sterile
Another use is the treatment of male insect pests with gamma radiation. This makes them sterile. They are then released to mate with female insects. The eggs these insects lay are unfertilised, so a generation of insects is wiped out.

Research uses of radioisotopes
Many radioisotopes are used in scientific research. The techniques described above are also used by research scientists.

Radioactive dating
Radioactive isotopes decay at a known rate, and so can be used to determine the age of things.

Carbon dating
Neutrons in cosmic rays from space are continuously bombarding nitrogen-14 in the atmosphere to produce carbon-14. All plants and animals contain carbon, and a fraction of this is the radioisotope carbon-14. In living things the relative amounts of carbon-14 and normal carbon-12 is constant.

The age of wooden objects found by archaeologists can be determined by carbon dating.

PHYSICS NOW!

Carbon-14 has a half-life of 5,760 years and turns into nitrogen-14 by emitting beta particles.

When the plant or animal dies, no further carbon is taken in. The carbon-14 already present in the dead body radioactively decays to nitrogen-14. The amount of carbon-14 relative to carbon-12 gives a measure of the age of a dead plant or animal sample.

A high level of carbon-14 means that the sample is of recent origin; a low level means that it is very old. This technique has been used to determine the age of bones, wood and other organic materials found by archaeologists.

URANIUM-238 DATING

Uranium-238 has a half-life of 4.5×10^9 years. It decays through a number of radioactive isotopes to end up as lead-206. Lead-206 is not radioactive. The relative amounts of uranium-238 and lead-206 are used to date the age of rock. The oldest rocks on earth have been dated as being 4,500 million years old. Rock samples taken from the moon have a similar age.

RADIOACTIVATION ANALYSIS

When a tiny sample of a substance is bombarded with neutrons, it turns into radioactive isotopes of the same elements. The half-lives of these isotopes and the wavelengths of the gamma rays emitted enable scientists to identify the substances and the amounts of them present. The sample used is about 10^{-12} g, and the test does not destroy the sample.

Effects of ionising radiation on your health

If you have ever been sunburned, you already have some idea of the effects of radiation. Sunburn is caused by the ultraviolet radiation emitted by the sun. This penetrates the skin and damages the cells inside. The ozone layer in the atmosphere of the earth screens us from much of the ultraviolet radiation. Your body can also protect itself if you give it time to develop a coloured layer underneath your skin: a suntan!

Sunstroke (severe sunburn) is extremely dangerous and can cause death. Long-term damage by ultraviolet radiation can cause skin cancer in some people. Irish people are genetically more susceptible to this than other people.

Ionising radiation is X-rays, alpha particles, beta particles, gamma rays and, indirectly, neutrons that lose energy by ionising the substances they pass through. The effects of ionising radiation are in many ways similar to sunburn.

All these radiations ionise the chemicals in the cells of the body. They produce new substances that cause harmful chemical reactions to take place and produce toxic (poisonous) substances. These toxic substances produce radiation sickness: nausea, vomiting, skin sores and loss of hair. If a lot of cells are destroyed or made incapable of repairing and replacing themselves, radiation causes death. High levels of radiation also kill the reproductive cells (the ova and the sperm) and cause sterility.

Some parts of the body are damaged by radiation more easily than others. Young cells, developing cells and rapidly dividing cells are damaged far more than mature cells. This explains why reproductive cells are seriously damaged by radiation. Where damage is caused to the DNA it can cause the cell to change its structure. Sometimes this kills the cell but it can cause cancer cells, and cause mutations in reproductive cells. The damaging effect of an absorbed dose of radiation depends on the parts of the body it hits.

Long-term exposure to even low-level radiation can lead to an increased incidence of some types of cancer.

Alpha particle radiation

Alpha radiation is stopped by the layer of dead cells above the live skin tissue. Alpha radiation is very dangerous if alpha emitters are taken into live tissue in a skin cut or breathed into the lungs in dust, liquid or gas. This is because it is a strongly ionising radiation and causes great damage to cells.

Beta particle radiation

Beta particles can penetrate about 1 cm of body tissue. Beta emitters endanger skin tissue, but do not affect the deeper organs of the body unless taken in through dust, liquids or gas.

Gamma radiation and X-rays

These radiations are similar. They differ only in their penetration and energy, gamma rays being the more penetrating and energetic. They can penetrate right through the body and so endanger all parts of the body. Gamma emitters are potentially more dangerous than X-rays, because they can be taken inside the body.

The damage caused to a person exposed to radiation depends on a number of factors:

1. The activity of the source of radioactivity — the more active the source the greater the damage.
2. The time exposed to the radiation — the longer the exposure to a particular source the greater the damage.
3. The sensitivity of the part of the body tissue exposed to the radiation.
4. The type of radiation — α, β, γ, x-rays or neutrons.

Radiation risks

It is important to realise that we are continuously exposed to low levels of radiation. Radiation from rocks, soil, concrete blocks, bricks and the atmosphere, and cosmic rays from space, continuously bombard us. The

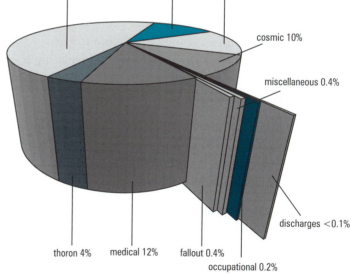

PHYSICS NOW!

human race and all other life on earth has evolved in this environment. This natural radiation, **background radiation**, has always been there.

In this century, humans have added to this radiation with medical X-rays, radiation from radioisotopes, radiation from television sets, radiation from nuclear power plants and radiation from the fall-out of nuclear weapons tests and explosions.

Experiment 37.1

AIM: To measure background radiation.

METHOD:
1. Set up a Geiger Counter as in diagram.
2. Record the count for one minute.
3. Repeat for a number of successive periods of one minute.
4. Draw up a table of your results.
5. Calculate the average count rate for background radiation.

Why do you think the count varies?

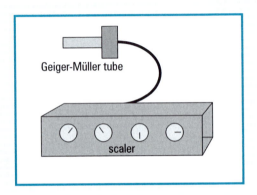

How serious are the risks?

The risk from medical X-rays is extremely small, and must be balanced against the greater danger from an untreated injury or illness. Modern radiography has reduced the exposure to very low levels.

Doctors have replaced X-rays with safer imaging techniques such as MRI scans, ultrasound scans and optical fibre scopes.

Nuclear magnetic resonance scans are also replacing X-rays. These scans surround the body with a very strong magnetic field, and use a radio-frequency coil to build up an image of the body.

The luminous material in old watches (radium mixed with a fluorescent substance) is no longer used. Radiation from TV sets has been greatly reduced in modern sets. Radiation from most man-made sources of this type has been reduced to insignificant levels.

RADON IS A PARTICULAR DANGER

One possible danger from radiation results from the draught-proofing of houses as an energy conservation measure. This reduces the number of changes of air in a given period, and so allows the build-up of a radioactive gas, radon-222, from the rocks and earth beneath the house and the bricks, stone or concrete walls. The radon level can be measured by the RPII (Radiological Protection Institute of Ireland) to find out if your home is at risk.

Uses of Radioisotopes and Radiation Hazards

Radon gas is an alpha particle emitter. Long-term exposure to radon gas can cause lung cancer. The amount of radon is greater in some parts of the country, particularly in areas over granite rock. Special measures must be taken to keep the radon levels low in homes in these areas. These include sealing floors and increasing the ventilation under floors.

Establishing safe levels

The best modern practice is to assume that there is no such thing as a safe dose of radiation. This means that all sources are kept safely contained and that radioisotopes are used only where there is a clear benefit.

Many natural radioactive substances are released into the air by mining and by burning fuels. Cigarettes release radioactive substances as well as cancer-causing chemicals into the air (and into your lungs if you smoke!).

The increase in coal and wood burning releases many radioactive isotopes into the atmosphere as gas or dust. This adds to the effects of coal mining and the non-radioactive effects of smoke and dust. Increased levels of carbon dioxide and acid rain from coal and wood burning is also damaging the environment. Many chemical compounds (cigarette smoking, asbestos, benzene, etc.), life style and other environmental factors are known to cause cancers and other illnesses.

Radiation protection

The best practice in radiation protection is as follows.
1. Assume that there is no safe dose.
2. Keep all unavoidable doses as small as possible.
3. Any deliberate exposure, such as using radioisotopes to diagnose illness, should have some clear benefit that outweighs the danger.

Handling radioactive sources

Exposure to radiation should be kept to a minimum. A large thickness of a good absorber such as lead should be placed between you and any source.

The possible dangers given above show the need for strict safety precautions in handling radiation.

1. Radioactive sources should be handled with long-handled tongs.
2. They should be stored in lead containers.
3. They should be stored in a place where persons are not usually present for long periods.
4. They should be clearly marked with the recognised international radioactivity symbol.
5. Lead-lined screens and lead-glass windows should be used when strongly radioactive sources are used for any length of time.
6. Liquid and gaseous radioactive sources must be used in a sealed container and prevented from escaping into the general working area.

International radioactivity symbol

Physics Now!

Remember that radioactive isotopes cannot be destroyed chemically or physically. Only time – sometimes thousands of years – will make them non-radioactive.

Radioactivity can be dealt with safely only when you know where it is.

Summary

- Artificial radioactivity is produced by bombarding non-radioactive isotopes with charged particles or neutrons.
- Radiation is used in medicine to treat cancers, diagnose diseases and produce images of the inside of the body.
- Radiation is used in industry in smoke detectors, as a power source, to detect leaks and to check welds.
- Radiation is used in agriculture to preserve food, in agricultural research and in pest control.
- Radiation is used in scientific research to date archaeological and geological materials and in radioactivation analysis.
- High levels of radiation kill cells.
- Long-term exposure to low-level radiation can lead to an increased incidence of cancer.

Short Questions

1. Radioisotopes are made by bombarding _____ isotopes with _____.
2. Gamma radiation emitted by _____ is used in hospitals to kill cancerous cells.
3. Iodine-131 is used to treat disorders of _____.
4. High levels of _____ radiation are used to sterilise syringes and scalpels.
5. A smoke detector contains the radioisotope _____.
6. Satellites are often powered by the radioisotope _____.
7. Radiation is passed through two packets, A and B. B shows a higher reading than A. Which packet is full?
8. Irradiated food is treated with _____ to kill _____.
*9. A sample of fresh wood gives a reading of 140 on a radiation counter. A sample taken from an archaeological dig gives a reading of 70. What is the likely age of the sample?
10. Uranium-238 decays to form _____.

Long Questions

1. Compare the damage done by α, β and γ radiation under the following headings: likely penetration of the body, damage done to cells. Outline how you could protect yourself from exposure to radiation.

2. Doctors have replaced X-rays with other forms of medical imaging devices. Name two of these devices. Outline how one of them works. Give one advantage of this method of imaging.
3. Radon-222 is known to increase the risk of lung cancer, especially in smokers. Where does radon gas come from? How does it build up in some homes? What measures could you take to reduce the level of radon gas?
4. Compare the dangers of radiation with the dangers of burning fossil fuels. How does burning fossil fuel add to the levels of radioactivity in the air? Outline the best safety practice in the use of radioactive isotopes.
5. What are radioisotopes? Explain the following statement. 'A certain radioisotope has a half-life of 300 days.' State *two* beneficial uses which are made of radioisotopes.
6. The diagram shows an arrangement for detecting the radiation emitted from a radioactive source, S. Name *two* types of radiation emitted from radioactive substances.

    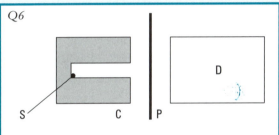

    D is a device for detecting the radiation emitted from the source S. name one type of detector which could have been used.

    A sheet of paper placed at P has no effect on the radiation reaching D. When the paper is replaced by a sheet of aluminium a few millimetres thick no radiation reaches D. Name the type of radiation being emitted by the radioactive source S.

    The radioactive source S is stored in a container C. Of what metal is the container usually made?

    Name the scientist who discovered radioactivity near the end of the nineteenth century.

    Mention one precaution which should be taken when dealing with radioactive substances.

Nuclear Energy

CHAPTER 38

Enormous amounts of energy are released in nuclear explosions; the same amounts are released over a much longer time in a nuclear reactor. The sun and the stars get their energy from nuclear reactions. All these are examples of mass turning into energy.

Einstein believed that mass and energy are simply different ways of looking at the same thing. He showed in his special theory of relativity in 1905 that mass and energy are related by the equation

$$E = mc^2$$

where E is energy, m is the mass of the body and c is the speed of light.

As the speed of light is very big, Einstein predicted that a small loss of mass would be accompanied by a big release of energy. This is the amount of energy equivalent to the loss of mass: the mass defect.

One result of this is that conservation of mass and conservation of energy, taken separately, do not work with nuclear reactions. Only conservation of mass–energy combined works with nuclear reactions.

Cockcroft and Walton's experiment

Mass–energy conservation was confirmed experimentally in 1932 by Cockcroft and Walton, who produced the first disintegration of a nucleus with an accelerated charged particle. They used an electrostatic generator to accelerate protons to energies of 600 keV. In a series of experiments they showed that when lithium is bombarded by protons, two α particles are emitted in opposite directions (i.e. momentum is conserved).

$$^{1}_{1}H + ^{7}_{3}Li \rightarrow ^{4}_{2}He + ^{4}_{2}He + Q$$

Albert Einstein 1879–1955
was probably the greatest theoretical physicist of the twentieth century. He developed mathematical models to explain physical phenomena, explained the photoelectric effect and stated the photoelectric law later verified experimentally by Millikan. Einstein developed the mass–energy equation $E = mc^2$, which predicted the possibility of nuclear fission. He explained the nature of space and time in the general theory of relativity, and predicted that light would 'bend' near a large mass. This was later verified experimentally, and is the reason why light does not escape from 'black holes'. Einstein was awarded the Nobel Prize for physics in 1921.

E. T. S. Walton (Ireland) 1903–1995 produced (with John Cockcroft) the first nuclear reaction using artificially accelerated particles, and also verified Einstein's mass–energy equation $E = mc^2$ experimentally. Walton is the only Irish Nobel laureate in science: he shared the 1951 prize for physics with Cockcroft.

The mass of the lithium nucleus and the proton that hits it is greater than that of the two α particles produced. The kinetic energy of the two α particles equals the loss of mass (calculated using Einstein's mass–energy equation, $E = mc^2$) in the reaction plus the kinetic energy of the proton. Cockcroft and Walton's experiment was the first direct confirmation of Einstein's prediction of the equivalence of mass and energy.

Fission

In 1934, Fermi bombarded thorium and uranium with neutrons. He found that the half-lives of the products were not those of any known radioactive isotope. He thought that elements of atomic number greater than 92 had been formed.

In 1939, Hahn and Strassman analysed the radioactive substances formed by the bombardment of uranium with neutrons. They found that barium-56 was one of the products. This led them to suggest that the uranium nucleus splits into two or more fragments when it is bombarded by neutrons. This is called fission.

Within months, bromine, molybdenum, antimony and iodine were identified as other fragments of the fission of uranium. Cloud chamber photographs were taken of the reaction and showed two particles moving in opposite directions at high speeds. This confirmed that fission took place when uranium was struck by a neutron.

Scientists soon found that great amounts of energy are released in nuclear fission. Frisch and Meitner measured the energy emitted with each fission of a single uranium atom. The fission energy of 200 MeV is enormous compared with the energy of chemical reactions, which release just a few electron volts.

Joliot, Curie, Halban and Kowarski showed in 1940 that two or three neutrons are emitted from the uranium nucleus during fission. A chain reaction, where each fission produces another fission, was shown to be possible.

Fission reactions can be caused by bombarding the nucleus with many different particles. Fissions caused by neutrons are the most important.

Fission: The splitting of the nucleus of a heavy element into two or more smaller nuclei with the emission of neutrons and a large amount of energy.

WHY DOES FISSION HAPPEN WITH LARGE ATOMS?
Extremely powerful nuclear forces hold the nucleus together. These forces are effective only at the very small distances that the nucleons (protons and neutrons) are from each other.

In large atoms, the nucleons are relatively far apart. The nuclear forces are not strong at these distances, so the repulsive forces between the protons tend to split the nucleus when a neutron hits it.

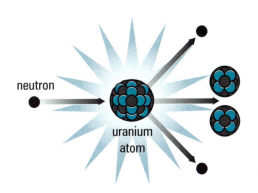

Enrico Fermi (Italy) 1901–1954
experimented on artificial radioactivity produced by bombarding elements with neutrons. He was awarded the 1938 Nobel Prize for physics for this work. Fermi carried out the first sustained nuclear fission reaction on 2 December 1942 in a reactor built in the tennis courts of Columbia University, USA.

A single atom of uranium 235 undergoing fission

Bohr's liquid drop model

Bohr pictured the nucleus as a spherical liquid drop which is continuously vibrating. When a neutron hits the nucleus it makes it vibrate faster and distort. If the distortion is sufficiently great, the nucleus splits into parts. This model is useful when considering nuclear fission.

Uranium fission

Uranium is the principal element used in fission. Natural uranium has three isotopes: U-238 (99·2%), U-235 (0·7%) and U-234 (0·006%). As the differences in mass are very small, the isotopes are very difficult to separate. The main isotopes, U-235 and U-238, behave differently when struck by neutrons.

U-238 undergoes radiative capture and very little fission.

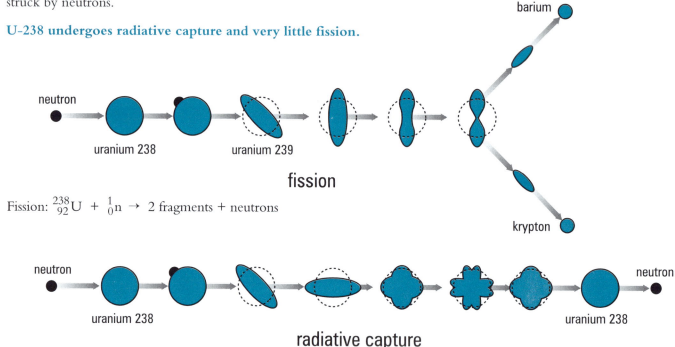

Fission: $^{238}_{92}U + ^{1}_{0}n \rightarrow$ 2 fragments + neutrons

Radiative capture: $^{238}_{92}U + ^{1}_{0}n \rightarrow ^{238}_{92}U + ^{1}_{0}n + \gamma$

Fission in U-238 needs neutrons with energy in excess of 1 MeV. Most of the neutrons emitted don't have this energy, so sustained fission in U-238 does not occur. Radiative capture is far more likely to occur with U-238.

U-235 undergoes fission and little radiative capture.

Fission: $^{235}_{92}U + ^{1}_{0}n \rightarrow$ 2 fragments + neutrons

Radiative capture: $^{235}_{92}U + ^{1}_{0}n \rightarrow ^{235}_{92}U + ^{1}_{0}n + \gamma$

Fission in U-235 takes place with both fast and slow neutrons. On average, slow neutrons produce 85% fission and 15% capture.

Slow neutrons (thermal) have energies similar to the kinetic energy of atoms at room temperature: about 0·025 eV. Fast neutrons have energy in excess of 1 keV.

Nuclear Energy

There are two important differences between U-235 and U-238.

U-238	(99·2%)	mainly radiative capture	fission with fast neutrons only
U-235	(0·7%)	mainly fission	fission with fast and slow neutrons

Chain reaction

For a self-sustaining reaction to take place, each fission must produce at least one further fission. This is called a chain reaction. Although 2–3 neutrons are emitted for each fission of a uranium nucleus, a chain reaction is not likely with natural uranium because neutrons are lost:

1. by radiative capture in U-238
2. by radiative capture in U-235
3. to nuclear reactions in the fission fragments
4. by leaving the surface of the uranium.

A chain reaction is achieved by using uranium enriched with more U-235. Uncontrolled fission chain reactions use pure U-235 or plutonium-239 (Pu-239). These fissile materials are used in nuclear weapons.

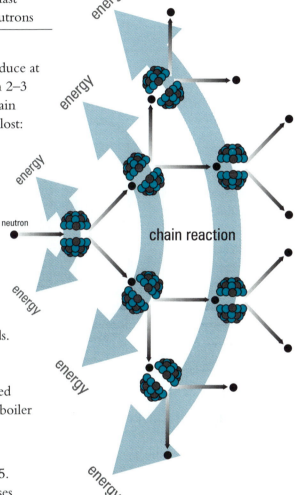

Nuclear reactors

A nuclear reactor produces energy by fission in uranium fuel rods. The energy is used to boil water and drive a steam turbine generator set. The reactor is made up of a core containing fuel rods, moderator, control rods and coolant. The core is surrounded by a containment vessel and shielding. Heat is transferred to the boiler by a heat exchanger.

Fuel rods

The fuel rods are made from natural uranium, enriched in U-235. About 3% to 4% U-235 is used in the enriched fuel. This increases the chances of fission taking place. The fuel rods are encased in a corrosion-resistant alloy.

When the reactor core is properly adjusted, the chain reaction is self-sustaining. The reactor is now 'critical'. If there are too few neutrons to maintain fission, the reactor is 'subcritical' and the nuclear reaction fizzles out. If too many neutrons are produced, the rate of fission increases and the reactor is 'supercritical'.

Moderator

The moderator rapidly slows down neutrons to the energy that allows fission to happen. The neutrons emitted in fission are fast neutrons (energy > 1 MeV). They have to be slowed down to energies below 5 eV for fission to happen. This prevents a lot of radiative capture of neutrons by U-238.

The moderator is a material such as graphite or heavy water that slows down the neutrons without undergoing nuclear reactions.

CONTROL RODS

Control rods are made from a neutron absorber such as cadmium or boron steel. The rods are adjusted by raising or lowering them into the reactor core so that just one fission-producing neutron results from each fission. This controls the rate of fission and so controls the energy production of the reactor.

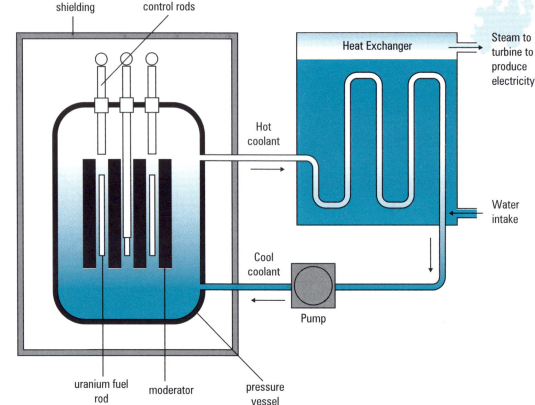

A reactor can be shut down in an emergency by dropping the control rods into the core. This absorbs all neutrons and stops fission.

In reactors where heavy water is used as the moderator, the reactor can be shut down by draining off the heavy water.

The core of the reactor is surrounded by a reflector of graphite, which scatters the neutrons back into the core. All the other materials are chosen so as not to absorb neutrons.

SHIELDING

The reactor core is contained in a sealed vessel. This prevents radioactive liquids and gases from escaping. Radiation does escape from the reactor core, and is contained by a thick concrete shield around the reactor. This protects workers in the nuclear power station from radiation.

Poor shielding, the lack of a containment vessel, bad safety practices and a poor design all led to the disastrous explosion of the Chernobyl nuclear reactor in April 1986.

Heat exchanger

A nuclear reactor does not heat the boiler directly. This is because the large number of neutrons in the reactor produce radioactive isotopes in any substance around it. The water (or other fluid) in the reactor flows through pipes and heats the boiler water indirectly. The radioactive isotopes are contained in the reactor water and pipes.

The steam produced by the boiler powers a generator. Nuclear power stations have powers of 1,000 megawatts or greater.

Problem

Calculate the energy released in the fission of 1 kg of uranium 235 when 200 MeV is emitted per fission event.

One mole of U-235 = 235 g

Number of moles in 1 kg = $\frac{1000}{235}$

Avogadro's number = $6 \cdot 023 \times 10^{23}$ per mole

Number of atoms in 1 kg of U-235 = $\left(\frac{1000}{235}\right) \times 6 \cdot 023 \times 10^{23}$

Total fission energy = $\left(\frac{1000}{235}\right) \times 6 \cdot 023 \times 10^{23} \times 200$ MeV
= $51 \cdot 26 \times 10^{25}$ MeV

1 MeV = $1 \cdot 6 \times 10^{-19} \times 10^{6}$ J = $1 \cdot 6 \times 10^{-13}$ J

$51 \cdot 26 \times 10^{25}$ MeV = $8 \cdot 2 \times 10^{13}$ J

Dangers of fission reactors

There are three big problems with fission reactors.
1. Even though many reactors have a good safety record, the potential for disaster is always there. The terrible destructive effects of the nuclear accident in April 1986 at the Chernobyl fission reactor are still being suffered.
2. Disposal of nuclear waste, including highly radioactive old nuclear reactors.
3. Reprocessing of used (spent) fuel rods from reactor cores.

Despite these problems, European countries such as France are almost totally dependent on nuclear power stations for their electricity supply. 95% of all electricity in France will be generated from nuclear energy in the early years of this century.

The effects of the nuclear reactor explosion at Chernobyl in 1986 are still being suffered in Belarus.

Nuclear waste

Nuclear waste comes from many sources. It includes strongly radioactive waste from reactors and weak radioisotopes from hospitals, research labs and industry. Nuclear waste is different from other waste for the following reasons.
1. Many radioactive isotopes remain radioactive for a long time: they have half-lives of thousands of years. They will have to be stored in a secure place away from people for thousands of years.
2. Radioactive waste produces a lot of heat, which can cause chemical

PHYSICS NOW!

reactions and lead to explosions that release the radioactive waste into the environment.

3. The containers used to store conventional waste will not last as long as the radioactive waste. Concrete-encased drums of radioactive waste dumped in the sea are known to have decayed.

Much of the low-level waste is buried in the ground. This waste contains cloth used to mop up radioisotope liquids, and clothing used by research workers. The same precautions must be taken as with toxic chemicals.

High-level waste is highly radioactive materials from nuclear reactors. There is at present no permanent storage facility for such waste. Scientists are experimenting on various methods of storage to see which ones are safest. One method is to turn the waste material into a glass-like substance and store it in old salt mines.

NUCLEAR WEAPONS

For a given mass of substance, a sphere has the smallest surface area for a neutron to escape. A chain reaction will occur in a sphere of fissile material if the mass is such that one neutron is produced per fission event. This is known as the critical mass. Masses less than the critical mass are subcritical. When a number of subcritical masses are brought together rapidly, they form a supercritical mass and a fast chain reaction releases enormous amounts of energy and radiation. This is what happens in nuclear explosions.

Fusion

Energy is released when light nuclei combine to form heavier nuclei. This process is called fusion. The nuclei must have very high energies to overcome the repulsive forces between the electric charges of the protons as the nuclei approach each other. Also, to sustain a fusion reaction the density of the nuclei must be great. In the sun and stars, fusion is responsible for the enormous energy output with little loss of mass. These self-sustaining fusion reactions require high temperatures and high density of particles. The sun has temperatures of millions of degrees and a high density due to great gravitational forces.

On earth these conditions have been achieved only in thermonuclear explosions. This is uncontrolled fusion: the temperature and density are achieved by exploding a fission bomb. Controlled fusion is far more difficult to achieve.

Fusion is the union of light nuclei to form a heavier nucleus with the emission of large amounts of energy.

$$^2_1H + ^2_1H \rightarrow ^3_2He + ^1_0n + \text{energy}$$

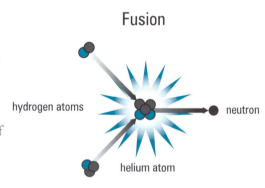

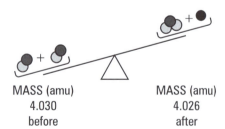

MASS (amu) 4.030 before

MASS (amu) 4.026 after

EXPERIMENTAL FUSION REACTORS

Experimental fusion reactors are attempting to produce sustained fusion of a plasma of hydrogen isotopes: a high-temperature mixture of deuterium and tritium. At temperatures of many hundred million degrees, all atoms are ionised and electrically charged. This plasma is kept in place in a doughnut-shaped tube called a tokamak with a powerful magnetic field.

Lithium metal is used as a heat exchanger because it is a good conductor of heat. Lithium also 'breeds' tritium when struck by neutrons. The tritium can later be extracted for use as fuel for further fusion.

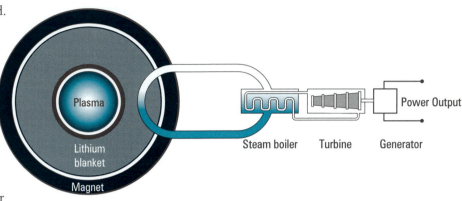

A fusion reactor

Present research on self-sustained fusion includes the use of magnetic fields as a container for the gas, and synchronised arrays of lasers to produce the required temperatures of several hundred million degrees: many times the temperature of the centre of the sun. When the JET (Joint European Torus) fusion reactor produced over a million watts for just two seconds in 1991, it was a major advance in fusion research.

Making fusion work in a controlled way is like making a small sun. It is one of the most challenging projects ever attempted by humans. Researchers hope to have a working fusion reactor sometime in the present century.

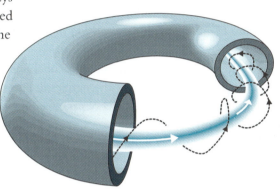

Tokamak

Problem

Calculate the energy released when two protons, one neutron and two electrons combine to form a helium-3 atom of mass 3·01603 a.m.u.

neutron:	1·008665 a.m.u.
proton:	1·007825 a.m.u.
electron:	0·0005486 a.m.u.

1 a.m.u. = $1·66 \times 10^{-27}$ kg

Mass 2p + 1n + 2e = 2(1·007825) + 1(1·008665) + 2(0·0005486)
= 3·0254122

Mass of helium-3 atom = 3·01603 a.m.u.

Mass defect = 0·00938 a.m.u. = $0·01557 \times 10^{-27}$ kg

Energy = mc^2 = $(0·01557 \times 10^{-27})(3 \times 10^8)^2 = 1·4 \times 10^{-12}$ J

PHYSICS NOW!

CONTROLLED FUSION IS ATTRACTIVE AS AN ENERGY SOURCE FOR FOUR REASONS

1. Low fuel cost: 700 g of deuterium could power a 200 MW station for 1 day.
2. Fuel is readily available from water: sufficient deuterium is available on earth to last for 2×10^4 million years at current energy consumption rates.
3. There are no radioactive wastes of long half-life to dispose of.
4. Fusion is not a chain reaction: it cannot get out of control.

Summary

- Einstein's mass–energy equation ($E = mc^2$): When a small amount of matter seems to disappear, a large amount of energy is released in its place.
- Fission: The splitting of the nucleus of a heavy element into two or more fragments with the emission of neutrons and a large amount of energy.
- Slow (thermal) neutrons have energies of about 0·025 eV.
- Fast neutrons are neutrons with energies in excess of 1 keV.
- Chain reaction: A reaction where each fission event produces at least one further fission.
- Fusion: The union of light nuclei to form a heavier nucleus with the emission of large amounts of energy.

SHORT QUESTIONS

Note:
$c = 3 \cdot 0 \times 10^8$ m s^{-1}
Charge on electron = $1 \cdot 60 \times 10^{-19}$ C
Masses: neutron, 1·008665 a.m.u.; proton, 1·007825 a.m.u.; deuterium, 2·0141 a.m.u. (1 a.m.u. = $1 \cdot 66 \times 10^{-27}$ kg)

1. The splitting of the nucleus of a heavy element with the emission of a large amount of energy is called _____.
2. What is meant by nuclear fission?
3. Neutrons with energies of about 0·025 eV are called _____.
4. What is meant by mass–energy conservation?
5. The union of light nuclei with the emission of large amounts of energy is _____.
6. Neutrons with energies in excess of 1 keV are called _____.
7. Fission and fusion are two processes by which energy may be released in nuclear reactions. What is the difference between them?
8. Complete the following nuclear reaction: $^{3}_{1}H + ^{2}_{1}H \rightarrow ^{4}_{2}He +$ _____.

9. Name two scientists who have played a major role in the field of nuclear physics.

*10. The difference between the mass of the reactants and that of the products in a nuclear reaction is 8.63×10^{-30} kg. Calculate the energy released in this reaction.

11. State one energy conversion that takes place in a nuclear reactor.

12. Albert Einstein deduced the following equation:
    (A) $E = \frac{1}{2}mv^2$, (B) $E = mc^2$, (C) $E = ma$, (D) $E = mgh$, (E) $E = hf$.

13. In a nuclear reactor the purpose of the moderator is to reduce (A) the temperature of the reactor, (B) the number of neutrons causing fission, (C) the rate at which energy is released, (D) the speed of the neutrons, (E) the supply of U-235.

*14. The energy released in a certain nuclear reaction was 2.5×10^{-12} J. Given that the speed of light in a vacuum, $c = 3.0 \times 10^8$ m s^{-1}, what was the change in mass?

Long Questions

1. (a) What is meant by (i) nuclear fission, (ii) mass–energy conservation?

    *(b) In a nuclear reaction the difference in mass between the reactants and the products is 8.63×10^{-30} kg. Calculate the energy produced in this reaction.

2. The following is an extract from a letter sent by Albert Einstein to President Roosevelt on 2 August 1939. Read the extract and answer the questions that follow.

    Sir
    Some recent work by E. Fermi and L. Szilard, which has been communicated to me in manuscript, leads me to expect that the element uranium may be turned into a new and important source of energy in the immediate future . . . In the course of the last four months it has been made probable – through the work of Joliot in France as well as Fermi and Szilard in America – that it may become possible to set up nuclear chain reactions in a large piece of uranium, by which vast amounts of power and large quantities of new radium-like elements would be generated. Now it appears almost certain that this could be achieved in the immediate future. This new phenomenon would also lead . . .

    (a) What is the 'new phenomenon' called?
    (b) How would you account for the release of 'vast amounts of power' from uranium?
    (c) What is meant by 'radium-like' elements?
    (d) Describe briefly how a substance can be checked for the presence of 'radium-like' elements.

⋆3. Calculate the energy of the emitted beta particle electron when a neutron decays into a proton.

⋆4. When a proton and a neutron combine to form deuterium, a gamma ray photon is emitted. Calculate the energy of the gamma photon, given that all the energy is emitted as a single photon.

⋆5. Calculate the energy released when two protons, two neutrons and two electrons combine to form a helium atom of mass 4·0026 a.m.u.

6. 'A nuclear fission reactor contains a fuel, control rods and a moderator.' Explain the underlined terms. Name a suitable fuel for a nuclear reactor.

   Give one advantage and one disadvantage of nuclear fission compared to nuclear fusion as a source of energy.

⋆7. The energy per fission for U-235 is 175 MeV. Calculate the energy released in the fission of 1 g of U-235.

⋆8. Two deuterium nuclei fuse with the emission of 3·3 MeV, according to:

$$^{2}_{1}H + ^{2}_{1}H \rightarrow ^{3}_{2}He + ^{1}_{0}n + 3\cdot3 \text{ MeV}$$

   Calculate the energy released per 1 g of deuterium.
   Compare this with the energy released in fission (question 7).

9. Complete the following nuclear reaction by replacing X with the appropriate symbol.

$$^{235}_{92}U + ^{1}_{0}n \rightarrow ^{141}_{55}Cs + X + 2^{1}_{0}n + 181 \text{ MeV}$$

   ⋆Given that the mass of the uranium and the caesium nuclei is 235·0439 and 140·9196 a.m.u. respectively, calculate the mass in kg of the nucleus X.

10. (a) When cobalt-59 is irradiated with neutrons, a radioactive isotope of cobalt is formed and a gamma ray photon is emitted. Write an equation to represent this reaction and give one use of the isotope formed.

    ⋆(b) The mass of the cobalt-59 nucleus is $9\cdot7859 \times 10^{-26}$ kg, the mass of the nucleus produced in the above reaction is $9\cdot9520 \times 10^{-26}$ kg and the mass of a neutron is $1\cdot6749 \times 10^{-27}$ kg. Calculate the energy of the photon produced in this reaction.

Inside the Atom (Option 1)

CHAPTER 39

The search for order

The ancient Greek philosopher Aristotle believed that all substances on earth were made from one or more of four basic substances: earth, air, fire and water. He believed that when rocks were heated (to make copper), the result was a combination of rock and fire: the metal copper. Other substances were formed from different combinations of the four basic substances. This was an attractive theory when few chemicals were known. Other Greek philosophers (Anaxagoras and Empedocles) believed that all matter was made of tiny 'seeds'. This idea was developed by Democritus and Leucippus, who suggested that all matter is formed from indivisible units: atoms.

Many techniques of refining and working metals and other substances were developed over the centuries by the Egyptians, Greeks, Romans and Arabs. This knowledge spread by contacts between different civilisations. Scientific study began in a systematic way in the middle ages.

In 1808 Dalton published his atomic theory, which stated that each atom has a characteristic mass and that atoms of elements are unchanged in chemical reactions. Dalton's atoms were solid and indivisible, and all matter was made from them. This theory has developed over the past two centuries and has led to our present understanding of the atom and chemical reactions.

The discovery of the electron, proton and neutron and Rutherford's nuclear model of the atom changed this picture. The model of the atom accepted by 1932 was that it was divisible. Scientists believed that these three particles (proton, neutron and electron) were the basic building blocks of all matter.

Conservation of momentum in nuclear reactions

When a nucleus emits an α particle, the nucleus recoils in the same way as a gun recoils when a shot is fired. The mass and velocity of the α particle and the mass of the new nucleus determine the recoil velocity. The process conserves momentum.

PROBLEM

Americium 241 emits an α particle with a velocity of 3×10^7 m s^{-1}. Calculate the recoil velocity of the resulting nucleus.

Nuclear equation: $^{241}_{95}\text{Am} \rightarrow\ ^{4}_{2}\text{He} +\ ^{237}_{93}\text{Np}$

Momentum before emission $\dot{=} 0$ (assume nucleus is at rest)
Momentum of α particle $m_1v_1 = (4)(3 \times 10^7)$
Momentum of neptunium nucleus $m_2v_2 = (237)(x)$
Conservation of momentum: momentum before = momentum after

$$0 = (4)(3 \times 10^7) + 237x$$

$$x = \frac{(4)(3 \times 10^7)}{237}$$

$$= 5.06 \times 10^5 \text{ m s}^{-1}$$

The nucleus of neptunium does not fly off at this velocity, because it is not on its own. This nucleus is just one among many millions of atoms of americium in the sample of radioactive material. The momentum of a single atom is rapidly transferred to the other atoms, and the overall effect is reduced by the number (and masses) of atoms present.

The neutrino

When β particles are emitted by radioactive decay, the range of velocities is extremely wide: from 30% to 70% of the speed of light. This leads to an enormous variation in the energy and momentum of the β particles. As the process leading to the emission is the same for a given nucleus, scientists had expected the β particles to have the same energy. The process seemed to contradict conservation of energy and conservation of momentum. This led Pauli to suggest (in 1930) that another particle – a neutrino (the name means 'little neutral one') – was emitted in the decay. When this is taken into account, energy and momentum are conserved.

Neutrinos are also emitted in other nuclear reactions involving electrons. The neutrino ($^0_0\upsilon$; υ is the Greek letter upsilon) has zero charge and almost zero mass, but has momentum and energy.

The neutrino is very difficult to detect because it has such a small mass and no electric charge. Millions of neutrino pass through your body each minute without any effect. Neutrinos can pass right through the earth without interaction.

Neutrinos were not discovered until 1957. A large number of neutrinos were detected in 1987 from the explosion of a star – a supernova.

Wolfgang Pauli (Austria) 1901–58 became famous for the 'Pauli exclusion principle' which states that no two electrons in an atom can have the same quantum number. In 1945 Pauli was awarded the Nobel Prize for physics for this work.

PROBLEM

The following nuclear equation describes the emission of a beta particle from a nucleus. Use the values for the masses given to calculate the energy released in the reaction.

$$^1_0\text{n} \rightarrow ^1_1\text{p} + ^0_{-1}\text{e} + ^0_0\upsilon$$

Masses: neutron, 1·008665 a.m.u.; proton, 1·007825 a.m.u.; electron, 0·0005486 a.m.u.

mass of proton + mass of electron = 1·0083736
mass defect = mass of neutron − (mass of proton + mass of electron)
= 1·008665 − 1·0083736 = 0·0002914 a.m.u.

The mass defect produces an equivalent amount of energy of about 271 keV. The emitted β particle has less energy than this. The difference is the energy of the neutrino.

> 1 a.m.u. is equivalent to an energy of 931 MeV.
>
> 1 a.m.u. = $1·660 \times 10^{-27}$ kg
>
> $E = mc^2 = (1·66 \times 10^{-27})(3·0 \times 10^8)^2$ J
>
> $= \dfrac{(1·660 \times 10^{-27})(3·0 \times 10^8)^2}{1.602 \times 10^{-19}} = 931$ MeV

Conservation of mass–energy

Enormous amounts of energy are released in nuclear explosions. The same amount is released over a much longer time in a nuclear reactor. The sun and the stars also get their energy from nuclear reactions. All these are examples of mass turning into energy.

Einstein believed that mass and energy are simply different ways of looking at the same thing. He showed in his special theory of relativity in 1905 that mass and energy are related by the equation $E = mc^2$, where m is the mass of the body and c is the speed of light. As the speed of light is very big, Einstein predicted that a small loss of mass would be accompanied by a big release of energy. This energy is the amount of energy equivalent to the loss of mass – the mass defect. The mass defect in most nuclear reactions is small, but the energy equivalent of this mass multiplied by the number of nuclei involved in the reaction is an enormous amount of energy.

Conservation of mass and conservation of energy taken separately do not work with nuclear reactions. Mass is not conserved because there is a mass defect, and energy is not conserved because energy is released when the mass defect turns into energy. Conservation of mass and conservation of energy are combined into conservation of mass–energy. This works when applied to nuclear reactions.

PROBLEM

Calculate the energy released in the following nuclear reaction:

$^{2}_{1}H + ^{6}_{3}Li \rightarrow ^{4}_{2}He + ^{4}_{2}He + Q$

Masses: deuteron, 2·014102 a.m.u.; lithium, 6·015125 a.m.u.

Sum of masses = 8·029227

2 × mass α particle = 8·005208 a.m.u.

Mass defect = 0·024019 a.m.u.

This is equivalent to 22·37 MeV

PHYSICS NOW!

Cockcroft and Walton split the nucleus

Mass–energy conservation was confirmed experimentally by Cockcroft and Walton in 1932. They produced the first artificial splitting of a nucleus with an accelerated charged particle: a proton.

They used an electrostatic generator (which they developed themselves) to accelerate protons to energies of about 600 keV. In a series of experiments they showed that when a lithium target is bombarded by protons, two α particles are emitted from the target in opposite directions. This was also the first artificial transmutation of an element.

Results:

$$^{1}_{1}\text{H} + ^{7}_{3}\text{Li} \rightarrow ^{4}_{2}\text{He} + ^{4}_{2}\text{He} + Q$$

1 MeV   17·3 MeV

1. Measurements of the velocities and directions of the α particles show that momentum is conserved.
2. The masses of the lithium nucleus and the proton that hits it are together greater than the masses of the two α particles produced.
3. There is a net gain in energy.

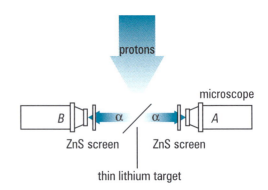

Cockcroft and Walton calculated the masses of the proton, lithium target and two alpha particles. Their estimate of the energy released, based on the atomic masses (as they were known at the time) was 14·3 ± 2·7 MeV.

We can calculate the energy released using modern values as follows.
$^{7}_{3}$Li: 7·016005 a.m.u.
$^{1}_{1}$H: 1·007825 a.m.u.
Sum of masses: 8·023830

2 × $^{4}_{2}$He: 8·005208 a.m.u.
Mass defect: 0·018622 a.m.u.

This 'missing' mass of 0·018622 a.m.u. is equivalent (from Einstein's mass–energy equation $E = mc^2$) to 17·3 MeV.

Cockcroft and Walton measured the kinetic energy of the two α particles from the ranges of the particles and their ionising effects. They found them to have a kinetic energy of 8·6 MeV each, i.e. a combined kinetic energy of 17·2 MeV. They concluded that this energy came from the conversion of mass into energy.

Cockcroft and Walton's experiment was the first direct confirmation of Einstein's prediction of the equivalence of mass and energy.

If you are really observant, you will ask 'what about the kinetic energy of the proton?'. Cockcroft and Walton took this energy into account in their calculations. The level of agreement they found between predicted and experimental results was sufficiently close to prove their explanation of the experimental results.

Inside the Atom (Option 1)

A machine to smash the nucleus

You cannot look into the nucleus of an atom. The only way scientists can find out what the nucleus is made of is by bombarding it with high-energy particles and observing what happens. One scientist described this process as like smashing two cars together and then examining the pieces thrown out of the crash to get an idea of the structure of the cars.

LINEAR ACCELERATORS

Cockcroft and Walton accelerated protons in a straight line, in a linear accelerator. These are still used to accelerate electrons: the Stanford Linear Accelerator in California is 3·2 km long, is absolutely straight and accelerates electrons to 50 GeV (99·9% of the speed of light). (1 GeV = 10^9 eV.)

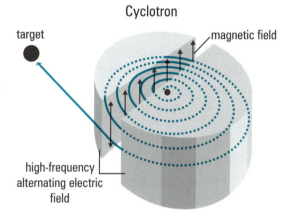

CIRCULAR ACCELERATORS

A more compact way of accelerating particles was developed in 1930 by Lawrence. The cyclotron he invented was about the size of a dinner plate.

1. The particles are charged and can be accelerated by an electric field. A magnetic field at right angles to the direction of the particles forces them into a circular path.
2. Each time they come to the gap between the two semicircles, the electric field accelerates them across the gap. The frequency of the electric field ensures that this happens at the correct moment.

Once cyclotrons began to accelerate particles to high velocities, one of the effects predicted by Einstein (in his theory of relativity) interfered with their usefulness. Einstein predicted that when a particle moves at a high velocity, its mass will increase. This meant that particles did not arrive at the gap in the cyclotron at the right time and so were not accelerated.

The **synchrocyclotron** adjusts the frequency to compensate for this effect and allow particles to accelerate to very high velocities. The **synchrotron** adjusts the strength of the magnetic field to keep the particles moving in phase.

Circular accelerators have developed from the plate-sized Lawrence cyclotron to the one 27 km in circumference built by CERN on the Swiss–French border near Geneva. This accelerates particles to energies of 500 GeV. Larger accelerators are planned to produce particle energies of 40 TeV. (1 TeV = 10^{12} eV.)

CERN is the European Organisation for Nuclear Research (Conseil Europeen pour la Recherché Nucleaire). International co-operation in scientific research enables

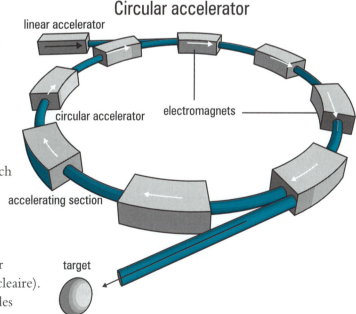

countries to pool their resources and build expensive facilities they could not afford individually. The JET (Joint European Torus) project on nuclear fusion is another example.

These large accelerators are used to slam high-energy protons into other protons and observe the reactions with detectors. They also use collisions between protons and other targets in experiments similar to the one carried out by Cockcroft and Walton, but with enormously greater energy.

Ernest O. Lawrence (USA) 1901–58 invented the cyclotron and was awarded the 1938 Nobel Prize for physics.

Summary

- Nuclear reactions conserve momentum.
- The neutrino ($_0^0\upsilon$) has zero charge and almost zero mass but has momentum and energy.
- Equivalence of mass and energy: $E = mc^2$.
- Cockcroft and Walton produced the first artificial splitting of a nucleus with an accelerated charged particle: a proton.
- Linear accelerators accelerate charged particles in a straight line.
- Circular accelerators (cyclotrons, synchrocyclotrons and synchrotrons) accelerate charged particles in circular paths.

Short Questions

1. In Dalton's model, atoms were _____.
2. Some nuclear reactions appear not to obey conservation of momentum. The _____ particle is emitted in these.
3. Scientists in 1932 believed that _____, _____ and _____ were the basic building blocks of all matter.
4. A mass defect of 0·0002914 a.m.u. is equivalent to an energy of _____ MeV.
5. The European Organisation for Nuclear Research is better known as _____.
6. The sun and the stars get their energy from _____ turning into _____.
7. The neutrino has a charge of _____ and a mass of _____.
8. Einstein showed that mass and energy are related by the equation _____.
9. The first artificial splitting of a nucleus with an accelerated charged particle was carried out by_____ in the year _____.
10. The cyclotron accelerates charged particles using _____.
11. Circular accelerators use _____ to keep particles in a circular path.
12. A superconducting supercollider (SSC) is planned to accelerate protons to energies of 40 TeV. What is 40 TeV in joules?

13. Complete the following nuclear reaction and comment on its historical significance.

$^{7}_{3}Li + \rightarrow ^{4}_{2}He + ^{4}_{2}He$

LONG QUESTIONS

1. Calculate the energy released in the following nuclear reaction:

   $^{7}_{3}Li + ^{1}_{1}H \rightarrow ^{4}_{2}He + ^{4}_{2}He + Q$

   Use the following nuclear masses:

   $^{7}_{3}Li = 7.016$ amu

   $^{1}_{1}H = 1.008$ amu

   $^{4}_{2}He = 4.004$ amu

   What is the historical significance of this reaction?

2. A carbon-12 atom recoils with a velocity of 6×10^6 m s^{-1} when struck head-on by a neutron. Calculate the velocity of the neutron. (Assume the mass of the neutron is 1, where the mass of an atom of C-12 is taken as 12.)

3. (a) The cathode ray tube and X-ray tube could be considered as electron accelerators. Explain how they accelerate electrons.
   (b) Describe how other charged particles are accelerated in circular accelerators using electric and magnetic fields.
   (c) When particles are accelerated to very high speeds, simple electric and magnetic fields are no longer adequate. Why? What changes are made to circular accelerators to overcome this effect?

4. Calculate the energy the bombarding neutron must have to cause the following nuclear reaction.

   $_{15}P^{31} + _{0}n^{1} \rightarrow _{14}Si^{31} + _{1}H^{1} + Q$

   The following are atomic masses. Nuclear masses (without electron mass included) should be used in your calculations. (Note that you can cancel electron masses on the left with those on the right.)

Mass $_{15}P^{31}$	=	30.98356 a.m.u.
Mass $_{0}n^{1}$	=	1.008665 a.m.u.
Mass $_{14}Si^{31}$	=	30.98515 a.m.u.
Mass $_{1}H^{1}$	=	1.007825 a.m.u.
Mass of electron	=	0.000549 a.m.u.

5. Calculate the energy released in the nuclear reaction

   $_{92}U^{238} \rightarrow _{90}Th^{234} + _{2}He^{4}$

   Use the following nuclear masses:

Mass $_{92}U^{238}$	=	238.05077 a.m.u.
Mass $_{90}Th^{234}$	=	234.04358 a.m.u.
Mass $_{2}He^{4}$	=	4.002604 a.m.u.

   Does all this energy go to give the kinetic energy of the α particle emitted? Explain your answer.

Fundamental Particles (Option 1)

CHAPTER 40

The belief that the proton, neutron and electron are the basic building blocks of matter did not last long. In the 1940s, studies of cosmic rays showed that many other sub-atomic particles also existed. By 1960, about 200 of these strange sub-atomic particles had been discovered. Scientists still believed that some elementary particles must exist. This belief led to the quark theory in 1963, which reduces the number of fundamental particles.

Antiparticles

Cosmic rays were discovered in the early twentieth century. Scientists working with radioactive substances found that electroscopes discharged more rapidly than normal leakage of charge could account for. They suggested this was due to background radiation from the earth. If this is true, the effect should decrease as you move further above the earth. The Austrian scientist Victor Hess tested this hypothesis by taking measurements while going up in a balloon. He found that the effect increased: the opposite of what was expected. Hess suggested the radiation was coming from outside the earth: **cosmic radiation**.

In 1928, Paul Dirac worked out mathematical solutions to formulas he derived. He found two values: one corresponding to the electron and the other to a positive particle identical in every other way to the electron. He suggested that every particle should have a corresponding antiparticle.

The first antiparticle was discovered by Anderson in cosmic rays in 1932. He found a particle with the same mass as the electron but with a positive electric charge. This positive electron is the **positron**.

Paul Dirac (England) 1902–1984 he predicted the existence of positrons and other antiparticles. He was awarded the 1933 Nobel Prize for physics for this work.

Carl David Anderson (USA) 1905–1991 was awarded the 1936 Nobel Prize for physics for his work on cosmic rays. Anderson discovered the positron — a positively charged electron.

Fundamental Particles (Option 1)

Converting Energy into Mass: Pair Production

Experimental work in the 1930s showed that electron–positron pairs are produced when high-energy photons pass close to a nucleus. This is another example of mass–energy equivalence. The photon disappears, replaced by two particles of equal mass and charge moving in opposite directions. Electric charge is conserved: the photon has zero electric charge and the sum of the two charges produced is also zero. Momentum is conserved because the two particles move with equal velocity in opposite directions. Mass–energy is also conserved in the reaction.

$$\gamma \rightarrow e^- + e^+$$

This process is called pair production. We can show that the minimum energy a photon must have for pair production is 1·02 MeV.

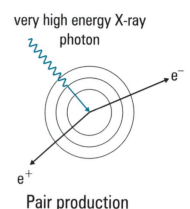

Pair production

Problem

An electron and a positron are produced from a photon in the electric field of the nucleus. What is the minimum energy the photon requires for this?

$$\gamma \rightarrow e^- + e^+$$

If we assume the two particles produced have zero kinetic energy:

mass of 2 electrons	=	2(0·0005486) a.m.u
	=	0·0010972 a.m.u.
Equivalent energy	=	1·02 MeV

Where the photon has energy greater than this, the excess shows as the kinetic energy of the particles.

Annihilation

When an electron and a positron meet, they annihilate each other and are replaced by two photons moving in opposite directions. Two photons are necessary for conservation of momentum. As the two photons have zero electric charge, charge is also conserved.

$$e^- + e^+ \rightarrow \gamma + \gamma$$

We have already calculated the mass–energy of the electron–positron pair to be 1·02 MeV. As this produces two γ ray photons, the energy of each photon must be 0·51 MeV.

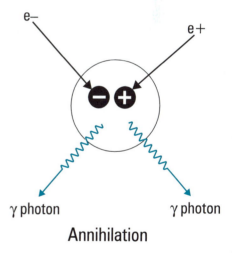

Annihilation

Antiprotons

It takes considerably more energy to produce a proton–antiproton pair, because the mass of a proton is nearly 2,000 times that of an electron. The antiproton was discovered in 1955 by Segré and Chamberlain. They used a 6·4 GeV proton beam to bombard a copper target. They produced a variety of particles in the process, and proved that one particle was a negative proton: the antiproton.

When a proton meets an antiproton they do not annihilate each other, but produce strange particles that in turn decay into other particles.

Physics Now!

One process is that the proton–antiproton pair react to form a pion–antipion pair. These in turn decay.

$$p^+ + p^- \rightarrow \pi^+ + \pi^-$$

Does antimatter exist?

The existence of antiparticles for each particle has led scientists to speculate on the existence of antimatter. An antimatter atom would contain negative protons in the nucleus orbited by positive electrons. Antimatter atoms would form antimatter molecules, and so on. When antimatter met matter the two would annihilate each other, releasing energy and particles. Scientists have found no evidence of antimatter existing anywhere in the universe.

Emilio Segré (USA) 1905–89 in 1955–: he and Chamberlain discovered the antiproton – a negatively charged proton. They shared the Nobel Prize for physics in 1959 for this work.

Owen Chamberlain (USA) 1920– discovered the antiproton with Segré. He also investigated interactions of antiprotons with hydrogen and deuterium.

High-energy collisions

Scientists studying cosmic rays (particles from the sun and stars that strike the earth) discovered many strange particles. These are produced by high-energy cosmic rays colliding with particles in the earth's atmosphere. One particle they found was the pion.

They found that pions are formed when high-energy protons in the cosmic rays collide. The pion is a very short-lived particle, and decays into another strange particle (a muon) and a neutrino in about 10^{-8} of a second. The muon decays after 10^{-6} seconds into an electron and two neutrinos. Many strange particles are found in cosmic rays. All have lifetimes of millionths of a second and decay into stable particles.

Particle	Antiparticle
electron e^-	positron e^+
proton p^+	antiproton p^-
muon μ^-	antimuon μ^+

Particle zoo

In 1940, scientists believed they had discovered the fundamental building blocks of all matter: protons, neutrons and electrons. Some strange particles were known at the time, but not a lot was known about them. About 20 years later the number of 'fundamental' particles had grown to 200, and more were being discovered. Most of these have been produced in high-energy collisions of protons and other particles using particle accelerators. Scientists doubted that there could be this number of fundamental particles.

Fundamental Particles (Option 1)

Scientists at CERN have blasted high-energy beams of protons into each other and produced many strange particles in the process. The greater the energy, the greater are the masses of the particles produced. This is easily understood when you consider Einstein's mass–energy equation: $E = mc^2$. Rearranging the equation, $m = \frac{E}{c^2}$. A particle of energy E in a collision can, in theory, produce an additional particle of mass $\frac{E}{c^2}$.

Problem

A 1·8 GeV proton strikes a hydrogen nucleus (a proton) and produces a proton, a sigma hyperon and a K meson. Estimate the mass of the K meson if 1 GeV is accounted for in the kinetic energy of the other two particles.

Mass of p^+ = 1·007825 a.m.u.
Mass of Σ^+ = 1·277940 a.m.u.

$$p^+ + p^+ \rightarrow p^+ + K^0 + \Sigma^+$$

$1\cdot8 - 1\cdot0 = 0\cdot8$ GeV $= 0\cdot8 \times 10^3$ MeV. This is converted to mass.

This is equivalent to a mass of 0·85929 a.m.u.
Mass of 2 protons and mass-equivalent of 0·8 GeV = 2·87494 a.m.u.
Mass of proton and sigma particle = 2·285765 a.m.u.
∴ Mass of K meson = 0·589175 a.m.u.

Problem

A photon strikes a hydrogen nucleus (a proton) and produces a neutral lambda hyperon and a K meson. Calculate the minimum energy the photon requires for this reaction.

Mass of p^+ = 1·007825 a.m.u.
Mass of K^+ = 0·530344 a.m.u.
Mass of Λ^0 = 1·198646 a.m.u.

$$\gamma + p^+ \rightarrow K^+ + \Lambda^0$$

Mass of $K^+ + \Lambda^0$ = 1·72899 a.m.u.
less mass of p^+ = 1·007825 a.m.u.
∴ Mass created = 0·721165 a.m.u.
→ Energy of photon must be at least 671 MeV

Proton–proton collisions

Scientists have produced a large number of strange particles by means of high-energy electron or proton collisions in accelerators. These are identical to the particles produced in cosmic rays. One high-energy reaction is a proton–proton collision that produces a pion, a proton and a neutron.

$$p^+ + p^+ \rightarrow \pi^+ + n^0 + p^+$$

How can this happen? Isn't the mass of the two protons that collide less than the mass of the proton and neutron? Where did the pion come from?

Mass of proton = 1·007825 a.m.u.

Mass of neutron = 1·008665 a.m.u.

2 × mass p = 2·01565

Mass p + n = 2·01649

Mass of pion = 0·150268

∴ Mass created = 0·151108

This is equivalent to 140·7 MeV.

The proton must have energy greater than this to produce pions in the collision reaction.

Einstein's mass–energy equation works both ways: mass changes into energy, but energy can also change into mass. When high-energy protons collide, some of the enormous energy changes into mass. In this reaction the mass is a proton, a neutron and a pion.

The mass of the pion is small compared to the proton or neutron. Much higher energies are needed to produce heavier particles. With energies of 6·4 GeV, proton–proton collisions produce proton–antiproton pairs. Many other strange particles (with lifetimes of 10^{-6} to 10^{-20} seconds) are produced in high-energy proton collisions.

EXAMPLES:

$p^+ + p^+ \rightarrow p^+ + p^+ + (p^+ + p^-)$: proton–antiproton pair produced

$p^+ + p^+ \rightarrow p^+ + p^+ + \pi^0$: neutral pion produced

$p^+ + p^+ \rightarrow d^+ + \pi^+$: deuteron (proton–neutron combination) and pion produced

$p^+ + p^+ \rightarrow p^+ + \Sigma^+ + K^0$: proton, sigma baryon and kaon (K meson) produced

Fundamental forces of nature

There are four basic, or fundamental, kinds of forces in nature: the strong nuclear force, the weak nuclear force, the electromagnetic force and the gravitational force.

Electromagnetic and gravitational forces are easy to observe and have been known for a long time. They have an effect at a great distance and cause many of the forces we see in everyday life.

Strong and weak nuclear forces were not discovered until the 20th century. These forces act on sub-atomic particles, and only at very short sub-atomic distances.

Fundamental Particles (Option 1)

Strong nuclear force

Extremely powerful nuclear forces hold the nucleus together. These forces are effective only at the very small distances the protons and neutrons are from each other. Beyond these distances they have no effect. The forces act equally on both neutrons and protons.

The strong force helps to explain why large nuclei are not very stable. Many of the particles in large atoms are far from each other in relative terms. The nuclear forces are not strong at these distances, and the repulsive forces between protons weaken the nucleus. These nuclei often undergo either alpha or beta decay.

Weak nuclear force

Weak nuclear forces are involved in beta decay. This is when a neutron decays into a proton, an electron (the β particle) and a neutrino pair. Weak nuclear forces are also involved in other nuclear reactions, including all reactions that involve neutrinos.

Electromagnetic force

Electromagnetic forces are forces between particles due to their electric and magnetic fields. They hold atoms and molecules together. The electromagnetic force obeys an inverse square law: it is inversely proportional to the square of the distance between the two charged particles. Electromagnetic forces act between protons (in the nucleus), but at short distances the strong nuclear force is 100 times stronger.

Gravitation

Every particle of matter in the universe is attracted to every other particle by a gravitational force. Newton's law of gravitation shows that gravitational forces are significant only with very big masses. The gravitational force obeys an inverse square law: it is inversely proportional to the square of the distance between the two masses. Gravitational forces have no significant effect on the structure of the atom or the nucleus.

PHYSICS NOW!

Force	Relative Strength	Range	Purpose
Strong nuclear force	1 Very strong	Very short distances	Holds proton and neutrons together in nucleus
Electromagnetic force	10^{-2} 100 times weaker than strong nuclear force	Extends over great distances; obeys inverse square law	Holds atoms and molecules together
Weak nuclear force	10^{-13} Weaker than electromagnetic	Very short distances	Involved in beta particle decay
Gravitational force	10^{-40} Weakest of fundamental forces	Extends over enormous distances; obeys inverse square law	Holds universe together

The ultimate structure of matter?

Matter seems to be built from two groups of particles: **hadrons** (nuclear particles) and **leptons** (non-nuclear particles).

Hadrons are all particles that are subject to the strong nuclear force. The name 'hadron' comes from the Greek word for 'strong'. There are over 200 hadron particles. Scientists have divided these into two general classes: the **baryons** ('heavy' particles) and the **mesons** (intermediate particles).

Baryons are all large mass particles: protons, neutrons and heavier. They are nucleons (protons and neutrons) and strange particles: hyperons (lambda, sigma, xi and omega particles). The hyperons have lifetimes of about 10^{-10} seconds and decay into nucleons and mesons. Each baryon is believed to have a corresponding antibaryon. Baryons are influenced by the strong nuclear force, and are a combination of three quarks.

Mesons are particles with masses between the electron and the proton. They are all strange particles (pions, kaons, etc.) of short lifetime. They are influenced by the strong nuclear force. Mesons are a combination of a quark and an antiquark.

Fundamental Particles (Option 1)

Leptons (meaning 'light' particles) are all particles that are not influenced by the strong nuclear force – electrons and neutrinos. They are indivisible and are fundamental particles. They are regarded as point objects.

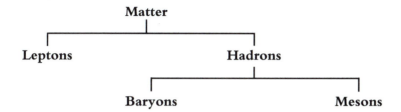

Quarks

A great number of strange 'fundamental' particles had been discovered by 1960. Scientists believed that not all of these could be truly fundamental. They began to search for some pattern and order. The leptons were not a problem: they were few in number, indivisible and were considered to be fundamental. The enormous number of heavy particles found was a problem.

Murray Gell-Mann and George Zweig proposed a model that reduced all these heavy particles to combinations of three fundamental particles. Gell-Mann named the particles 'quarks'.

This name has nothing to do with physics. Gell-Mann had an interest in linguistics, and came across the word in *Finnegans Wake* by James Joyce ('Three Quarks for Muster Mark').

The three-quark model was soon found to be inadequate, and was rapidly extended to six quarks (and six antiquarks). The quarks are named Up, Down, Strange, Charmed, Top and Bottom. (The names have no significance other than that of distinguishing the different properties of these quarks.)

Quarks have a fractional electric charge: some have $\frac{1}{3}$ electron charge; others have $\frac{2}{3}$.

Murray Gell-Mann (USA) 1929– : Gell-Mann and George Zweig independently developed the quark theory to explain the organisation of particle families.

Quark	Charge	Antiquark	Charge
Up (u)	$+\frac{2}{3}$	Up ($\bar{u}$)	$-\frac{2}{3}$
Down (d)	$-\frac{1}{3}$	Down ($\bar{d}$)	$+\frac{1}{3}$
Strange (s)	$-\frac{1}{3}$	Strange ($\bar{s}$)	$+\frac{1}{3}$
Charmed (c)	$+\frac{2}{3}$	Charmed ($\bar{c}$)	$-\frac{2}{3}$
Top (t)	$-\frac{1}{3}$	Top ($\bar{t}$)	$+\frac{1}{3}$
Bottom (b)	$+\frac{2}{3}$	Bottom ($\bar{b}$)	$-\frac{2}{3}$

All heavy particles are combinations of quarks. Baryons are combinations of three quarks; mesons are a quark–antiquark pair.

BARYONS

Particle	Quarks	Charge
Proton	uud	$+\frac{2}{3} + \frac{2}{3} - \frac{1}{3} = +1$
Neutron	udd	$+\frac{2}{3} - \frac{1}{3} - \frac{1}{3} = 0$
Σ^+	uus	$+\frac{2}{3} + \frac{2}{3} - \frac{1}{3} = +1$
Σ^-	dds	$-\frac{1}{3} - \frac{1}{3} - \frac{1}{3} = -1$

MESONS

Particle	Quark–antiquark	Charge
π^+	$u\bar{d}$	$+\frac{2}{3} + \frac{1}{3} = +1$
π^-	$\bar{u}d$	$-\frac{2}{3} - \frac{1}{3} = -1$
K^+	$u\bar{s}$	$+\frac{2}{3} + \frac{1}{3} = +1$
K^-	$\bar{u}s$	$-\frac{2}{3} - \frac{1}{3} = -1$

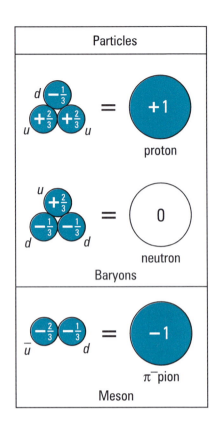

It is important to realise that the best that scientists can do is to build up a picture or model based on the information available at the time. As further information becomes available, this model may have to be changed. In some cases the model may be abandoned completely in favour of a new model that explains the facts better.

Matter is now seen as being made up of leptons and baryons. Leptons are fundamental particles and are not subject to the strong nuclear force. Baryons are composed of quarks. The fundamental particles are six quarks and six leptons and their antiparticles. All common matter is made up of just four fundamental particles: the leptons – electrons and neutrinos – and the up and down quarks. Protons and neutrons are composed of up and down quarks.

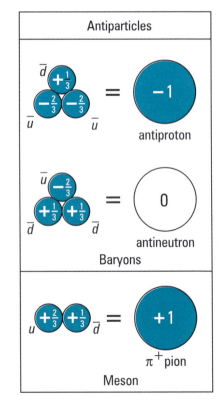

Six quarks	Six leptons
Up (u)	Electron
Down (d)	Electron neutrino
Strange (s)	Negative muon
Charmed (c)	Muon neutrino
Top (t)	Negative tau
Bottom (b)	Tau neutrino

Six antiquarks	Six antileptons
Up ($\bar{u}$)	Positron
Down ($\bar{d}$)	Electron antineutrino
Strange ($\bar{s}$)	Positive muon
Charmed ($\bar{c}$)	Muon antineutrino
Top ($\bar{t}$)	Positive tau
Bottom ($\bar{b}$)	Tau antineutrino

Summary

- Cosmic radiation is radiation that comes from outside the earth.
- Electron–positron pairs are produced when high-energy photons pass close to a nucleus.
- An electron and a positron annihilate each other and are replaced by two photons moving in opposite directions.
- The greater the energy of a beam of protons, the greater are the masses of the particles produced.
- A particle of energy E in a collision can, in theory, produce an additional particle of mass $\frac{E}{c^2}$.
- There are four fundamental forces in nature: the strong nuclear force, the weak nuclear force, the electromagnetic force and the gravitational force.

PHYSICS NOW!

- Baryons are all large-mass particles, are influenced by the strong nuclear force and are a combination of three quarks.
- Mesons are particles with masses between the electron and the proton, are influenced by the strong nuclear force and are a combination of a quark and an antiquark.
- Leptons are fundamental particles that are not influenced by the strong nuclear force.
- Quarks have a fractional electric charge of $\frac{1}{3}$ or $\frac{2}{3}$ electron charge.
- The fundamental particles are six quarks and six leptons.

SHORT QUESTIONS

1. Radiation coming from outside the earth is _____.
2. A particle with a positive electric charge and the same mass as the electron is a _____.
3. Dirac suggested in the year _____ that every particle should have _____.
4. The quark theory was worked out by _____ and _____ in 1963.
5. The minimum energy a photon must have for electron-positron pair production is _____ MeV.
6. All heavy particles are combinations of _____.
7. An atom with antiprotons in the nucleus and positrons orbiting it is called _____.
8. Mesons are a combination of _____.
9. Why are two photons always emitted in electron–positron annihilation?
10. Quarks were named from a line in _____ by the Irish author _____.
11. Strange particles are produced in _____.
12. A positive electron is a _____.
13. The strong nuclear force acts on _____ and _____ and is effective at _____ distances..
14. The greater the _____ of a proton beam, the greater is the _____ of the particles produced.
15. _____ are a combination of three quarks.
16. The fundamental particles are _____ and _____.

Fundamental Particles (Option 1)

Long Questions

1. Complete the following table.

Force	Strength	Range	Purpose
Strong nuclear force	Very strong		
	Weaker than electromagnetic	Very short distances	
	100 times weaker than strong nuclear force		Holds atoms and molecules together
	Weakest of fundamental forces		Holds universe together

2. A Σ^0 (sigma) particle decays into a Λ^0 (lambda) particle with the emission of a photon. Calculate the energy of the photon.
$\Sigma^0 \rightarrow \Lambda^0 + Q$
Mass Σ^0 = 1·278994 a.m.u.
Mass Λ^0 = 1·197753 a.m.u.

3. Identify the following particles as either baryons or mesons, and give the electric charge of each particle.

Combination of quarks	Type of particle	Charge
uud		
uus		
u$\bar{s}$		
u$\bar{d}$		
dds		
$\bar{u}$d		
udd		
$\bar{u}$s		

387

4. A π^+ meson decays into a μ^+ meson and a neutrino. Calculate the energy Q released in this decay.
$\pi^+ \to \mu^+ + \upsilon + Q$
Mass π^+ = 0·149856 a.m.u.
Mass μ^+ = 0·113627 a.m.u.

5. A proton and an antiproton annihilate each other in a collision that produces two photons. Calculate the energy of the emitted photons. (Mass of proton (and antiproton) = 1·007825 a.m.u.)

6. A π^0 meson decays to give two photons. Calculate the energy of each photon.
Mass π^0 = 0·144916 a.m.u.

7. How many electron–positron pairs could be produced from a 143 MeV photon? (Mass of electron (and positron) = 0·0005486 a.m.u.)

8. A kaon K^0 decays to give a pion–antipion pair. Calculate the energy released in this decay.
$K^0 \to \pi^+ + \pi^- + Q$
Mass K^0 = 0·530261 a.m.u.
Mass π^+ = 0·149856 a.m.u.
Mass π^- = 0·149856 a.m.u.

Answers to Long Numerical Questions

Chapter 1
3. Absolute 0.5 m s^{-1}. Relative 1 m s^{-1}
5. (a) 30 cm
   (b) (i) 30 cm, real, inverted, same size as object
   (ii) 60 cm, real, inverted, magnification 3
   (iii) 30 cm behind the mirror, virtual, erect, magnification 3
6. 6 cm from mirror, magnification $\frac{2}{3}$
7. (a) Virtual, erect, diminished
   (b) Real, inverted, same size as object
8. Magnification 3
9. 15 cm
10. Concave
11. 32 cm, 32 cm, 16 cm
12. 20·2 cm

Chapter 2
1. 41° 48′
2. 8 m below the surface
3. $\frac{3}{2}$ and 1 cm
5. 2×10^8 m s^{-1}
7. 1·29, 51°
8. 1·34
10. 1·5
11. 1·33
12. 1·414
13. 1·6
14. 2·3 m
15. 2 m
16. 4° 47′
17. 80° 30′

Chapter 3
1. real, inverted, 33·33 cm from the lens. Magnification 2/3
2. Virtual, 7·5 cm from lens
3. 15 cm, 60 cm from lens
4. 2 cm, 7·5 cm
5. 10 cm, 20 cm in front of lens
6. 3·2 cm, 4
7. 30 cm, 15 cm
8. 25 cm × 25 cm, 16·7 cm
9. 8 cm
10. 3·375 cm from lens
11. 11·25 cm, 15 cm from screen. $\frac{1}{3}$ size of object
12. 9 cm
13. 40 cm
14. 8 cm, 24 cm
15. 5·3 cm, 5 cm

Chapter 5
2. (c) (i) 0·5 m (ii) 330 m s^{-1}
3. (i) 243° 30′ because Sin 43° 30′ is not twice Sin 17° 15′
   (ii) 593 nm
4. 570 nm
5. 19° 3
6. 590 nm
7. 430 nm
8. 5700 lines per cm
9. 509 nm
10. 606 nm

Chapter 7
1. 1100 Hz
2. Sound
3. 0·25 m
4. 0·3 sec
5. 32 beats per sec
6. 82·5 Hz, 165 Hz, 247·5 Hz
7. 0·1 m, 0·8 m, 1·6 m s^{-1}, 2 Hz
8. 34 Hz
9. 450 Hz
10. 58 cm, 22·5 N
11. 480 Hz
14. 515 Hz
15. (a) 532·25 Hz (b) 471·43 Hz
16. 1214 Hz, 850 Hz
19. 37·8 m s^{-1}

Chapter 8
1. (a) 20 N 36° 52′ North of West
   (b) 150 N 36° 52′ West of South
   (c) 20·25 N 32° 57′ North of West
2. 54 N 22° North of West
3. 1000 N
4. (i) 3464 N (ii) 2000 N

Chapter 9
1. 50 m, 7·07 s
2. 3·5 m s^{-2}, 8·57 s
3. 75 m, 5 s
4. 5 m s^{-2}, 10 m
5. 2·48 s
6. 7·07 s, 100 m
7. No. Stopping distance 96 m. Yes. Car going slower at impact.
8. (a) ab, 2 m s^{-1} (b) cd, 1 m s^{-1}
   (c) bc, de, 300 s (d) ef (e) 100 m
   (f) 100 m (g) 500 s
9. 0·25 m s^{-2}
11. 135 m
12. 68·6 m s^{-1}, 63·7 m

13. (a) 20·4 m (b) 14·14 m s^{-1}
    (c) 4·08 s
14. 304 m
15. 60 m s^{-1}, 175 m

Chapter 10
1. 2·5 m s^{-2}
2. 19 N, 310 m
3. 15 N
4. 2500 N, 4 s
5. 37·5 s
6. (i) 600 N (ii) 1500 N, 60 kg
7. 0·23 m s^{-2}
8. 4 m s^{-2}, 40 N, 50 m
9. 20/3 m s^{-1}
10. 18 kg
11. 0·19 m s^{-1}, 0·6 m s^{-2}
12. 0·29 N
13. 2 m s^{-2}, 4 N
14. 42 s
15. 0·18 N

Chapter 11
1. 1 N
2. 980 N
3. 400 N, 700 N
4. 350 N, 70 N
5. 1·1 N

Chapter 13
1. 25 J
2. 2450 J
3. 32·66 W
4. 0 J, 0·3 J, 0·15 J, 0·15 J
5. 2·613 × 10^3 W
6. 20 m s^{-1}
7. 18 J
8. 1764 J, 176·4 W
9. (a) 1·96 J (b) 1·47 J
11. 112·5 kJ, 22·5 kW
12. 135 kJ, 2700 N
13. 54·9 : 1, 8·55 × 10^{-13} J, 1·59 × 10^7 m s^{-1}, 2·89 × 10^5 m s^{-1}
14. 1225 W
15. (a) 6·25 m s^{-1} (b) 93·75 J
16. 35·79 J

17. 124·5 W
18. 1·8 × 10^3 N
19. 0·5 m, 50 N
20. 29·5 m s^{-1}

Chapter 14
1. 555·55 cm^3
2. 4·272 kg
3. 1·045 g cm^{-3}
5. 49 N, 1·96 N cm^{-2}, 1·96 N cm^{-2}, 3920 N
7. An increase of 5 mm of mercury

Chapter 15
3. 12·5 N
4. 7·743 m s^{-2}
5. 3·66 m s^{-2}
6. 164·3 years
7. (f) 0·08 N
9. 5·5 × 10^3 kg m^{-3}
10. 6·232 m s^{-2}
12. 1·7 m s^{-1}. The angle is too large
13. (i) 0·94 m (ii) 0·85 m North East
14. 3·74 × 10^8 S
16. 3·05 m s^{-1}, 11·6 m s^{-2}, 2·8 N

Chapter 18
1. 88 kJ
2. 1·08 × 10^7 J
3. 1866·66 W
4. 1·89 × 10^4 J
6. 0·186 K
7. (a) 50 J (b) 15 kJ
   (d) 937·5 J kg^{-1} K^{-1}
8. (a) (i) 322·92 J (ii) 6665·4 J.
   (b) 296076 J kg^{-1}
9. 2309·2 kJ kg^{-1}
10. 1·16 °C
11. 4·04 kg
12. 61 °C
13. 28·17 °C
14. 10·32 °C
15. 6·75 × 10^5 J
16. 37·5 °C
17. 48 °C

18. (a) 4210·5 J kg^{-1}K^{-1}
    (b) 2105 J kg^{-1}K^{-1}
19. 3·2 °C
20. 38·6 g, 76·2 °C, 7·6 °C
22. 1·495 × 10^3 W, 2·395 K

Chapter 20
1. +2
2. 80 × 10^{-6} N
3. 1 × 10^4 NC^{-1}
4. 24 J
5. 6·0 × 10^{-11} C
6. 16F newtons
   7·5 × 10^{-10} NC^{-1}
7. 5 × 10^{-10} NC^{-1}
8. (a) 8·36 × 10^{-10} C
   (b) $\frac{2\cdot 5}{4}$ × 10^{-6} N
11. 200 × 10^{-3} N
    1·6 × 10^6 V
12. 150 × 10^{-3} J
13. 4 × 10^{10} J
    4 × 10^4 A
14. (i) 9·9 × 10^6 NC^{-1}
    (ii) 58·8 NC

Chapter 21
1. 18 Ω
2. 6 Ω
3. 1 A, 4 V (4 Ω resistor)
   0·66 A, 2 V (3 Ω resistor)
   0·33 A, 2 V (6 Ω resistor)
4. 0·09 A
5. 1·59 A through 3 Ω
   1·06 A through 6 Ω
   3·18 V
11. (i) 3 Ω
    (ii) 2 A

Chapter 23
1. 0·42 mm
   1·06 × 10^{-6} Ω.m
3. 1·12 × 10^{-6} Ω.m
5. 60 Ω
6. 3·6 × 10^3 Ω
7. 19 Ω
9. 4·8 × 10^{-5} Ω.m

Answers to Long Numerical Questions

10. $2 \cdot 5 \times 10^{16}$ Ω
11. 0·32 mm

Chapter 24
1. 6 Ω
2. 1200 J
3. 1·5 A
   15 V
4. 36·4 A
5. 0·5 W
6. At 240 V : I = 0·42A, R = 576 Ω (fixed)
   at 220 V : I = 220/576 = 0·38 A
   Lower current, less heat so lasts longer
7. 4·78 Kg
8. 22 Ω
9. 0·6 A, 2,88 W

Chapter 25
2. 1×10^{-3} T
3. 10 mA
   $F = 2 \cdot 3 \times 10^{-1}$ N
   $T = 3 \cdot 4 \times 10^{-2}$ Nm
7. 2·4 N

Chapter 26
4. $1 \cdot 5 \times 10^{-3}$ Nm
5. 0·48 A
10. 54 Ω, 0·108 V, 4946 Ω

Chapter 27
2. E = –NBlv
   I = E/R = (NBlv)/R
   F = NBIl = NB ((NBlv)/R)l
4. 400 V
5. 5·76 V, 4 V, 27·5 V, 240 V, 500 turns
7. 7·2 V
9. –80 V, 0·05 A

Chapter 28
2. 75 turns
3. 120 V
   83 %

6. 0·2 A
   500 V
   50 V
7. 75 %
11. (a) 45·5 A, 0·025 A
    (b) 6·2 kW; $1 \cdot 9 \times 10^{-3}$ W

Chapter 29
2. 1 µF
4. 0·2 C
5. 2 V
6. 25 V
7. 12×10^{-3} C, 4·8 A
8. 12·5 J, 2500 seconds
9. 7×10^{-5} C
10. 895 V, 0·025 C
11. 0·05 C

Chapter 31
2. 240 Ω
7. 240 Ω

Chapter 32
1. I = Q/t = Ne/t
   N/t = n
   so that I = ne
   n = I/e

Chapter 33
1. $0 \cdot 62 \times 10^{-19}$ J
3. $1 \cdot 5 \times 10^{19}$
4. $5 \cdot 8 \times 10^{-19}$ J
   $0 \cdot 8 \times 10^{-19}$ J
5. $7 \cdot 5 \times 10^{14}$ J
   0·023 J
8. $6 \cdot 2 \times 10^{-11}$ m
   $3 \cdot 1 \times 10^{-11}$ m
9. 0·02 J s^{-1}
10. 9×10^{-16} J
    $0 \cdot 62 \times 10^{-19}$ J

Chapter 36
1. 1/8
2. 7/8
5. 1/16
6. 56 hours

7. 1/2, 1/8
9. 11,400 years
12. (i) $1 \cdot 35 \times 10^{11}$ s^{-1}
    (ii) $5 \cdot 1 \times 10^{10}$ s
13. $5 \cdot 1 \times 10^{10}$ s
14. (i) $3 \cdot 7 \times 10^{-3}$ s^{-1}
    (ii) $3 \cdot 6 \times 10^{13}$

Chapter 38
1. $7 \cdot 8 \times 10^{-13}$ J
3. $4 \cdot 35 \times 10^{-14}$ J
5. $4 \cdot 7 \times 10^{-12}$ J
7. $7 \cdot 2 \times 10^{10}$ J
8. $7 \cdot 95 \times 10^{10}$ J
9. $1 \cdot 54 \times 10^{-25}$ kg
10. $1 \cdot 25 \times 10^{-12}$ J

Chapter 39
1. $1 \cdot 2 \times 10^{-12}$
2. $7 \cdot 8 \times 10^{7}$ ms^{-1} (if we assume neutron is absorbed by C–12).
4. $3 \cdot 0 \times 10^{-14}$ J
   (Negative sign means that neutron that strikes the phosphorus nucleus must have this energy if the nuclear reaction is to take place.)
5. $6 \cdot 83 \times 10^{-13}$ J

Chapter 40
2. $1 \cdot 2 \times 10^{-11}$ J
3. baryon, +1
   baryon, +1
   meson, +1
   meson, –1
   baryon, –1
   meson, +1
   baryon, 0
   meson, –1
4. $5 \cdot 4 \times 10^{-12}$ J
5. $1 \cdot 5 \times 10^{-10}$ J
6. $1 \cdot 1 \times 10^{-11}$ J
7. 280 particles, 140 pairs
8. $3 \cdot 43 \times 10^{-11}$ J.

Index

absolute zero, 142
absorption spectra, 50
acceleration, 75
    in a circle, 127
    due to gravity, 78
accommodation, 30
alpha particles, 327
alternating current, generator, 261
ammeter, moving coil, 242
    moving iron, 243
ampere, 235
amplitude, 36
AND gate, 293
angular velocity, 125
annihilation, 377
antinode, 58
antiparticles, 376
apparent depth, 14
Archimedes' Principle, 121
artificial radioactivity, 348
atmospheric pressure, 119
atomic number, 338

back, emf, 240
band spectrum, 50
barometer, aneroid, 120
    mercury, 119
baryons, 382
base current, 289
beats, 57
becquerel, 342
bel, 62
beta particles, 328
bias, forward, 281
    reverse, 282
bimetallic strip, 136
bonding, electrical, 198
Boyle's law, 141
Brownian motion, 161

camera, 33
capacitance, 270
capacitors, 269
    and a.c., 274
    and d.c., 274
    energy stored in, 273
    parallel plate, 271
    uses of, 275
carbon-dating, 351
cathode rays, 301
cathode-ray tube, 306
cells, simple, 190
centripetal force, 126
chain reaction, 361
charge density, 174
charging by friction, 168
    by induction, 172
circuit breakers, 197
circuits, integrated, 294
circular motion, 125
cloud chamber, 326
Cockroft and Walton's experiment, 358, 372
collector current, 288
commutator, 239
concave mirror, 4
conduction (heat), 147
conductors (electric), 170
conservation of energy, 104
    of mass–energy, 358, 373
    of momentum, 88
constant-volume gas thermometer, 143
continuous spectrum, 50
convection, 148
converging lens, 23
convex mirror, 7
cosmic rays, 376
Coulomb's law, 181
couples, 99

critical angle, 16
critical mass, 364
current, electric, 189
cyclotron, 373

dead time, 331
decay constant, 342
decibel, 62
density, 117
depletion layer, 281
detectors, 330
diffraction, 39
diode, 280
dipole, magnetic, 206
direct current motor, 239
dispersion, 46
displacement, 75
doping, 279
Doppler effect, 61
dry cell, 191
dust precipitator, 185

earthing, 198
earth's magnetic field, 208
eddy currents, 263
Einstein's photoelectric law, 313
electric charge, 171
    fields, 182
    field line, 183
    field strength, 183
electrolysis, 227
electromagnetic, induction, 248
    relay, 238
    spectrum, 47
electromotive force (emf), 189
electron, charge of, 301
    charge to mass ratio, 303
    energy of, 302
electroscope, 171
emission spectra, 50

Index

emitter current, 288
energy, 102
    and mass, 358
    conservation of, 104
    kinetic, 103, 107
    potential, 106
extrinsic conduction, 279
eye, 30

farad, 270
Faraday's butterfly net experiment, 174
    law of induction, 249
fibre optics, 17
fields, electric, 182
    magnetic, 204
fission, 359
Fletcher's Trolley, 85
flotation, law of, 122
flux, magnetic, 207
force, 84
    between charges, 181
    centripetal, 126
    nuclear, 381
    on charge in magnetic field, 234
    on conductor in magnetic field, 232
forward bias, 281
Fraunhofer lines, 50
frequency, 36
    fundamental, 55
friction, 110
fundamental forces, 380
fuse, 197
fusion, 364

G (gravitational constant), 127
g experiment, 78
galvanometer, moving coil, 241
gamma radiation, 329
gates, logic, 292
    uses of, 296
Geiger-Müller tube, 330
generator, a.c., 261
geostationary orbit, 129
gravitation, 127

gravity, centre of, 96
greenhouse effect, 48

hadrons, 382
half-life, 342
half-wave rectifier, 285
harmonics, 55
heat, 136
heat capacity, 153
heat, latent, 156
heat pump, 160
holes, positive, 280
house wiring, 196
hydrometer, 122

ideal gas, 142
    scale, 143
impulse, 87
induction, electrostatic, 172
    mutual, 254
    self, 255
induction coil, 260
    uses of, 261
induction motor, 264
inductors and a.c., 255
infra-red, 48
insulators, electric, 170
    heat, 150
integrated circuits, 294
interference, 36
intrinsic conduction, 278
isotopes, 338

jet engine, 90
joule, 106
Joule's law, 224
junction diode, 280

keepers, 208
Kelvin scale, 143
Kepler's laws, 127
kilowatt hour, 227
kinetic energy, 103, 107
    theory, 161

latent heat, 156
lead-acid accumulators, 191
Leclanche (dry cell) cell, 191
lens converging, 23
    diverging, 23
Lenz's law, 249
leptons, 382
lever, 96
light-dependent resistor (LDR), 216
light emitting diode (LED), 282, 286
lightning conductor, 175
line spectrum, 50
logic gates, 292
longitudinal waves, 35
loudness, 54
loudspeaker, moving coil, 241
luminous, 1

magnetic fields, 204
    flux density, 207
magnets, 204
magnifying glass, 31
mains tester, 199
majority charge carriers, 280
mass, 84
    energy, 358
    number, 339
mercury thermometer, 138
mesons, 382
microscope, compound, 31
microwaves, 49
minority charge carriers, 280
mirrors, plane, 4
    concave, 4
    convex, 4
moments, principle of, 98
momentum, conservation of, 88
motor, d.c., 239
    induction, 264
moving coil galvanometer, 241
    speaker, 241
moving iron meter, 243
mutual induction, 254
myopia, 30

n-type semiconductor, 279
neutron, discovery of, 337
neutrino, 370
newton, unit, 85
Newton's laws of motion, 85
    of gravitation, 127
nodes, 58
NOT gate, 294
nuclear fission, 359
    fusion, 364
    reactors, 361
nucleus, 336

ohm, unit, 193
Ohm's law, 193
ohmmeter, 244
optical fibres, 17
OR gate, 293
overtones, 55

pair production, 377
    annihilation, 377
p-type semiconductor, 279
parallax, 2
pascal, unit, 119
peak value (emf), 251
pendulum, simple, 79
periodic time, 125
permittivity, 181
photocell, 314
photodiode, 282, 287
photoelectric effect, 311
    equation, 313
photons, 313
pitch, 54
Planck's constant, 312
    quantum theory, 312
planetary motion, 127
p–n junction, 280
point discharge, 174
polarisation, light, 41
potential difference, 186
    divider, 219
potential energy, 106
potentiometer, 220

power, 109
    electric, 225
    ionising, 325
pressure, 118
    in fluids, 120
primary colours, 46
principle of moments, 98
protons (Rutherford's experiment), 337
pure spectrum, 46

quality of sound, 54
quantum theory, 312
quarks, 383
quenching process, 331

radial circuit, 196
radial magnetic field, 239
radians, 125
radiation, electromagnetic, 47
    heat, 148
    infra-red, 48
    ultraviolet, 48
radioactivation analysis, 352
radioactive decay, 342
radioactivity, 323
    artificial, 348
    health effects, 352
    ionising, 325
    penetrating, 324
radiative capture, 360
radioisotopes, 348
radon, 354
reactors, fission, 361
    fusion, 364
real image, 4
    depth, 14

rectifier, bridge, 286
    half-wave, 285
reflection, laws of, 1
    total internal, 16
refraction, laws of, 13
refractive index, 13
relay, electromagnetic, 238
residual current device (RCD), 199

resistance, 292
    and temperature, 214
resistivity, 213
resistors, in parallel, 194
    in series, 194
    light-dependent, 216
resolution of vectors, 72
resonance, 56
reverse bias, 282
rheostat, 194
ring main circuit, 196
Rutherford and Royd's experiment, 327
Rutherford's scattering experiment, 336

saturation current, 305
scales of temperature, 138
scalars, 70
secondary colours, 46
semiconductors
    n-type, 279
    p-type, 279
short sight, 30
simple harmonic motion, 131
simple pendulum, 79
Snell's law, 13
solar constant, 150
solenoid, 206
    magnetisation by, 207
solid state detector, 331
sound, velocity of, 58
specific heat capacity, 155
spectra, 50
spectrum, electromagnetic, 47
speedometer, 264
stability, 96
static electricity, 168
    problems with, 176
stationary waves, 58
strain gauge, 217
strong nuclear force, 381

telescope, astronomical, 32
temperature scales, 140
tesla, 207

tester, mains, 199
thermionic emission, 304
    uses of, 307
thermistors, 215
thermometers, 138
thermopile, 150
thermostat, 136
Thomson's experiment, 302
threshold frequency, 312
timbre, 54
torque, 97
torque of motor and 'back'
    emf, 240
total internal reflection, 16
tracers, radioactive, 351
transformers, 252
    efficiency of, 263
transistors, 288
    applications of, 290
    switching action of, 289
transverse waves, 35
truth tables, ogic gates, 294

U-values, 150
ultrasonics, 55
ultraviolet, 48
universal gravitation, 127
uranium, 360

Van de Graaff generator, 176
vectors, 70
    resolution of, 72
velocity, 72
    linear, 72
    angular, 125
    of sound, 58
    terminal, 112
virtual image, 4
viscosity, 112
volt, 190
voltage amplifier, 290
    inverter, 292
voltameter, 228
voltmeter, 243

watt, 225
waves, 35
    electromagnetic, 47
    longitudinal, 35
    transverse, 35
wave theory of light, 37
wavelength of light, 40
weak nuclear force, 381
weber, 250
weight, 84
wheatstone bridge, 216
    uses of, 217
work, 106
    function, 306

X-ray tube, 316
X-rays, 315
    uses of, 317

Young's equation, 39

zero potential, 186

CD Contents

Acceleration, to measure
Acceleration, proportional to force
Boyle's Law, to verify
Conservation of momentum
Calibration curve of thermometer
Current varies with potential difference, to show that
Focal length – concave mirror
Focal length – converging lens
Fundamental frequency with length, variation of
Fundamental frequency with tension, variation of
g – free fall
g – pendulum
Joule's Law, to verify
Laws of equilibrium
Refractive index – glass block
Refractive index – liquid
Resistance of a conductor varies with temperature
Resistance of a thermistor varies with temperature
Resistivity in a wire, to measure
Snell's Law, to verify
Specific Heat Capacity of a metal
Specific Heat Capacity of water
Specific Latent Heat of fusion of ice
Specific Latent Heat of vaporisation of water
Velocity of sound, resonance tube
Velocity, to measure
Wavelength of light, to measure

INSTALLATION

The sections below assume that the presentation is on a CD-ROM in drive D. If the presentation is on some other drive, substitute the appropriate drive letter.

To run presentation directly from CD-ROM
This CD-ROM has been made to 'Autorun'. This means that the presentation starts automatically on most computers when the disc is inserted into the CD-ROM drive. If the presentation fails to load automatically on your computer, you can start it running by:

- Clicking the **Start** button and choosing **Run**. Then type **D:\Setup** and then click **OK**.
  or
- Double click on **My Computer** and then on the CD-ROM drive (usually D:) and double click on the *Physics Now!* icon.